ZBrush Cookbook

Practical step-by-step recipes for creating production-ready creatures for VFX and animation

Andrea Salvatori

<packt>

ZBrush Cookbook

Portfolio Director: Rohit Rajkumar
Relationship Lead: Tanisha Mehrotra
Program Manager: Sandip Tadge
Content Engineer: Shreya Sarkar
Technical Editor: Tejas Mhasvekar
Indexer: Manju Arasan
Proofreader: Shreya Sarkar
Production Designer: Ajay Patule
Growth Lead: Chayan Majumdar

First published: August 2026

Production reference: 1130826

Published by Packt Publishing Ltd.
Grosvenor House
11 St Paul's Square
Birmingham
B3 1RB, UK.

ISBN 978-1-83620-761-0
`www.packtpub.com`

To my wife, my daughters, my parents, and my entire family.

Thank you for your endless love, patience, and unwavering support that made this journey possible. This book is dedicated to you.

And to every artist chasing the dream of working in this extraordinary industry. I know how difficult the journey can be, because I've walked that path too. Never stop creating, never stop learning, and never stop believing in your work.

– Andrea Salvatori

Foreword

Sculpting is an art form as old as mankind. When talking about traditional stone statues, it's often said that it isn't about adding shape – it's about discovering the form already waiting beneath the surface. Whether working with physical clay or digital pixels, the art lies in translating bones, muscles, fat, and skin into a static sculpture.

But even more than that, it is about crafting emotions – giving life to what once existed only in the mind of storytellers or filmmakers.

In the realm of high-fantasy filmmaking, creatures aren't just drawn; they are built, breath by breath, scale by scale. In his *ZBrush Cookbook*, Senior Creature Artist Andrea Salvatori opens his digital workshop to reveal the techniques and workflows he used when sculpting some of the most iconic dragons for HBO's *House of the Dragon*. One of the basic principles behind the creatures in the world of *Game of Thrones* is to ground mythical creatures in real-world animal biology to achieve believable muscle movement and structure.

Follow Andrea in this comprehensive guide, which takes you step-by-step through his industry-grade creature sculpting workflow using Maxon ZBrush.

Get inspired, learn, or refine an art form that has been around for centuries, combining a solid foundation of science, a deep knowledge of anatomy, an eye for detail, and the creativity of an artist.

Unleash your inner dragon. Master the digital clay!

Sven Martin

Visual Effects Supervisor at Pixomondo

Foreword

I can only say good things about Andrea, personally and professionally.

I had the pleasure of working with him at different studios and on different projects, and his dedication to what he does is truly outstanding.

As a CG Supervisor, I could rely completely on him to ensure the creatures and characters were transposed from the 2D concept art into the 3D models, and the result was always as expected: excellent.

Having him as the lead for modeling on my last project was a great mix of creativity and technical skills and, of course, fabulous guidance to the modeling team.

I can only recommend that people follow Andrea's guidance to learn how to model properly in ZBrush, through the lens of a real production pipeline, with all the pro tricks and tips that only an expert like him can provide.

The importance of having a guide like this for anyone who wants to learn from real production experience cannot be overstated. It provides a strong foundation for the current ZBrush landscape, with the support of practical exercises that explain the real-world modeling workflow for characters and massive creatures in Hollywood VFX productions and AAA games.

Luca Candela

CG Supervisor at Blur Studios, former Head of Department of Lighting, Compositing, and Lookdev at Axis Studios

Foreword

Before I ever spoke to Andrea, I was astounded by his work.

Our interview process was such a pleasure, and I knew I had struck gold.

At the time, we had a small team on the project, but Andrea was the glue, building and bridging connections between departments. I cannot recall a single meeting where we didn't laugh as a group!

His skills were exceptional, but he was always humble and, most importantly, he was patient and willing to teach. Through his passion and knowledge, I got to see others grow day by day.

It really was a beautiful thing.

Beyond work, we bonded, and I am very happy to call Andrea a true friend. He taught me how to make an authentic carbonara – just the right amount of cream (zero). In return, I introduced him to Irn-Bru and whisky.

A proper trade of culture and creative passions.

I feel honored to know him and even more so to have been asked to write this.

Anyone willing to take the time to read or listen to the guidance of Andrea is in seriously good hands, and I personally would take great notice of any recommendation that ever comes from this fine gentleman.

Drew Robertson

CG Supervisor at DIGIC Pictures

Contributors

About the author

Andrea Salvatori is a Senior Creature Artist, Digital Sculptor, and 3D Modeler with more than 10 years of experience in the visual effects industry. Throughout his career, he has specialized in creating creatures, characters, and hard-surface assets for feature films, television productions, and AAA projects.

Andrea has contributed to internationally acclaimed productions including *House of the Dragon* (2022), *Love, Death & Robots Season 4* (2025), *The Rings of Power Season 3* (2026), *The Boys Season 5* (2026), *Raised by Wolves* (2020), *Carnival Row Season 2* (2023), *Gran Turismo* (2023), *Captain America: Brave New World* (2025), and *The Dog Stars* (2026). During his career, he has collaborated with leading studios such as Pixomondo, Blur Studio, Axis Studios, and Untold Studios.

Alongside his production work, Andrea has spent more than a decade teaching digital sculpting and production workflows through universities, professional academies, and specialized masterclasses. His teaching philosophy is based on explaining not only how to use the tools, but also why professional production workflows are built the way they are.

This book brings together the experience, techniques, and practical lessons he has gained throughout his career, with the goal of helping artists build production-ready workflows and develop the skills needed to work in the film, VFX, and game industries.

Before anything else, I would like to thank my family. Their patience, understanding, and constant support made this project possible. Writing a book while balancing work, teaching, and family life is a challenge that no one accomplishes alone. To my wife, my daughters, and everyone close to me, thank you for encouraging me throughout this journey and for supporting the countless hours I dedicated to this project.

I would also like to express my sincere gratitude to the entire Packt team for giving me this incredible opportunity. Publishing a book has been a personal dream for many years, and seeing that dream become a reality is something I am deeply grateful for. Thank you for your guidance, trust, professionalism, and support throughout the entire process.

As I worked on these chapters, I often found myself wanting to add more recipes, more exercises, and more production examples. The world of creature creation is incredibly vast, and every topic covered in this book could easily become a book of its own. At some point, I realized that the most important goal was not to cover everything, but to provide a practical and solid foundation that you could immediately apply to your own projects.

If a single chapter helped you solve a problem, improve your workflow, or look at creature creation from a different perspective, then this book has accomplished its purpose. Sharing the knowledge I have gathered through years of sculpting, teaching, and collaborating with talented artists around the world has been a privilege.

About the reviewers

Maxime is a French freelance 3D artist whose career spans film, luxury, 3D printing, and real-time production. After discovering 3D as a hobby in 2011, he turned his passion into a profession in 2014 and has since worked with clients in France and internationally, including those in Australia and Canada. Blending technical expertise with artistic creativity, he also teaches at several 3D schools in France.

A long-time ZBrush enthusiast, he develops plugins for the software, including a widely used tool that streamlines 3D-printing workflows. He previously served as a technical reviewer for *Sculpting in ZBrush Made Simple* by Lukas Kutschera (Packt Publishing).

Tiziano Palumbo is a Lead Character Artist at Platige Image with extensive experience creating high-end digital characters and creatures for games, cinematic trailers, film, and television. He specializes in sculpting, modeling, texturing, shading, grooming, and character development, with a strong foundation in anatomy and traditional sculpture. Throughout his career, he has contributed to projects including *The Witcher IV*, *Call of Duty: Black Ops 6* and *7*, *Call of Duty: Modern Warfare III*, *Warhammer 40,000: Dawn of War IV*, and *Prehistoric Planet*. He also mentors aspiring artists in creature sculpting and character development.

Table of Contents

Chapter 3: Blocking Complex Areas: Hands, Mouth, and Functional Structures 99

Chapter 4: Retopology in Maya: Understanding Topology Theory and Creating Clean Geometry for Animation 117

Preface

When I first discovered digital sculpting more than 20 years ago, learning resources were extremely limited. There were no comprehensive online courses, very few books, and only a handful of tutorials available. Most of what I learned came from experimentation, observing the work of other artists, making mistakes, and gradually understanding why certain workflows produced better results than others.

As the years passed, the amount of educational content grew enormously. Today, information is everywhere. However, I noticed that many resources still focus on showing which buttons to press rather than explaining the reasoning behind professional decisions. Understanding why a workflow works is often more valuable than simply knowing how to execute it.

That realization became one of the main reasons for writing the *ZBrush Cookbook*.

Throughout these chapters, I won't simply show you which buttons to press or which brushes to use. Instead, I'll share the production mindset I've developed over more than a decade working on creatures for films and television. Every workflow, decision, and technique presented in this book comes from real production experience, where efficiency, organization, and problem-solving are just as important as artistic skill.

My hope is that this book will help you become not just a better ZBrush user but also teach you how to think like a production artist. Whether you're creating your first creature portfolio or preparing for a career in VFX, animation, or games, I hope these recipes will give you practical tools, greater confidence, and the curiosity to keep learning long after you've finished the final chapter.

Who this book is for

This book is intended for digital sculptors, creature artists, character artists, and 3D modelers who already have a basic understanding of ZBrush and want to develop production-ready workflows used in the film, VFX, and game industries.

While beginners can still follow many of the concepts presented throughout the book, readers will benefit most if they are already familiar with ZBrush's interface, navigation, brushes, and fundamental sculpting tools. Rather than focusing on explaining every feature of the software, this book emphasizes the reasoning behind professional workflows, helping readers understand not only how to perform a task but also why a particular approach is used in production.

Whether you are an art student with prior ZBrush experience, a freelancer looking to refine your workflow, or a junior to intermediate creature artist preparing for a professional career, the recipes in this book will provide practical techniques, production insights, and industry-proven workflows that can be immediately applied to your own projects.

What this book covers

Chapter 1, Set up and Best Practices for a Production-Ready Creature, introduces the software, project organization, essential references, and best practices for building a solid foundation before starting any creature sculpt.

Chapter 2, Blocking with DynaMesh and ZSpheres: Establishing Primary Shapes, explains how to establish proportions, silhouette, and primary forms using an efficient blocking workflow that can be refined throughout production.

Chapter 3, Blocking Complex Areas: Hands, Mouth, and Functional Structures, focuses on sculpting the most challenging anatomical regions while maintaining correct proportions, functionality, and production-ready forms.

Chapter 4, Retopology in Maya: Understanding Topology Theory and Creating Clean Geometry for Animation, teaches the principles of animation-friendly topology and demonstrates how to build clean, efficient meshes using Maya's **Quad Draw** tools.

Chapter 5, UV Mapping with UDIMs: Fixing Distortions and Optimizing Workflow, covers professional UV layout techniques, UDIM organization, texel density, and strategies for creating clean UVs suitable for production assets.

Chapter 6, Using Layers in ZBrush: Correct Workflow for Primary, Secondary, and Tertiary Details, demonstrates how to organize sculpting layers, preserve flexibility, and progressively develop surface detail using a non-destructive workflow.

Chapter 7, Creating Custom Brushes and Insert Meshes for Creature Tertiary Details, explores how to build reusable brushes, custom alphas, and Insert Meshes to speed up production while adding believable tertiary details.

Chapter 8, Dividing the Model to Maximize Resolution, explains how to organize SubTools and subdivision levels efficiently to maximize sculpting resolution while maintaining a responsive and production-friendly scene.

Chapter 9, Exporting Meshes and Creating Maps for Texturing and Lookdev, shows how to prepare production-ready assets by exporting meshes and generating Displacement, Normal, Cavity, and other essential maps for texturing and look development.

To get the most out of this book

To get the most out of this book, you should already be familiar with the **ZBrush** interface and understand the basic sculpting workflow, including navigation, brushes, SubTools, and subdivision levels.

Basic knowledge of **Autodesk Maya**, particularly polygon modeling and Viewport navigation, is also recommended as several chapters rely on Maya for retopology, UV mapping, and mesh preparation.

Note that this book focuses on production workflows and assumes that readers already know the fundamentals of both ZBrush and Autodesk Maya.

Software/Hardware covered in the book	OS Requirements
Autodesk Maya (2024 or later)	Windows, Mac OS X
Maxon ZBrush (2024.0 or later)	Windows, Mac OS X
Adobe Photoshop (2024 or later)	Windows, Mac OS X
PureRef (latest version)	Windows, Mac OS X

The following table summarizes the minimum software versions and the recommended hardware specifications for completing the recipes in this book.

Hardware	Minimum	Recommended	Optimal
CPU	Quad-core processor	Modern 6-core processor	Modern 8-core (or higher) processor
RAM	16 GB	32 GB	64 GB
GPU	Dedicated GPU	Dedicated GPU with 8 GB VRAM	Dedicated GPU with 12 GB VRAM or more
Storage	SSD	NVMe SSD	High-speed NVMe SSD

Before starting the exercises, ensure that ZBrush and Autodesk Maya are correctly installed and activated. A graphics tablet is highly recommended for sculpting, although a mouse can be used for the early chapters.

Some chapters also reference third-party utilities such as **PureRef** (free) and **PolyRaven** (commercial; available for a fee), which can be installed as needed when they are introduced in the book. Download links and installation guidance are provided where required.

Note that the author acknowledges the use of cutting-edge AI, such as ChatGPT, with the sole aim of enhancing the language and clarity within the book, thereby ensuring a smooth reading experience for readers. It's important to note that the content itself has been crafted by the author and edited by a professional publishing team. Packt does not accept AI-generated content that replaces expert authorship.

Download the example code/resource files

This book includes a complete downloadable code/resource bundle containing all the example projects and files used throughout the chapters. We recommend downloading the bundle so you can follow along smoothly and experiment with the examples.

Use the bundle as a practical starting point. Modify it, extend it, and apply what you learn by creating your own variations as you progress through the chapters.

Get the code/resource bundle

If you bought the book directly from Packt:

1. Go to `packtpub.com`.
2. Click your profile picture and select **Your Orders**.
3. Find this book and click **Download Code**.

If you bought this book from Amazon or any other channel partner:

1. Go to `packtpub.com/unlock` or scan the following QR code:

2. Search for this book.
3. Sign up or log in to your free Packt account.
4. Upload your proof of purchase and download the code/resource bundle locally.

Usage note: You're free to use and modify this code/resource for personal learning and non-commercial projects. The downloadable assets are organized into chapter-wise folders. Some folders are shared across multiple chapters when the same files are reused (for example, `Chapter02_03`, `Chapter04_05`, and `Chapter06_07`). It also contains the final creature model in Maya (`dragonCrest_approved.fbx`) for your reference. Refer to the *Technical requirements* section at the beginning of each chapter to identify the folder and assets required for that chapter.

Download the color images

Some screenshots contain detailed ZBrush interface elements that may be easier to inspect in the included color PDF edition, which supports zooming. Your purchase includes a color, DRM-free PDF copy of this book, ideal for viewing color images, screenshots, and diagrams. Refer to the *Free benefits with your book section* at the end of the *Preface* to unlock your PDF copy.

Conventions used

There are several text conventions used throughout this book.

`CodeInText`: Indicates code words in text, database table names, folder names, filenames, file extensions, pathnames, dummy URLs, user input, and X (formerly Twitter) handles. For example: "Default labels such as `pCube1`, `Merged2`, or `PM3D_Sphere3` give you no information about what the object actually is."

Bold: Indicates a new term, an important word, or words that you see on the screen. For instance, words in menus or dialog boxes appear in the text like this. For example: "Activate **PLine** in the **Draw** | **Floor** panel to display a perspective line between the camera and the mesh. "

> **Note**
>
> Warnings or important notes appear like this.

> **Tip**
>
> Tips and tricks appear like this.

Sections

In this book, you will find several headings that appear frequently (*Getting ready*, *How to do it...*, *How it works...*, *There's more...*, and *See also*).

To give clear instructions on how to complete a recipe, use these sections as follows:

Getting ready

This section tells you what to expect in the recipe and describes how to set up any software or any preliminary settings required for the recipe.

How to do it...

This section contains the steps required to follow the recipe.

How it works...

This section usually consists of a detailed explanation of what happened in the previous section.

There's more...

This section consists of additional information about the recipe in order to make you more knowledgeable about the recipe.

See also

This section provides helpful links to other useful information for the recipe.

Get in touch

Feedback from our readers is always welcome.

General feedback: If you have questions about any aspect of this book or have any general feedback, please email us at `customercare@packt.com` and mention the book's title in the subject of your message.

Errata: Although we have taken every care to ensure the accuracy of our content, mistakes do happen. If you have found a mistake in this book, we would be grateful if you reported this to us. Please visit `http://www.packt.com/submit-errata`, click **Submit Errata**, and fill in the form.

Piracy: If you come across any illegal copies of our works in any form on the internet, we would be grateful if you would provide us with the location address or website name. Please contact us at `copyright@packt.com` with a link to the material.

If you are interested in becoming an author: If there is a topic that you have expertise in and you are interested in either writing or contributing to a book, please visit `http://authors.packt.com/`.

Subscribe to Game Dev Assembly Newsletter!

We are excited to introduce **Game Dev Assembly**, our brand-new newsletter dedicated to everything game development. Whether you're a programmer, designer, artist, animator, or studio lead, you'll get exclusive insights, industry trends, and expert tips to help you build better games and grow your skills. Sign up today and become part of a growing community of creators, innovators, and game changers.

Scan the QR code to join instantly!

https://packt.link/gamedev-newsletter

Free benefits with your book

This book includes free benefits designed to support your learning and help you apply what you learn effectively. Activate them now for instant access (see the *How to unlock* section for instructions).

Here's a quick overview of what you can instantly unlock with your purchase:

How to unlock

Scan the QR code (or go to `packtpub.com/unlock`). Search for this book by name, confirm the edition, and then follow the steps on the page.

UNLOCK NOW

Note: Have your invoice handy. Purchases made directly from the Packt website don't require an invoice.

Share your thoughts

Once you've read *ZBrush Cookbook*, we'd love to hear your thoughts! Scan the QR code below to go straight to the Amazon review page for this book and share your feedback.

https://packt.link/r/1836207611

Your review is important to us and the tech community and will help us make sure we're delivering excellent quality content.

1

Set up and Best Practices for a Production-Ready Creature

Welcome to the *ZBrush Cookbook*!

In this first chapter, we'll explore the essential setup and best practices needed to begin sculpting a **production-ready creature**. Developing precision from the very beginning is not about being pedantic, but about training the mindset required to operate within complex, high-end production pipelines. Clean setups, consistent organization, and technical discipline allow artists to work faster and more reliably, and to integrate smoothly with large teams and demanding studio standards. Hence, the recipes in this chapter are valuable not just for aspiring professionals but also for hobbyists and junior artists who want to develop studio-ready workflows.

We'll begin by tailoring ZBrush for performance, structuring clean project directories, and setting up Maya for seamless interoperability. By understanding how these early technical steps influence the entire production chain, you will build a foundation that allows you to work faster and cleaner within high-end production pipelines.

Here are the recipes that we'll cover in this chapter:

- Customizing the ZBrush interface for creature production
- Organizing files for a clean and consistent workflow
- Setting up a project in Maya using correct scale and unit conventions
- Keeping ZBrush responsive with high-resolution assets
- Using naming conventions for both ZBrush and Maya
- Importing and exporting assets between ZBrush and Maya

Note

Download the code/resource bundle and the PDF version of this book

Your purchase includes a DRM-free PDF copy of this book, the code/resource bundle, and a range of exclusive benefits. To unlock everything, follow the *Free benefits with your book* section in the *Preface*.

Technical requirements

To follow the recipes in this chapter, make sure you have the following software, tools, and hardware ready. These will ensure a smooth and stable workflow across all the recipes in the book:

- **ZBrush 2024** or later, with all updates installed. It will be used for digital sculpting, layering, and displacement map generation.
- **Autodesk Maya 2024** or later, properly configured to handle scene scale and asset exchange.
- **Organized project folders**, including directories for:
  - `/ztl` (ZBrush Tools)
  - `/fbx_obj` (Interchange geometry)
  - `/ma_mb` (Maya scenes)
  - `/maps` (Textures and displacement maps)
- **Custom ZBrush interface assets**: Brushes, hotkeys, and UI layouts (for example, **DynaMesh**, **ZRemesher**, **Del Hidden**)
- **Naming convention guide**: Use consistent suffixes such as `_DYNA`, `_GEO`, or `_APPROVED` for production clarity

Hardware recommendations are as follows:

- **CPU**: Intel i7/i9 or AMD Ryzen 7/9 series
- **RAM**: Minimum 16 GB (32 GB recommended)
- **GPU**: Dedicated OpenGL 3.3+ graphics card with ≥ 4 GB VRAM
- **Storage**: SSD with at least 50 GB free space for ZBrush temp and autosaves
- **Tablet**: Wacom or equivalent with pressure sensitivity

You can download the example project files for this book by following the instructions in the *Download the example code/resource files* section in the *Preface* of this book.

This chapter's code/resource files are included in the downloadable code/resource bundle.

Note that some screenshots in the chapters contain detailed ZBrush interface elements that may be easier to inspect in the included color PDF edition, which supports zooming. Refer to the *Preface* for details on accessing your PDF copy.

Customizing the ZBrush interface for creature production

Let's get started customizing the ZBrush interface! This is where every sculpting session begins and where efficiency can make the biggest difference during production. Before focusing on anatomy and detail, it's essential to design an interface that supports your daily workflow – one that keeps all critical tools within reach and minimizes menu searching. ZBrush is extremely flexible: panels can be rearranged, shelves reorganized, and new menus created to match the specific needs of a professional artist.

Because ZBrush offers hundreds of buttons and submenus, the default layout can often feel overwhelming or cluttered. A tailored interface solves this by exposing only the features you use most: **DynaMesh**, **ZRemesher**, **Polygroups**, **Layers**, and sculpting brushes that define your process. Decluttering the workspace will allow you to reduce distractions and maintain focus on the forms rather than the interface itself.

In this recipe, we'll build a practical creature-oriented layout that consolidates SubTool and Layer management, exposes essential Polygroup tools for mesh control, and assigns shortcuts for speed. You'll learn how to create a custom menu, save it as your personal UI preset, and ensure it loads automatically each time ZBrush starts.

Getting ready

Before customizing the ZBrush interface, ensure you have the following setup:

1. ZBrush is open and reset to its default interface, so you begin from a clean layout. This will allow you to clearly see which panels and buttons you want to rearrange for your own workflow.
2. At this stage, load a simple Sphere or any clean PolyMesh3D. This allows you to immediately customize the ZBrush interface while clearly evaluating panel layout, visibility, and tool access.
3. Finally, ensure that your `ZStartup` folder is writable, as we'll save our custom UI there later.

Figure 1.1 shows an overview of the default ZBrush interface before any customization is applied:

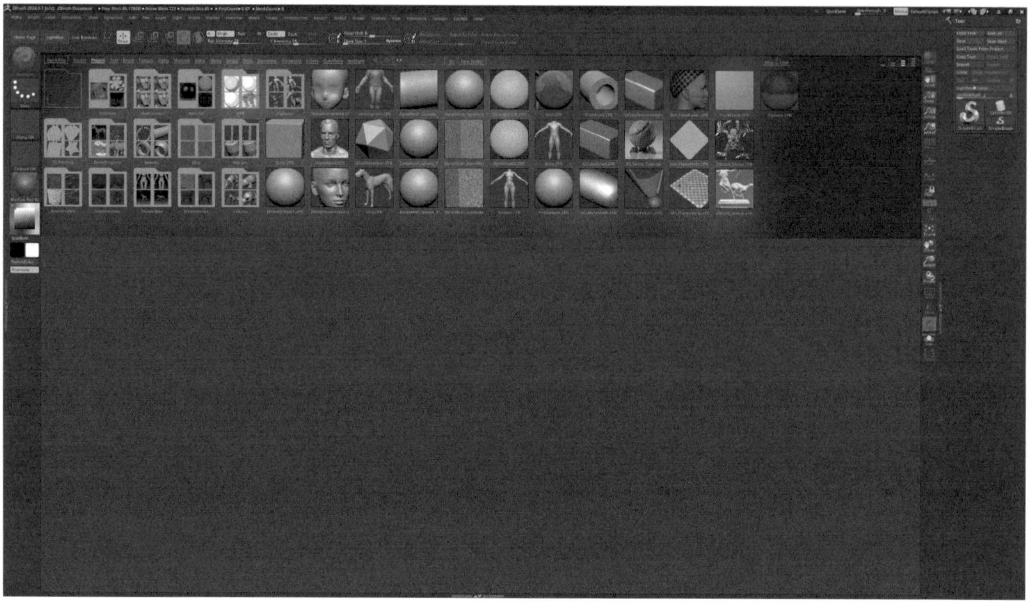

Figure 1.1 – Overview of the default ZBrush interface before customization

How to do it...

Let's start customizing the interface so it matches the way you actually sculpt. Follow these steps to customize the ZBrush interface and adapt it to a creature production workflow:

1. Open **Preferences** | **Config** | **Enable Customize**. ZBrush will enter an editable mode that allows you to move, add, or remove buttons anywhere in the interface.
2. While **Customize Mode** is active, hold *Ctrl* + *Alt* and simply drag any button, brush, or material to your preferred location. This could be on the top bar, side shelves, or custom trays. For example, you can drag **DynaMesh**, **ZRemesher**, or **Auto Groups With UV** from their menus directly into your main shelf.

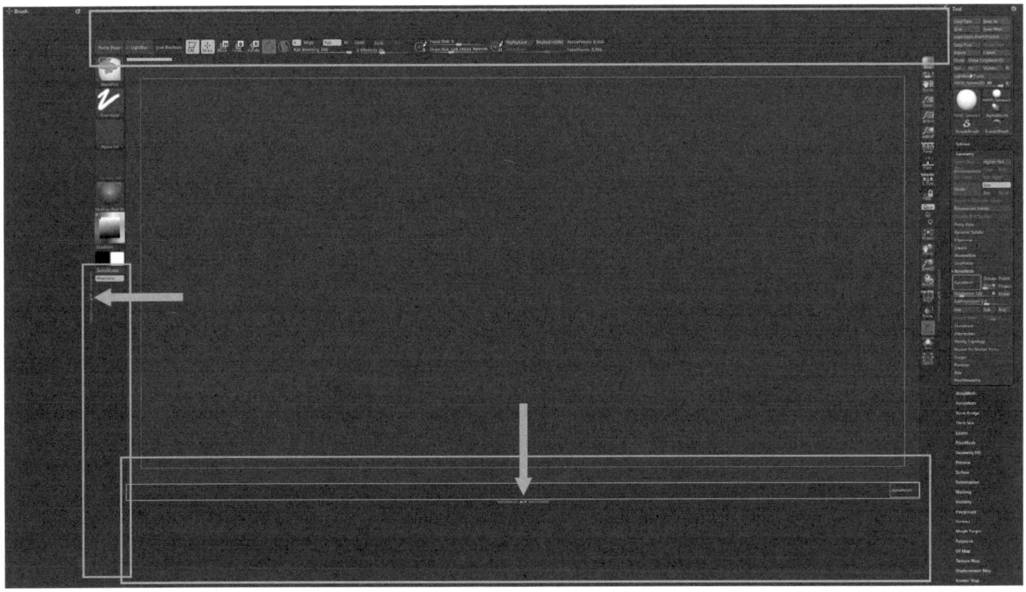

Figure 1.2 – Valid drop zones highlighted while Customize Mode is active in ZBrush

While **Customize Mode** is active, valid drop areas are highlighted, indicating where buttons and tools can be placed within the ZBrush interface. These areas can be resized to reclaim unused space, allowing you to organize menus on the left and create custom button shelves along the bottom without affecting the sculpting canvas.

3. Add the brushes you rely on daily to the lower shelf:
    - **ClayBuildup** for muscle definition
    - **DamStandard** for wrinkles and sharp creases
    - **Move** and **Move Topological** for adjusting silhouettes
    - **Inflate** to emphasize volumes

4. From **Tool | Geometry**, drag **DynaMesh**, **ZRemesher**, and **Mirror And Weld** into your interface. This avoids constant panel switching during blocking or cleanup. *Figure 1.3* shows **DynaMesh** settings docked in the UI to speed up remeshing and volume iteration during early sculpting:

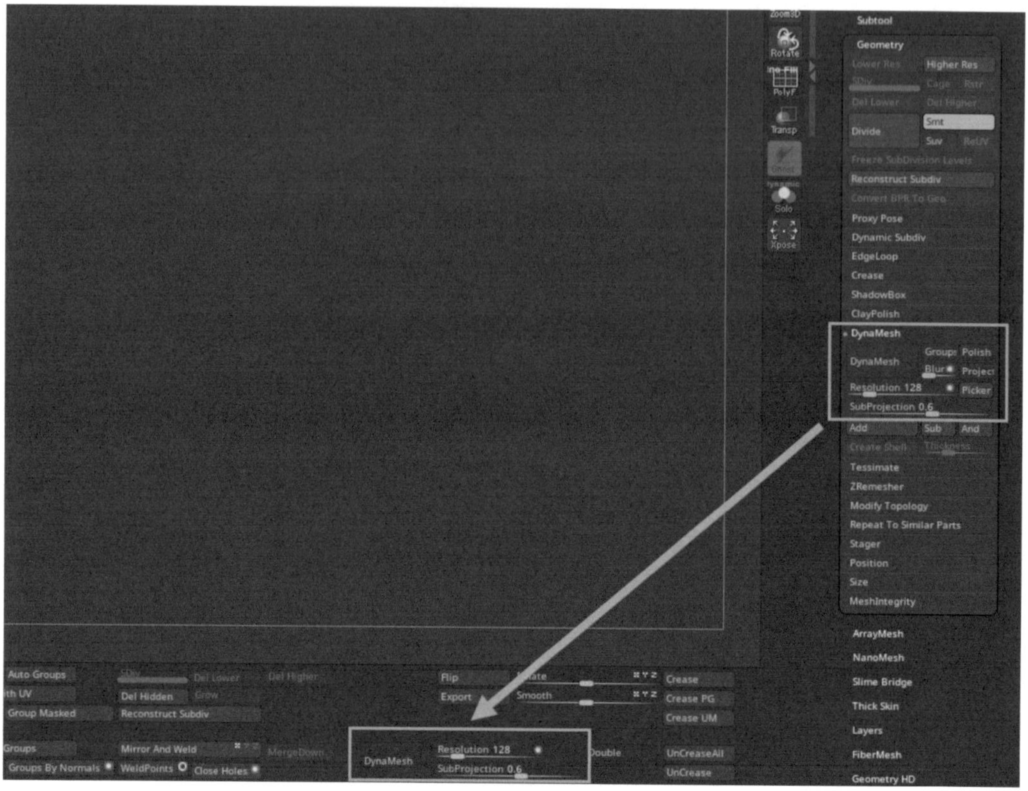

Figure 1.3 – Docking DynaMesh settings in the UI

Figure 1.4 shows the **ZRemesher** controls added to the custom interface for quick access during blocking and retopology checks:

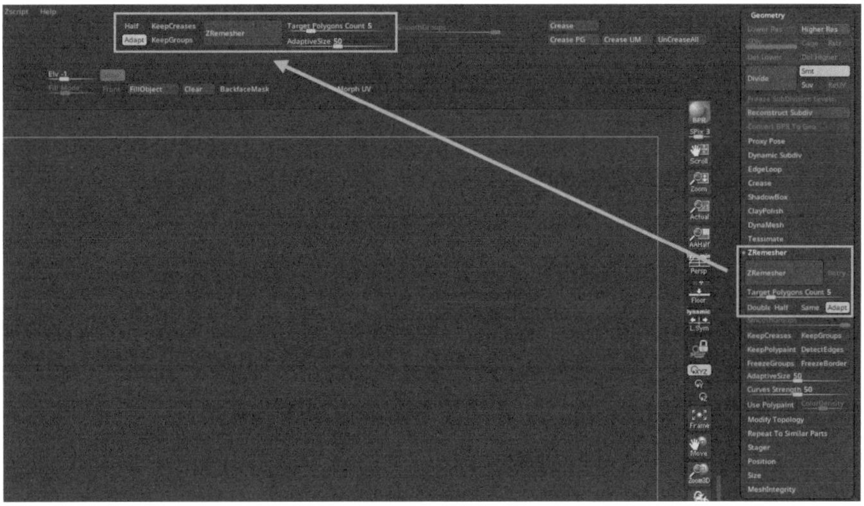

Figure 1.4 – Adding ZRemesher controls

Figure 1.5 shows **Modify Topology** tools placed on the lower shelf, with **Mirror And Weld** positioned for fast symmetry fixes and geometry cleanup without opening panels:

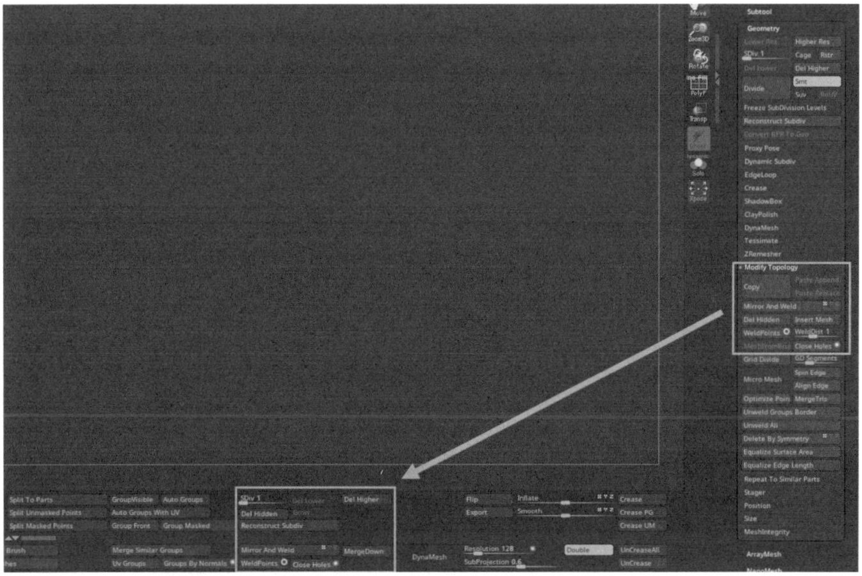

Figure 1.5 – Placing Modify Topology tools on the lower shelf

> **Note**
>
> Placing tools such as **Divide**, **Del Lower**, **Del Higher**, **Del Hidden**, **Weld Points**, **Merge Down**, and **Mirror And Weld** in this area gives you immediate control over cleaning, separating, or merging geometry. This is especially useful when working on low-poly meshes, preparing clean SubTools, or fixing symmetry issues without interrupting your sculpting flow.

5. Drag your favorite shaders, like **MatCap Grey**, **BasicMaterial**, and **SkinShade4**, into the interface using *Ctrl* + *Alt* and *drag*. You can even assign a few alternate shaders to hotkeys (for example, 1 = **MatCap Grey**, 2 = **BasicMaterial**) to instantly switch between them.

> **Tip**
>
> Keep one neutral and one colored material visible at all times. This helps evaluate both surface contrast and color variation when working on fine tertiary details.

6. Still in **Customize Mode**, bring **Del Hidden**, **Groups by Normals**, and **Auto Groups With UV** into view. These are used frequently during subdivision cleanup and mesh organization.
7. When the interface feels comfortable, exit **Customize Mode** by toggling **Enable Customize** off. Then, go to **Preferences** | **Config** | **Store Config** to save your setup permanently. ZBrush will now load it automatically every time you start the software.

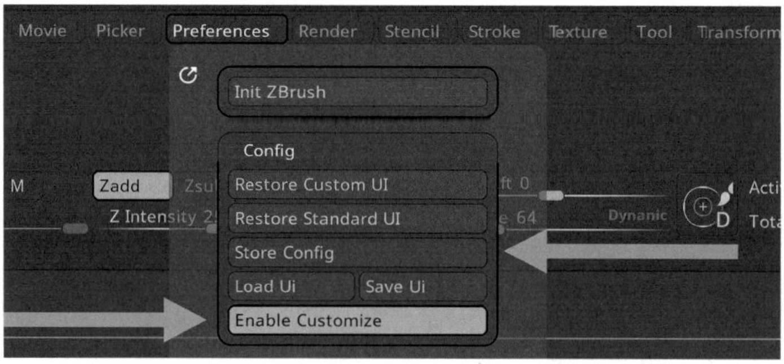

Figure 1.6 – Exiting Customize Mode and saving the UI layout

Note

Make a backup copy of your `.cfg` file located in `ZStartup/ConfigFiles`. ZBrush updates can overwrite your layout during installation.

How it works...

Now, let's understand the underlying logic behind interface customization and how it supports speed, clarity, and stability during creature production.

ZBrush's interface was designed to be modular. Each tray, shelf, and menu can be reorganized to reflect the natural flow of your sculpting process. The principle is simple: place the most frequently used tools (such as **DynaMesh**, **ZRemesher**, or **Mirror And Weld**) where your hand instinctively reaches during production. This ergonomic optimization directly impacts speed, especially when working with dozens of SubTools or switching between primary and tertiary detailing.

Materials as visual feedback

Including **MatCap Grey**, **BasicMaterial**, or **SkinShade4** in your interface isn't only aesthetic, but also functional. Creature modeling often requires constant evaluation of surface tension and readability under different lighting conditions. Quick access to materials lets you switch between neutral and colored shaders instantly, helping you spot sculpting inconsistencies or areas lacking definition. A matte shader is perfect for checking form, while a reflective one emphasizes silhouette and depth.

Workflow stability and iteration

A personalized UI also stabilizes your mental workflow. Since all tools, layers, and materials are always visible, you maintain continuity between creative and technical phases. This reduces context switching, prevents errors like accidentally enabling **Record** on the wrong layer, and improves rhythm during sculpting sessions. Saving your setup through **Preferences** | **Config** | **Store Config** ensures that every session opens exactly as you left it, maintaining consistency across projects.

There's more...

Here are some practical recommendations for managing and refining your ZBrush interface to help you stay organized and efficient across different stages of a creature production workflow:

- **Backup your custom interface**: Always export your ZBrush UI once it's finalized by going to **Preferences** | **Config** | **Save UI**. Store the file in a safe location, such as a shared studio folder or version-controlled repository. This prevents loss of your optimized setup after software updates or reinstallation.
- **Multiple layouts for different stages**: You can create separate configurations for *blocking*, *detailing*, and *presentation*. For example, a minimalist layout for early sculpting and a full layout for high-resolution detailing can make your workflow faster and cleaner. *Figures 1.7* and *1.8* show examples of different types of layouts:

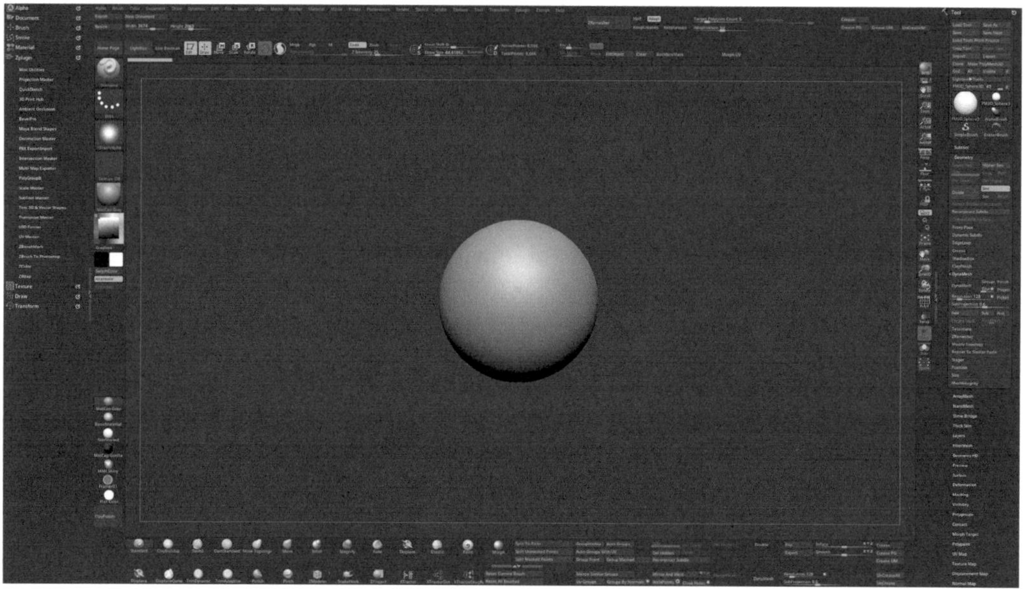

Figure 1.7 – Overview of ZBrush interface for a blocking-focused layout

Figure 1.8 – Overview of ZBrush interface for high-resolution detailing layout

- **Keep it simple**: Avoid overcrowding the interface with rarely used buttons. A focused workspace reduces visual fatigue and keeps you engaged on form and anatomy instead of the UI.

Organizing files for a clean and consistent workflow

Keeping your files organized from the beginning of your creature project is essential for a smooth and professional workflow. Whether you're working alone or as part of a larger team, clean file structure and clear naming conventions ensure that your assets can be easily understood, modified, and integrated across departments from sculpting and texturing to rigging and rendering. Thinking ahead not only saves time later but also makes you a more production-ready artist.

This recipe will guide you through best practices for structuring project folders, naming files, and organizing elements inside Maya and ZBrush.

Getting ready

Make sure you have the following setup before you begin:

- A clear project folder ready on your drive, preferably on an SSD for faster access.

- You'll need both **ZBrush** and **Maya** installed and configured to use **meters** as the unit scale.
- Have your reference board open in **PureRef**, and prepare a base project folder where all files, from sculpts to exports, will be organized.

How to do it...

Let's follow these steps to build a clean and scalable folder structure that will serve as the backbone of your creature production:

1. Begin by creating a main directory named after your creature. This folder will act as the root of your project. For example, if your asset is a thorny dragon, name the folder `thornyDragon`. Inside, create a set of subfolders that reflect each stage of production, as shown in *Figure 1.9*:

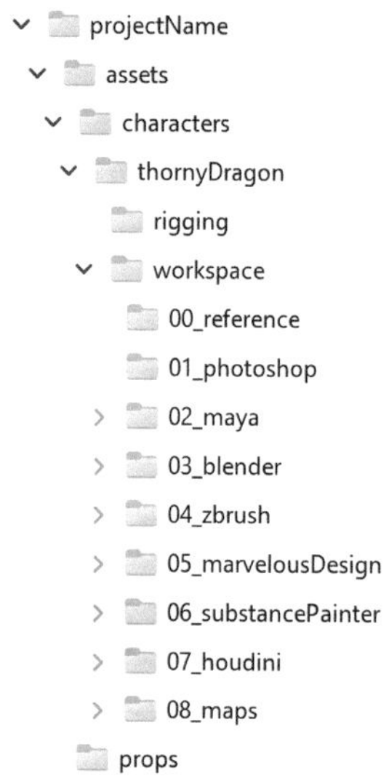

Figure 1.9 – Example of a well-organized creature project directory structure

This modular hierarchy can easily scale with the project. If new departments join the pipeline, such as rigging or lookdev, you can simply add new folders without disrupting the existing structure.

> **Tip**
>
> Keep all folders lowercase and avoid spaces in names. Use underscores or camelCase for clarity when projects move between software.

2. Inside each folder, use a consistent and descriptive naming pattern. This helps both you and your teammates understand what a file contains at a glance. The recommended syntax is:
   `<assetName>_<fileType>_v###.ext`

   Where:

   - `assetName` identifies your creature (for example, `dragon`, `golem`, `marineSoldier`)
   - `fileType` describes the content (for example, `sculpt`, `geometry`, `retopo`, `uvs`, `texture`)
   - `v###` tracks the version number, padded with zeroes (for example, `v001`, `v002`)

   Here are some practical examples:

   - `dragon_sculpt_v001.ZTL`
   - `golem_geos_v002.ma`
   - `marineSoldier_uvs_v003.obj`
   - `hydra_tx_v006.spp`

How it works...

The logic behind this method is simple: each folder represents a stage in the pipeline, and each filename tells a small story about what it contains. The root folder acts as your project's foundation, while subfolders mirror the journey of your asset through different departments, from sculpting in ZBrush to look development in Substance 3D Painter and animation preparation in Maya. This modular organization means you can move files between software or share them with other artists without breaking paths or references.

Another advantage of a structured file system is scalability. If your creature project expands, you can simply add new folders, for example, `Rig`, `Groom`, or `CFX`, without breaking the logic of the existing structure. This modular approach mirrors real studio pipelines, allowing your personal workflow to integrate seamlessly into larger production environments.

Additionally, file naming follows principles of clarity and version control; we'll discuss this in detail in the *Using naming conventions in ZBrush and Maya* recipe later in the chapter.

There's more...

To avoid rebuilding the same structure for every new creature, consider creating a reusable base project folder template. A predefined hierarchy with consistent subfolders for ZBrush, Maya, Substance 3D Painter, exports, and references allows you to start each project immediately with a production-ready setup.

Using templates improves consistency across assets, reduces setup time, and minimizes organizational errors, especially when switching between multiple projects or revisiting older work. Remember that in studio pipelines, standardized folder structures are essential for scalability and collaboration.

See also

For file naming, see the *Using naming conventions in ZBrush and Maya* recipe.

Setting up a project in Maya using correct scale and unit conventions

With a clean file structure in place, the next step is configuring Maya to ensure assets move consistently and predictably through the production pipeline. This process is often overlooked, yet it forms the foundation of a clean, reliable, and production-ready workflow. By disabling unnecessary plug-ins and optimizing preferences, you'll reduce startup times, avoid crashes, and keep the workspace focused on modeling and lookdev tasks.

These small adjustments can dramatically improve stability and performance, especially when dealing with high-resolution geometry or complex UDIMs. Even if you're working on a single asset, the same structure used in large studios applies here. By the end of this recipe, you'll have a fully optimized Maya environment that launches quickly, runs efficiently, and integrates seamlessly into your production pipeline.

Getting ready

Before we begin, make sure you follow these steps for an optimal setup:

1. Maya should be closed, and any open scenes should be saved. We'll be adjusting global preferences and plug-in settings, so it's wise to back up your current configuration from `Documents/maya/<version>/prefs/`.
2. Once the above step is done, reopen Maya with a clean scene to ensure a fresh start. Throughout this process, keep an eye on stability – some changes might require a quick restart to take effect. Having a neutral workspace ready will make it easier to follow the upcoming steps safely and without interruptions.

How to do it...

Follow these steps to turn Maya into a fast, predictable workspace that matches your creature pipeline:

1. Launch Maya and open **Windows | Settings/Preferences | Plug-in Manager**.
2. You will see two checkboxes per item: **Loaded** (active now) and **Auto Load** (loads at startup). Uncheck both for plug-ins you don't need during sculpting and lookdev work. Typical candidates are `stereoCamera.mll`, `dx11Shader.mll`, `bifrostGraph.mll`, `mash.mll`, and `xgenToolkit.mll` if you are not grooming. Keep essentials such as `objExport.mll` for ZBrush handoff and your renderer (for example, `mtoa.mll for Arnold`).

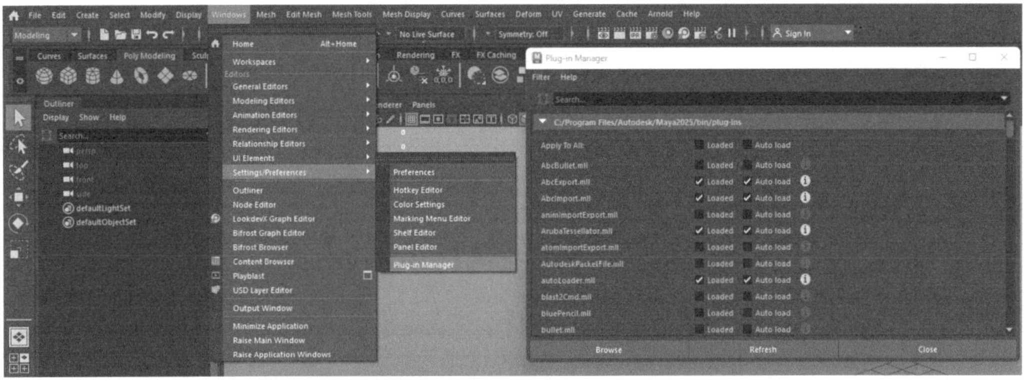

Figure 1.10 – Plug-in Manager with unused entries unchecked

3. Confirm the change by closing the **Plug-in Manager**. If Maya prompts for a restart, accept it. On relaunch, you should notice a shorter startup and a lighter memory footprint, which helps when opening heavy scenes with multiple UDIMs.
4. Next, open **Windows | Settings/Preferences | Preferences**. In the left panel, choose **Settings**, then under **Working Units** set **Linear | Meters**. Leave **Angular** and **Time** as they are unless a specific rig or animation requires otherwise.

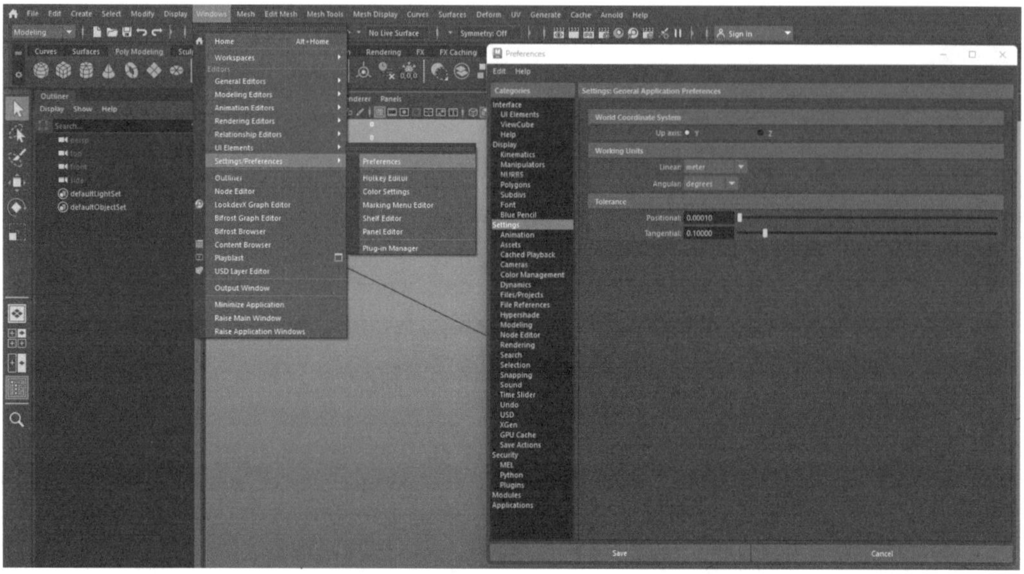

Figure 1.11 – Preferences with Linear Units set to Meters

> **Note**
>
> Never scale the whole model to fix unit mismatches. Adjust the *project units* instead. Manual scaling often breaks rigging, simulation, and displacement depths downstream.

5. Click **Save** at the bottom of the dialog.
6. Create a compact shelf for the actions you repeat every day. Right-click the shelf tabs and choose **New Shelf**; name it **CreatureTools**.
    1. To add a command, hold *Ctrl* + *Shift* and click the menu item you want.
    2. Add the core set most creature artists use:
        - **Mesh | Combine, Mesh | Separate**
        - **Edit | Delete by Type | History**
        - **Modify | Center Pivot**
        - **Modify | Freeze Transforms**
        - **Display | Heads Up Display | Poly Count**
        - **Edit Mesh | Extrude**
        - **Edit Mesh | Bevel**

- **Edit Mesh | Insert Edge Loop**
- **Edit Mesh | Target Weld**
- **Mesh Tools | Multi-Cut**
- **Mesh Display | Soften Edge**
- **Mesh Display | Harden Edge**

If you rely on an exporter or a small MEL or Python utility, add those tools here as well.

Figure 1.12 – A "CreatureTools" shelf with utilities

7. Test the shelf by importing a simple OBJ and running each button once. The goal is muscle memory: one click to *clean history*, one to *center the pivot*, one to *freeze transforms*, and you are ready to export or send to ZBrush.

> **Tip**
>
> Keep the shelf minimal. Five to eight buttons you use constantly are faster than twenty you might use. You can always extend it later.

8. Save the environment so it sticks. Go to **Windows | Settings/Preferences | Preferences** and click **Save Preferences**. This writes your current units, shelf layout, and general options to disk.
9. Back up the key files so you can recreate this setup on any machine. In `Documents/maya/<version>/prefs/`, copy: `shelves/shelf_CreatureTools.mel` (your shelf), `userHotkeys.mel` (if you mapped any), `prefs/userPrefs.mel` (global options). Store them in a folder named, for example, `Maya_Setup_Backup`, or sync them to cloud storage.

Figure 1.13 – Preferences folder with shelf and hotkey files highlighted

10. To verify everything, restart Maya one last time. Confirm that unused plug-ins remain disabled, the **Status Line** shows **m** for meters in the unit readout, and your **CreatureTools** shelf is present and functional.

With this single pass, Maya becomes lean, consistent with ZBrush and the rest of your pipeline, and ready for high-resolution creature work without the usual friction.

How it works...

Everything we've done in this setup contributes to one simple goal: stability. Disabling unnecessary plug-ins helps us to reduce Maya's memory footprint and startup load, allowing the program to focus entirely on what matters: handling geometry, managing scene data, and exporting clean assets to ZBrush or downstream departments. Each plug-in that loads in the background consumes CPU and RAM, so even if you never use **Bifrost**, **XGen**, or **MASH**, they still occupy valuable resources. Streamlining Maya ensures those resources are fully available to your sculpting workflow.

Setting Maya's scale to **meters** is just as crucial. While ZBrush doesn't use real-world units, the scale at which a model exists affects everything that comes later, from brush behavior and displacement depth to simulation accuracy and rendering consistency. Keeping a unified measurement system across the pipeline prevents displacement maps from appearing exaggerated or flattened and eliminates the need to rescale meshes every time you export or re-import between software.

The custom shelf ties it all together by turning repetitive menu commands into one-click actions. Instead of wasting seconds navigating through nested options for **Combine**, **Delete**, **History**, or **Freeze Transforms**, those tools are always visible and ready. Over a day of production work, that translates into minutes saved, and over a project, hours. It also gives you a rhythm: your technical steps become muscle memory, keeping you focused on creative decisions instead of interface management.

Finally, saving and backing up your preferences transforms this configuration into a portable workspace. Whether you move to a different computer, reinstall Maya, or work in a studio lab, you can restore your familiar environment instantly. That reliability builds confidence: every time Maya opens, it behaves the same way, with the same tools and scale, aligned to your creature pipeline.

> **Note**
>
> If you work across multiple versions of Maya, always test your configuration after migrating preferences. Some plug-ins or shelf scripts may change paths between releases, so verifying them early can save hours of debugging later.

There's more...

Once your Maya setup is stable, a few small habits can help you maintain consistency over time and make your configuration easier to reuse, share, and troubleshoot. The following practices focus on keeping your environment clean, repeatable, and production-friendly:

- **Share your setup**: Once you've refined your Maya configuration, it becomes easy to share it with teammates or students. A standardized environment reduces confusion in production, ensuring everyone exports at the same scale and uses the same optimized settings. Simply zip your `prefs` folder and send it along with a short readme explaining the setup.
- **Create a startup preset**: You can automate the launch of your preferred layout by saving a `.mel` or `.py` script that loads your shelves, units, and custom hotkeys. This allows Maya to open directly into your creature-ready workspace every time.
- **Keep it clean**: Over time, plug-ins and scripts can accumulate inside your **Preferences** folder. It's a good idea to periodically reset Maya's **Preferences** and reapply only what's essential. This helps prevent crashes and keeps the software running smoothly.

Keeping ZBrush responsive with high-resolution assets

Working with high-resolution geometry is one of the most demanding aspects of digital sculpting, but it does not automatically require constant optimization. ZBrush is designed to handle dense meshes efficiently, and in many cases, a clean workflow is enough to maintain good performance without touching advanced settings.

This recipe focuses on understanding *when* performance optimizations are actually needed and how to apply them selectively. Rather than forcing technical tweaks at every stage, you'll learn practical techniques to keep ZBrush responsive only when heavy geometry, multiple SubTools, or detailed refinement passes begin to impact interactivity.

The goal is not to permanently restrict your setup, but to know which levers to pull when responsiveness drops, allowing you to preserve a smooth creative flow while still pushing high-resolution assets comfortably, even on modest hardware.

Getting ready

Follow these steps to prepare your workspace:

1. Start from a clean and distraction-free environment. Make sure unnecessary background applications are closed and that your project is stored on a fast local drive, preferably an SSD.
2. Inside ZBrush, work only with the SubTools you need at that moment and avoid enabling features you are not actively using.

This simple preparation is often enough to keep the interface responsive without changing your workflow. The optimizations covered in this recipe should be applied only when performance starts to drop.

How to do it...

This section offers a small set of targeted actions to keep ZBrush responsive when working with high-resolution assets. Each step focuses on reducing the amount of geometry and background processing ZBrush needs to evaluate at any given time. Apply them selectively based on where performance begins to drop:

- Start by separating your creature into logical SubTools so you can push resolution only where needed. Open **Tool | SubTool**, then use **Split | Split to Parts or Split | Group Split** if Polygroups are already defined. Keep natural regions such as head, torso, limbs, tail, and membranes as separate SubTools. This allows you to sculpt high-density detail in one area without forcing the entire creature to update at the same resolution.

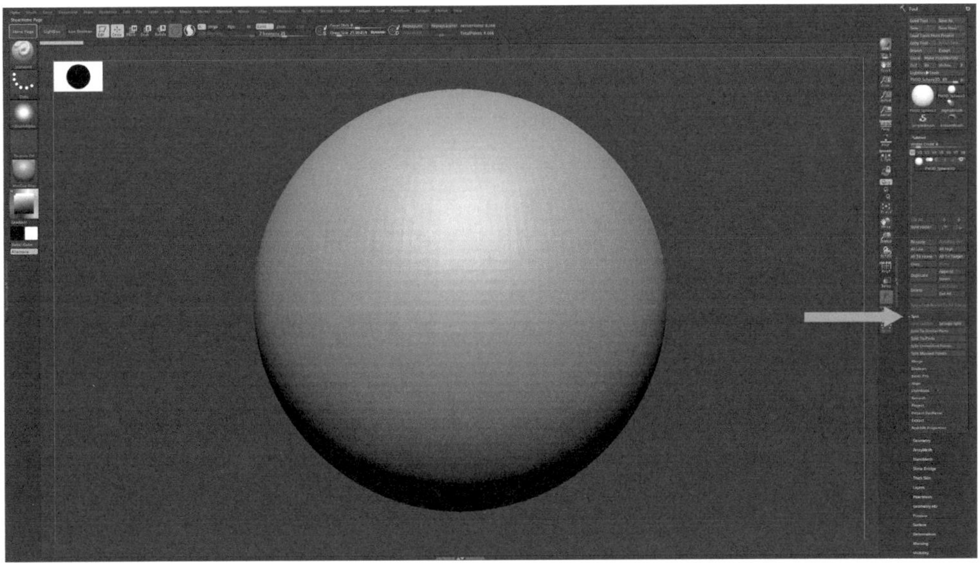

Figure 1.14 – Position of the Split options inside the Tool | SubTool menu in ZBrush

- Hide everything you are not sculpting. Hold *Ctrl* + *Shift* and *click* on the canvas or SubTool you want to isolate. Use *Ctrl* + *Shift* and *click* on an empty canvas to reveal all again. ZBrush evaluates only visible polygons, so isolating a single SubTool can immediately free CPU and memory, often resulting in the biggest performance gain.

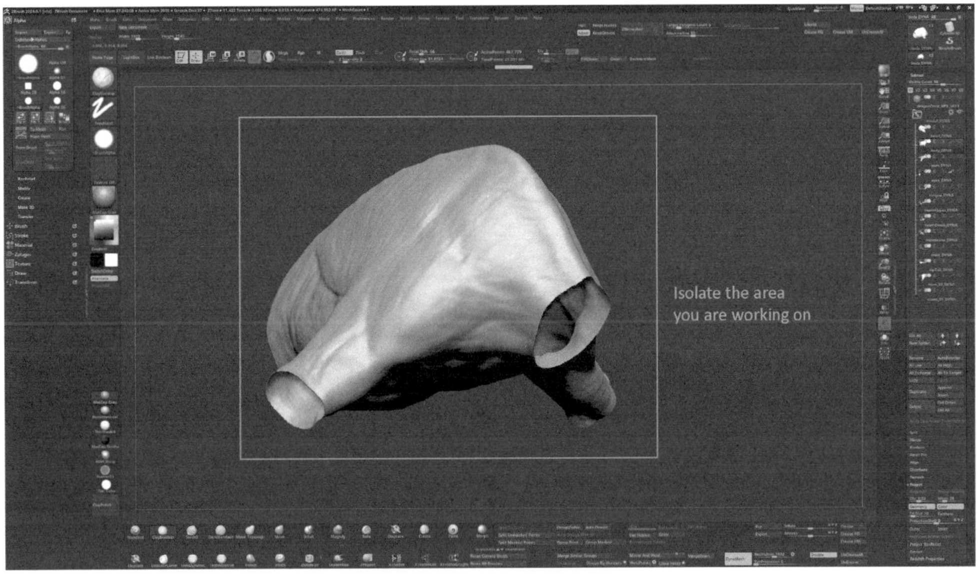

Figure 1.15 – Isolating the active SubTool

- Use **Solo** mode selectively (**Transform | Solo**). The **Solo** button hides all other SubTools and displays only the active one. This can be useful for quick isolation, but it is often better to manually hide unnecessary SubTools instead. Keeping nearby parts visible helps maintain spatial context while still reducing the amount of geometry ZBrush needs to evaluate.

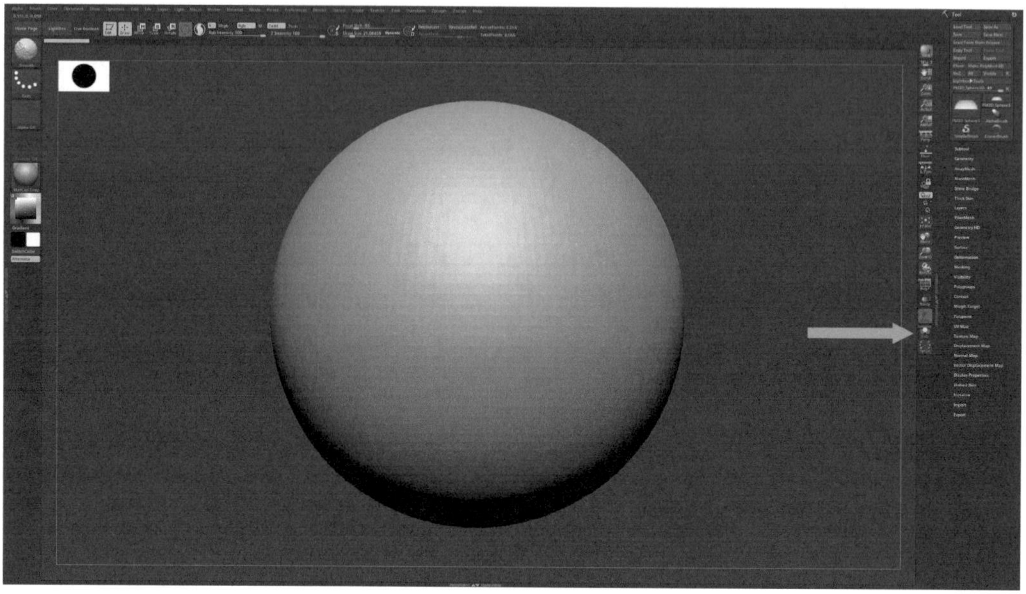

Figure 1.16 – Position of the Solo button on the right shelf of the ZBrush interface

- Use *Shift* + *D* to step down and *D* to step up through subdivision levels. Keep a medium level active for navigation and broad edits, and switch briefly to the highest level only for targeted detailing. This keeps brush response crisp and Viewport interaction smooth. Avoid sculpting and navigating at the highest subdivision level unless necessary.

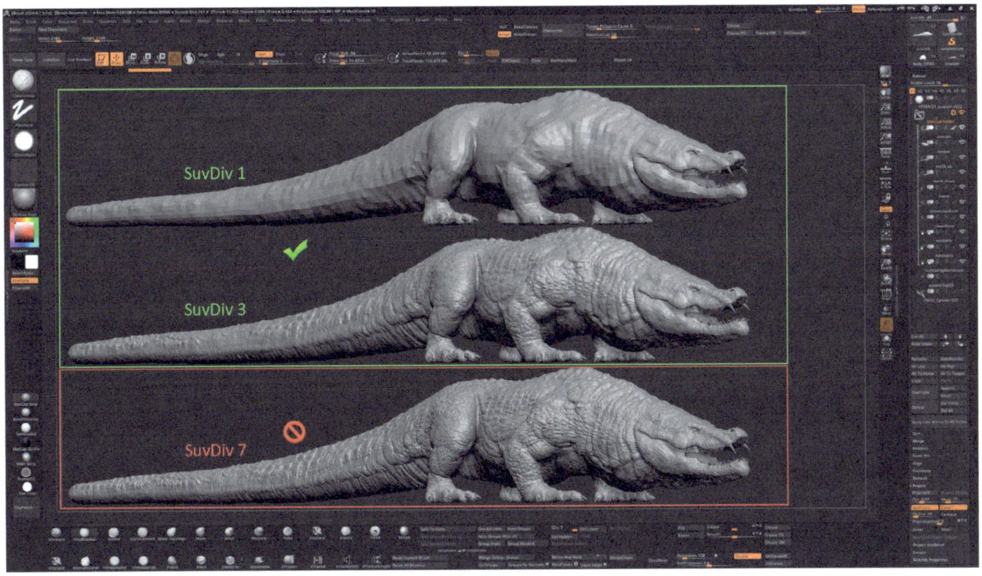

Figure 1.17 – Managing subdivision levels for performance

- Go to **Tool** | **Geometry** | **Dynamic Subdiv** and make sure **Dynamic Subdivision** is turned off while sculpting. **Dynamic Subdivision** adds a real-time smoothing preview that is recalculated every frame. Enable it only briefly when checking surface continuity or presentation.

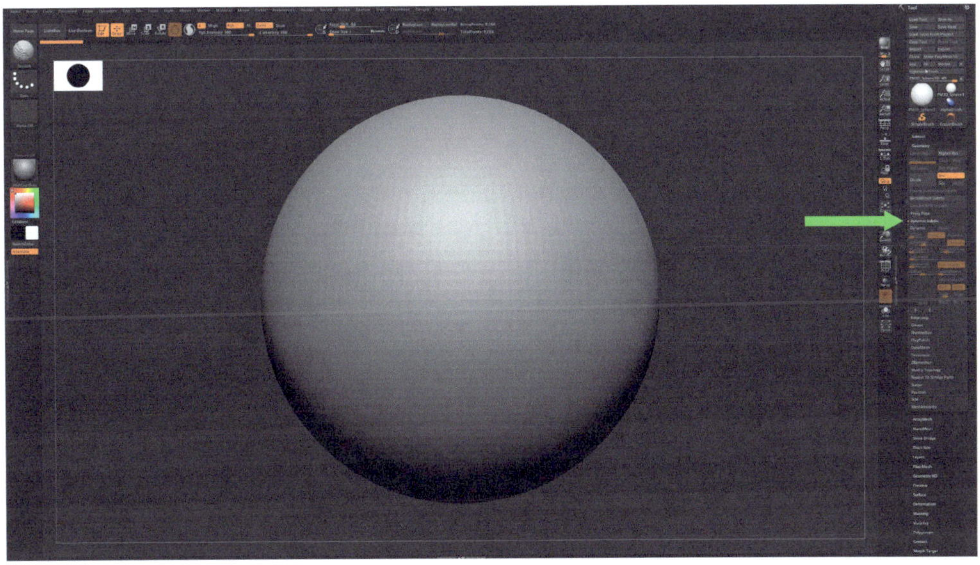

Figure 1.18 – Position of the Dynamic Subdivision option inside the Tool | Geometry menu

- Check the top bar and make sure **Live Boolean** is turned off unless you are actively performing Boolean operations. **Live Boolean** continuously evaluates mesh intersections in the background. For organic creatures, leaving it disabled avoids unnecessary performance overhead.

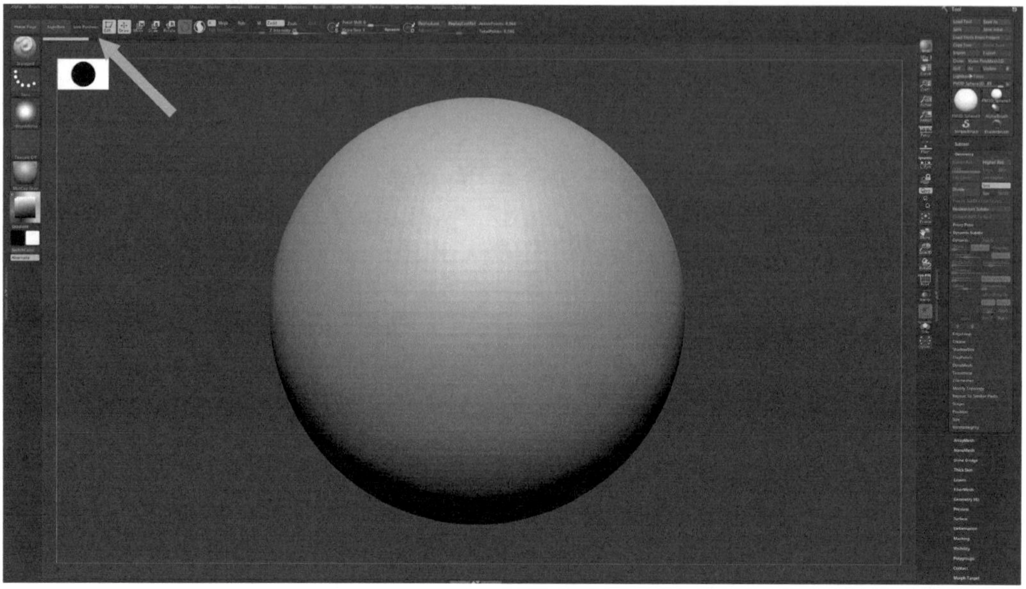

Figure 1.19 – Position of the Live Boolean button in the upper-left section of the ZBrush interface

- Go to **Preferences | Undo History** and set Max Undo to a reasonable range, typically `20` to `40`. Optionally, disable undo for SubTool switching. Every undo step stores a full mesh state. Instead of relying on long undo chains, save incremental versions of your file at key milestones.
- Create Layers for specific refinement passes, such as wrinkles or corrective edits, using **Tool | Layers**. Avoid keeping many high-resolution layers active at the same time. Once a pass is approved, use **Bake All** to commit the changes and free memory. Rename layers clearly so they remain easy to track.
- Open **Preferences | Performance** and ensure **MultiThreaded** and **MultiDraw** are enabled. Check that **Active Cores** matches your system's logical core count. If the value looks incorrect, restart ZBrush to refresh detection.
- Keep auxiliary geometry lightweight. For reference meshes or accessories you are not actively sculpting, reduce their cost. Use **ZPlugin | Decimation Master** to lower

resolution, or remove unnecessary hidden geometry after splitting. A lean SubTool list improves navigation, saving, and loading times.

- Go to **Preferences | QuickSave** and choose sensible intervals, such as every 10 to 15 minutes, with a limited number of stored files. Keep projects on a fast local SSD to avoid save-related slowdowns.

> **Tip**
>
> For very large projects, especially complex creature assets like the one used throughout this book, disabling **QuickSave** entirely can sometimes result in a more stable experience. Automatic saves may momentarily freeze the interface or, in extreme cases, contribute to crashes on heavy files. This approach is recommended only if you are disciplined about saving your work manually and using incremental versions regularly.

By applying these steps selectively, you ensure that ZBrush spends its resources only on the geometry under your brush at that moment. The result is a responsive Viewport, cleaner interaction, and the ability to push high-resolution detail comfortably, even on non-high-end machines.

How it works...

ZBrush performance is directly affected by how much geometry and how many operations it needs to evaluate at the same time. When working on dense assets, slowdowns usually occur because multiple SubTools, subdivision levels, layers, undo states, and background features are being processed simultaneously, and not because of polygon count alone.

The optimizations applied in this recipe all work by reducing the active workload at any given moment. Splitting geometry into SubTools, hiding unused parts, navigating at lower subdivision levels, and disabling real-time features temporarily allow ZBrush to focus its resources only on the visible, editable data under the brush.

Using naming conventions in ZBrush and Maya

Whether you're working in Maya or ZBrush, adopting a clear and consistent naming structure ensures that your files, assets, and hierarchies are understandable to you as well as every other artist, rigger, or technical director down the pipeline. Poor naming slows down production, causes confusion, and can even break automated tools or scripts that rely on predictable asset names.

This recipe will provide practical naming systems tailored to each software, ZBrush and Maya, explaining when and how to use them and why adopting a disciplined naming habit is a mark of a reliable production artist.

Figure 1.20 shows an example of a production-ready **Outliner** in Maya:

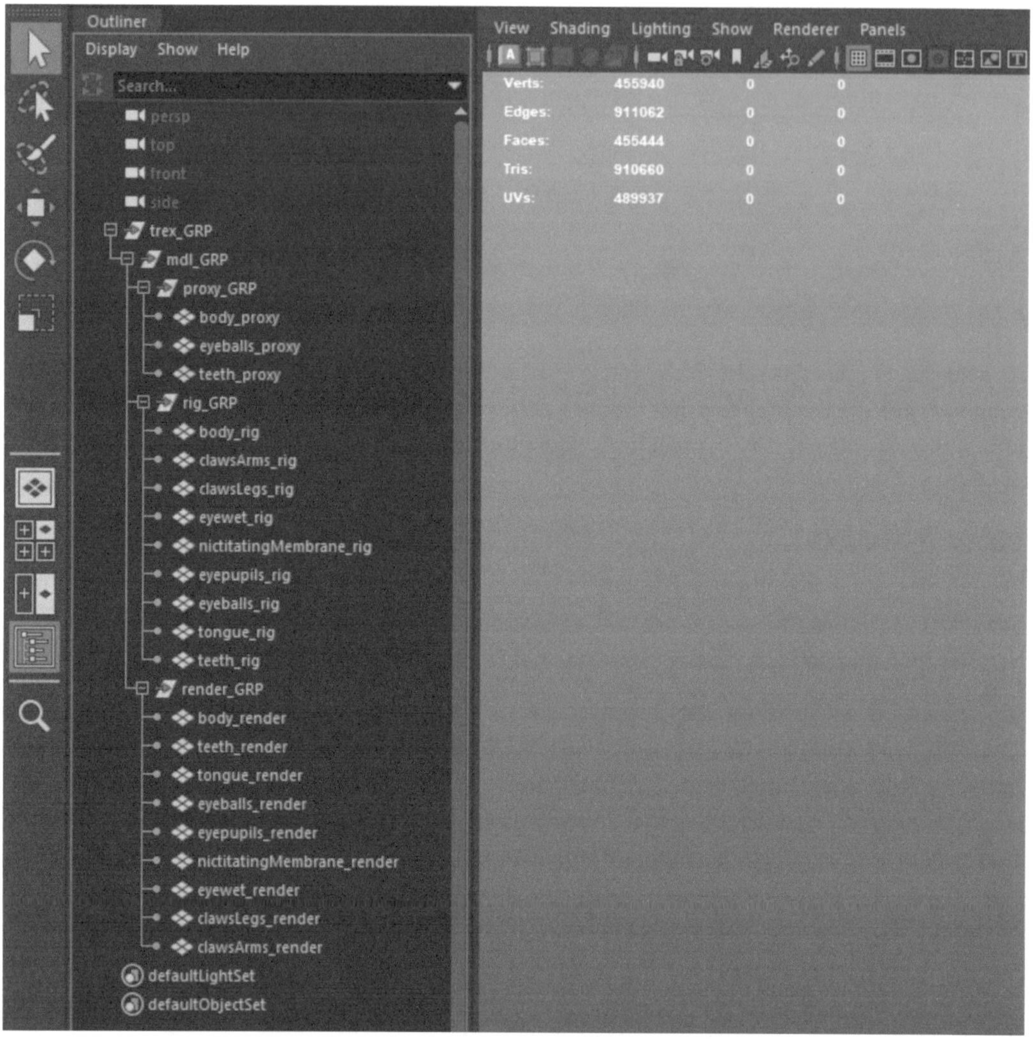

Figure 1.20 – Production-ready Maya Outliner with clear, consistent naming conventions

Getting ready

Take a moment to organize your current scene or project:

- Open both your ZBrush SubTool list and your Maya **Outliner**, and observe how your objects are currently labeled.
- If you notice generic names such as `pCube1`, `polySurface2`, or `SubTool_Extract_001`, take note of them, as these are common sources of confusion in production scenes.

Figure 1.21 shows a Maya **Outliner** with generic names like `pCube2` and `pCylinder2` before cleanup:

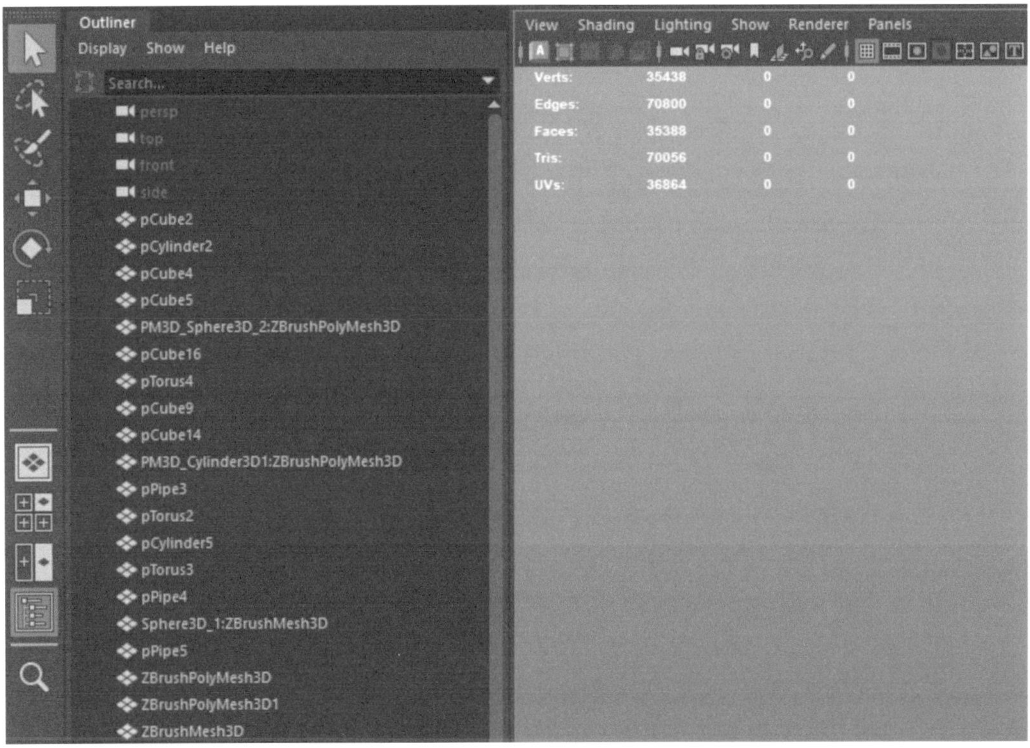

Figure 1.21 – Default Maya Outliner showing messy names before cleanup

How to do it...

Follow these steps to implement practical naming conventions in both ZBrush and Maya to turn complex scenes into readable, production-ready assets:

1. Start by examining your current scene and spotting unclear names. Default labels such as `pCube1`, `Merged2`, or `PM3D_Sphere3` give you no information about what the object actually is.
2. Rename these labels immediately (as you'll learn in the next steps). Your goal is that anyone opening the file can identify every element at a glance.
3. In ZBrush, names are your only organizational tool since the SubTool list is flat and doesn't support hierarchy. Use a compact format that describes both the part and its production status:
   `[partName]_[status]_[optionalVersion]`

   Where:

   - The first term defines the part: head, wing, tail, etc.
   - The second defines where it stands in the workflow:
     - `DYNA` for DynaMesh sculpting
     - `POLY` for retopologized models
     - `GEO` for clean final geometry
     - `APPROVED` once it's validated for production
   - The optional version tag, such as `_v02`, helps track iterative exports. For example, `jaw_DYNA`, `armL_POLY`, `eye_GEO`, `horn_APPROVED`.

   To see how naming directly affects readability inside ZBrush, compare the SubTool lists in *Figure 1.22*. The left one uses clear, production-ready names, while the right shows default, unstructured SubTool naming.

Figure 1.22 – A production-ready ZBrush SubTool list (left) and a poorly named one (right)

4. When working in **Maya**, your naming system can take advantage of hierarchy and suffixes. Adopt a structure that keeps logic consistent:

```
assetName_part_function_suffix
```

For example, `dragon_head_high_GEO`, `dragon_armL_proxy_GEO`, or `dragon_eye_CTRL`. The suffix defines the object's role: `GEO` for geometry, `GRP` for groups, `JNT` for joints, `CTRL` for controls, and `LOC` for locators.

This approach ensures that scripts, riggers, and exporters always know what each object represents.

5. Keep consistency between software. If your SubTool in ZBrush is called `tail_GEO`, make sure the same name appears once imported into Maya. This simple alignment eliminates mismatched references and speeds up the exchange between departments such as lookdev, rigging, or lighting.
6. Test your naming logic on a real export. Move a few SubTools from ZBrush into Maya and check if each name still makes sense contextually. If you can immediately tell what's in progress, what's clean and what's ready to publish, without checking the model, your naming is doing its job.

How it works...

Naming conventions might seem like a small organizational habit, but in production they act as invisible glue holding the entire pipeline together. From sculpting to rigging, shading, or rendering, every stage depends on how easily assets can be identified, referenced, and replaced. When your naming is predictable, software scripts can find the right objects automatically, and artists down the line can open your files without hesitation or cleanup.

In *ZBrush*, consistent naming compensates for the lack of hierarchy. Because the SubTool list is flat, a clear name like `head_GEO` or `tail_DYNA` becomes your only visual cue for understanding which meshes are in progress or finalized. This structure also simplifies exporting: if every clean mesh ends in `_GEO`, you can batch-export only production-ready elements without touching your sculpting drafts. It's a lightweight, manual pipeline that saves hours over the course of a project.

In *Maya*, naming conventions become even more powerful. Here, suffixes and hierarchical grouping allow technical artists to automate complex tasks such as binding geometry, linking materials, or exporting joints. For instance, a script doesn't need to guess what's a mesh and what's a control – it just reads `_GEO` or `_CTRL` and processes accordingly. The entire workflow becomes safer, faster, and less dependent on human interpretation.

Finally, once your convention is in place, stick to it. Consistency is far more valuable than complexity. Whether you're a freelancer working alone or part of a large studio, predictable naming builds trust, prevents errors, and accelerates production hand-offs. It's a silent signal to supervisors and TDs that your assets are reliable, and that you are too.

Beyond technical benefits, good naming communicates intent. Seeing `_POLY` or `_APPROVED` instantly tells your team whether an asset is still being refined or ready for the next department. These cues replace uncertainty with confidence and let you focus on creativity instead of file management.

> **Tip**
>
> **Pro-tip**: Consider documenting your naming rules in a short internal *pipeline guide* or even a simple one-page chart showing examples for ZBrush and Maya. It becomes the reference that every new artist will thank you for later.

See also

- For file-level naming, folder structure, and versioning, see the *Organizing files for a clean and consistent workflow* recipe.
- For preparing a clean scene before applying naming conventions, see the *Setting up a project in Maya using correct scale and unit conventions* recipe.

Importing and exporting assets between ZBrush and Maya

Moving assets between ZBrush and Maya is one of the most common and critical tasks in any production pipeline. Sculptors, modelers, and lookdev artists frequently pass geometry back and forth, refining details in ZBrush, checking proportions or scale in Maya, or preparing clean topology for rigging.

To keep this exchange seamless, it's essential to understand the right tools and export options to maintain a direct connection between both programs without losing fidelity or wasting time troubleshooting errors. Even minor inconsistencies can lead to costly issues down the line: misplaced meshes, mismatched scales, or broken UVs.

In this recipe, we'll explore the main methods for transferring data between ZBrush and Maya, including **GoZ**, ZBrush's dedicated live connection system, the **FBX ExportImport plug-in**, and ZBrush's built-in Import/Export tools for OBJ and FBX files. We'll discuss when to use each approach, their common pitfalls, and how to ensure both applications interpret your assets consistently.

Figure 1.23 shows a side-by-side Maya and ZBrush view used to verify the correct scale and alignment using a **1.80 m** human reference:

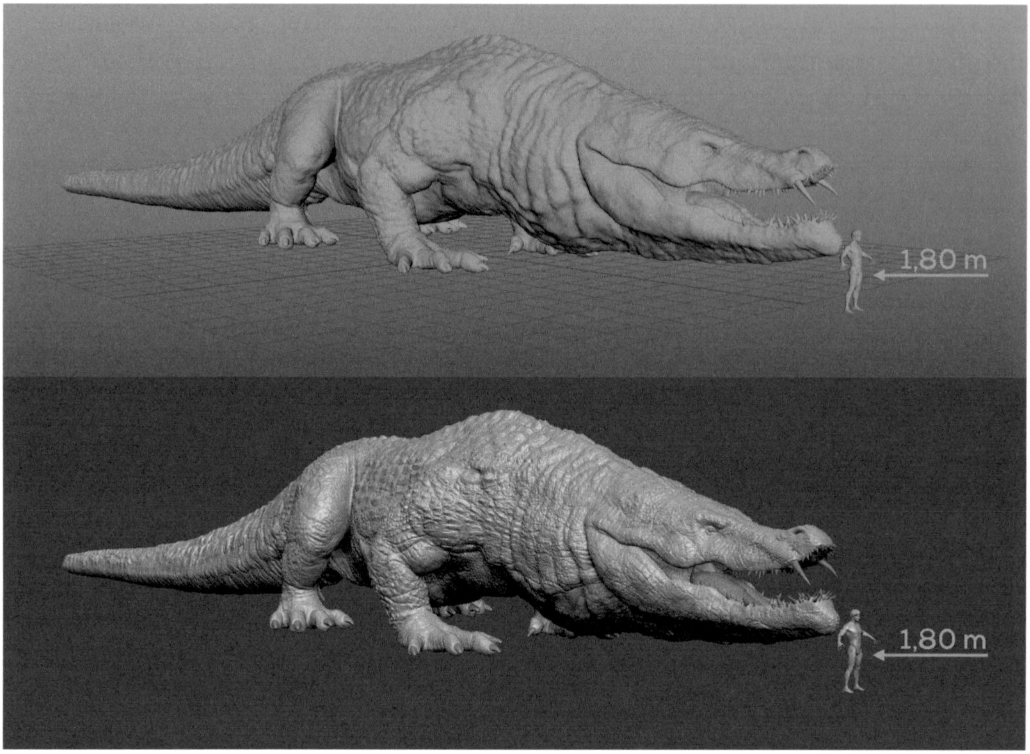

Figure 1.23 – View of Maya (top) and ZBrush (bottom) with the same model

Tip

ZBrush includes ready-to-use human reference tools. You can find the default human models in **LightBox | Tool**, under assets such as `NickZ_HumanMale`, `NickZ HumanFemale`, or similar demo figures. These models are ideal for quick scale checks before exporting to Maya. More details are in the *How to do it...* section of the recipe.

Getting ready

Having a tidy, predictable scene on both ends ensures that the import-export process remains stable and reproducible across the pipeline:

1. Ensure both ZBrush and Maya are set to compatible units and scales: **meters** are recommended for production consistency.
2. Check that your mesh is clean, with no hidden geometry, multiple subdivision levels, or unused layers that could cause export errors.
3. It's also good practice to name SubTools clearly and freeze transformations in Maya before transfer.

How to do it...

Let's have a look at the steps to establish a clean, predictable method for transferring geometry between Maya and ZBrush, while avoiding the most common issues, such as scale mismatches, misplaced pivots, or broken hierarchies.

Preparing and exporting geometry from Maya

To prepare your geometry for export from Maya, follow these steps:

1. Begin by cleaning your Maya scene. Delete unused nodes, references, or cameras that might interfere with export.
2. Select the asset you want to send to ZBrush and check that transformations are frozen and history is cleared. You can do this by going to **Modify** | **Freeze Transformations**, followed by **Edit** | **Delete by Type** | **History**. This ensures the exported mesh represents only the visible, finalized geometry and prevents any hidden data from shifting or breaking on import.

3. Next, check your scene scale. Both Maya and ZBrush can work correctly with real-world units, but the communication between the two software packages during mesh imports and exports can sometimes behave unpredictably, especially when using OBJ or FBX files. In some situations, this may result in unexpected x100 scale mismatches or inconsistent asset sizes across the pipeline.

   To keep the workflow cleaner and more predictable, many creature artists prefer working in meters inside Maya. Go to **Windows** | **Settings/Preferences** | **Preferences** | **Settings** | **Working Units**, and under **Linear**, choose **meter** (see *Figure 1.24*). This helps maintain more consistent asset behavior across sculpting, rigging, simulation, and rendering workflows.

Figure 1.24 – Maya Preferences panel with Linear Units: Meters highlighted

4. With your model selected, decide which format best suits your purpose. For single meshes or static models, use **OBJ**; it's simple, lightweight, and highly reliable. For multi-part assets or if you need to preserve grouping or naming, choose **FBX**.
   To export, go to **File** | **Export Selection**, then pick the format from the dropdown:
   - **OBJ export**: Enable **Groups and Materials** if you want to preserve organization, as shown in *Figure 1.25*:

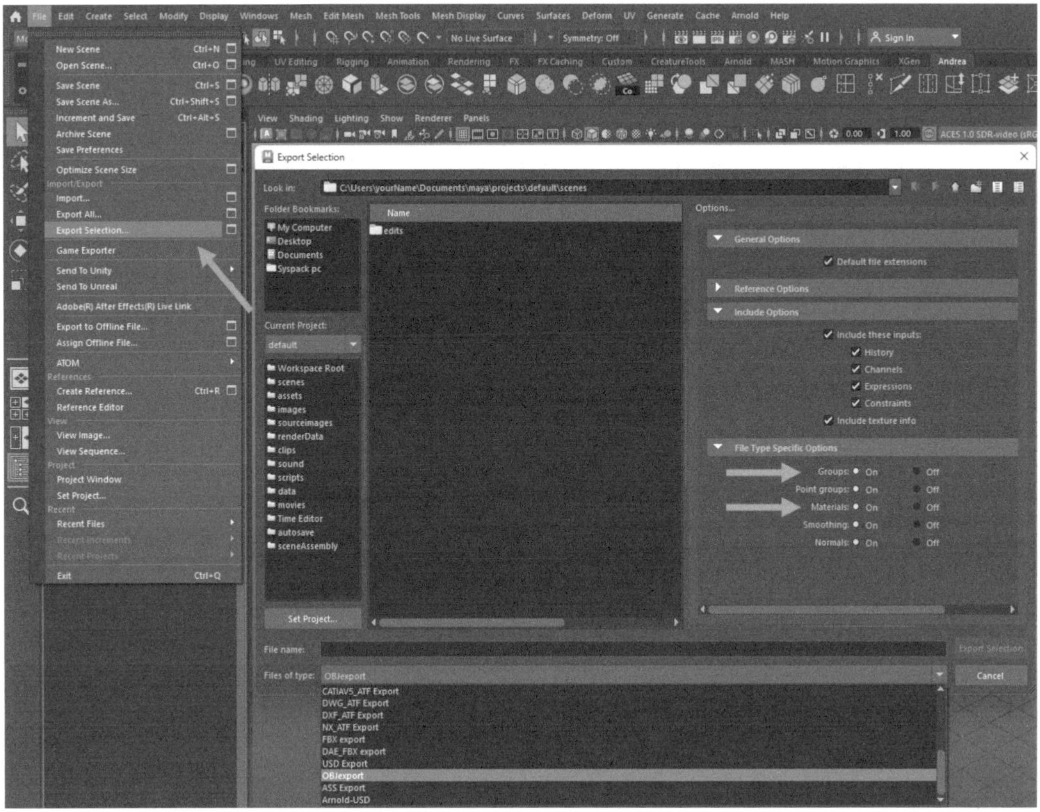

Figure 1.25 – Exporting the mesh with Groups and Materials enabled to preserve asset organization

- **FBX export**: Disable animations, cameras, and lights (see *Figure 1.26*); keep only geometry data. Check **Smoothing Groups** and **Tangents and Binormals** (see *Figure 1.27*) if you plan to bring the asset back for shading or rigging later.

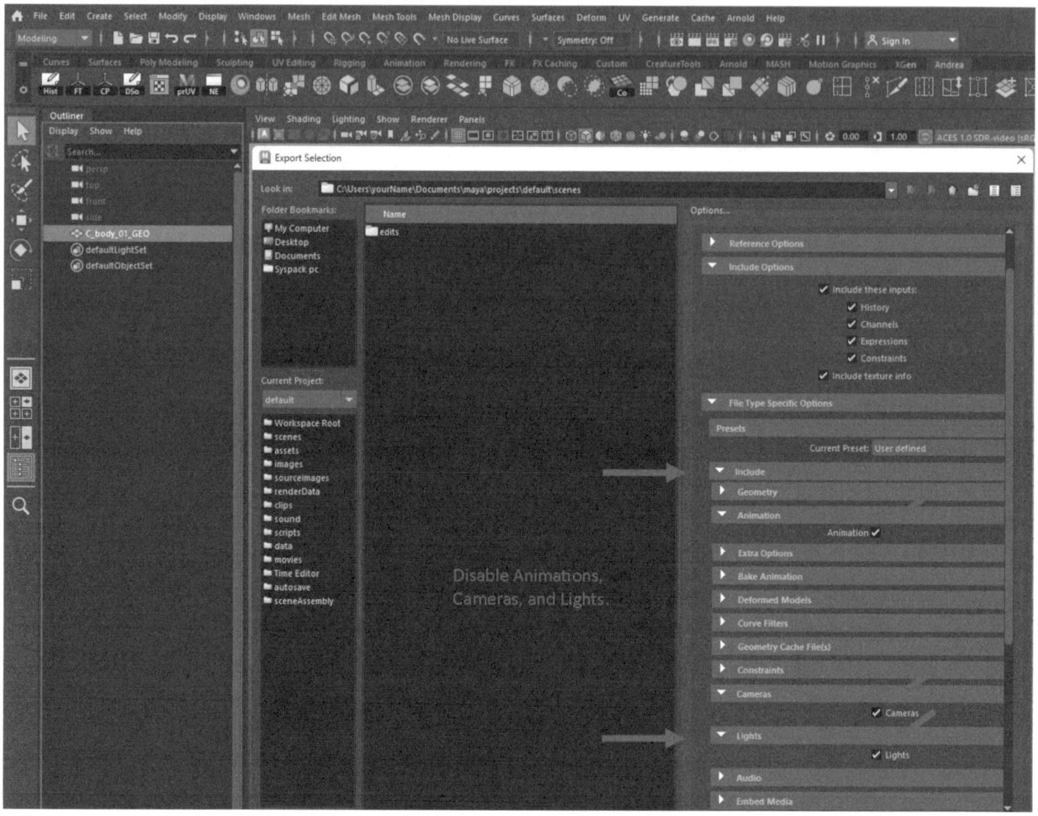

Figure 1.26 – Disabling animations, cameras, and lights to export clean geometry

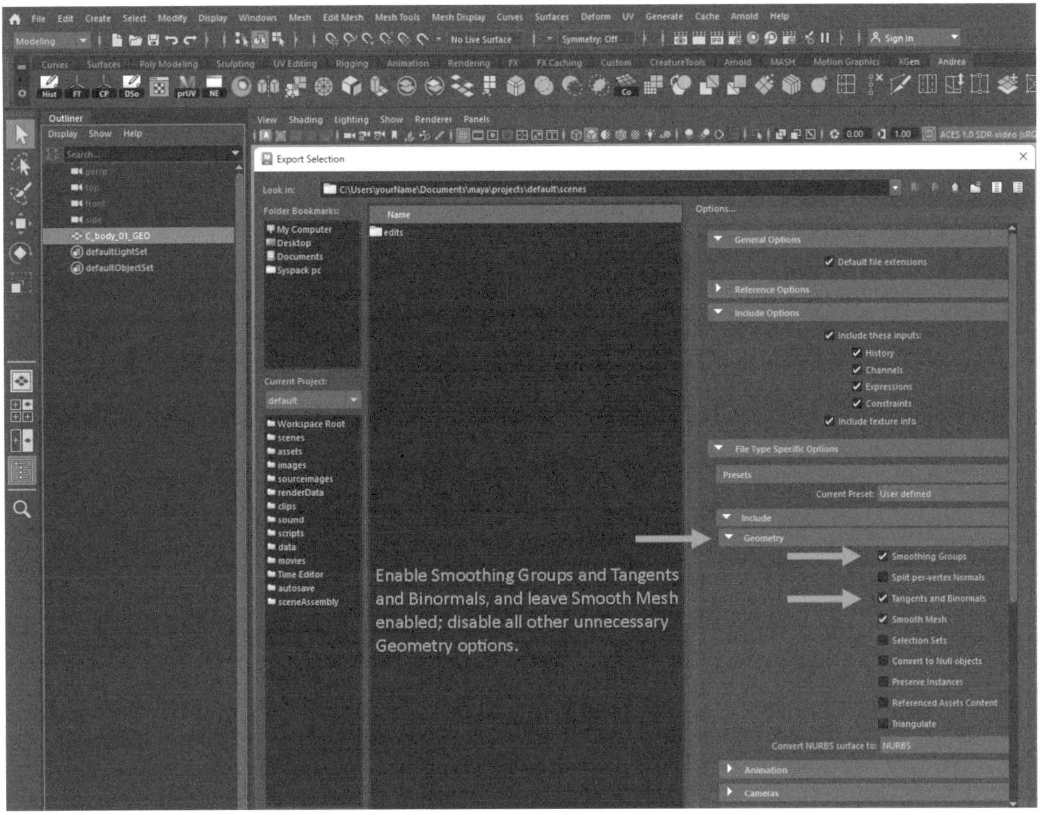

Figure 1.27 – Export Selection dialog with Geometry options enabled to preserve smoothing groups and tangents and binormals

5. If you are exporting for sculpting symmetry in ZBrush, it's helpful to center your pivot to the origin before saving. Use **Modify | Center Pivot**, then in the **Channel Box**, set the **Translate X, Y, Z** values to `0`. This guarantees perfect symmetry alignment when you import into ZBrush.

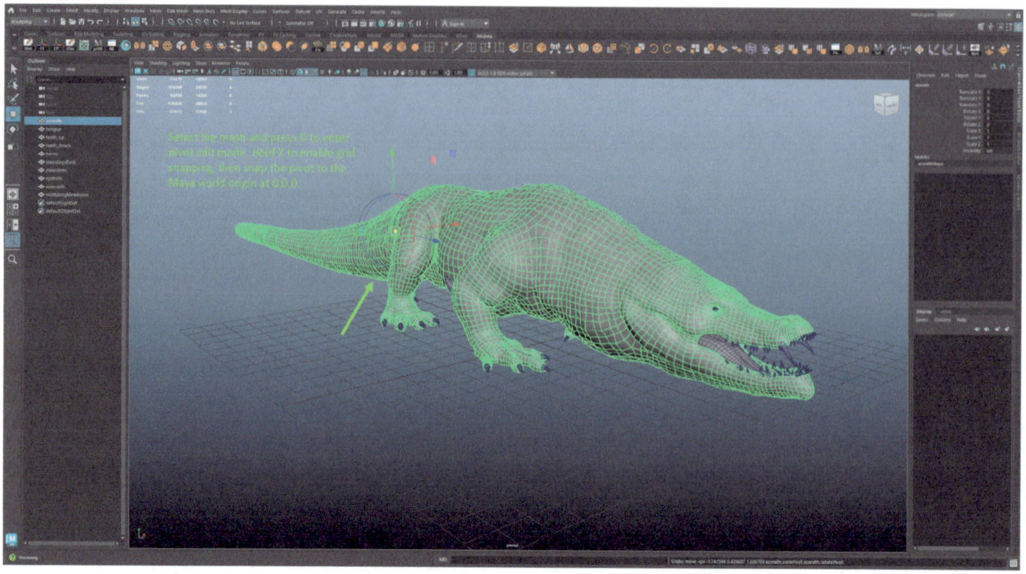

Figure 1.28 – Enter pivot edit mode in Maya (D key) and snap the pivot to the world origin at (0, 0, 0)

Figure 1.29 shows the pivot aligned to the Maya world center:

Figure 1.29 – Pivot aligned to the Maya world center; exit pivot edit mode to finalize the transformation

6. Now switch to ZBrush. If you're importing a single static object, use the OBJ method. Go to **Tool | Import**, then navigate to your exported file. ZBrush will load the mesh as a new Tool. Rename it immediately, for example, `dragon_body_POLY`, and save it as a `.ZTL` file. This simple step keeps your file library organized and prevents overwriting default Tool names like `PolyMesh3D`.

Importing multi-part assets with FBX

To import a multi-part asset into ZBrush using FBX, follow these steps:

1. For more complex multi-mesh assets, use the **FBX ExportImport** plugin. Navigate to **ZPlugin | FBX ExportImport**, click **Import**, and configure the options before confirming (see *Figure 1.30*):
   - Enable **Import Mats as SubTools** if your FBX uses different material assignments and you want each material region imported as a separate SubTool. This is especially useful when working with production assets that have already been combined into a single mesh but still use multiple materials to define different parts.
   - Enable **Import Mats as Polygroups** if you want the material assignments to be converted into Polygroups, making it easier to isolate, mask, or edit specific regions without manually rebuilding the separation.

Figure 1.30 – ZBrush FBX ExportImport plugin with the options configured

2. If the model imports at the wrong size, adjust **Scale** within the plugin. ZBrush interprets 1 Maya meter as 100 internal units. When working in Maya, always remember that assets coming from ZBrush usually need to be scaled *100×* to match real-world units. The safest workflow is to center the pivot on the asset and apply the scale there.

> **Tip**
>
> If you don't want to modify the original pivot, place the mesh inside a group node and apply the 100× scale to the group instead. This keeps the geometry untouched while preserving the correct scale for rigging, lookdev, and export.

3. Once imported, inspect your model in ZBrush. Press *F* to frame all geometry. If the mesh seems missing or floating far away, it may have retained Maya's world-space offset. You can correct this by opening **Tool** | **Geometry** | **Modify Topology** | **Position**, and setting the **XYZ** position fields to `0`.

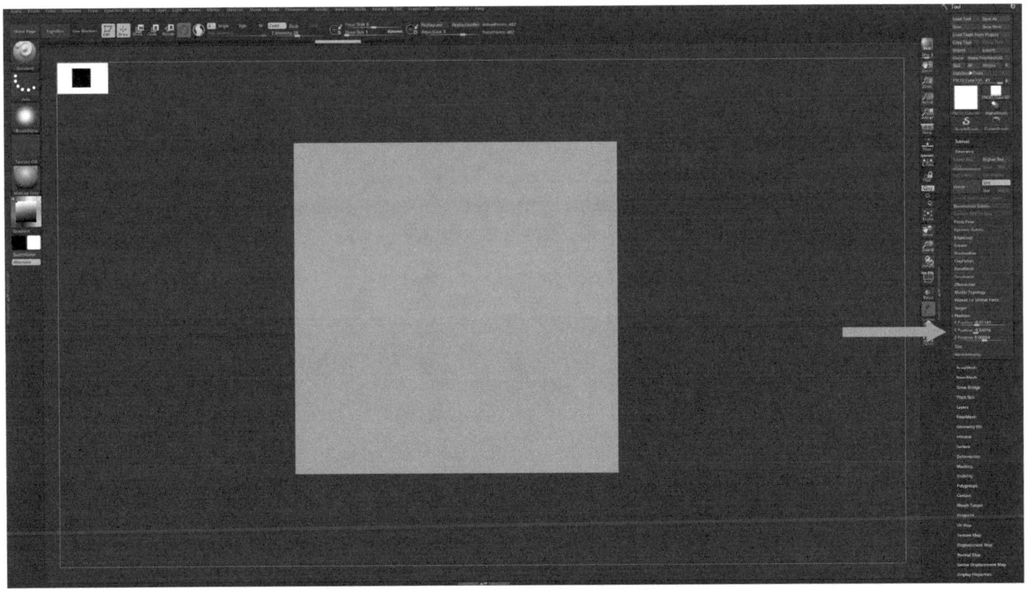

Figure 1.31 – Position controls are used to correct minor mesh offsets after importing assets into ZBrush

Note

When working between Maya and ZBrush, position values can easily become inconsistent, especially on the Y and Z axes. Because the two applications handle world space differently, an asset may appear correctly framed in ZBrush while still carrying non-zero position offsets. For a clean and predictable pipeline, always ensure that **Position X** is set to **0** in ZBrush. This is critical for reliable re-imports into Maya and helps prevent issues during rigging, lookdev, and export.

4. At this point, test the scaling. Switch to the **Transpose** tool and compare your creature against a known reference, such as ZBrush's default human mannequin. Open **LightBox**, go to the Tool tab, and load `HumanMaleAverage.ZTL`.

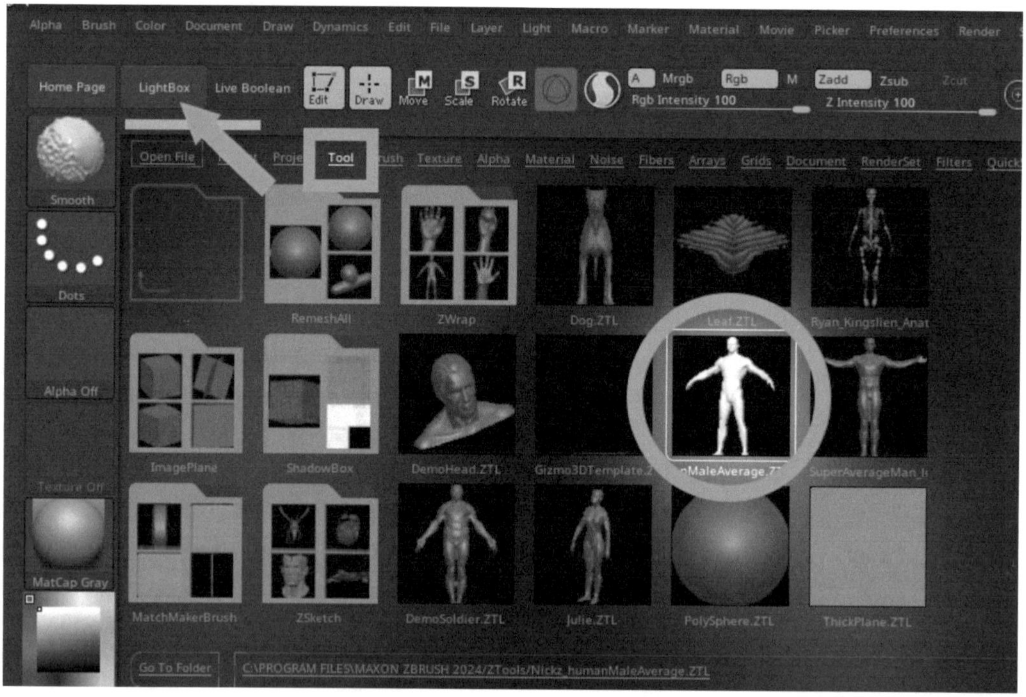

Figure 1.32 – Loading the default human mannequin (HumanMaleAverage.ZTL) from LightBox

5. If it's 100× larger or smaller, you can fix it by opening **ZPlugin** | **Scale Master** and clicking **Set Scene Scale**. This resizes your tool correctly relative to real-world proportions.

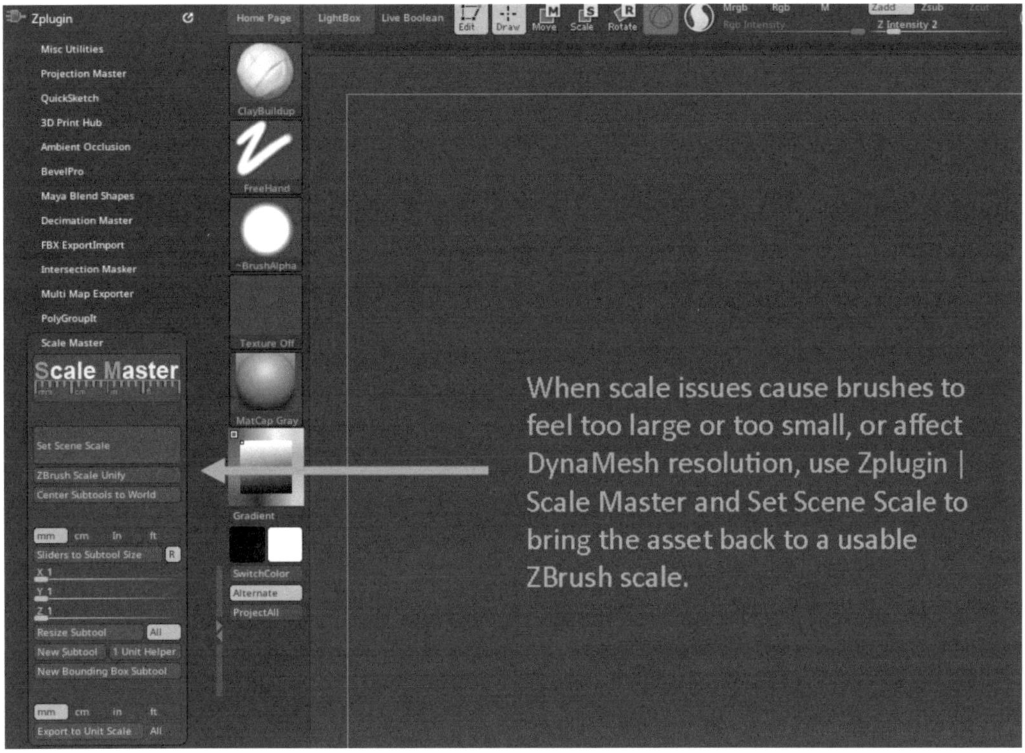

Figure 1.33 – Scale Master panel

Using GoZ for quick iteration (with limitations)

For users preferring quick iteration, ZBrush also offers **GoZ**, an automatic send/receive bridge to Maya. Follow these steps to use it:

1. To configure it, go to **Preferences** | **GoZ** and click **Update All Paths** so ZBrush can detect Maya's installation.
2. Once linked, pressing the **GoZ** button sends the selected SubTool to Maya with one click.

However, GoZ can be unreliable. It may cause scale inconsistencies, merge grouped meshes, or even break after software updates. Use it only for small, experimental workflows or concept modeling. For production assets, stick to the manual OBJ/FBX pipeline.

Troubleshooting common problems

The following tips address some common import problems:

- If you encounter the common *100× scale issue* (your imported model appears huge), don't panic. It's usually caused by Maya exporting in centimeters or ZBrush interpreting FBX units incorrectly. Return to Maya, verify that your units are set to **meters**, and re-export. Alternatively, correct it inside ZBrush using **Scale Master** | **Resize SubTool**.
- Another common issue is *offset meshes*: objects imported far from the origin. In that case, use **Frame All** (*F*) to locate them, or manually move the pivot back to (0,0,0) using the Gizmo. You can also duplicate the SubTool, zero its position, and delete the misplaced version.
- For occasional *FBX import crashes*, reopen the file in Maya and re-export using an older FBX version (2014/2015). Remove animation or camera data before saving. If the crash persists, revert to an OBJ export; it handles static geometry safely and avoids plugin instability.

By following these steps, you maintain a clean, predictable exchange pipeline between Maya and ZBrush, one that works reliably across studios, machines, and software versions.

How it works...

When exchanging data between Maya and ZBrush, the key challenge lies in how each program interprets *units*, *hierarchy*, and *transformation* data. Maya operates in real-world linear units (centimeters or meters) while ZBrush uses an internal unitless system. This mismatch is what leads to most scaling and alignment errors during import and export. By standardizing your Maya scene to meters, you ensure that both applications speak the same *language* of scale, allowing your creature to retain its real proportions when moving between sculpting, rigging, or rendering stages.

File formats also play a crucial role. The **OBJ format** is intentionally simple: it carries vertex positions, UVs, and materials without hierarchy or transform data. This makes it extremely stable and predictable, perfect for sculpting or displacements. The **FBX format**, on the other hand, supports multiple meshes, pivots, and animation layers, but with that flexibility comes complexity. Because FBX embeds extra scene data, even a small inconsistency (like Maya exporting in centimeters) can cause ZBrush to interpret the model at 100× scale.

Finally, while **GoZ** offers the convenience of automated transfer, it lacks the control and reliability required for production pipelines. It handles the process through temporary caching and background conversions, which makes it prone to breaking after software updates or when dealing with heavy, multi-SubTool creatures.

OBJ remains the safest choice for single meshes or sculpting passes, while FBX is your friend for multi-part assets or structured production work. GoZ can still be useful for concepting and fast iteration, but always test scale and naming before integrating it into your professional workflow.

There's more...

In production, consistency across artists and departments is more important than speed. Even if GoZ seems faster at first, relying on manual OBJ or FBX exports ensures that your assets remain versionable, testable, and pipeline-safe. Always save your export presets in Maya; this allows everyone in your team to use identical settings for scale, smoothing, and grouping, minimizing discrepancies between files.

Another advanced tip is to maintain a dedicated `exchange` folder for Maya–ZBrush transfers. Keep both your exported meshes and imported **ZTools** there, organized by version numbers (for example, `dragon_body_POLY_v002.obj`, `dragon_body_GEO_v003.ztl`). This habit not only keeps your project clean but also provides a reliable rollback history, which can be a lifesaver if something goes wrong late in production.

An important aspect is understanding the difference between saving **Maya scenes** and **ZBrush files**. In Maya, artists usually work with `.ma` or `.mb` files. A `.ma` **(Maya ASCII)** file stores the scene in a readable text format. It is easier to debug, safer for version control systems, and often preferred in production pipelines because corrupted sections can sometimes be manually fixed. A `.mb` (**Maya Binary**) file instead stores the scene in a compressed binary format, which is generally smaller and faster to save, but much harder to recover if corrupted.

In ZBrush, the most common formats are `.ZTL` and `.ZPR`. A `.ZTL` **(ZTool)** saves only the selected tool or SubTool hierarchy, making it lighter and more practical for production workflows. A `.ZPR` **(ZProject)** instead stores the entire scene, including lights, materials, undo history, and all loaded elements. While this can be useful for presentations or backups, it often generates unnecessarily heavy files that become difficult to manage in production.

For most creature workflows, saving clean `.ma` scenes and lightweight ZTools is usually the safest and most efficient approach.

2

Blocking with DynaMesh and ZSpheres: Establishing Primary Shapes

Starting gently (as we always do), we'll begin building the foundation of every successful creature sculpt: the **blocking phase**. In this chapter, we'll focus on using **ZSpheres** and **DynaMesh** to establish strong primary shapes before moving into secondary and tertiary sculpting. The goal is to help you create a solid base mesh that supports believable anatomy, balanced proportions, and flexibility for iteration.

You'll learn how to use **ZSpheres** efficiently to build a clean armature and when to rely on **DynaMesh** for organic massing. We'll explore how to sculpt readable silhouettes, merge volumes seamlessly, and decide the right time to remesh your model for refinement. Whether you're blocking a four-legged beast or a fantasy dragon, gaining proficiency in this phase will give you full control over your creature's design and structural integrity.

Figure 2.1 shows an example of the blocked creature base you will build with **DynaMesh** and **ZSpheres** in this chapter:

Figure 2.1 – Example of a blocked creature base

In this chapter, we'll cover the following recipes:

- Setting up image references for accurate blocking
- Using ZSpheres for a fast base and as a support tool in DynaMesh
- Sculpting primary shapes with DynaMesh and Sculptris Pro (Body)
- Sculpting the head from a sphere
- Creating membranes and wings

By the end of this chapter, you'll have a clean, production-ready creature base that serves as a strong foundation for further sculpting and detailing.

Technical requirements

Before you start, make sure you have the listed tools and assets installed and ready to use.

The `Chapter02_03` folder in the GitHub repository includes the following assets:

- `dragonCrest_concept.png`: This is the main concept artwork.
- `dragonCrest_side.jpg`: It provides the side-view reference used throughout the chapter.

- `dragonCrestHead_side.jpg` and `dragonCrestHead_side_openMouth.jpg`: They show the head with the mouth closed and open for anatomical reference.
- `dragonCrest_skeleton.png`: This is the skeletal reference.
- `dragonCrest_ZGrid_v001.zgr`: This is a ZBrush Grid file used to correctly align the reference images.
- `dragonCrest_zSpheres_v001.ztl`: It contains the ZSpheres rig used to build the base structure.
- `dragonCrest_dynamesh_v001.ztl`: This is a decimated mesh that can be used as a reference for the initial A-pose and overall proportions, although these will naturally evolve during the sculpting process.

You can download the example project files for this book by following the instructions in the *Download the example code/resource files* section in the *Preface* of this book.

This chapter's code/resource files are included in the downloadable code/resource bundle.

Required software and tools

- A pressure-sensitive graphics tablet like **Wacom** or equivalent is highly recommended.
- **PureRef** (`www.pureref.com`) for organizing and referencing anatomical images and concept art.

Setting up image references for accurate blocking

Accurate image references are the foundation of a clean and production-ready sculpt. Whether you're working from your own concept or a provided studio turnaround, properly aligned image planes in ZBrush eliminate structural inconsistencies from the very beginning. Without correct alignment, **Front** and **Side** views rarely match perfectly, proportions drift, feet may not sit correctly on $Y = 0$, and primary forms can become distorted early in the blocking stage. Fixing these issues later often requires reshaping large areas of the model, which can cost hours of rework.

Therefore, this step is about defining scale, balance, and grounding from the very start. By setting up precise reference sheets, you can evaluate the silhouette, volume distribution, and anatomical flow before committing to shape refinement.

In this recipe, we'll prepare the reference sheets in Photoshop and correctly place them in ZBrush using the **Draw | Floor system**. This built-in reference plane lets you display and align concept images accurately within the 3D Viewport. The goal is to ensure your creature aligns perfectly to world space, with its feet resting on $Y = 0$, and proportions ready for a clean sculpting pass.

Getting ready

Before importing any references into ZBrush, it's important to clarify a production reality: you rarely receive a perfect front, side, and top turnaround. In many cases, especially in early concept stages, you only have a strong 3/4 hero illustration. While visually appealing, a single 3/4 view is not structurally reliable for precise proportion control.

For this chapter, the blocking workflow will be demonstrated using a dedicated creature asset called `dragonCrest`, named after its distinctive dorsal crests. The original concept was developed by **Lestoidea** (`https://www.artstation.com/anhe`), a creature-focused concept artist with a strong sense of anatomical rhythm and silhouette design. The initial brief required a wingless dragon with integrated membrane structures and an elongated body plan.

Figure 2.2 illustrates `dragonCrest`'s (the creature model you'll be working on in this book) primary design reference, defining silhouette, proportions, and overall creature language:

Figure 2.2 – dragonCrest 3/4 hero concept (Image courtesy of Lestoidea)

Since a 3/4 illustration alone would not provide sufficient structural clarity for blocking, I requested a clean **Side** view specifically for proportion control. This is a common production step: when a concept is visually strong but not technically complete, additional orthographic support is developed before sculpting begins.

Figure 2.3 shows a primary structural reference for spine alignment, skeletal placement, and length proportions:

Figure 2.3 – dragonCrest orthographic side view

In the case of `dragonCrest`, the **Side** view is the most structurally important reference. The creature develops primarily along its length, meaning that spine curvature, chest depth, pelvis placement, and tail balance are better evaluated in profile than from the front. The 3/4 image will still be used to validate volume and design intent, but the **Side** view will drive the initial blocking decisions.

Before importing side references into ZBrush, always align the ground plane precisely at the *vertical center* of the canvas. In this workflow, the image was prepared in Photoshop with the ground line placed exactly at mid-height. This ensures that, once imported, the creature's feet will rest correctly on *Y = 0* in Maya, maintaining consistent world-space alignment across the pipeline.

The texture was created at 2048 × 2048 resolution. This is intentional. When using the **Draw | Floor** system in ZBrush, reference images are internally limited to 2K resolution. Preparing the reference at 2K avoids unnecessary scaling and preserves clarity without wasting memory.

Figure 2.4 shows the finalized 2048 × 2048 side reference sheet prepared for ZBrush import, with the ground line aligned to mid-canvas for consistent world-space positioning:

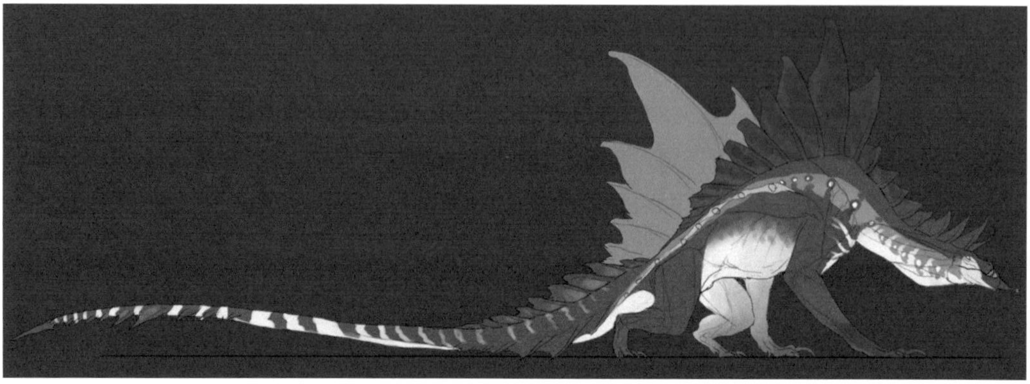

Figure 2.4 – Side reference 2048 x 2048 aligned in Photoshop and prepared for import

Proper alignment at this stage prevents downstream issues such as floating characters, incorrect pivot positioning, or scale inconsistencies during export.

How to do it...

Let's now go step by step to import and align orthographic reference images (**Front**, **Side**, and **Top** views) using the **Draw | Floor** system, so the creature matches the turnaround at a production level.

This method is ideal for blocking your creature with precise proportions and anatomical clarity. You will load front, side, and top sheets, align the ground line to $Y = 0$, and lock camera views for precise checks while blocking the wingless, membrane-limb dragon.

1. Open the **Draw** palette and enable **Floor**. It is used to verify correct ground positioning before blocking.

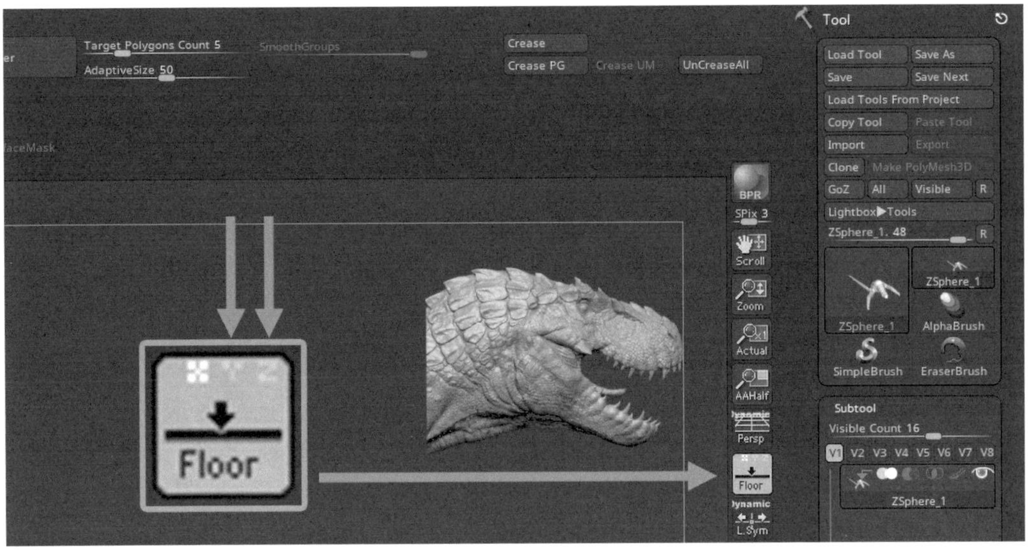

Figure 2.5 – Floor activated for world-space alignment

2. Activate the grid and switch the camera to an orthographic **Side** view. The **Floor** will act as your world reference, helping you verify that the creature's feet sit correctly on *Y = 0*. Correct axis activation ensures accurate orthographic reference alignment.
   Make sure the **Floor** axes you need are enabled. In many setups, *Y* and *Z* are disabled by default, so the grid may appear only partially visible. If you are working with **Front** or **Top** references, click the *Y* and *Z* axis toggles directly on the **Floor** controls to enable them and display the full ground reference.

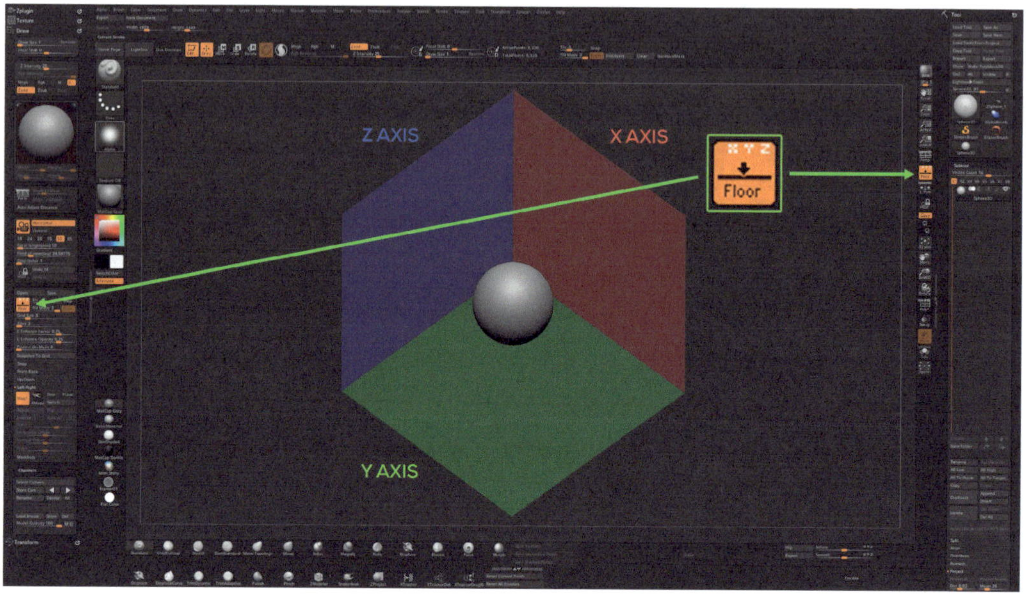

Figure 2.6 – Y and Z axes enabled on the Floor grid

3. Load the images into their channels. Use the **Map1/Map2** buttons under **Front-Back**, **Left-Right**, and **Up-Down** to assign the correct file to each view. If a sheet appears mirrored or inverted, use **Switch**, **Flip**, or **Rotate** in the same section.

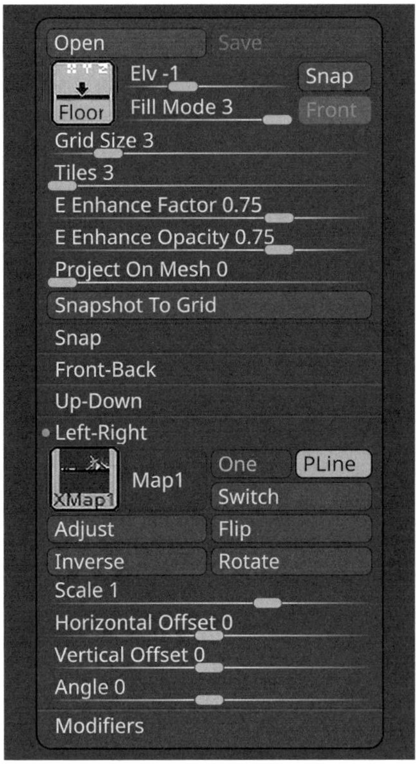

Figure 2.7 – The Front-Back, Left-Right, and Up-Down channels

> **Tip**
>
> Files in PNG, JPG, or PSD formats are fine.

4. If you aligned and centered the images correctly in Photoshop, you can leave **Scale, H Offset,** and **V Offset** at their default values. The references should already match across views, and adjusting offsets at this stage often introduces inconsistencies rather than fixing them.

> **Tip**
>
> If your front and side photos were shot with different focal lengths, there could be a minor perspective mismatch. Favor the **Side** view for skull length and limb reach, and use the **Front** view for width and stance symmetry. Consistency beats averaging everything.

5. In the **Draw** | **Floor** section, locate **Fill Mode** and set it to 3. This mode allows the reference image to display as an overlay behind the mesh, enabling proper visual comparison during blocking. **Fill Mode** controls how the reference interacts with the model:

    - **Mode 0** displays the grid only
    - **Mode 1** and **Mode 2** partially fill the plane but do not allow enhanced image blending
    - **Mode 3** activates full image blending controls, enabling **E Enhance Opacity** and **E Enhance Factor**

    Without **Fill Mode** set to 3, the **Enhance** parameters will remain inactive.

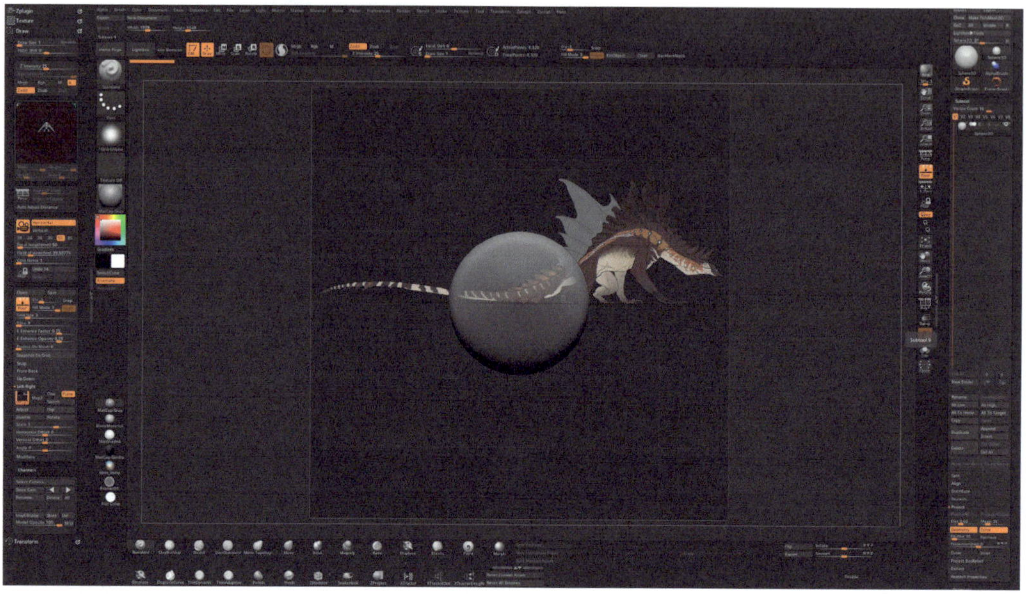

Figure 2.8 – Mode 3 enables image blending controls, activating E Enhance Opacity and E Enhance Factor for reference visibility

6. Adjust reference visibility. Once **Fill Mode** is set to 3, use **E Enhance Opacity** and **E Enhance Factor** to control how the reference interacts visually with the mesh.
    - Lower **E Enhance Opacity** if the image overpowers the sculpt
    - Increase **E Enhance Factor** to strengthen contrast and improve readability

   Keep **Project On Mesh** disabled, since the reference is used strictly for alignment, not projection.

7. The **Snap** option in the **Draw | Floor** panel does not control camera alignment. It controls whether the **Floor** plane dynamically snaps to the active mesh. When **Snap** is enabled, the **Floor** updates automatically as you sculpt, keeping the grid aligned to the mesh's bounding space. This can be useful when blocking base forms and ensuring the model remains grounded during early proportional adjustments.
   However, for precise reference alignment, **Snap** should be disabled. Keeping it off prevents the **Floor** from shifting as the mesh changes, ensuring that *Y = 0* remains a stable world-space reference throughout the blocking phase.

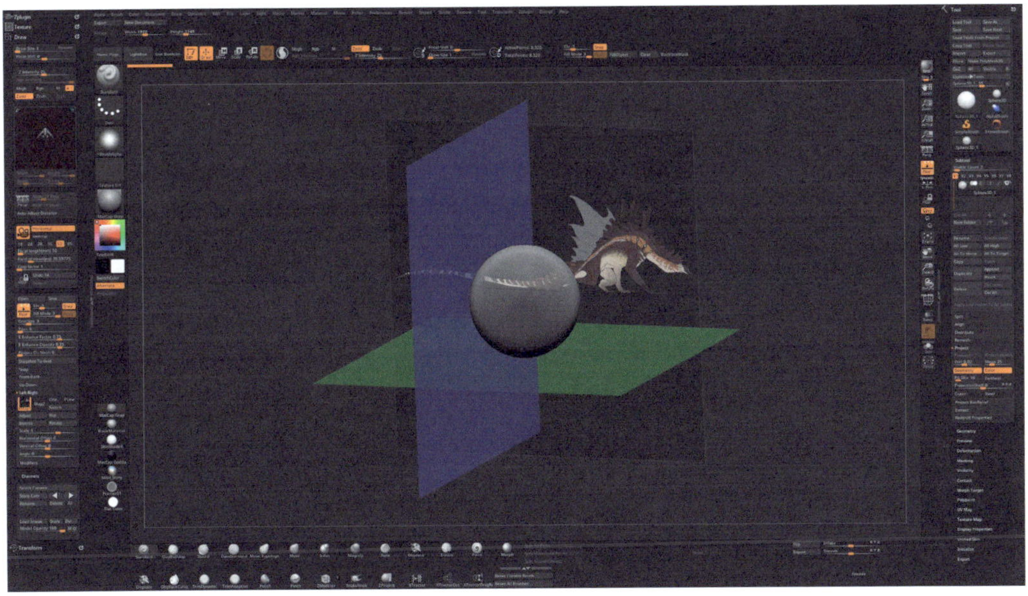

Figure 2.9 – With Snap active, the Floor dynamically updates and follows the mesh as it changes

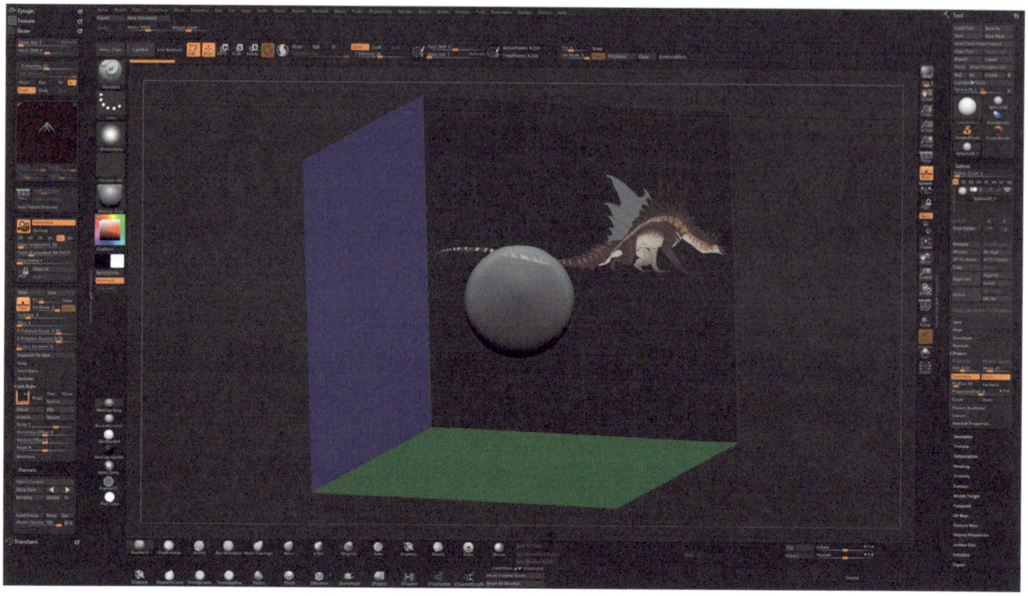

Figure 2.10 – With Snap turned off, the Floor remains fixed in world space

8. Use **PLine** for proportional checks. Activate **PLine** in the **Draw** | **Floor** panel to display a perspective line between the camera and the mesh. This tool helps visualize depth relationships and confirm that major landmarks align correctly in space. Unlike the grid, **PLine** gives you a directional visual cue, making it easier to understand volume relationships in 3D rather than relying only on flat orthographic comparison.

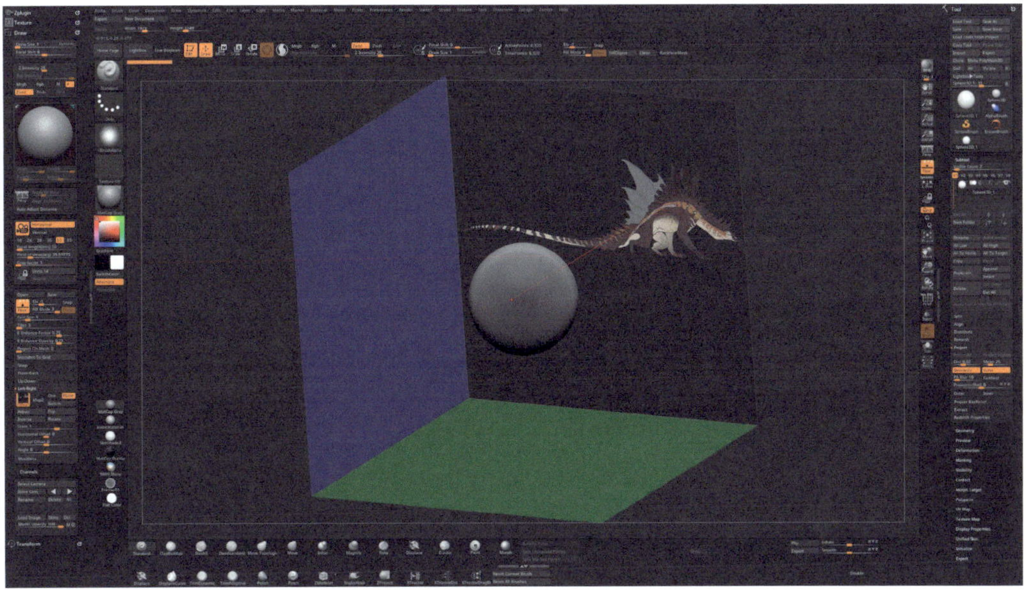

Figure 2.11 – PLine active, showing depth alignment between reference and mesh

9. Save your reference setup properly. If you prepared 2048 × 2048 images in Photoshop and aligned them correctly, you can preserve this configuration using **Draw** | **Save**. This stores the **Floor** and reference alignment without saving unnecessary geometry.
10. If the references were not pre-aligned in Photoshop, you can manually adjust **Scale**, **Horizontal Offset**, **Vertical Offset**, and **Rotation** inside the **Draw** panel, then save the configuration using **Draw** | **Save**. This allows you to reload the setup every time you reopen ZBrush using **Draw** | **Load**, maintaining consistency without rebuilding the alignment from scratch.
    Saving the entire project as a `.ZPR` file will also preserve the reference setup, but it stores all loaded tools and scene data, which can unnecessarily increase file size and clutter your workflow.

Note that you must never scale the sculpt to fit a misaligned sheet. Fix the sheet alignment in the **Grid** controls first. Scaling the mesh now will cause world-space inconsistencies and break the *Y = 0* grounding when exporting to Maya later.

How it works...

ZBrush's **Draw | Floor** system functions as a world-space anchoring tool that allows you to align orthographic references directly to the global axes of the scene. When configured correctly, the **Floor** becomes a stable spatial framework for proportional blocking.

Each reference image is mapped to a specific axis plane such as **Front-Back**, **Left-Right**, or **Up-Down**. Because these planes are tied to world coordinates rather than Viewport overlays, alignment remains consistent as you rotate the camera and switch between orthographic views.

Unlike traditional image planes in other software, the advantage of the **Floor** system is that it keeps your **Front**, **Side**, and **Top** views perfectly aligned to real axes. This allows you to compare views with precision and maintain structural consistency across planes.

When **Fill Mode** is set to 3, the reference can be displayed transparently behind the mesh, enabling continuous visual comparison while sculpting. This makes it possible to evaluate proportions and volume relationships without losing surface readability.

The **Snap** option does not control camera alignment. It controls whether the **Floor** dynamically updates to follow the mesh. When **Snap** is enabled, the **Floor** recalculates its position as the model changes. While this can be useful in early exploratory stages, it should remain disabled during precise blocking. Keeping it off ensures that the world reference remains clearly visible and stable throughout the process.

The **PLine** tool adds a perspective depth indicator between the camera and the mesh. While the **Floor** helps with planar alignment, **PLine** helps you evaluate spatial relationships. It supports proportional awareness in depth, which is essential when translating flat reference drawings into solid volumes.

This workflow reinforces three-dimensional thinking. When working with two or more orthographic references, every volume must agree in 3D space. A form that works in **Side** view must also work in **Front** and **Top**. You are not adjusting silhouettes independently, but also constructing volumes that hold up across axes.

By configuring the **Floor** system correctly, you are building a structured 3D foundation that ensures consistency from blocking through retopology, UVs, and further production stages.

Using ZSpheres for a fast base and as a support tool in DynaMesh

ZSpheres are one of the most efficient ways to block the structure of a creature before moving into **DynaMesh**. They allow you to define gesture, balance, and anatomical rhythm using a lightweight system that's easy to adjust. Base meshes built from primitives often lose gesture and proportion flexibility, while **ZSpheres** preserve structural flow and make early adjustments faster and cleaner.

In this recipe, you'll use **ZSpheres** to create the main body mass of the dragon, that is, the torso, limbs, tail, and the base for its wing membranes, while maintaining symmetry and proportion against your reference grid. This approach ensures that the creature's pose and flow feel natural from the start, giving you a solid foundation for later refinement. Once the overall silhouette is established, you'll convert the structure into **DynaMesh** to continue sculpting freely.

> **Note**
>
> **ZSpheres** will be used only for the body. The head will be sculpted separately from a sphere to allow more precise surface control and detailing in the *Sculpting the head from a sphere* recipe later in the chapter.

Getting ready

All companion files are available in the book's GitHub repository. To access the repository link, follow the steps in the *Download the example code/resource files* section in the *Preface*.

For this recipe, you'll find the following in the `Chapter02_03` folder:

- **The reference images**: `dragonCrest_concept.png`, `dragonCrest_side.jpg`, and `dragonCrest_skeleton.png`
- **The ZBrush Floor grid**: `dragonCrest_zGrid_v001.zgr`
- **The starting ZSphere file**: `dragonCrest_zSpheres_v001.ztl`

These files follow the naming convention introduced in *Chapter 1* to maintain a consistent production workflow.

If you download and use these files, either keep the same naming convention to stay aligned with the examples in this book or rename them according to the workflow explained in the *Organizing files for a clean and consistent workflow* recipe in *Chapter 1*.

Before starting, set up your scene the following way:

1. Make sure your reference grid is active and aligned, as it will guide the proportions of your **ZSpheres** armature.
2. Set the model's symmetry along the *X*-axis (**Transform** | **Activate Symmetry**) and enable the **Floor** grid to keep orientation consistent.
3. Create a new tool and select **ZSpheres** from the **LightBox** or the **Tool** palette. This clean starting point will allow you to focus purely on building the body rhythm before switching to **DynaMesh** for sculpting.

Figure 2.12 shows the initial ZSphere armature aligned to the creature's side-view silhouette before conversion to **DynaMesh**:

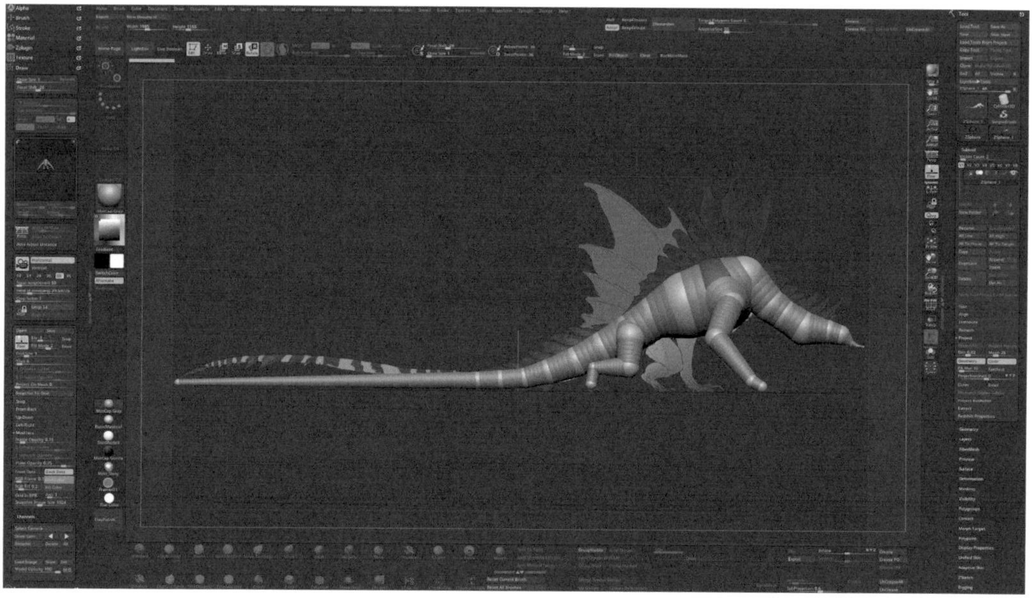

Figure 2.12 – Example of how ZSpheres should follow the concept

How to do it...

Using **ZSpheres** to build a creature base is about thinking like an animator or rigger. The process involves you defining the way the creature moves and carries its weight. In this section, we'll block out the body of our dragon using **ZSpheres**, following the silhouette of the concept while maintaining symmetry and balance across the spine, limbs, and tail:

1. Start by selecting **Tool** | **ZSphere**, then click and drag in the canvas to place it.
2. Enter **Edit mode** (press *T*) immediately so you can modify it. This first ZSphere acts as the root of the body, positioned roughly at the creature's chest. This is the point from which all other limbs will grow.

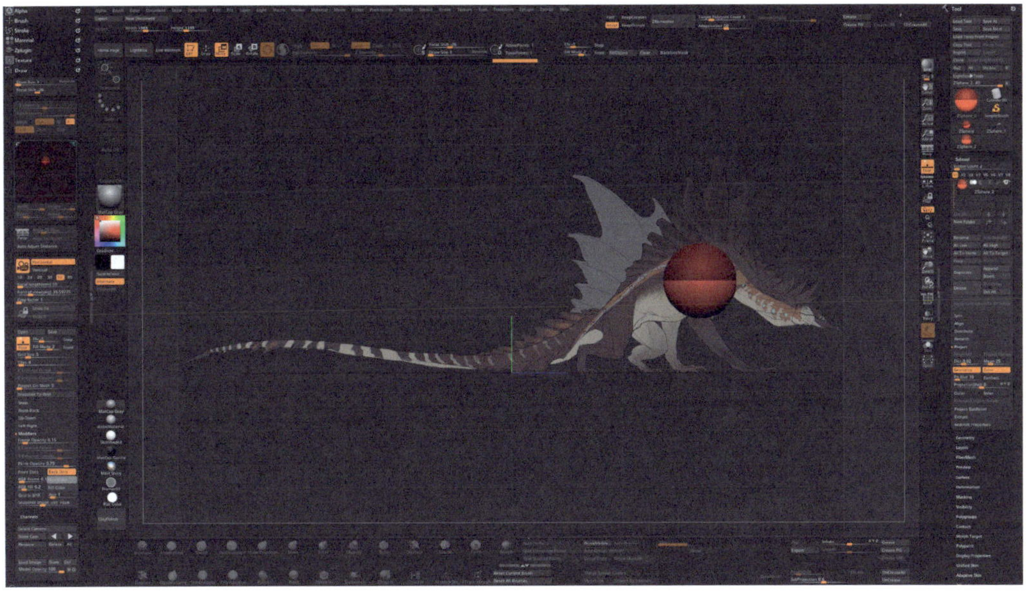

Figure 2.13 – First ZSphere placed at chest level aligned to side-view reference

Note

If the colored axis lines on the **Floor** planes become visually distracting while blocking your forms, go to **Draw | Modifiers** and set **Axis** to `0`. This removes the axis guides from the planes without disabling the **Floor** itself, keeping your orthographic references clean and easier to read while sculpting.

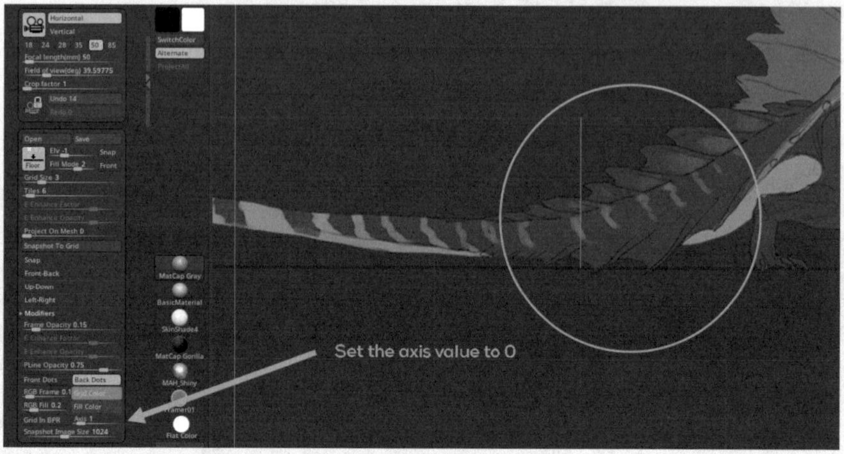

Figure 2.14 – Example of removing Cartesian axis lines from the Floor by setting Axis to 0

3. Use **Draw** (press *Q*) to add 5 to 6 **ZSpheres** along the spine, following the gesture line in **Side** view.
4. Use **Gizmo 3D Move** (press *W*) to adjust curvature and ensure the posture feels dynamic. If needed, use **Scale** (press *E*) to resize individual **ZSpheres** and better define the proportions before generating the **Adaptive Skin**.

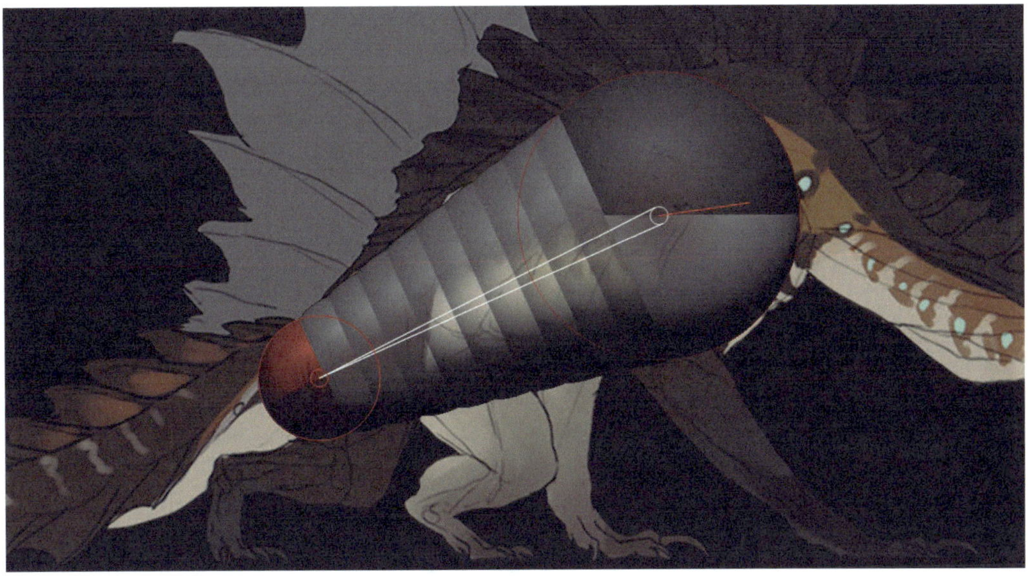

Figure 2.15 – The white line represents the parent-child relationship that defines the ZSphere hierarchy

> **Note**
>
> In addition to **Draw** (*Q*), **Move** (*W*), and **Scale** (*E*), ZBrush also provides the **Rotate** (*R*) tool. Unlike **Move** and **Scale**, **Rotate** does not simply rotate a single ZSphere (individual **ZSpheres** themselves cannot actually be rotated). Instead, it changes the orientation of the connected ZSphere chain while preserving the parent-child relationship. Understanding this behavior is essential when building more complex ZSphere rigs, even though in this recipe we will primarily use **Draw**, **Move**, and **Scale**.

5. Activate **Adaptive Skin** by clicking on **Tool | Adaptive Skin** (press *A*) to preview the adaptive skin and check that the silhouette flows naturally from hips to neck.

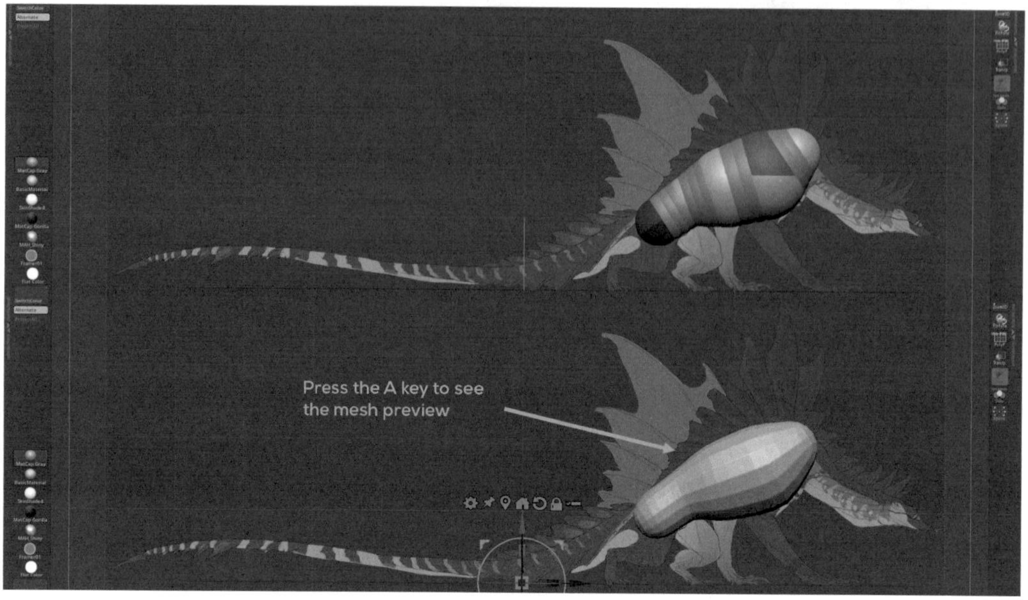

Figure 2.16 – Building the torso with ZSpheres and previewing the mesh

6. Add a ZSphere at hip level to clearly define the pelvic mass.
7. From this sphere, create a new ZSphere that represents the base attachment of the tail.
8. Then place a smaller ZSphere at the very end of the tail and position it according to the concept silhouette.

9. Instead of scaling each intermediate sphere manually, insert additional **ZSpheres** between the base and the tip to follow the tail curvature more accurately.
   This method keeps the volume transition homogeneous and progressively decreasing from the attachment to the tip, avoiding inconsistent scaling that can create irregular thickness along the tail. Apply the same approach to the neck and head.

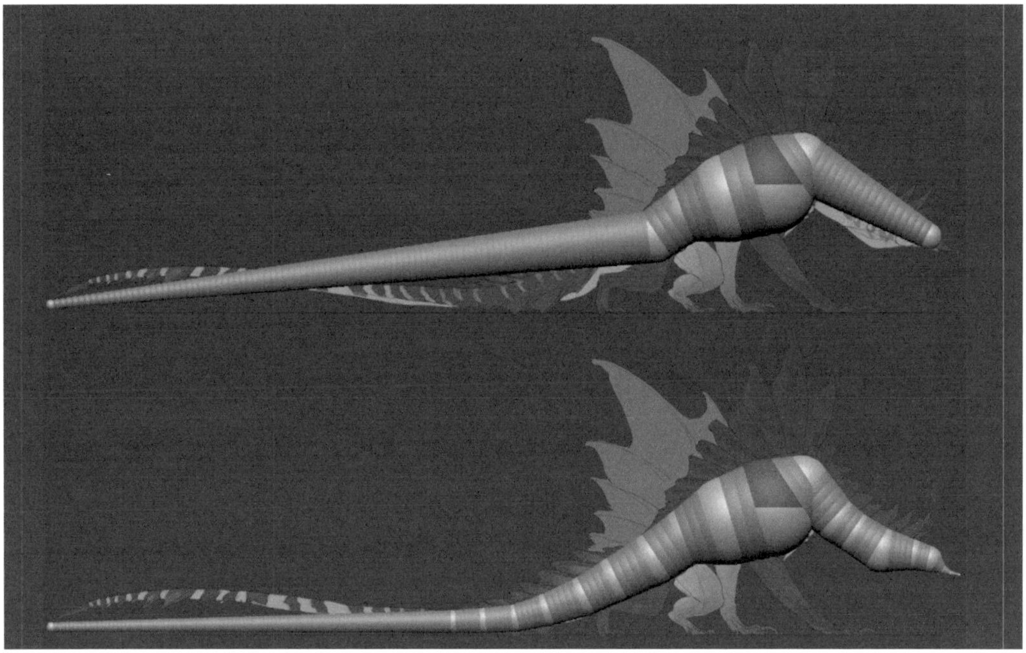

Figure 2.17 – Defining the tail structure from hip to tip, refining curvature to match the reference silhouette

10. With symmetry active (press *X*), draw arms from the shoulder sphere and legs from the hips. Limit each limb to 2 or 3 **ZSpheres** per segment to keep the structure simple. Adjust the joints so the pose matches the **Front** and **Side** views from your reference grid.

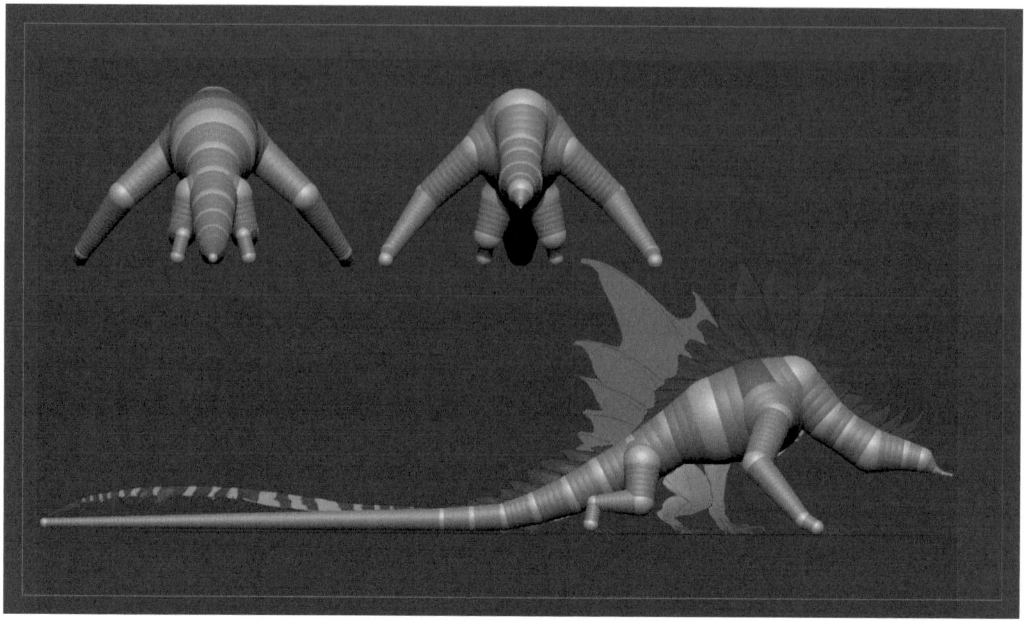

Figure 2.18 – ZSphere limb placement, defining shoulders and hips

11. Rotate to **Front** and **Top** views to verify balance. The ZSphere skeleton should feel centered, with even spacing between legs and a stable silhouette. If any limb drifts off-axis, reposition it using **Gizmo 3D Move** (press *W*) before generating geometry.
12. When satisfied, go to **Tool | Adaptive Skin**, set **Density** to 3 or 4, and click **Make Adaptive Skin**. A new tool, `Skin_ZSphere_1`, will appear; select it to begin your DynaMesh sculpting pass. Then activate **DynaMesh** and increase the resolution to `1024` to establish a solid base for refining primary forms.

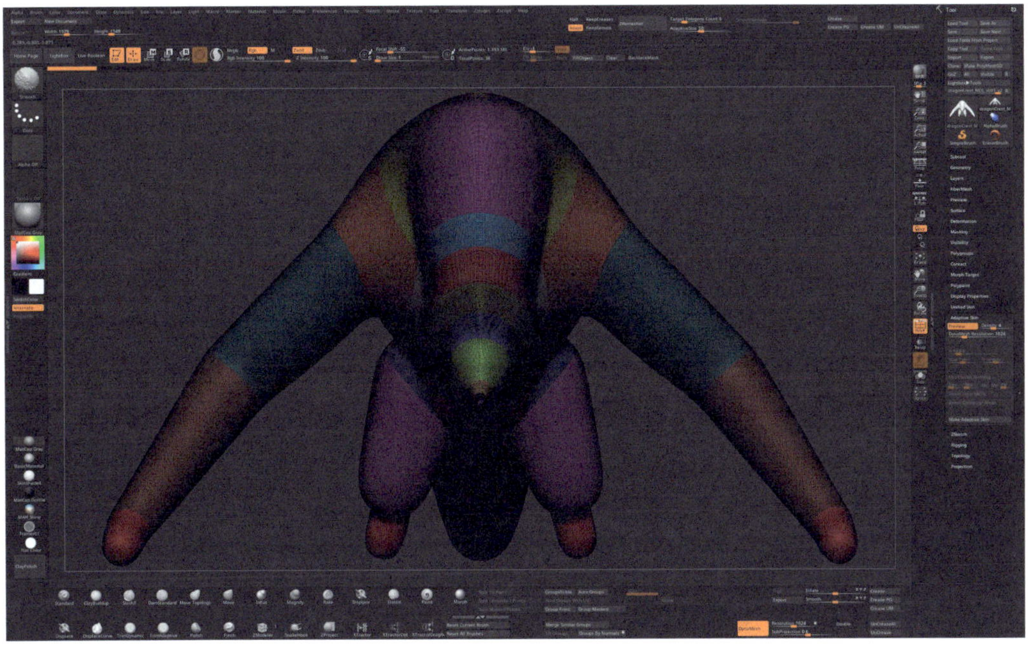

Figure 2.19 – Adaptive Skin generated from ZSpheres (Density 4) with DynaMesh set to 1024 for primary form refinement

Keep the ZSphere layout as lightweight as possible. Fewer spheres mean smoother transitions when converted to **DynaMesh**, preventing unnecessary pinching or lumpy topology during sculpting.

How it works...

ZSpheres work as a procedural skeleton inside ZBrush, defining both proportion and motion logic before any sculpting begins. Each ZSphere represents a joint or mass, linked through a parent–child hierarchy that mimics how a rigger defines bones. This makes it possible to adjust the creature's posture and gesture at any moment without breaking its structure. When you preview the **Adaptive Skin**, ZBrush interpolates smooth surfaces between spheres, allowing you to focus on anatomical rhythm instead of topology.

For our dragon, this method ensures that the torso, hips, and limbs follow a believable line of action while maintaining symmetry. It also helps establish realistic joint spacing: shoulders, elbows, and knees fall naturally along the skeletal arc you've built. The simplicity of the ZSphere armature keeps the mesh lightweight and flexible, perfect for a later transition to **DynaMesh**, where true sculpting detail begins.

Unlike building directly from primitives, ZSpheres encourage you to think structurally about pivot points, balance, and weight distribution. This mindset translates directly into cleaner forms once converted, resulting in a model that behaves predictably under deformation or posing.

Figure 2.20 compares a ZSphere blockout with one built from primitives, showing the stronger gesture flow achieved through the ZSphere workflow:

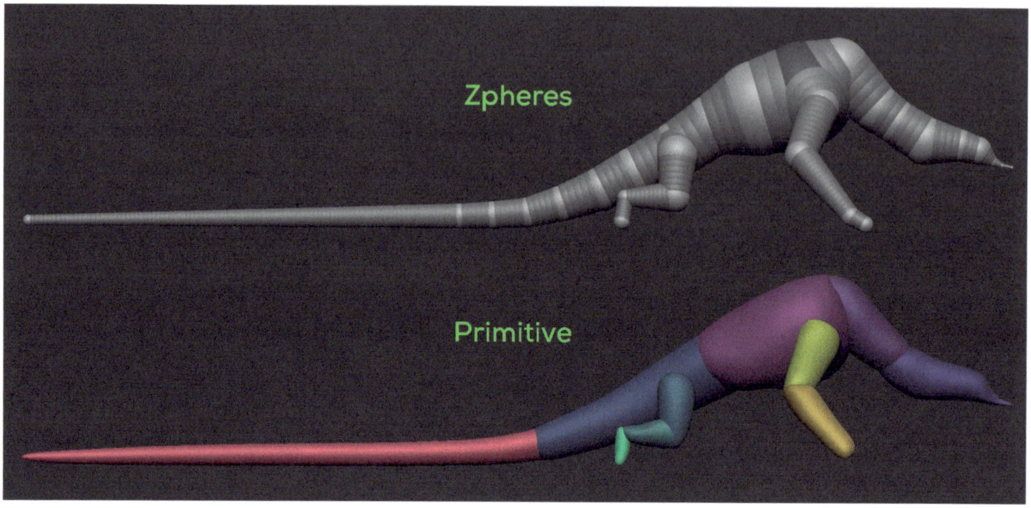

Figure 2.20 – A DynaMesh sculpt built from ZSpheres vs. one started from a primitive

Sculpting primary shapes with DynaMesh and Sculptris Pro (Body)

Before adding secondary forms or fine details, it's crucial to establish strong, clean primary shapes. In this recipe, you'll learn how to use **DynaMesh** and **Sculptris Pro** to define the main body of our creature: the wingless dragon. **DynaMesh** allows you to merge and reshape volumes freely, maintaining even topology as you block the silhouette, while **Sculptris Pro** offers flexibility for subtle adjustments without subdividing.

Keeping the head as a separate SubTool is ideal at this stage. This is because the facial area requires a higher **DynaMesh** resolution to sculpt structural elements such as eyelids, nostrils, and mouth openings with sufficient definition. If the head remained attached to the body, increasing the resolution to support these features would unnecessarily raise the density of the entire mesh, making the blocking phase heavier and less responsive. By isolating the head, you can locally increase resolution only where needed, ensuring better control over complex areas such as the mouth, nostrils, and eyes.

At this stage, fingers and membranes are intentionally not defined yet. The focus is strictly on establishing clear primary masses. Introducing smaller elements too early would interfere with proportion control and silhouette clarity. These components will be developed in the later recipes, once the main volumes and anatomical relationships are solid.

By understanding this workflow, you'll be able to sculpt confident, readable forms that support anatomy and gesture from the very first pass.

Figure 2.21 shows the blocked **DynaMesh** dragon base from multiple angles, with the head kept as a separate SubTool for higher-resolution sculpting:

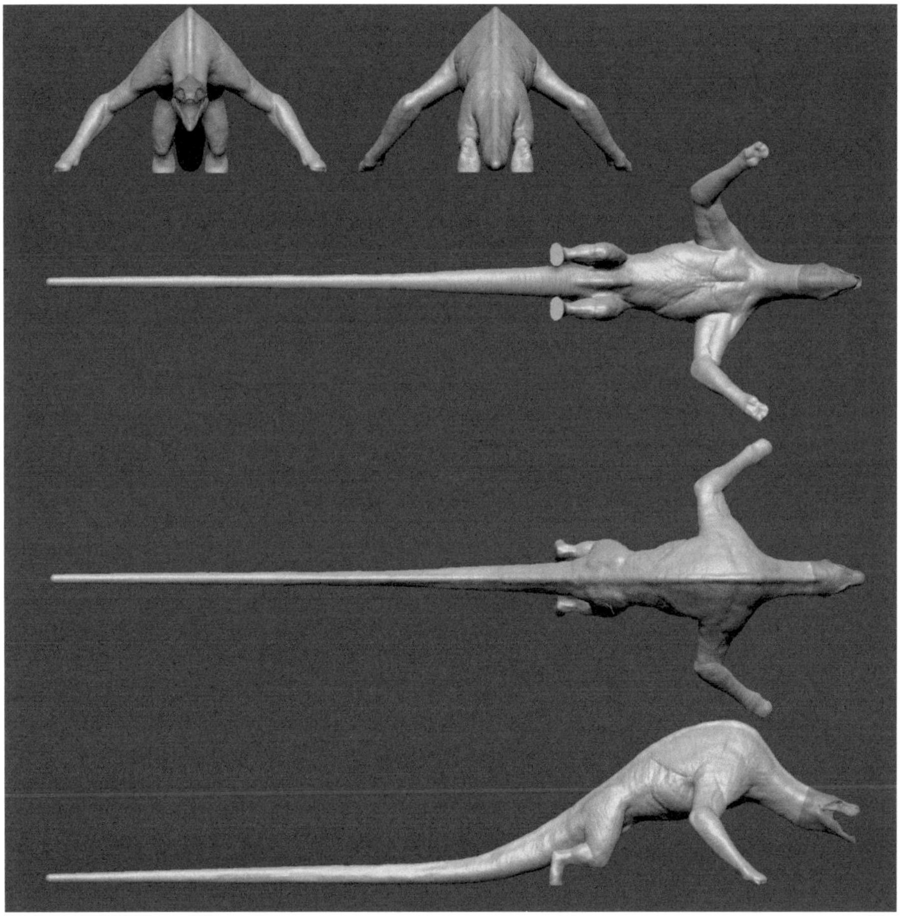

Figure 2.21 – DynaMesh dragon base with a separate head SubTool

Getting ready

Before you start blocking, ensure the scene is prepared for sculpting:

1. Make sure your creature's **DynaMesh** base is clean and responsive.
2. Use the mesh converted from **ZSpheres** as your body foundation and duplicate it to create a separate **SubTool** for the head.
3. Keep the **DynaMesh Resolution** at `256` to `1024` to maintain fluid sculpting while preserving major volumes and enabling **Symmetry** to keep anatomy balanced from the start.

To support this workflow, I have prepared a file with all the main pieces separated and ready for inspection and download: `dragonCrest_dynamesh_v001.ztl` from the chapter folder (see *Technical requirements* section for details). The file will allow you to review the structure and analyze how each volume is organized before moving forward.

How to do it...

Once your **DynaMesh** base is ready, start shaping the main muscle masses that define your creature's anatomy. This stage is about gesture, rhythm, and weight flow rather than fine detail. For large-scale creatures, managing resolution efficiently is crucial. **DynaMesh** gives you uniform topology, while **Sculptris Pro** lets you locally add density where you need more precision. Follow these steps:

1. Begin with a **DynaMesh Resolution** of `256` to `1024`. Use the **ClayBuildup** Brush to establish primary anatomical volumes: torso, shoulders, hips, and thighs. Work broadly, layering strokes along muscle direction. Keep the surface raw and fibrous; visible brush strokes will help you read tension and structure later.

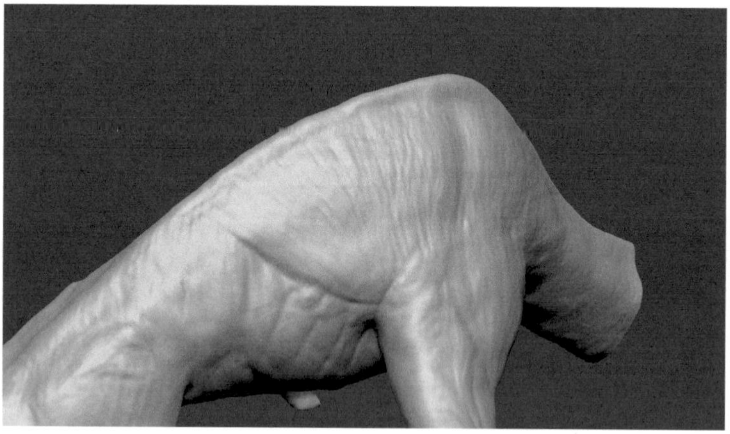

Figure 2.22 – Early ClayBuildup pass showing chest masses roughly defined

2. Switch to the **Move Topological** Brush to refine the silhouette and gesture. Adjust the spine arch, tail curvature, and balance of the limbs in **Side** and **Front** views.
3. When you need significantly more local definition, especially for smaller details that require tighter surface control during blocking, temporarily enable **Sculptris Pro** from the top bar. This mode dynamically adds topology only where you sculpt, increasing density under the brush without affecting the rest of the mesh.
   For example, if you want to introduce sharper rib separations, subtle bony landmarks, or early secondary forms that require more precision than your current **DynaMesh** resolution allows, activate **Sculptris Pro** and sculpt directly on the area. You will notice the topology becomes denser only where needed. At this stage of our dragon, we are still focusing on primary forms, so **Sculptris Pro** is not necessary. However, we will use it later when working on the head, where smaller anatomical structures require higher local definition and more controlled topology density.

> **Tip**
>
> Use **Sculptris Pro** with a small brush radius to refine edges and anatomical transitions. The *smaller* the brush radius, the *higher* the localized tessellation. This is ideal for large creatures that need detail only in specific areas, such as joints or facial planes.

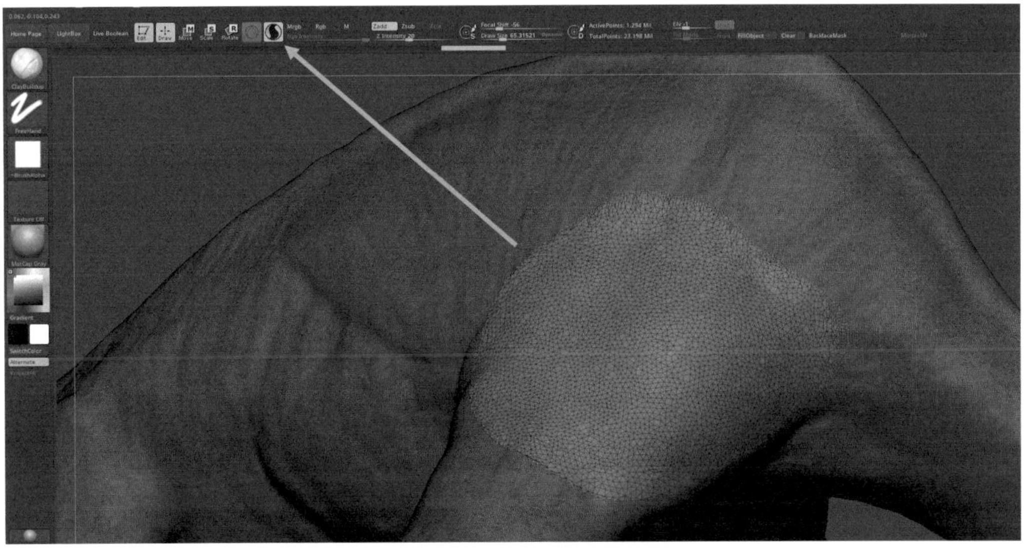

Figure 2.23 – Sculptris Pro enabled, showing localized topology increase on the ribcage

> **Note**
>
> If **DynaMesh** is active, remember that every time you re-run **DynaMesh**, the topology generated by **Sculptris Pro** will be redistributed evenly across the entire surface. This means you lose the local density advantage created by **Sculptris Pro**.
>
> For this reason, use **Sculptris Pro** either before committing to a final **DynaMesh** pass or after your primary **DynaMesh** stage is complete.

4. Remesh with **DynaMesh** only when necessary, that is, after major shape changes, not after every stroke. Overusing it can erode volume and flatten detail. Find a steady rhythm of *sculpt → adjust → remesh*, checking that those thin areas like membranes, wings, elbows, or ankles retain volume. If they collapse, reinforce them with **Inflate** or **Move** Brush before refreshing the mesh.
5. Keep monitoring performance: large creatures can quickly reach heavy polygon counts. After using **Sculptris Pro** sparingly, return to **DynaMesh** for unifying the topology before saving or subdividing. The goal is to balance freedom and control, maintaining enough density for readable anatomy without choking memory.

How it works...

In this workflow, **DynaMesh** and **Sculptris Pro** serve two different but complementary purposes.

DynaMesh supports structural freedom during the primary phase. It allows you to reshape large volumes without being constrained by topology, keeping proportions and gesture flexible while blocking the anatomy. **Sculptris Pro** adds controlled local refinement. Instead of increasing resolution across the entire mesh, it introduces density only where higher precision is required. Together, they create a hierarchy of control: **DynaMesh** preserves global volume consistency, **Sculptris Pro** enables localized definition.

This balance keeps the sculpt lightweight, editable, and production-ready. Density is introduced intentionally, not uniformly, allowing the model to transition cleanly into subdivision, retopology, or posing stages without unnecessary complexity. For large creatures like our dragon, this approach ensures readable anatomy, stable proportions, and clean topology throughout the sculpting process.

Sculpting the head from a sphere

The head defines the creature's *personality*, *rhythm*, and *scale*. Starting it from a simple sphere gives you full freedom to sculpt without the constraints of topology inherited from the body mesh.

In this recipe, we'll create the dragon's head as a separate **SubTool**, focusing on clean volumes, readable anatomy, and the balance between structure and expression. Working independently allows for higher resolution where it matters most, around the mouth, eyes, and cranial plates, while keeping the rest of the body lightweight.

Using the **ClayBuildup** Brush for major planes and **Slash3** for defining bone transitions and jaw separation, you'll learn how to capture form tension and secondary rhythm even at this early stage. The goal is not to finish the head but to establish strong shapes that integrate smoothly with the body once merged back into **DynaMesh**.

Getting ready

Before sculpting the head, prepare a clean starting mesh. You can either create it as a standalone exercise or insert it into your existing dragon scene:

1. If you want to start from scratch as a separate exercise: Select **Tool** | **Sphere3D**, then click **Make PolyMesh3D** to convert it into editable geometry.

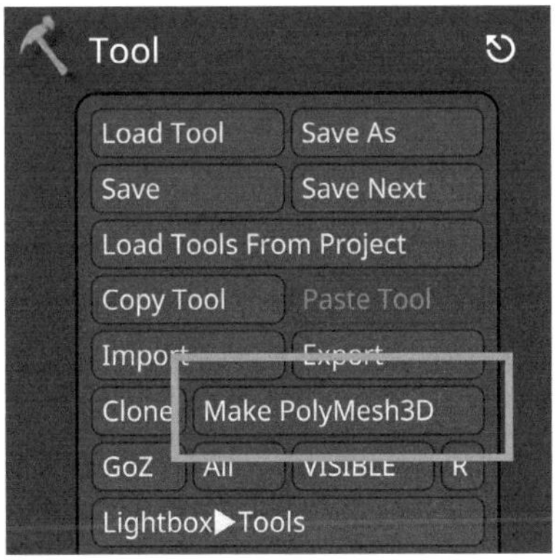

Figure 2.24 – Using Make PolyMesh3D to convert the mesh into editable geometry

2. If you are adding the head to your existing dragon body, go to the **SubTool** panel, click **Append** or **Insert** in **Tool** | **Append** or **Tool** | **Insert**, choose **Sphere3D**, and the new mesh will be ready to sculpt.

3. Position and scale the sphere in the following way:
    1. If you are following the previous dragon workflow, place it near the creature's neck area according to your reference grid.
    2. If working independently, simply center it in the scene and scale it proportionally to your concept.
4. Enable **Symmetry** (press *X*) to maintain bilateral balance.
5. Activate **DynaMesh** and set a medium resolution, around 256–384, to maintain responsiveness while capturing clear primary forms around the jaw and eye sockets.

You may download the prepared starting file from the GitHub repository if you prefer to continue with the exact setup used in this chapter. The file follows the naming convention explained in the *Organizing files for a clean and consistent workflow* recipe in *Chapter 1*. If you use it, you can either keep the same naming logic or adapt it to your own structured pipeline.

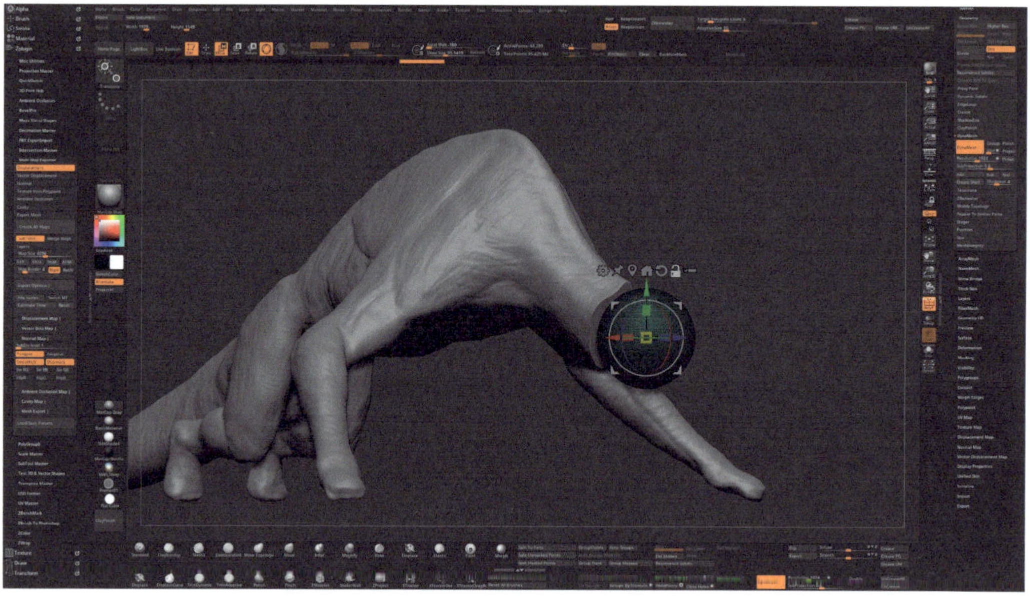

Figure 2.25 – Head sphere added as a separate SubTool and ready for DynaMesh sculpting

How to do it...

Let's start sculpting the head from a clean sphere to give the creature a strong focal point and a believable cranial rhythm. The process begins with rough anatomy and gesture, then evolves into clear planes and defined muscle flow using **ClayBuildup**, **Move**, and **Slash3** brushes. Follow these steps:

1. Insert a **Sphere3D**, convert it to a **PolyMesh3D**, and activate **DynaMesh** at a medium resolution (around `1024–2048`).
2. Use the **Move** Brush to stretch the sphere slightly forward, shaping the basic head volume. Block the main proportions, the cranium, snout, and jaw – without focusing on symmetry or detail yet.

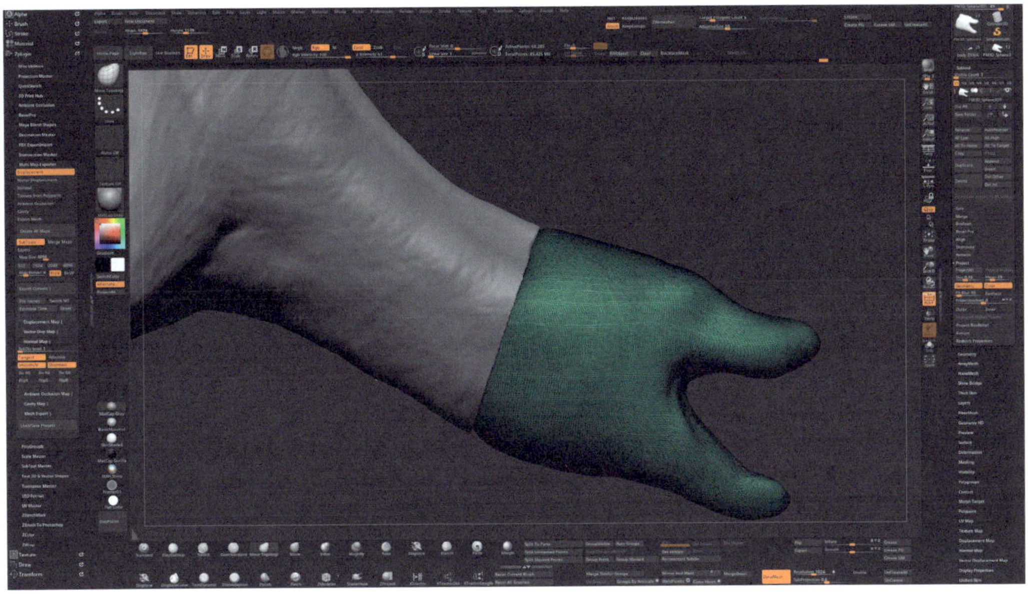

Figure 2.26 – Initial sphere reshaped into a head silhouette using Move Brush

3. Switch to the **ClayBuildup** Brush and begin establishing the main structural planes of the head: forehead, cheekbones, jawline, and temporal region.
4. Keep strokes broad and directional to define mass and tension. Think about the skull beneath the surface to maintain believable anatomical flow.
5. Then use the **Move Topological** Brush to refine proportions and silhouette. Pull the muzzle forward, shape the brow ridge, and adjust the back of the skull to balance the profile. For dragons and other large creatures, slightly exaggerate the jaw and zygomatic arches to reinforce strength and character.
6. Work back and forth between the **ClayBuildup** and **Move Topological** brushes, constantly checking the **Side** view to ensure the silhouette remains clear and readable.

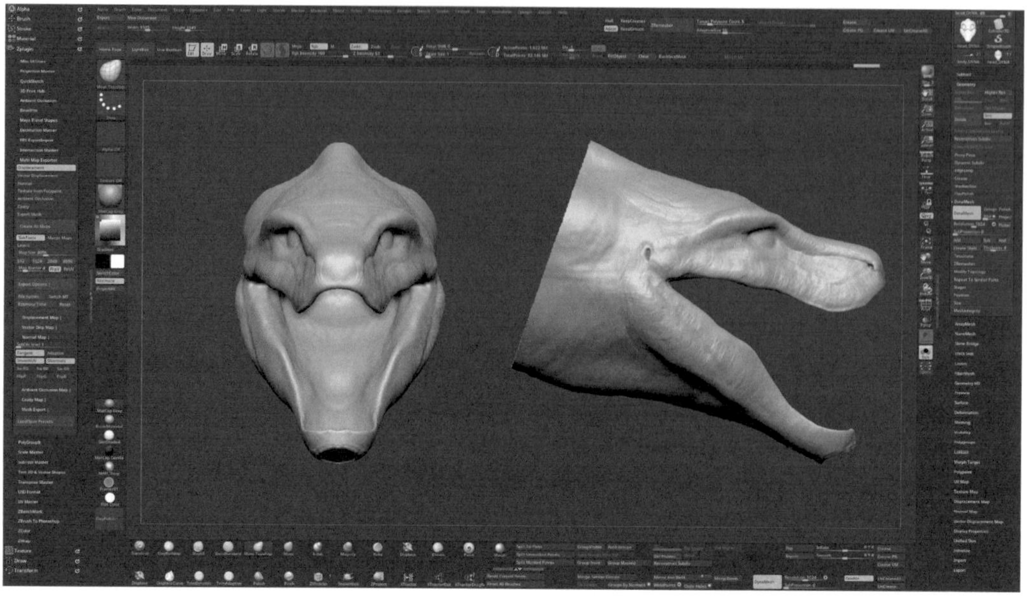

Figure 2.27 – Side and Front view showing blocked cranial planes and corrected jaw projection

7. Insert temporary eye spheres to establish gaze, orbital structure, and eyelid support. Append a new **Sphere3D** as a SubTool and convert it to **PolyMesh3D**. Subdivide the sphere 3 to 4 times to maintain better topological definition when scaling and positioning it inside the eye socket. Scale it down and position it inside the eye socket area using **Gizmo 3D Move** and **Scale**.
8. Position the eye according to your concept reference. Switch to **Side** view and follow the silhouette arc visible in the profile image. That cranial curve tells you how large the eye should be. The sphere must sit naturally inside that arc, supporting the orbital cavity instead of breaking the silhouette.
9. Duplicate the sphere to the opposite side using **Tool** | **Geometry** | **Modify Topology** | **Mirror And Weld**, or position both eyes manually with symmetry active. Keep the eye spheres as separate SubTools.
10. Now use the **Paint** Brush directly, then paint a simple black pupil at the center. Keep it minimal. This is not for rendering, but for structural reading.

Figure 2.28 – Example of a painted eye position

These temporary eye spheres are not decorative. They are fundamental for sculpting believable eyelids and for defining the brow ridge. The eyelids must wrap around a solid spherical volume. Without this anchor, they tend to collapse or lose anatomical tension. The brow mass also depends on the eye's placement to establish proper shadow and expression.

Study reptilian references such as Komodo dragons or large snakes. Observe how the eyelids hug the globe tightly and how the brow ridge compresses the upper lid. Use the side silhouette to judge orbital depth and eye scale before refining any secondary forms.

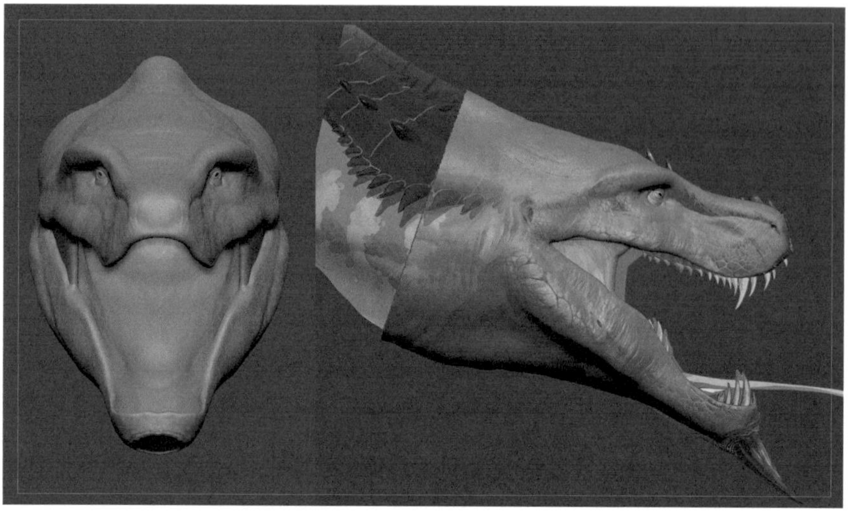

Figure 2.29 – Temporary eye spheres positioned inside the orbital cavity, aligned with side-view silhouette and concept proportions

11. Activate **Sculptris Pro** when refining smaller features such as nostrils, eye sockets, or the mouth corners. This dynamically increases local tessellation where more density is needed, perfect for capturing sharper forms without remeshing the entire head. Once refined, toggle **Sculptris Pro** off to maintain fluid performance.

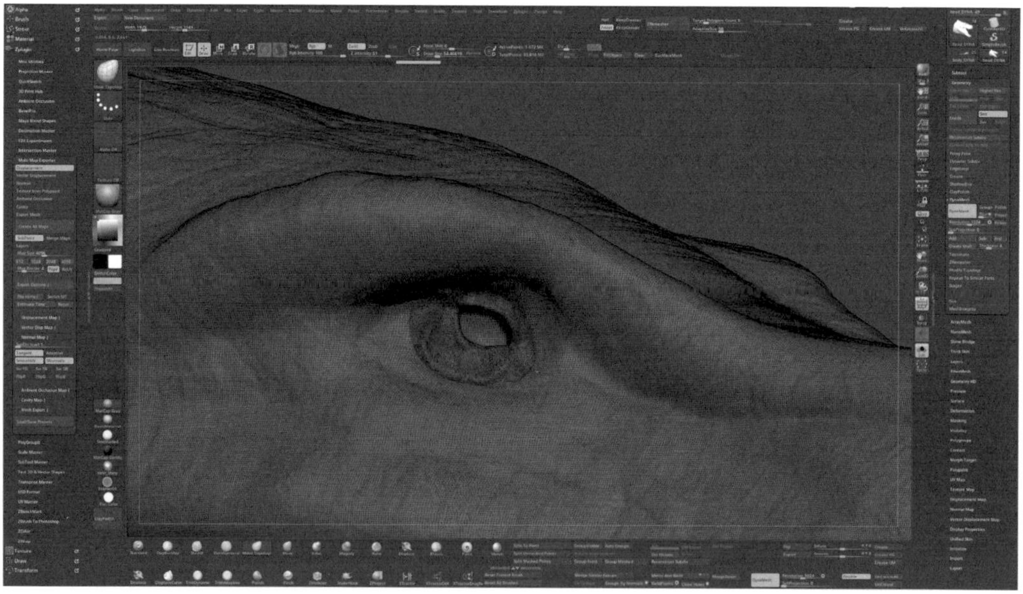

Figure 2.30 – Localized tessellation from Sculptris Pro around nostril and eye ridge

12. Use the **Slash3** Brush at low intensity (`10-20`) to carve clean separations such as the jawline, mouth crease, and cranial plate divisions. You can also use **Slash3** to incise the nostrils and define the eyelid separations with controlled, deliberate strokes. Unlike the **DamStandard** Brush, **Slash3** produces wider and more stable cuts, ideal for establishing clear anatomical transitions and readable structural landmarks during early detailing.

> **Tip**
>
> Use short, confident strokes that follow anatomy lines. This will help you preserve edge tension once you move to tertiary detailing.

13. Follow the natural anatomical flow and avoid overcutting. Defining smaller areas such as the eyes and nostrils early, even with subtle wrinkles or edge indications, can also support the retopology phase later in *Chapter 4*. Clear structural separations give you visual guidance for where edge loops will likely need to flow, helping you anticipate topology layout and maintain cleaner deformation around key facial features.

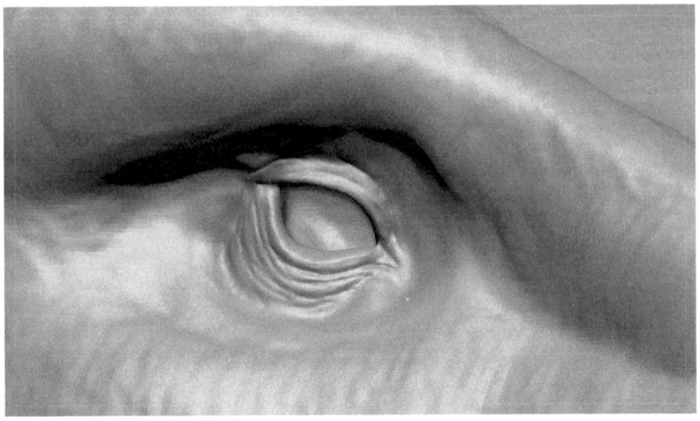

Figure 2.31 – Slash3 strokes defining eyelid lines

> **Tip**
>
> Use the **Slash3** Brush in **ZAdd** mode with controlled strokes, then lightly smooth (hold *Shift* while dragging with the left mouse button (or pen), and set **Smooth Strength** `20` to `30`) the surrounding transition to soften sharp edges without losing the main separation. Alternating between carving and smoothing helps maintain clean edge definition around eyelids and mouth borders.

14. Reassess proportions from **Front** and **Side** views, keeping the head aligned with the reference grid. Rotate constantly in perspective mode to ensure that volume reads well from every angle. If the mesh begins to stretch, remesh once with **DynaMesh** to restore even topology.
15. To define the inner mouth membranes, append a **Cube3D** as a new SubTool.
16. Position the cube inside the mouth cavity and scale it using **Scale** until it becomes thin and elongated, matching the intended membrane thickness.
17. Adjust its placement with **Gizmo 3D Move** so it follows the curvature between the upper and lower jaws. If needed, ensure perfect symmetry by using **Tool | Geometry | Modify Topology | Mirror And Weld**.

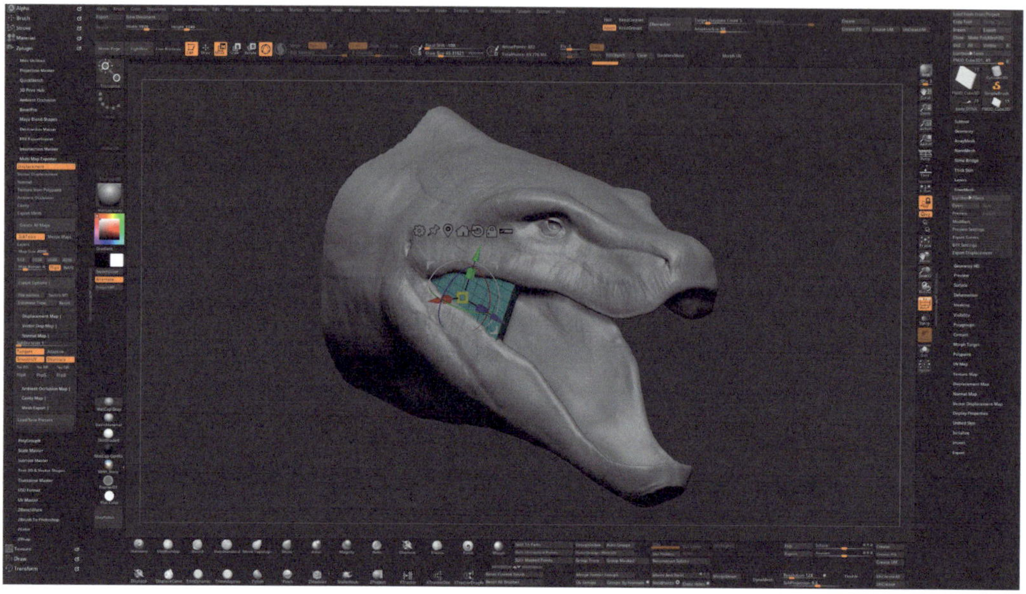

Figure 2.32 – Cube3D positioned inside the mouth cavity, scaled and shaped to establish the inner membrane before merging

18. Make sure the correct axis is selected, usually *X*, so the cube mirrors properly across the central plane.

Note

Mirror And Weld operates based on the symmetry axis. If you're working with off-center SubTools, such as detached horns, claws, teeth, membranes, or other separate production assets, activate **Transform | Activate Symmetry** and enable **L.Sym** (or **Local Symmetry**) before performing the mirror.

Note that **Local Symmetry** allows **Mirror And Weld** to follow the SubTool's local axis instead of the global world axis, which is especially useful when working with off-center elements.

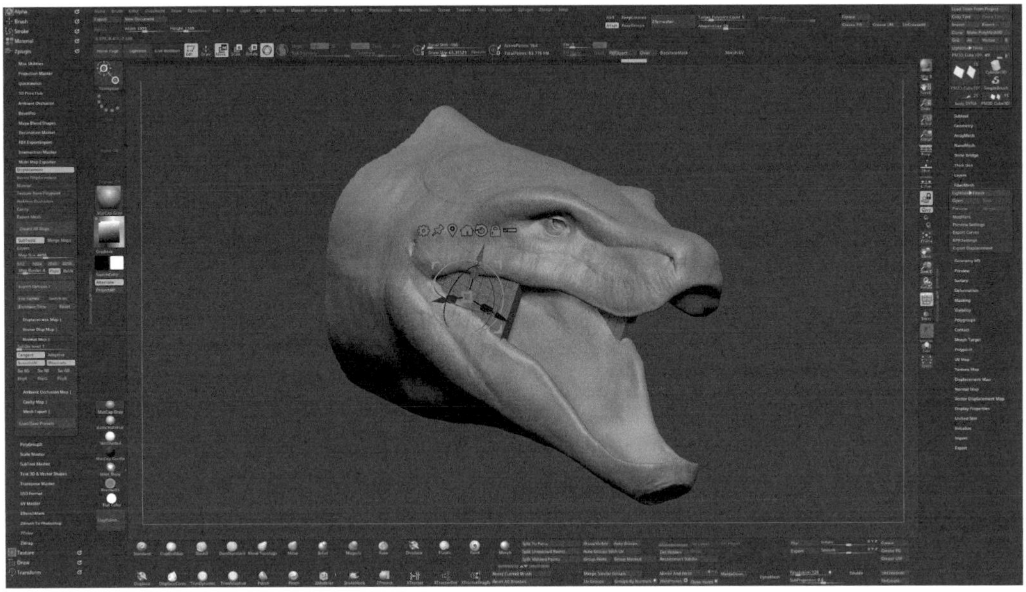

Figure 2.33 – Membrane geometry mirrored across the X axis using Mirror And Weld to ensure perfect symmetry and proper alignment with the jaw curvature

19. Once the membrane shape is correctly aligned, merge the membrane SubTool with the head SubTool using **SubTool | Merge Down**.

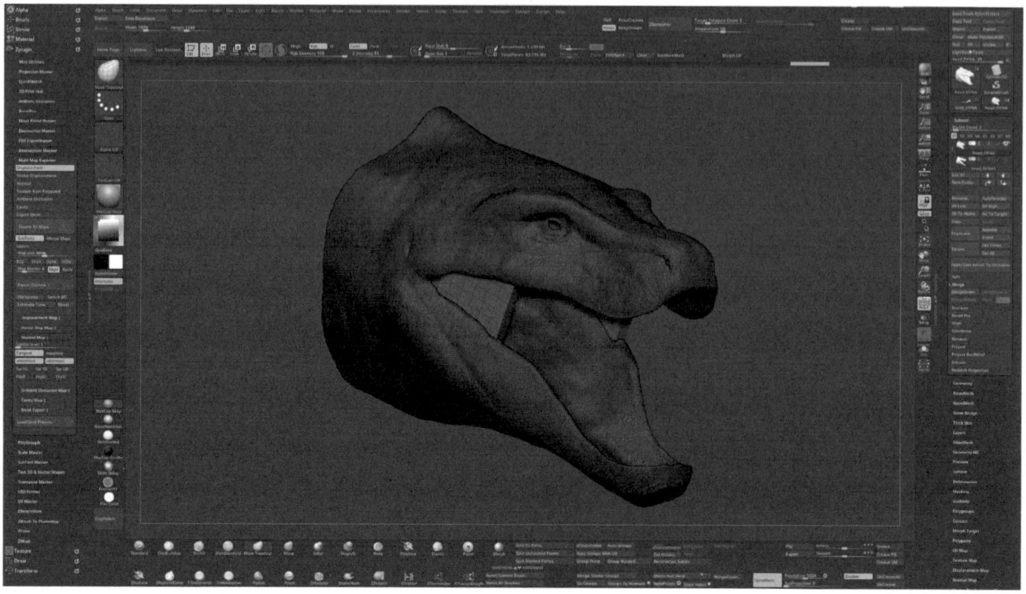

Figure 2.34 – Membrane SubTool merged with the head using Merge Down, preparing the mesh for unified topology

20. After merging, activate **Tool | DynaMesh** to fuse the geometries into a single unified mesh. This step attaches the membrane seamlessly to the head structure.
21. Finally, smooth the rigid edges left from the original cube and refine the transitions to make the membrane feel organic and integrated into the surrounding anatomy.

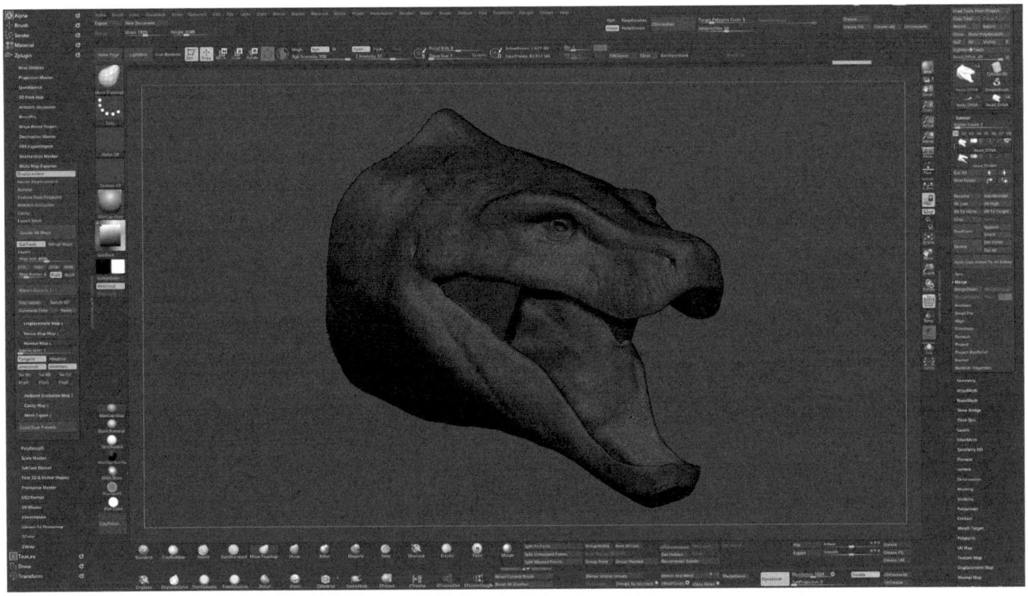

Figure 2.35 – DynaMesh activated to fuse the membrane with the head, followed by smoothing to soften the original cube edges and create organic transitions

How it works...

Starting the head from a separate sphere is primarily a resolution control strategy. Facial features such as nostrils, eyelids, lip folds, and fine-scale details require significantly higher density than the torso. Keeping the head as a separate SubTool allows you to push resolution where needed without increasing polygon count across the entire character.

DynaMesh ensures stable primary volume construction, while **Sculptris Pro** temporarily increases tessellation only in localized areas. This keeps the mesh efficient and responsive during blocking, while still allowing sharp definition in critical facial zones.

The **ClayBuildup** Brush defines mass and anatomical flow, the **Move Topological** Brush adjusts proportion without stretching nearby regions, and **Slash3** establishes structural separations that help clarify plane transitions early. Using the **Slash3** Brush instead of **DamStandard** prevents overly sharp micro-cuts and preserves clean form hierarchy.

Maintaining the head as a separate element through the retopology stage also improves control during downstream production. It allows independent topology density, cleaner loop planning around facial landmarks, and more predictable deformation later in rigging.

Creating membranes and wings

Membranes are one of the most recognizable features in creature design, from dragon wings to gliding flaps or webbed limbs. They combine structural tension with delicate, paper-thin surfaces that must feel believable both at rest and in motion.

In this recipe, we'll explore how to efficiently block out membranes using a **mask-and-extract workflow**, allowing you to sculpt clean, flat surfaces that retain their shape under deformation. This method will be very simple and will provide us with the basis to create membranes and wings with a perfectly straight structure, which is essential for the parts concerning rigging and simulations.

You'll also learn how to integrate the membranes with existing body geometry, define supporting bones or claws using **ZSpheres**, and adapt the shape to curved silhouettes without losing thickness control. The goal is to create elegant, functional membranes that look natural and remain technically sound for rigging and animation.

Figure 2.36 shows the extracted membrane shapes positioned along the dragon's spine during the blocking stage:

Figure 2.36 – Membrane masks blocked along the spine before extraction

Getting ready

Before diving in, set up your scene and materials properly:

1. Make sure your creature's body is properly blocked and positioned in world space, with **Symmetry** enabled. You should already have a clear understanding of how the membranes connect between limbs, torso, or tail before proceeding.
2. Keep a clean top or side view of your concept art visible for accurate alignment, especially when working with symmetrical wings or vertical membrane structures.
3. Decide whether your membrane should follow a *curved* surface or remain structurally *straight*.
   This decision must originate from the concept. In many production cases, wings and membranes are modeled in a neutral straight configuration to simplify rigging, deformation, and simulation. However, if the concept establishes curvature as part of the character's anatomical language or silhouette, the technical strategy must adapt accordingly.

Figure 2.37 – Wings modeled in a straight pose (Image courtesy of Ernesto Santini)

4. In this project, the membrane follows the relaxed curvature of the spine. This choice was defined at the concept stage and the modeling approach was built around it. The key principle is aligning technical decisions with design intent while remaining aware of downstream implications.

5. Keep Maya open as well, since some steps will be performed there to build and precisely control the base of the curved membrane before bringing it back into ZBrush for the sculpting phase.
6. If you plan to sculpt directly, prepare a **Plane3D** tool or a separate **SubTool** with sufficient resolution to support masking, shaping, and extraction without stretching the surface.

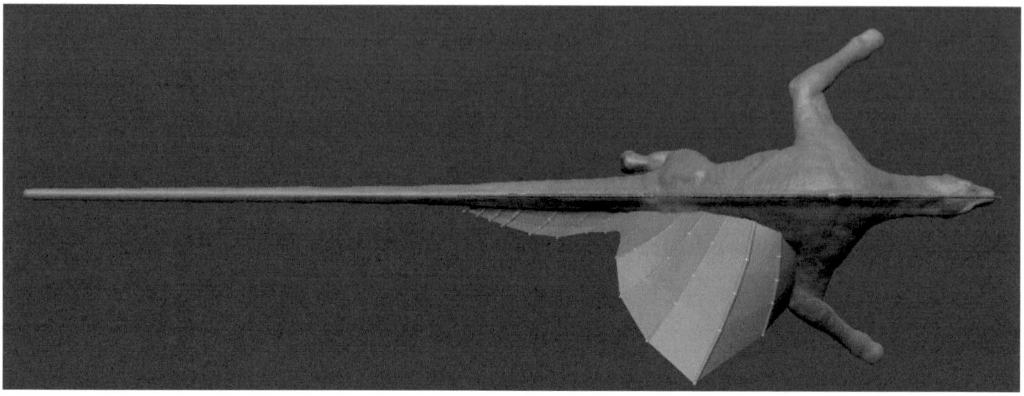

Figure 2.38 – Top-view reference with planned membrane connections between limbs and torso

How to do it...

We'll build creature membranes using a structural plane-and-extract workflow, starting from the central dorsal crest and then moving to the lateral membranes. The goal is to construct clean, thin, production-ready surfaces before adding structural support and organic refinement. By the end of this recipe, you'll understand a repeatable system that can be adapted to crests, gliders, tail fins, or any tension-based membrane structure. Now let's get started.

Blocking and extracting the central crest

We begin with the central crest, building it from a subdivided plane masked in strict orthographic view, then extracting thickness and reinforcing it with ZSphere-based supports that follow the dorsal spine. Once this method is clear, we'll apply the same logic to the lateral membrane, constructing it only on the left side and mirroring it afterward to maintain precision and control. Follow these steps:

1. Start by inserting a new plane. Go to **Tool** | **SubTool** | **Insert** and select **Plane3D**. This will create a new SubTool in your current tool.

2. With the new **Plane3D** SubTool selected, position it at world center. Activate the Gizmo by pressing *W*, then check the **Transform** palette to ensure the plane is aligned at *X = 0*.

   This is not related to symmetry. The plane must sit exactly on the central world axis because the dorsal crest will be generated along the spine, and the dragon's body is already aligned at *X = 0*. Keeping the plane centered ensures structural coherence when integrating the crest with the body.

3. Rotate the plane using the Gizmo so its normal faces the correct working direction. From this point onward, consistently work from the left side, which will act as your reference orientation during masking.

4. Now increase the plane resolution. Go to **Tool** | **Geometry** | **Divide** and click **Divide** *6 to 7 times*. This subdivision level is intentional. The added density is required for precise masking when tracing the concept silhouette before extraction.

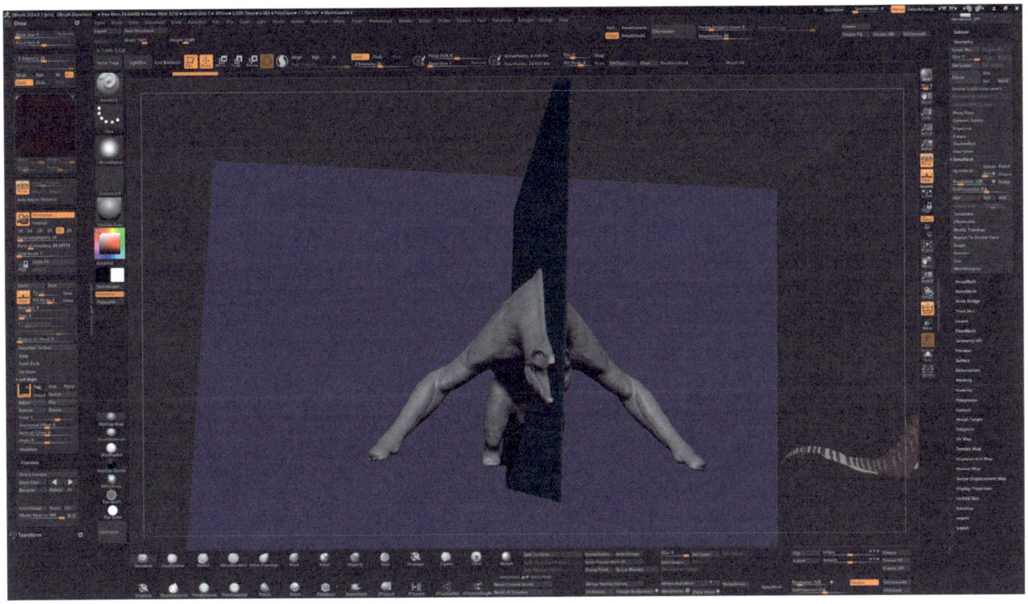

Figure 2.39 – Plane3D inserted as a SubTool, aligned at X = 0, subdivided and ready for masking in strict side view

5. Switch to a perfectly orthographic side view. Activate your **Floor** with the **Side** reference as explained in the *Setting up image references for accurate blocking* recipe and set **Fill Mode** to 3. Make sure the side reference is aligned correctly before proceeding.

6. To use **Mask Lasso**, hold *Ctrl* to temporarily activate the masking mode. While holding *Ctrl*, go to the top menu and open **Stroke**. Change the stroke type from the default (usually **Freehand** or **Dots**) to **Lasso**.
7. Now, still holding *Ctrl*, click and drag to draw a lasso shape that follows the membrane silhouette directly over the reference. Because you are in strict orthographic **Side** view with **Fill Mode** 3 active, the mask will project cleanly and accurately.

   Avoid rotating the camera while masking. Work entirely from the locked **Side** view. Leave a thin unmasked rim along the attachment area where the membrane connects to the body. This rim becomes your structural transition after extraction and DynaMesh.

Figure 2.40 – Side reference visible in the background through Draw | Floor; crest silhouette masked on the subdivided Plane3D in strict orthographic side view

Tip

You do not need to complete the entire mask in a single stroke. It is often more accurate to build the silhouette in multiple passes. Hold *Ctrl* to add to the mask progressively, refining complex curves step by step. If needed, hold *Ctrl* + *Alt* to subtract from the mask and correct small areas. Working in controlled sections improves precision and reduces silhouette errors.

8. Go to **Tool | SubTool | Extract**. In the **Extract** panel, set a **Thickness** value appropriate to your scale (`0.001-0.003` relative to your scale, and if it doesn't match, remember that you can always scale it on the *X*-axis) and keep **S Smt** set to **OFF**. The thickness should extend enough to intersect cleanly with the structural supports you previously created, such as the dorsal spine supports or membrane bones, ensuring proper integration later.
9. Click **Extract** to preview the thickness. At this stage, carefully evaluate whether the generated thickness penetrates correctly into the supporting structures without exceeding the intended volume. Adjust the Thickness slider if necessary.
10. Once satisfied with the preview, click **Accept**. ZBrush will generate a new SubTool containing the extracted membrane geometry.
11. Select the newly created SubTool and immediately activate **Tool | Geometry | DynaMesh** to weld borders and unify topology. Without **DynaMesh**, the extracted shell may contain unstable edge transitions.

Figure 2.41 – Extract preview adjusted for correct structural intersection, then accepted and unified with DynaMesh

Tip

If masking yields stair-stepped edges, sharpen the mask (*Ctrl* + *click*) once, then **Blur** it once before **Extract**. This produces a crisp but not jagged border that remeshes beautifully.

Creating the structural support system

Before building the membrane surface, we first need a structural support system that will define tension, curvature, and attachment flow along the creature's back:

1. Create the supporting structure using **ZSpheres**. Insert a new ZSphere tool at the world center and activate **Symmetry** by pressing *X*. Build a continuous central spine that follows the dorsal flow, then branch outward to form the structural elements supporting the membrane. Think in terms of one coherent skeletal system rather than separate floating bones.

Figure 2.42 – ZSphere chain forming a continuous dorsal structure with branching supports

2. With the **ZSpheres** tool active, go to **Tool | Adaptive Skin** in the right-hand **Tool** palette.
3. Set **Density** to 3 and **DynaMesh Resolution** to `1024`, then click **Preview** to evaluate the generated mesh. If the structure looks correct, click **Make Adaptive Skin**. ZBrush will generate a new tool, typically named `Skin_ZSphere_1`, in the **Tool** palette.
4. Now we'll add the newly created structural mesh (typically named `Skin_ZSphere_1`). Switch back to your main dragon Tool, then go to **Tool | SubTool | Insert** and choose the newly created `Skin_ZSphere_1` from the list. This will insert the structural mesh as a new SubTool inside your main model.
5. Before creating the membrane plane in Maya, export both the dragon body and the structural supports from ZBrush. Select the body SubTool and go to **Tool | Export**, choosing **OBJ** as the file format. Save it with a clear name such as `body_DYNA.obj`.
6. Then select the structural support SubTool, which is the DynaMeshed spine structure, and again go to **Tool | Export,** saving it as a separate file, for example `spikes_DYNA.obj`. Export each SubTool individually so that body and structure remain separate objects once inside Maya.

Building and integrating the lateral membrane

With the support structure prepared, we can now build the lateral membrane in Maya, shape its curvature in low poly, and reintegrate it into ZBrush as a unified sculptable surface:

1. Switch to Maya and import the files one at a time using **File | Import.** First load the body OBJ, then repeat the process for the structural supports. Once both meshes are in the scene, verify that the scale is consistent, that they are aligned in world space, and that no transforms are offset. If necessary, freeze transforms and reset pivots before proceeding.
2. Now create the membrane surface. Go to **Create | Polygon Primitives | Plane**. With the plane selected, open the **Channel Box** and set **Subdivisions Width** = `1` and **Subdivisions Height** = `1`. Starting with a single quad is important because we want full control over curvature without unnecessary density. Scale the plane so it spans the entire membrane area between the supporting spikes.

3. To position it precisely, press *V* to activate vertex snap and move the plane so its edge aligns at the center between the spikes. Place it slightly above the midpoint of the structural supports. This offset is intentional because later, when we add thickness, the membrane will naturally embed into both the dragon body and the support structure.

Figure 2.43 – Plane snapped between spikes and positioned slightly above midpoint

4. Instead of globally subdividing, add control only where needed. Activate **Mesh Tools | Multi-Cut** tool and insert two vertical cuts across the plane, roughly at one-third intervals. These cuts provide enough geometry to shape the curvature without overcomplicating the topology.
5. Switch to the **Move** tool and adjust the new vertices so the plane follows the anatomical curve defined by the spikes. The rule is simple: *use as few polygons as possible to define broad arcs, and only increase density where curvature changes direction*. Continue this process along the full span of the membrane until the surface reads cleanly from the **Side** view.

Figure 2.44 – Two vertical cuts inserted and vertices adjusted to follow the curvature

> **Tip**
>
> Always shape curvature in low poly before increasing density. Dense geometry makes surfaces harder to control and introduces subtle waves that become visible during rigging.

6. Select the membrane mesh and go to **Edit Mesh** | **Extrude**. Adjust the extrusion so the plane extrudes downward into the spike structure. Make sure the thickness is sufficient to sit properly between the supports without intersecting incorrectly.
7. After extrusion, check the normals. If they are facing the wrong direction, go to **Mesh Display** | **Reverse**. You can verify orientation using **Display** | **Polygons** | **Face Normals** if needed.
8. With the membrane modeled, export it back to ZBrush. Select the mesh and go to **File** | **Export Selection**, choosing the **OBJ** format. In ZBrush, return to the `dragonCrest` tool, then go to **Tool** | **SubTool** | **Append** and add any temporary primitive (I usually use a **Sphere3D**). Then, select the newly appended SubTool and use **Tool** | **Import** to load the membrane as a new SubTool.

9. Position it correctly and use the **Move** Brush to refine any intersections where the membrane does not perfectly contact the body or the structural spikes. At this stage, focus only on clean structural integration, not surface detailing.
10. Once satisfied, activate **DynaMesh** on the membrane SubTool at a resolution comparable to the body.
11. Then use **SubTool | Merge Down** to merge it with the main body, and reapply **DynaMesh** to unify everything into a single clean sculptable volume. This step ensures the membrane, body, and supports become one coherent structure ready for further refinement.

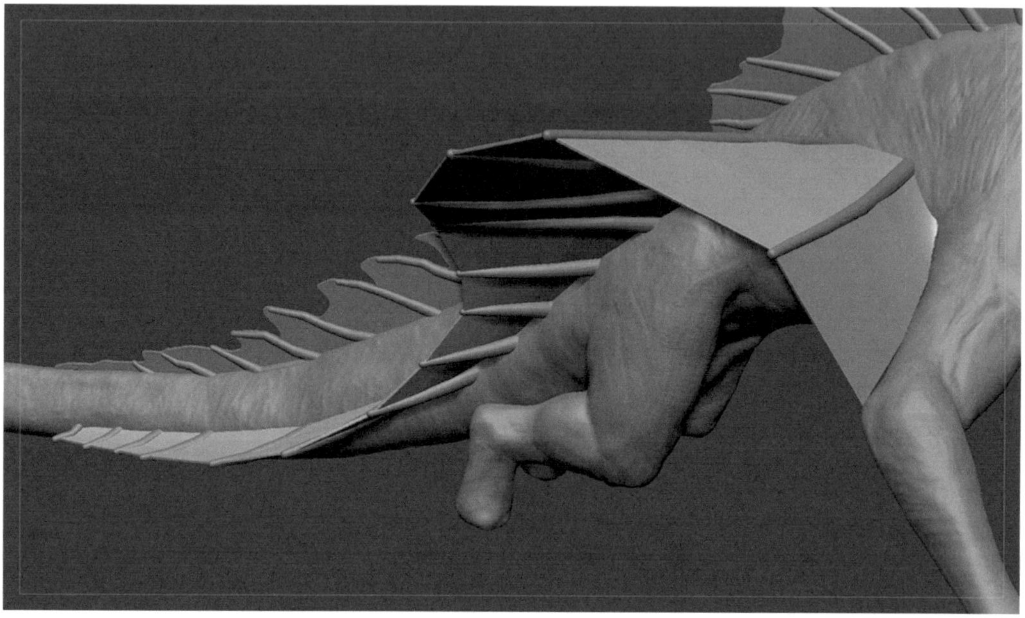

Figure 2.45 – Membrane thickness validated in ZBrush and aligned to integrate cleanly with the underlying support structure

> **Note**
>
> Resist the urge to sculpt folds at this stage. Membranes must remain *as flat as possible* before rigging; tension and wrinkles should come from deformation, not from the base model. When in doubt, remesh to re-flatten and re-establish the clean silhouette.

12. For the tail fins, the logic is identical to the central crest. They follow the same process used for the central crest. The only difference is that the plane is created from a **Top**

view instead of a **Side** view. Model only one side, then after DynaMesh unification use **Tool | Geometry | Modify Topology | Mirror And Weld** to generate the opposite side and finally collapse everything again into the main body.

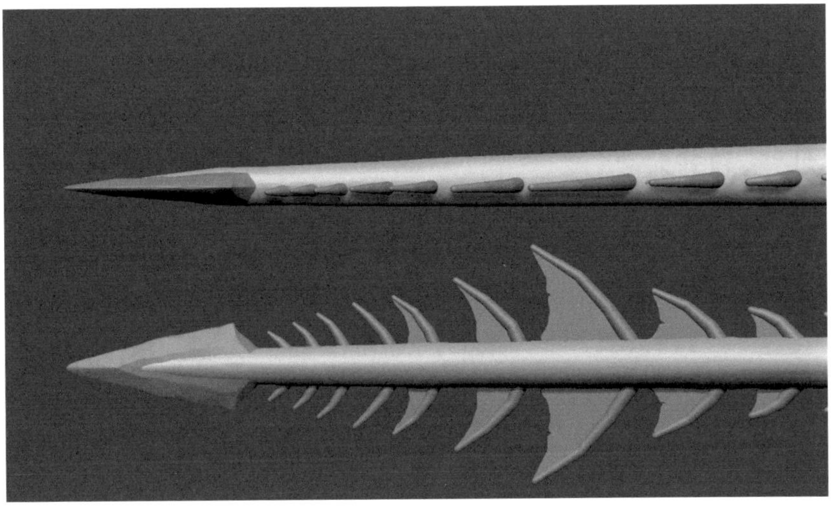

Figure 2.46 – Tail membranes constructed from low-poly planes, aligned between structural spines and adjusted to follow the curvature and tension flow of the tail

How it works...

Membranes are all about the balance between geometry, simplicity, and structural tension. The reason we use a *mask and extract workflow* is to create thin, controllable geometry that behaves predictably when deformed later in rigging. Unlike sculpted **DynaMesh** volumes, a plane offers a consistent polygon layout with even thickness and predictable surface flow. This ensures that, when animated, the membrane bends and stretches smoothly without collapsing or folding in unpredictable ways.

By starting with a low-poly plane in Maya, you gain precise control over curvature and silhouette before adding any unnecessary geometry. This approach also makes it easier to position the membrane accurately between the supporting spikes using vertex snapping and to generate a perfectly uniform thickness through polygon extrusion.

While the same result can be achieved entirely in ZBrush, Maya provides a higher level of geometric precision during this structural stage. Once the foundation is complete, the membrane can be returned to ZBrush, where DynaMesh and sculpting tools are better suited for integrating it organically with the rest of the creature. Extracting from masks adds real thickness—small, but essential for visual realism and deformation. The key is restraint: even the thinnest surface needs a defined shell to catch light correctly and avoid transparency artifacts when rendered.

Using **ZSpheres** as support structures introduces a believable sense of anatomy. Their parent-child hierarchy makes it easy to define natural tapering, that is, thicker at the base, thinner at the tip, thereby mirroring the way real bone or cartilage supports tensioned tissue. Once converted to mesh, these spines become anchors for the membrane, guiding both visual weight and rigging logic. The contrast between rigid supports and flexible sheets creates that dynamic *sail* effect typical of dragons or gliding creatures.

This workflow also keeps the model technically clean. Each membrane remains a separate SubTool, easy to isolate for UVs or retopology, while maintaining a clear relationship with its structural base. The combination of flat geometry, accurate alignment, and well-placed supports ensures that the membranes not only look elegant in sculpt but also deform correctly once animated.

3

Blocking Complex Areas: Hands, Mouth, and Functional Structures

In creature production, not all parts of a model are solved with the same approach.

After completing the large-scale blocking covered in *Chapter 2*, the workflow naturally shifts toward smaller, functionally critical anatomical areas. These regions often contain complex, repetitive structures, such as fingers, claws, and teeth, where maintaining anatomical consistency across similar elements becomes essential.

Hands, claws, teeth, gums, and the internal mouth are critical regions that can easily break the credibility of the entire creature if handled incorrectly. Unlike large body masses, these parts demand a clean structure, precision, and a clear understanding of how forms connect and behave.

In this chapter, we shift from global blocking to a more focused approach, tackling complex areas that require tighter control over shape definition and spatial relationships. The goal is to build clean and readable forms that will support later stages such as retopology, deformation, and texturing.

One key aspect we will explore is how to build these elements efficiently by starting from simple base meshes that can be reused and adapted. This approach allows you to structure teeth, claws, and fingers quickly, while maintaining consistency across similar anatomical parts. Instead of rebuilding everything from scratch, you will learn how to establish a solid base and then customize it to fit each specific area, preserving visual consistency while still leaving room for variation and artistic control.

Figure 3.1 shows how reusable base meshes can be used to establish consistent teeth forms during the blocking stage:

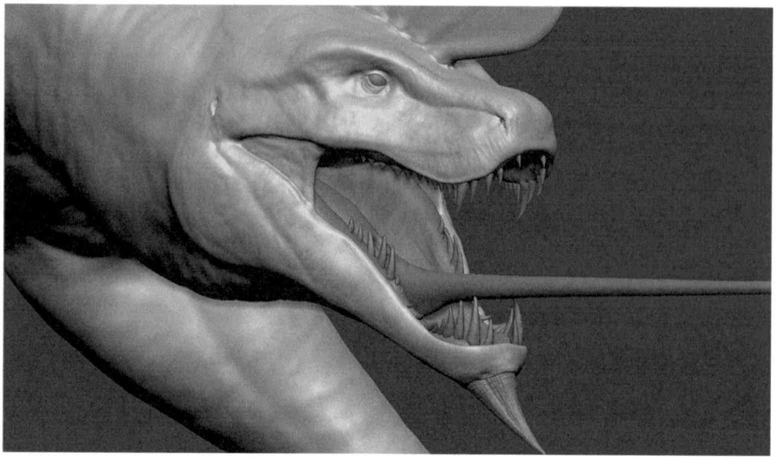

Figure 3.1 – Blocking the teeth using simple base meshes

In this chapter, we'll focus on these workflows in the recipes:

- Blocking hands and fingers for creatures
- Blocking the internal mouth, teeth, and tongue

By the end of this chapter, you will have a solid strategy to handle the most delicate parts of a creature, improving both the clarity of your sculpt and the reliability of your workflow in a production environment.

> Note
>
> **Download the code/resource bundle and the PDF version of this book**
>
> Your purchase includes a DRM-free PDF copy of this book, the code/resource bundle, and a range of exclusive benefits. To unlock everything, follow the *Free benefits with your book* section in the *Preface*.

Technical requirements

All the files required for *Chapters 2* and *3*, including base meshes and supporting assets, can be downloaded from the book's GitHub repository. Since both chapters use the same files, please refer to the *Technical requirements* section in *Chapter 2* for the complete list of assets.

Additionally, refer to the guidelines provided in *Chapter 2* regarding the software setup, scale, and general workflow.

You can download the example project files for this book by following the instructions in the *Download the example code/resource files* section in the *Preface* of this book.

This chapter's code/resource files are included in the downloadable code/resource bundle.

Blocking hands and fingers for creatures

Hands and **claws** are among the most intricate areas to sculpt on any creature, often requiring a careful balance between anatomy, rhythm, and functional design.

In this recipe, you'll learn how to efficiently block out fingers and appendages using a modular workflow built around a reusable neutral finger base. By sculpting one clean, well-proportioned finger and adapting it through duplication and transformation, you'll drastically reduce sculpting time while maintaining consistency across all digits.

This approach ensures each claw or finger shares the same structural logic, bones, joints, and curvature, while still allowing for variation in length and proportion. You'll also explore how to integrate these elements smoothly with the palm, creating a solid, production-ready foundation for both realistic and stylized creatures.

Figure 3.2 shows the final blocked hand structure created from a reusable neutral finger base, demonstrating the modular workflow covered in this recipe:

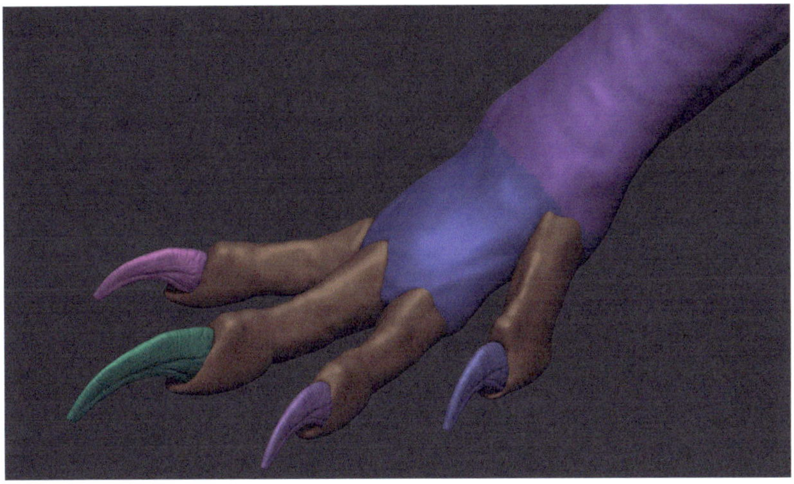

Figure 3.2 – Neutral finger sculpt duplicated and adapted to create a dragon's clawed hand

Getting ready

Before sculpting, make sure you are working on the prepared base file `dragonCrest_dynamesh_v001.ztl` (see the *Technical requirements* section in *Chapter 2*), which contains the simplified hand blockout and a neutral finger SubTool ready for duplication. If you are joining this recipe independently, open this file to match the exact setup used in this chapter.

Before sculpting, prepare the hand area and reference setup as follows:

1. Open your creature project and verify that the simplified hand blockout and neutral finger SubTool are available.
2. Enable **Symmetry** (press *X*) and confirm that your anatomical reference sheets are correctly aligned.
3. Prepare a simplified hand or paw blockout with the correct palm proportions and finger-root spacing.
4. Create a separate **Sphere3D** or **Cylinder3D** SubTool that will serve as the reusable neutral finger base.

How to do it...

Instead of sculpting each digit individually, we'll start from a reusable *neutral finger* base that can be duplicated and adjusted across the hand. This workflow keeps proportions consistent while allowing for natural variation between claws, thumbs, and support digits. We'll build the hand in three main stages.

Creating the master finger

Let's begin by building a neutral finger that will serve as the reusable base for the rest of the hand:

1. Begin by inserting a **Sphere3D**.
2. Convert it to **PolyMesh3D** and activate **Symmetry**.
3. Mask half of the sphere cleanly across its center by holding *Ctrl* and dragging a straight mask. The masked side will remain stable and act as the finger base.
4. Press *W* to activate the **Gizmo 3D Move** tool. Using the axis handles, translate the unmasked half along the primary finger direction.
   Because the deformation is axis-based and not brush-driven, the volume stretches evenly, preserving clean topology and a stable cylindrical profile. Keep the base slightly thicker and allow the translated section to taper subtly toward the tip. Clear the mask once the elongated finger volume is established.

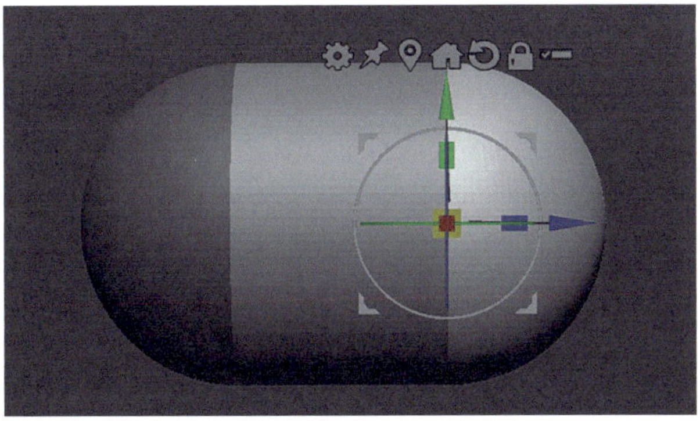

Figure 3.3 – Elongated base sphere forming a tapered finger segment

5. Duplicate the mesh directly inside the same SubTool by holding *Ctrl* while dragging one of the **Gizmo 3D Move** (press *W*) axis handles.
   This creates a clean copy without generating a new SubTool, keeping the structure compact and easier to manage during early blocking.
6. Repeat this duplication two or three times to establish the basic phalangeal segments.
7. Use the rotation rings of **Gizmo 3D** to slightly rotate each duplicated segment, building a natural finger arc. Avoid perfect alignment. Subtle angular variation creates a more believable gesture and prevents mechanical stiffness.
8. Allow the segments to overlap slightly at the joints. This intentional intersection ensures smoother transitions once the forms are unified with **DynaMesh**. At this stage, focus on overall rhythm and proportion rather than anatomical precision.

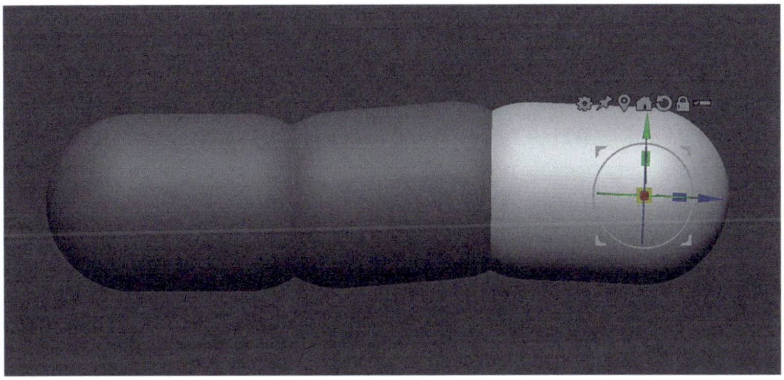

Figure 3.4 – Three spheres placed in a gentle curve, defining the main finger shape

9. Merge the parts into a single SubTool (**SubTool | Merge Down**) and activate **DynaMesh** at a medium resolution (around 256). This creates a continuous surface ideal for sculpting.
10. With the **ClayBuildup** Brush, define the main knuckles and add a slight bulge where tendons would emerge. Smooth with *Shift* and reinforce the joint lines using the **Slash3** Brush.
11. Keep the finger in a neutral pose. Use the **Inflate** Brush to balance volume across the joints and ensure the finger tapers cleanly toward the tip. A good test is to check the silhouette from the side: each joint should slightly offset the next, avoiding stiffness. This will be your *master finger*, ready for duplication across the hand.

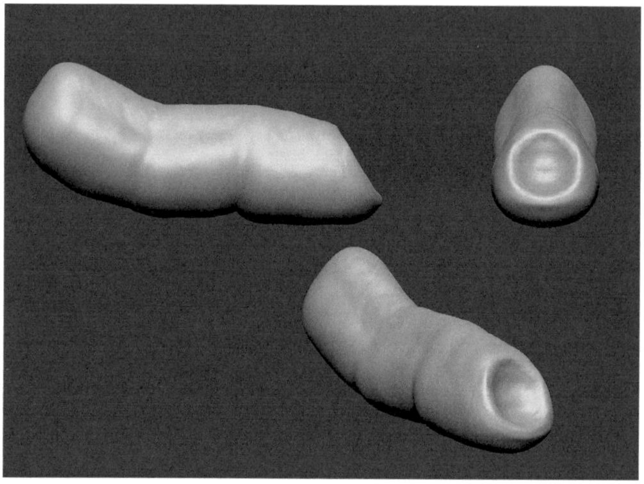

Figure 3.5 – Views showing clean taper and offset silhouette

Building the hand structure

With the master finger now complete, we can duplicate and adapt it to establish the hand structure and flow:

1. Instead of creating new SubTools, duplicate the master finger directly inside the same SubTool by holding *Ctrl* while dragging one of the **Gizmo 3D Move** axis handles. This keeps all digits structurally unified and easier to manage during early blocking.
2. Position each copy to establish the overall spacing and proportion of the hand. From one duplication to the next, adapt the finger rather than leaving it identical.
3. Use **Gizmo 3D Move** (press *W*) to slightly adjust orientation and curvature, then refine mass differences with **ClayBuildup** Brush where needed.

The thumb or inner claw usually requires a broader base and a more forward-oriented angle to suggest gripping capability. Subtle sculptural adjustments between copies prevent the hand from feeling mechanically repeated. Natural variation at this stage immediately improves realism and anatomical credibility.

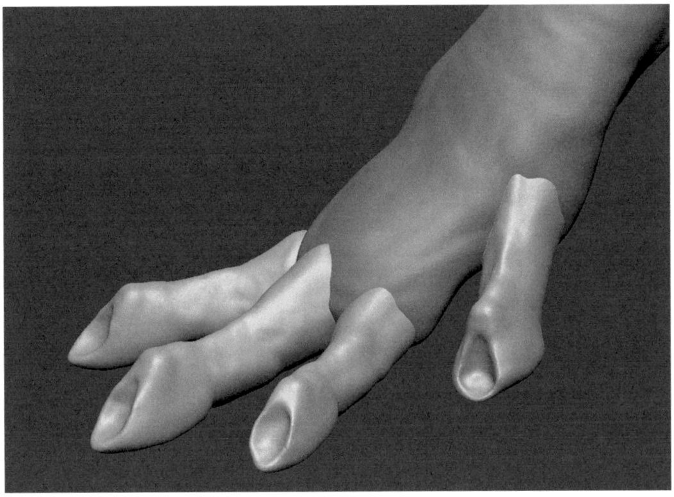

Figure 3.6 – Duplicated fingers positioned along the palm with unique curvature

> **Tip**
>
> When sculpting claws or digits, exaggerate curvature slightly more than in real anatomy. Once posed or smoothed in later stages, this exaggeration will translate into a more dynamic, natural result.

4. Build the palm or hand base from a low-resolution block (**DynaMesh** or **ZSphere** structure). Place it roughly beneath the roots of the fingers and merge the SubTools once everything aligns.
5. Use **DynaMesh** again to weld the transitions, then sculpt over the joints with the **ClayBuildup** Brush to unify the hand flow.

   The same process applies to the rear paws: start from a simplified base mass, align it under the digit roots, merge, re-**DynaMesh**, and refine the anatomical transitions to maintain consistent structural flow between the front and back limbs.

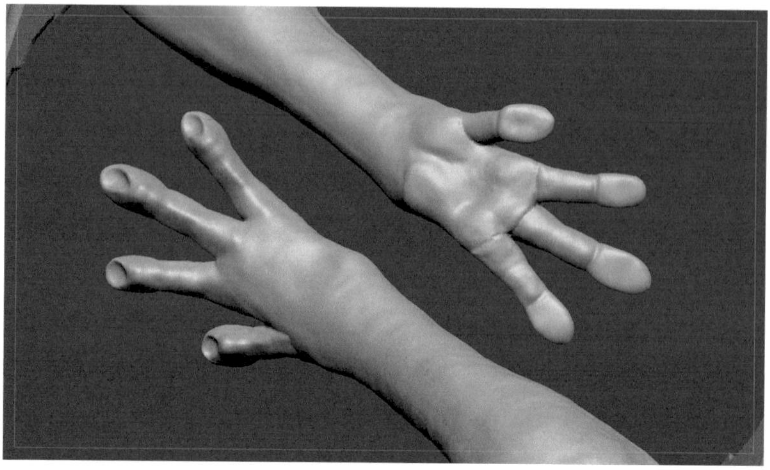

Figure 3.7 – Merged hand and fingers forming a cohesive blocking silhouette

Sculpting the claws

Finally, we'll create the claws and integrate them naturally into the fingertips to complete the blocking stage.

1. For claws or elongated fingertips, start by inserting a **Sphere3D** and positioning it at the world center in ZBrush.
2. Convert it to **PolyMesh3D** and activate **Symmetry**.
3. Using the **Move** Brush, stretch and shape the sphere into a tapered claw form, defining the overall silhouette and curvature first.
4. Once the primary shape is established, use the **ClayBuildup** Brush to clean and reinforce the structural planes. Refine the base thickness and establish a clear transition from root to tip. Keep the volume readable and avoid overworking the surface at this stage.
5. Switch to the **Slash3** Brush to introduce secondary structural details early on. Use controlled strokes to define subtle keratin separations, ridge indications, or light surface tension lines. These early structural marks help the claw read as a material rather than as a generic cone.
6. If additional refinement is needed at the tip, activate **Sculptris Pro** with a small brush size to locally increase tessellation. This allows you to sharpen points or define splits without remeshing the entire hand.
7. Keep transitions smooth; each claw should grow naturally from the fingertip rather than appear attached.

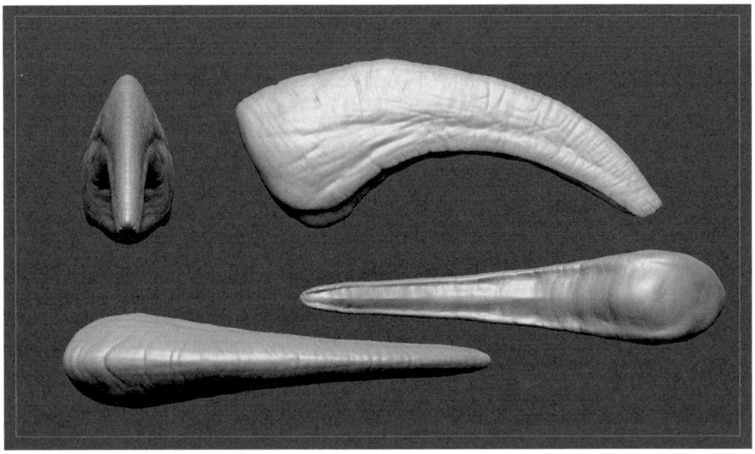

Figure 3.8 – Final claw structure after primary shaping, structural cleanup, and secondary detailing

8. Check the structure from all views. The rhythm of the fingers should flow like a fan, converging at the wrist. Adjust each digit's angle so that all arcs lead toward a common pivot point. This ensures the hand reads well when posed later. If necessary, re-**DynaMesh** and lightly polish to restore even topology.

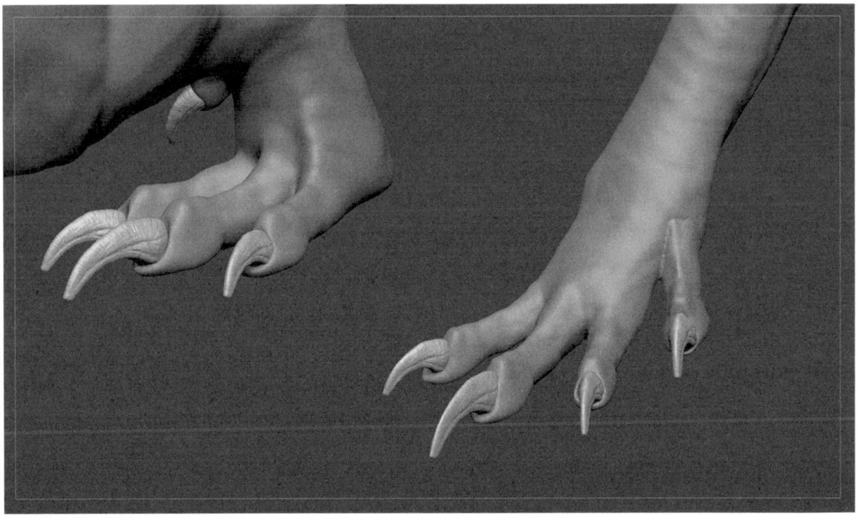

Figure 3.9 – Front and rear dragon paws showing integrated claw structure, base thickness, and secondary keratin detailing

How it works...

Building a modular *neutral finger* before detailing each digit mirrors how real production pipelines approach anatomy reuse. By sculpting one clean, anatomically balanced base, you define all the key proportional rules – joint spacing, curvature, taper, and silhouette rhythm – that will remain consistent across the entire hand or paw. This prevents small structural mismatches that often occur when sculpting each finger independently. It also speeds up iteration, since any correction to the master finger can be instantly propagated through duplication.

Using **DynaMesh** early keeps the mesh unified and flexible. This allows you to blend phalange segments smoothly, preserving volume continuity across knuckles and joints. The reason we use the **Slash3** Brush instead of the **DamStandard** Brush here is precision at the blocking stage: **Slash3** creates wider, cleaner cuts that read as planar separations rather than sharp creases. This reinforces the illusion of underlying bone and tendon transitions while maintaining smoothness for future subdivisions.

The neutral pose of the finger is another critical factor. It ensures deformation consistency once the model is rigged or posed later. A straight, relaxed arc minimizes stretching at the joints and serves as a reliable foundation for both sculpting and retopology. This principle scales perfectly from human hands to reptilian claws or even alien appendages; anatomical rhythm and tension always follow the same logic of curvature and hierarchy.

By duplicating and adjusting this base finger for each digit, you preserve the overall harmony of the hand while introducing natural variation. It's a modular mindset: one that matches both how real anatomy works and how production pipelines manage efficiency. Once combined with a **DynaMesh** palm, the hand becomes a single organic unit ready for secondary sculpting, surface detailing, or even **ZRemesher** retopology.

There's more...

The following best practices will help you keep claws and nails structurally clean and consistent, as well as make them easier to refine during later production stages:

- **Reuse a neutral claw base across all digits**: The same modular logic used for fingers applies directly to claws and nails. Production efficiency comes from building one clean, well-tapered neutral claw and reusing it across all digits. Instead of sculpting each nail from scratch, duplicate and adapt the base claw, adjusting length, rotation, and curvature while preserving structural consistency.

- **Use DynaMesh to maintain surface continuity**: Working inside **DynaMesh** allows you to merge, refine, and re-establish surface continuity without worrying about topology breaks.
- **Maintain clear structural thickness**: A believable claw begins with visible thickness at the base and transitions into a sharper, thinner tip. Thickness defines how light reacts and how the form reads in motion. After adjusting curvature or elongating the silhouette, re-run **DynaMesh** to unify the surface before refining secondary details.
- **Preserve anatomical consistency**: Claws emerge from the final phalanges and follow the same directional rhythm as the underlying bone. Slight variation in rotation and curvature prevents mechanical repetition while preserving overall harmony.
- **Enable Backface Masking when refining thin structures**: When refining thin structures, enable **Brush | Auto Masking | BackfaceMask**. This prevents unwanted deformation on the opposite side of the mesh and ensures cleaner edge definition.

Blocking the internal mouth, teeth, and tongue

The internal mouth is one of the most expressive areas of a creature, defining how believable a roar, snarl, or breath feels on screen. Treating it as a structural element rather than an afterthought ensures that every later phase, from detailing to rigging, remains grounded in logic.

In this recipe, we'll block out the gums, tongue, and teeth inside the existing head cavity, focusing on clean geometry and correct spacing for deformation. The workflow follows a modular approach, with each part – tongue, gums, and teeth – built as a separate SubTool for better control.

You'll learn how to sculpt the tongue with strong gestures, duplicate and align teeth for both arcs, and connect them smoothly to the gum line using **DynaMesh**. This approach prevents one of the most common issues in creature sculpting: mouths that feel hollow, overcrowded, or structurally disconnected, which later cause deformation and shading problems. This foundation will later support precise secondary sculpting, proper retopology, and realistic shading behavior.

Figure 3.10 shows the blocked internal mouth structure, demonstrating the placement and integration of the tongue, gums, and teeth:

Figure 3.10 – Blocked dragon mouth showing teeth and tongue placement in side and three-quarter views

Getting ready

This recipe assumes you are working from the base head file `dragonCrest_dynamesh_v001.ztl` (see the *Technical requirements* section in *Chapter 2*) with the head already blocked and the mouth cavity roughly established. If you are jumping directly to this section, open this file to match the setup used in the following steps.

Before blocking the internal mouth, prepare your scene as follows:

1. Isolate the head SubTool and make sure **Symmetry** is enabled along the *X*-axis.
2. Create a clean cavity inside the mouth using **Move** and the **ClayBuildup** brushes, ensuring there's enough space to fit the gums and tongue.
3. Keep the mouth slightly open; this makes it easier to work inside and visualize deformation.
4. Prepare three new SubTools: one *sphere* for the tongue, one *plane* or *cylinder* for the gums, and one *sphere* for the first tooth that will later be duplicated.
5. Set **DynaMesh** resolution between 256 and 384 for balanced responsiveness while sculpting overlapping surfaces.

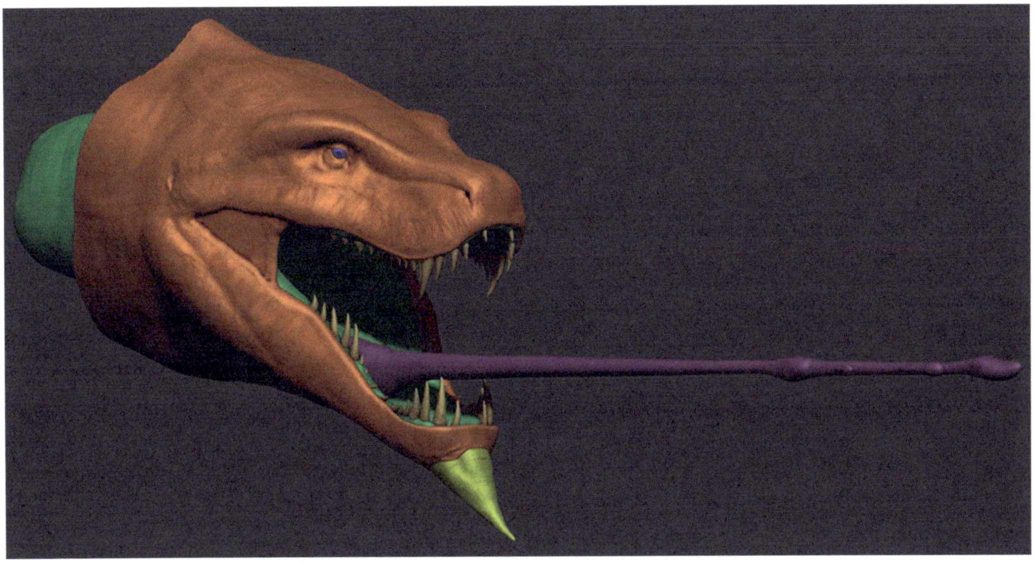

Figure 3.11 – Head cavity opened and base SubTools for tongue, gums, and first tooth positioned for blocking

How to do it...

A functional mouth should feel like a system of interconnected surfaces that can open, stretch, and compress believably once animated. You're not chasing detail yet, just the big shapes that define tension, flow, and volume. Let's go through it step by step:

1. Isolate the head SubTool and slightly open the mouth if needed to clearly access the internal area. Using the **Mask** Brush (press *Ctrl*), carefully mask the inner mouth region directly on the existing mesh. Follow the natural curvature between the upper and lower jaws, defining the internal membrane area with clean, controlled masking.

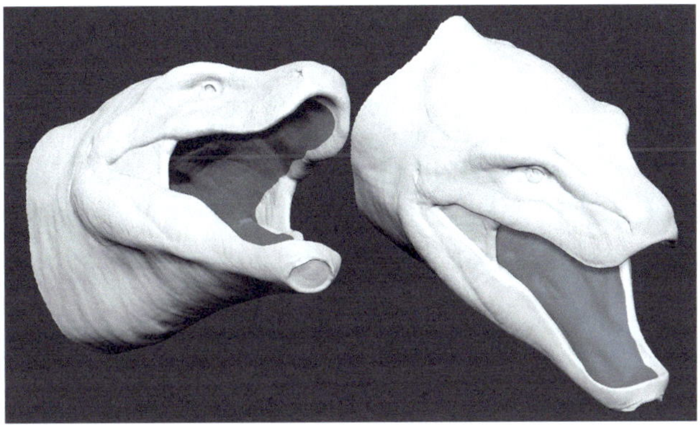

Figure 3.12 – Example of how to mask the inside of the mouth

2. With the area masked, go to **Tool | SubTool | Extract** and generate the internal mouth surface. Keep the thickness subtle and avoid excessive offset. Accept the extraction and ensure the new geometry remains clean and readable. At this stage, the goal is simply to establish a continuous internal cavity that structurally belongs to the skull.

> **Note**
>
> Enable **Brush | Auto Masking | BackfaceMask** only when working on thin surfaces where the front and back faces are very close together, such as gums, tongues, eyelids, or membranes. This prevents your brush from accidentally affecting the opposite side of the mesh. Disable it again when returning to thicker volumes, where unrestricted brush movement provides better sculpting control.

3. Refine the extracted surface using the **ClayBuildup** Brush to build volume where needed, especially along the gum lines and transition zones.
4. Use the **Move** Brush to adjust curvature and overall flow, and **Smooth** sparingly to soften harsh edges while preserving thickness. Focus on creating a clear concave interior that feels anatomically grounded and ready for the tongue and teeth placement.

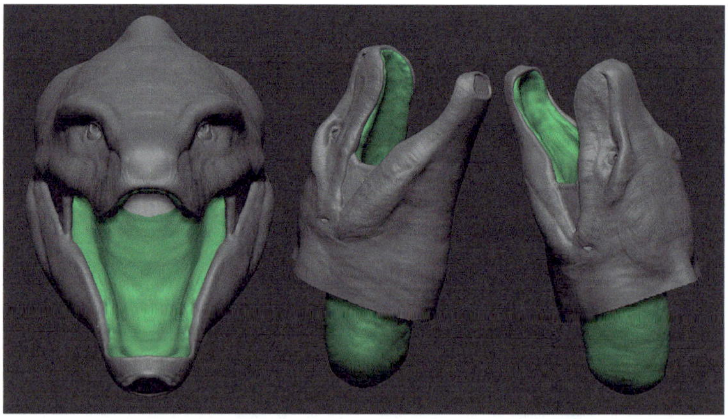

Figure 3.13 – Masked area extracted and refined to form a structurally integrated internal mouth cavity

5. Now add the tongue as a new SubTool, starting with a simple **ZSphere** chain. Place the first ZSphere at the base of the throat and extend additional ZSpheres forward to define the overall length and curvature of the tongue. Focus on gesture and flow rather than thickness at this stage.

6. Once the structure feels natural, open **Tool** | **Adaptive Skin** and click **Make Adaptive Skin** to generate the mesh.
7. Switch to **Edit** mode and refine the form using the **ClayBuildup** Brush to reinforce volume along the central mass and base attachment. Avoid making it too flat; the tongue should feel muscular and slightly tensioned.
8. Use the **Slash3** Brush at low intensity to define a subtle central groove and hint at surface tension lines. Keep the top plane soft and organic. The tongue should press gently against the lower gums and flow dynamically toward the tip, rather than lying rigid or detached inside the cavity.

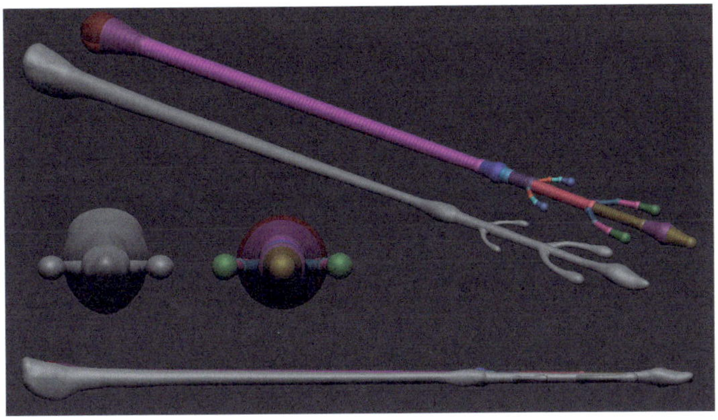

Figure 3.14 – Tongue created from a ZSphere chain, converted with Adaptive Skin, and refined with ClayBuildup and Slash3

9. Create a single `tooth` from a low-resolution sphere. Use the **Move** Brush to stretch it, then refine its base with the **TrimDynamic** Brush and light **Slash3** Brush cuts to separate the root from the crown.
   You're defining the shape's rhythm more than its polish; think of how it fits within the jaw curvature rather than as an isolated piece.

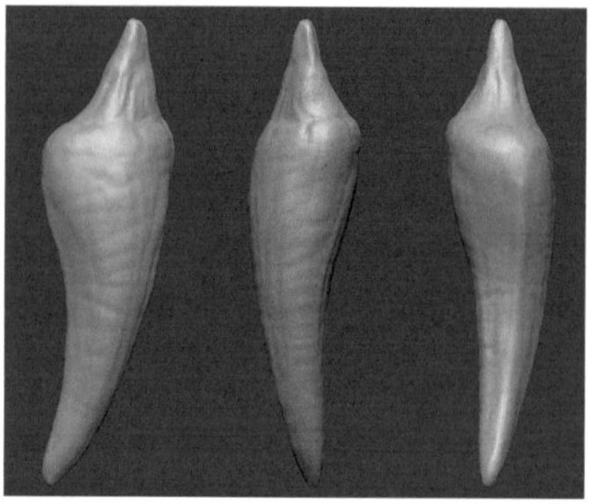

Figure 3.15 – Basic tooth sculpted from a sphere showing root and crown structure

10. Duplicate the tooth along the gum line using *Ctrl* + **Gizmo 3D Move**. Slightly vary their scale and rotation to avoid a uniform look.

> **Note**
>
> The *Ctrl* + **Gizmo 3D Move** duplication workflow only works on SubTools without subdivision levels. If your mesh already contains subdivisions, use **Tool | SubTool | Duplicate** instead, then position the copy with the **Gizmo 3D Move**.

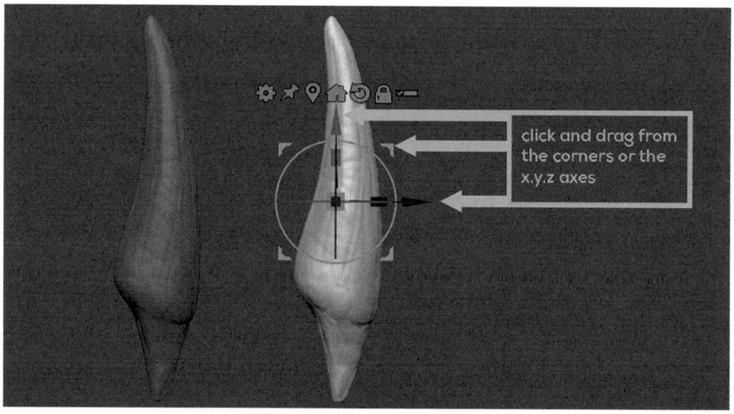

Figure 3.16 – Duplicating a tooth using Ctrl + Gizmo 3D Move

11. For larger canines or fangs, use the **SnakeHook** Brush to extend and curve the tooth, ensuring it follows the direction of the jaw flow. Imperfection here adds life; no two teeth should look identical.

Tip

The chin spike can be approached using the same workflow as a tooth or a claw. Instead of sculpting it from scratch, build it as a clean, tapered modular element, focusing on base thickness, curvature, and flow. Treat it as a structural extension of the jaw rather than a decorative add-on. This ensures consistent material language across teeth, claws, and spikes, reinforcing anatomical credibility and surface coherence.

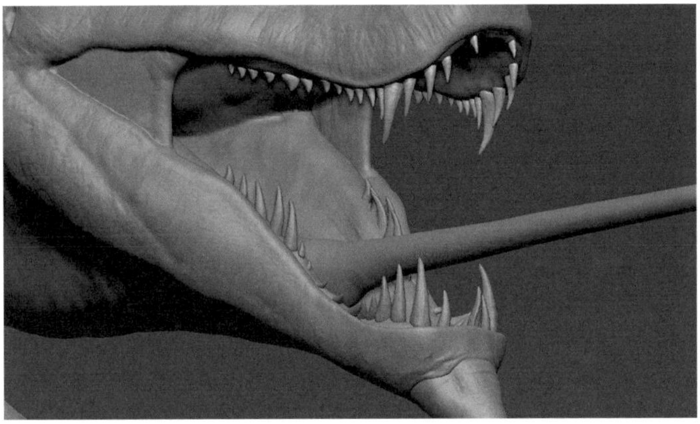

Figure 3.17 – Duplicated teeth placed along the upper and lower gums, following the mouth's arc

12. Finally, inspect the sculpt from three-quarter and side views. The upper teeth should slightly overhang the lower, while the tongue presses softly against the base of the mouth. These overlaps create the sense of tension that makes a mouth feel alive even in a static pose. If needed, slightly exaggerate the curves for clarity. Strong primary shapes will guide all later detailing.

How it works...

The mouth is one of the most deformable areas of a creature's anatomy, so its structure must support compression, sliding contact, and wide opening without breaking visual logic. Blocking the gums, tongue, and teeth as separate, controllable elements early on creates a clean, flexible foundation that supports both sculpting and later deformation.

Using **Extract** to generate the inner mouth surface ensures that the cavity follows the existing jaw curvature instead of being rebuilt manually. This produces cleaner transitions, preserves the surrounding anatomy, and provides a solid foundation for positioning the gums, tongue, and teeth throughout the rest of the workflow.

The gums establish the structural base of the mouth interior. Their curvature determines how natural the bite and jaw compression will feel. A slightly concave upper gum and a more convex lower gum simulate how real jaws close and slide against each other, giving weight and direction to the dental arches.

The use of the **Slash3** Brush reinforces soft anatomical separations that remain readable after remeshing, creating clear structural landmarks for refinement. Likewise, creating the tongue from a simple **ZSphere** chain and converting it with **Adaptive Skin** provides a clean, evenly distributed mesh that is fast to reshape as the mouth evolves. Refining the teeth with the **TrimDynamic** Brush establishes clear primary planes before adding smaller surface details, making the overall forms easier to read and iterate during production.

The **SnakeHook** Brush is particularly effective during the blocking stage, where large proportional changes are still expected. It excels at pulling and stretching volumes to create horns, large scales, claws, teeth, or other elongated anatomical forms much faster than the **Move** Brush. In some situations, it can also be used as a more aggressive version of the **Move** Brush to quickly reposition and extend existing geometry. For best results, use it on **DynaMesh** models or at medium subdivision levels (around 3 or 4), where the mesh can still deform freely without compromising fine details.

The tongue acts as both a volume balancer and a visual anchor. When properly arched and placed in contact with the lower gums, it introduces subtle tension that makes the mouth feel alive. If it sits too low or too flat, the interior loses depth and elasticity.

Blocking the teeth individually preserves control over spacing and silhouette rhythm. Slight overlaps between upper and lower arches create a funnel toward the throat, reinforcing anatomical coherence and believable motion.

4

Retopology in Maya: Understanding Topology Theory and Creating Clean Geometry for Animation

In this chapter, we will explore one of the most important steps in the production workflow: **retopology**, the process of rebuilding a clean and optimized mesh over a high-resolution sculpt. After completing your high-resolution sculpt in ZBrush, it is essential to rebuild the geometry with clean and optimized topology to make it ready for animation and deformation. Good topology ensures smooth rigging, efficient UVs, and predictable results during rendering.

We will begin with the theory behind clean topology, understanding how n-gons, triangles, and poles affect the mesh and how to recognize and correct them. You will then learn how to use Maya's **Quad Draw** tool to create clean, manual topology. Finally, we will discuss how to organize loops around joints and muscles to ensure believable deformation during animation.

The goal of this chapter is to provide you with solid foundations in retopology, helping you understand how to build clean topology and why different production contexts require different approaches. In particular, we will clarify the differences between topology used in VFX, animation, and real-time gaming, so you can make informed decisions based on your target pipeline.

The recipes in this chapter are designed to give you practical control over both general topology and more complex areas, such as membranes, eyes, claws, teeth, tongue, and gums, allowing you to work in a more precise and predictable way in production.

In this chapter, we'll cover the following topics and recipes:

- Understanding topology issues: N-gons, triangles, and poles
- Identifying and fixing N-gons, poles, and triangles
- Using the Quad Draw tool for manual retopology
- Handling topology in complex areas: eyes, eyelids, ears and nose, claws and teeth, as well as tongue and gums

Technical requirements

To complete this chapter, you will need the following setup:

Software:

- **Autodesk Maya 2024** or later (for retopology and modeling)
- **ZBrush 2024** or later (for projection and topology validation)

Add-ons and tools:

- **Quad Draw** tool (within Maya's **Modeling Toolkit**)

System recommendations:

- System recommendations are the same as described in *Chapter 1*. Refer to its *Technical requirements* section for details.

Assets:

- The high-resolution sculpt of the spinal ridge gliding dragon

All working files used in this chapter are available in the book's GitHub repository. The `Chapter04_05` folder in the repository includes the following assets:

- `checker_uv.jpg`: A directional UV checker texture used to identify UV stretching, distorted shells, incorrect texel density, and inconsistent UV orientation during the retopology and UV validation workflow.
- `dragonCrest_retopology_uvset_v001.fbx`: This is the production-ready retopology of the `dragonCrest` creature used throughout *Chapters 4* and *5*. The same file also includes the complete UV layout required for the UV workflow in *Chapter 5*.

You can download the example project files for this book by following the instructions in the *Download the example code/resource files* section in the *Preface* of this book.

This chapter's code/resource files are included in the downloadable code/resource bundle.

Understanding topology issues: N-gons, triangles, and poles

In any professional production pipeline, **topology** defines how a mesh will behave once it is deformed, rigged, and subdivided. A clean quad-based surface is essential for predictable results in animation and shading. Poor topology looks messy, and it can break your workflow. In animation, it can cause unstable deformations, unwanted creasing, and loss of volume in critical areas such as joints or facial regions. In shading, it can generate visible artifacts and inconsistencies across the surface.

From a sculpting perspective, topology is equally important. Polygons that are too stretched or elongated create an uneven surface distribution, making it difficult to apply consistent detail. This becomes especially problematic when sculpting skin details such as wrinkles, pores, or scales, where uniform polygon density is required to achieve clean and controlled results.

Before moving into the practical steps in the *Identifying and fixing N-gons, poles, and triangles* recipe, it is important to clearly define the main types of polygons you will encounter:

- **N-gons** are polygons with more than four sides. They are often created during fast modeling or Boolean operations and can lead to unpredictable shading and subdivision results.
- **Triangles** are polygons with three sides. While not inherently incorrect, they can introduce pinching and shading artifacts, especially when placed in areas that require smooth deformation.
- **Poles** are vertices where the number of connected edges is different from four. In a quad-based topology, the most common cases are 3-edge and 5-edge poles. These are typically used to redirect edge flow or close loops.

From my own experience, you may sometimes hear the terms **E-pole** and **N-pole** used informally. In some cases, a 5-edge pole is referred to as an *E-pole*, often associated with edge redirection during operations such as extrusions, while a 3-edge pole may be called an *N-pole*, as these configurations frequently appear in areas like the nose when building facial topology. However, this terminology is not standardized and can vary between artists and studios. Poles with six or more connected edges are generally avoided in organic modeling, especially in deforming areas, as they tend to create visible pinching and instability in both sculpting and animation.

Another important issue to be aware of is the presence of **non-planar polygons**, also known as **unfolded faces**. This occurs when the vertices of a polygon do not lie on the same plane, causing the surface to twist in 3D space. *Figure 4.1* shows how a polygon can appear correct from one angle but reveal structural issues when viewed from another:

Figure 4.1 – Example of a non-planar polygon viewed from different angles

While this problem may not always be immediately visible from a single view, it can lead to shading artifacts, unstable subdivision, and unpredictable deformation. For this reason, it is essential to regularly check your topology from multiple angles and ensure that faces remain evenly distributed and structurally consistent.

Understanding how these elements affect the mesh is the first step toward building clean, production-ready topology.

Identifying and fixing N-gons, poles, and triangles

The objective of this recipe is to understand how different polygon types affect the structure of a mesh. As discussed in the previous section, **N-gons**, **triangles**, and **poles** can create shading artifacts and unpredictable deformations when the model is animated.

In this recipe, you'll learn how to identify these issues, understand when they are acceptable, and how to fix them to maintain clean, animation-ready geometry.

Getting ready

Before we begin, follow these steps to set up your environment:

1. Open Autodesk Maya and create a simple polygonal object, such as a *cube* or *sphere*. These primitives will be used to demonstrate common topology issues in a controlled environment.
2. Make sure **Wireframe** on **Shaded** and **Viewport Statistics** are enabled so that you can easily visualize edges and vertex connections.

This setup will help you understand how N-gons, triangles, and poles appear in a mesh before moving to more complex models later in the chapter.

How to do it...

Let's start this recipe by creating a few simple topology errors directly in **Maya**. This will help you understand how N-gons, triangles, and poles form, how to recognize them in the Viewport, and why they create problems in animation and shading:

1. We'll begin by creating an **N-gon**. In **Face** mode, select the top face of the cube and activate the **Multi-Cut** tool.
2. Start from one corner of the face and draw a diagonal toward one of the other three edges, creating a new internal edge that splits the surface.
3. Then, delete the two faces created by the diagonal so that only the outer border remains.
4. After that, double-click on one of the border edges to select the entire edge loop of the top opening.
5. With the loop selected, use **Mesh** | **Fill Hole** to close the surface. This will generate a single face with five sides, creating your first N-gon.

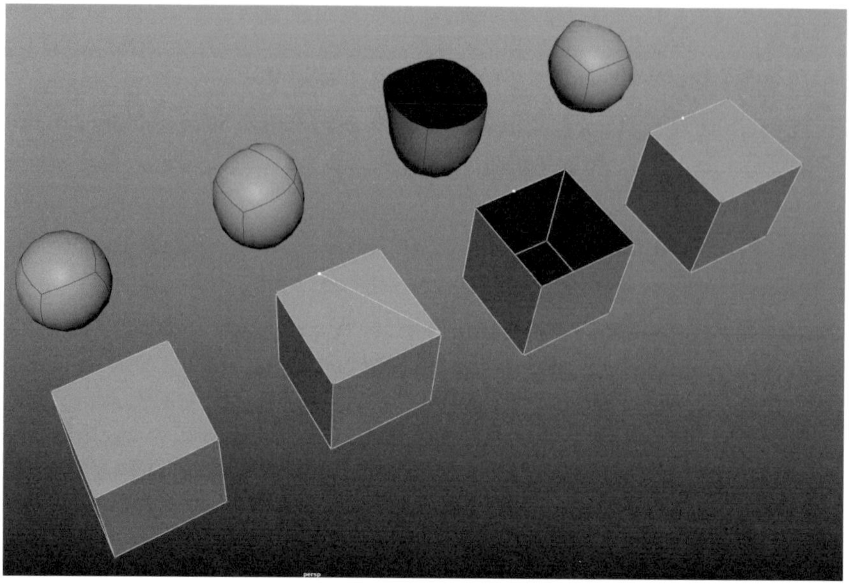

Figure 4.2 – Step-by-step creation of an N-gon from a quad surface and its behavior under subdivision

Next, let's observe how a triangle behaves:

1. Using the same cube, stay in **Face** mode and activate the **Multi-Cut** tool.
2. Draw a diagonal from one corner of the top face to one of the opposite edges, creating a triangle within the surface.
3. Press *3* on the keyboard to switch to **Smooth Preview** mode, allowing you to see both the low-resolution topology and the smoothed result at the same time.
   Notice how the presence of the triangle slightly affects the surface curvature, making it less even, compared to a clean quad-based surface. While this does not necessarily break the model, it introduces a change in the surface flow that must be carefully evaluated depending on the context.

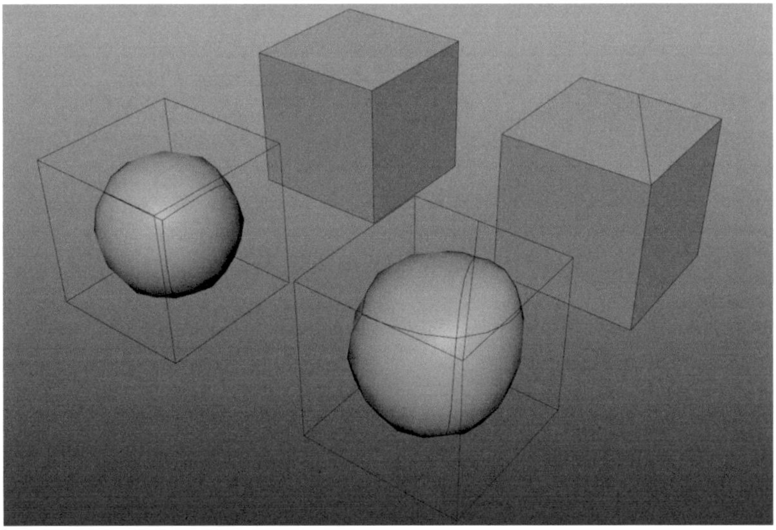

Figure 4.3 – Triangle on a quad surface showing curvature irregularity in smooth preview

Now let's move to poles:

1. Create a **Plane** with a quad grid (for example, 3 x 3 subdivisions) and select the central face.
2. Extrude the central face upward using the **Extrude** tool. This simple operation will automatically generate vertices where multiple edges meet.
   Observe the resulting topology: at the base of the extrusion, you will notice different types of poles forming naturally. Some vertices will have three connected edges (3-edge poles), while others will have five connected edges (5-edge poles), as the edge flow is redirected around the extrusion.
3. Press *3* to activate **Smooth Preview** and observe how the surface behaves. Notice how the curvature changes around these poles, creating subtle pinching and tension in the surface.

Figure 4.4 – Poles created by extruding a central face on a quad grid, forming 3- and 5-edge poles

> **Tip**
>
> Keep poles away from bending or stretching areas, as they create uneven edge distribution and can lead to pinching when the surface is smoothed.

Finally, let's explore what happens when too many edges converge at a single vertex.

1. In Maya, go to **Create** | **Polygon Primitives** | **Cylinder** and add a cylinder to the scene.
2. By default, the **Subdivisions Axis** is set to `20`, which is already sufficient for this example. You can keep this value or adjust it as needed, as long as it does not drop below 6.
3. Switch to **Face** mode and look at the top of the cylinder. You will notice that all the surrounding edges converge into a single central vertex, creating a high-valence pole. In this case, more than six edges meet at the same point, which is where topology typically starts to become problematic.
4. Press *3* to activate **Smooth Preview** and observe the result. The surface will show visible pinching and uneven curvature around the center, as the edge flow collapses into a single point.

   This example highlights how high-density poles can disrupt surface continuity. While this topology is acceptable for simple primitives or non-deforming objects, it is not suitable for clean subdivision or organic modeling, where even edge distribution is required.

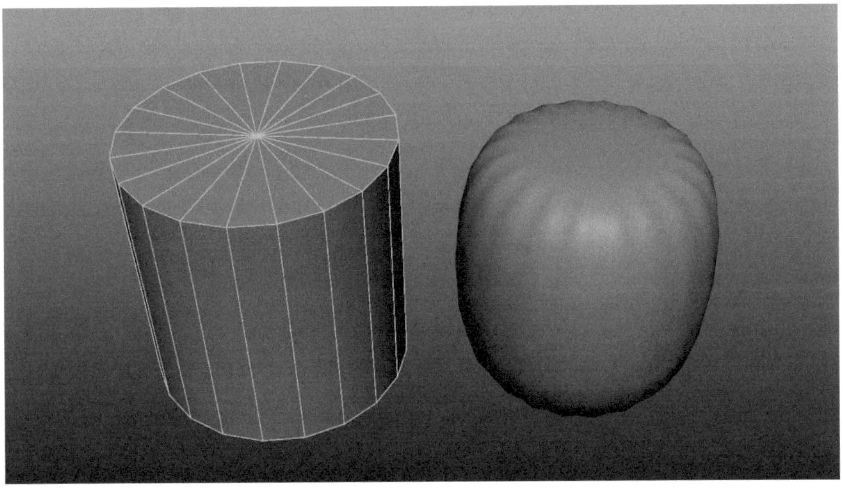

Figure 4.5 – Base cylinder with edges converging into a single vertex (left); Smooth Preview showing visible pinching (right)

> **Tip**
>
> In production topology, always aim to keep four edges per vertex whenever possible. This ensures predictable deformations, especially when the mesh is subdivided or used for animation.

How it works...

In this recipe, we intentionally introduced topology issues on simple primitives to observe how they affect the surface under subdivision. Let's break down what is happening in each case and why these results are problematic in production.

Starting with the *cube* used to create an N-gon, we added a diagonal and then rebuilt the surface into a five-sided polygon. When this mesh is subdivided, the N-gon is automatically converted into triangles. This conversion is not consistent and depends on the software, which leads to unpredictable results. This is why, in production, N-gons are avoided, as they break edge flow and create instability across different tools.

In the second *cube* example, we introduced a *triangle* by adding a diagonal edge. When switching to smooth preview, you can clearly see that the surface is no longer perfectly even. The triangle changes how the surface interpolates, creating a slight irregularity in curvature. While this may seem subtle, in a real production asset, this can affect shading, deformation, and even texture distribution.

Moving to the *plane* example, where we extruded the central face, we generated poles naturally. At the base of the extrusion, some vertices have three edges, while others have five. These poles, often referred to as 3-edge and 5-edge poles, are an inevitable part of topology, as they are required to redirect edge flow.

They are not inherently problematic, but their usage must be controlled. In production, the goal is to keep their number as low as possible and to avoid placing them too close to each other. Ideally, poles should not share the same face and should be spaced by at least two edge loops to prevent tension from concentrating in a single area.

When poles are placed too close together, their influence overlaps, creating visible pinching and uneven surface behavior when the mesh is smoothed, as shown in *Figure 4.6*:

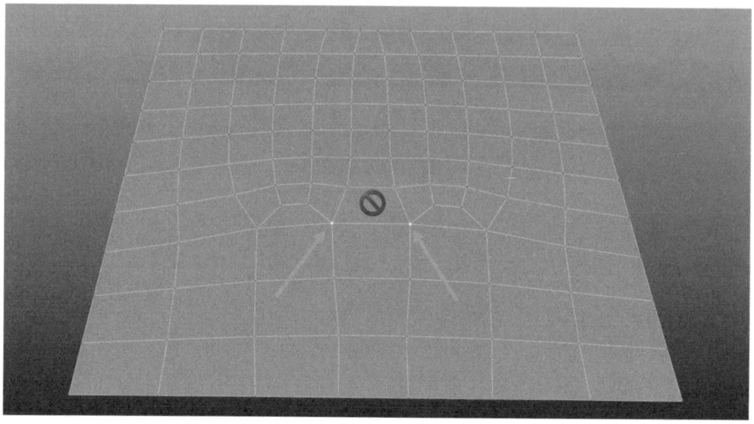

Figure 4.6 – Poles placed too close, creating pinching and tension

This behavior becomes more extreme when too many edges converge into a single vertex, as shown in the *cylinder* example. On the top cap of the cylinder, all edges meet at one central point, creating a high-valence pole. When **Smooth Preview** is activated, the surface collapses toward that vertex, producing visible pinching and uneven curvature. This is a clear example of why vertices with six or more connected edges should be avoided in organic modeling.

In production, these issues translate into real problems. N-gons create unpredictable subdivision, triangles disrupt surface flow, and poorly placed poles introduce pinching in deformation areas. While some of these elements can be used in controlled situations, especially in hard surface or game assets, they must be carefully managed.

The goal of clean topology is not perfection for its own sake, but control. A well-structured quad-based mesh allows predictable deformation, consistent shading, and stable results across the entire pipeline.

Using the Quad Draw tool for manual retopology

Manual retopology (or **manual retopo**) is one of the most fundamental tasks in creature modeling. It's where sculptural freedom meets technical precision. By rebuilding your mesh with clean, quad-based geometry, you ensure that your asset can deform properly during animation, subdivide cleanly in ZBrush, and remain usable across departments like rigging, lookdev, and FX.

This recipe will focus on how to approach manual retopo using Maya's **Quad Draw tool**, an interactive retopology tool that allows you to rebuild geometry directly on top of a high-resolution mesh by placing and adjusting vertices and faces with precision.

You'll learn how to control edge flow around areas of deformation (shoulders, hips, jaw, and digits), how to build efficient topology for wings and membranes, and how to respect the vertex count limits that will help you reach maximum subdivision levels in ZBrush (for example, ~100 million points from a ~24,000 vertex base mesh).

A completed retopology of the dragon is shown in *Figure 4.7*. By the end of this recipe, you will have rebuilt a clean, animation-ready mesh with proper edge flow, organized deformation loops, and a topology optimized for subdivision and the next stages of the production pipeline. Throughout the recipe, we will build this result progressively, one section at a time.

Figure 4.7 – Clean quad topology supporting edge flow, deformation, and subdivision

Getting ready

Before starting the retopology process, make sure your dragon sculpt in ZBrush is clean and finalized in its primary forms, as this version will be used as the reference for rebuilding the mesh.

Since high-resolution sculpts are usually too heavy to manage efficiently in Maya, a lighter, decimated version of the model will be prepared in the *How to do it...* section. This decimated mesh will serve as a projection surface during retopology, allowing you to work smoothly while preserving the original shape.

Because the creature is anatomically symmetrical, you will work on only one half of the character during retopology. This approach significantly speeds up the process, reduces complexity, and ensures consistent results across both sides. The completed half will later be mirrored to reconstruct the full model, which will also simplify the UV layout process.

Once imported into Maya, the mesh should be treated only as a reference and never edited directly, as all new topology will be built on top of it.

> **Tip**
>
> For better performance and control, you can cut the decimated mesh in ZBrush and keep slightly more than half of the model. This provides a safety margin along the symmetry line and helps avoid alignment issues when mirroring.
>
> Working on a half model also improves accessibility, making it easier to properly retopologize complex areas such as the inside of the mouth, the inner thigh, and under the armpits. When the retopology is complete, you can mirror the result to reconstruct the full mesh.

How to do it...

Before moving into Maya, we first need to prepare a decimated version of the sculpt directly in ZBrush. This step is essential to keep the scene responsive while preserving enough detail for accurate projection during retopology.

Preparing a decimated version of the sculpt

Follow these steps to create a decimated version of your sculpt for export and further processing:

1. Open your dragon sculpt in ZBrush and make sure all SubTools are visible and ready for export. For each SubTool, go to **ZPlugin** | **Decimation Master** and click **Pre-process Current** to analyze the geometry.
2. Once the preprocessing is complete, set a decimation percentage that keeps a good balance between performance and detail. As a general rule, aim for a mesh between `400,000` and `800,000` points per object. For example, if your **DynaMesh** is around 8 million points, a value between 5% and 10% is usually a good starting point.

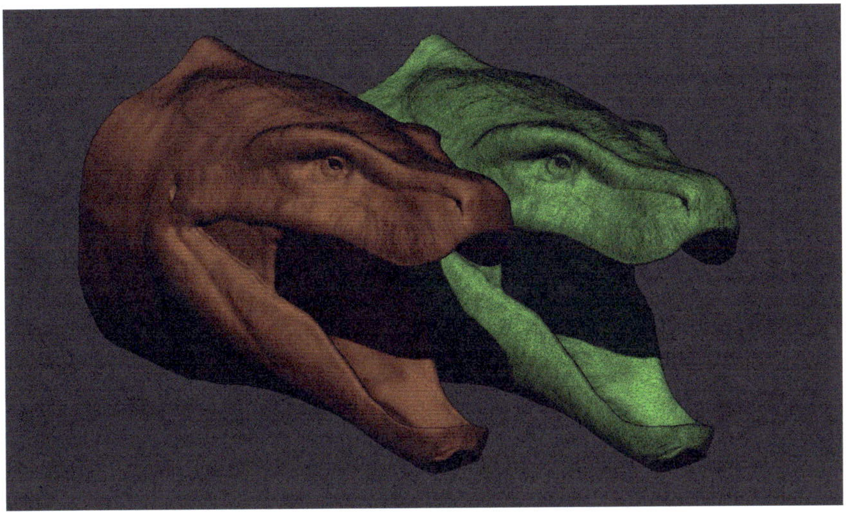

Figure 4.8 – High-resolution DynaMesh sculpt (left); Decimated mesh preserving the shape with a much lower polygon count (right)

3. Click **Decimate Current** and repeat the process for each SubTool.

> **Tip**
>
> **Decimation Master** also provides **Pre-process All** and **Decimate All**, allowing you to process all visible SubTools automatically. Although this can save time, I usually prefer to decimate each SubTool individually. For example, the dragon's head requires much more geometric detail than the body, so I can assign a higher polygon count to the head while keeping the body lighter. This gives us complete control over the polygon budget and ensures each part of the model contains only the detail it actually needs.

4. Once all elements are decimated, export each object as an OBJ by going to **Tool | Export**, making sure to keep consistent naming. These decimated meshes will be used as the high-resolution reference inside Maya.
5. Import your decimated OBJ files into Maya and organize them in the **Outliner**. To do this, go to **File | Import** and select one of the exported OBJ files from ZBrush. Make sure the file type is set to OBJ, then confirm the import.
6. Repeat the process for all the decimated SubTools. Once all meshes are in the scene, select them in the Viewport or **Outliner**, press *Ctrl* + *G* to group them, and rename the group `dynamesh_GRP` in the **Outliner** (see *Figure 4.9*).

This ensures a clean setup and clearly separates the high-resolution reference from the retopology you will create next.

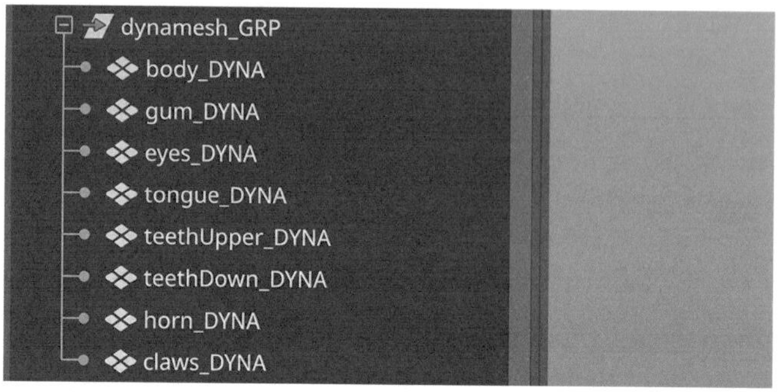

Figure 4.9 – Outliner showing dynamesh_GRP

Using the Quad Draw tool

Before starting to build the main deformation loops, it is important to understand how the **Quad Draw** tool works. Taking a few minutes to become familiar with its core controls will make the retopology process much faster and more intuitive.

1. Start by selecting the main body of your creature in the Viewport or **Outliner**.
2. With the mesh selected, enable **Make Live** from the **Modeling Toolkit**, so it becomes your projection surface. This allows all new topology to snap directly onto the sculpt. In *Figure 4.10*, the selected mesh is highlighted as an active projection surface:

Figure 4.10 – The Make Live button in the Modeling Toolkit

3. Activate the **Quad Draw** tool from the **Modeling Toolkit**. You can now begin placing points directly on the live surface by clicking with the left mouse button. These points will become the foundation of your new topology.

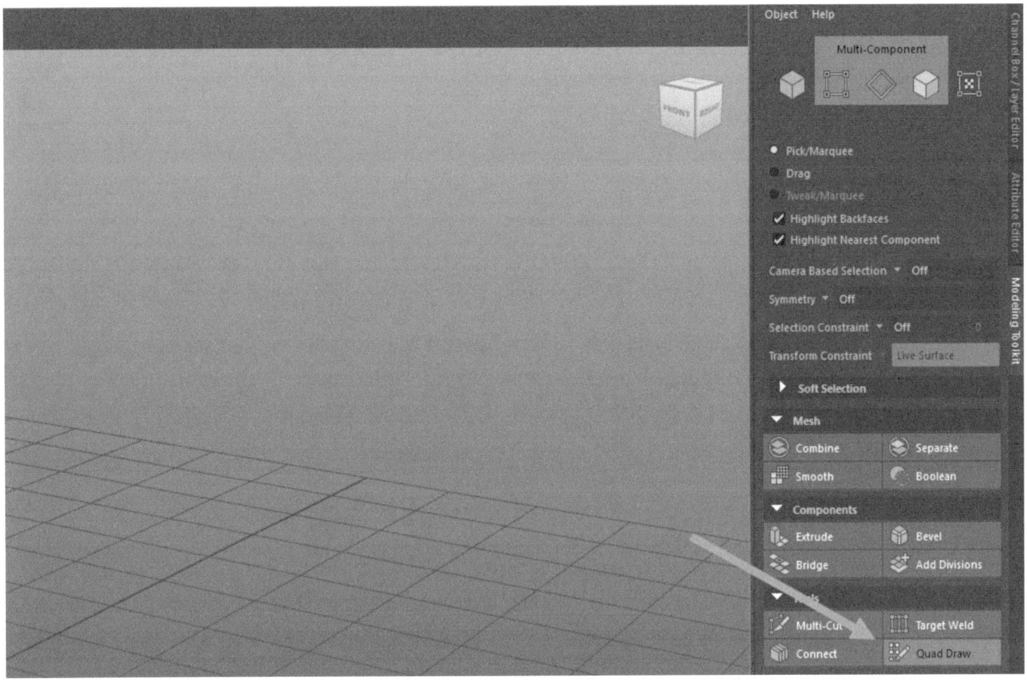

Figure 4.11 – The Quad Draw tool inside the Modeling Toolkit panel in Maya

4. To remove a point, hold *Ctrl* + *Shift* and click on it. To create a polygon, place four points and hold *Shift* while clicking inside them to generate a quad.

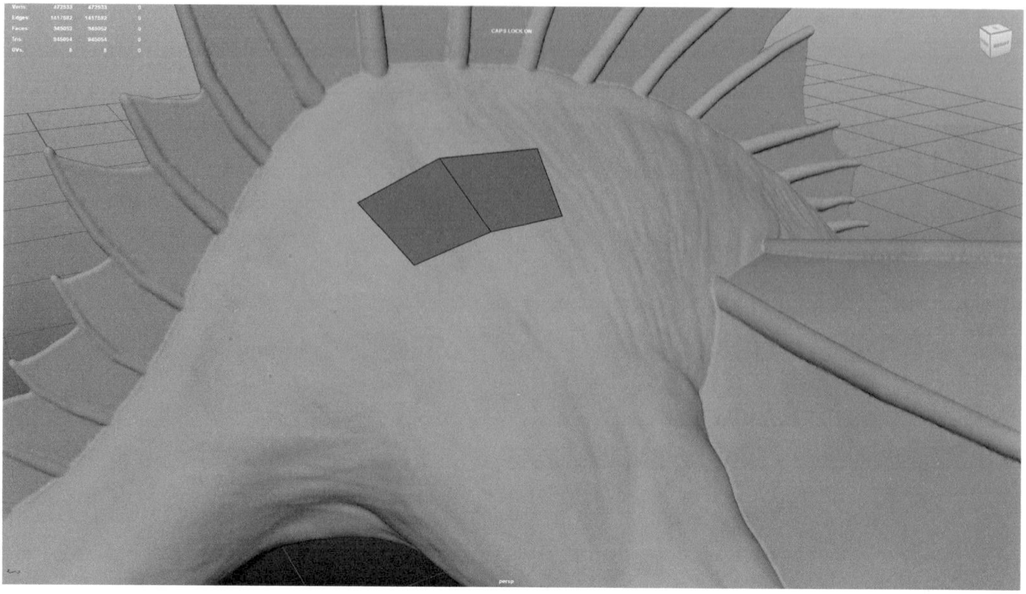

Figure 4.12 – Placing points and generating quads

5. To adjust your topology, you can move vertices directly by clicking and dragging them on the surface.
6. If you need to reposition a polygon, you can move one of its vertices, an edge, or the entire polygon. The adjacent geometry will automatically follow the selected component, making it easy to adjust the local topology.
   For more controlled adjustments, enable **Soft Selection** (press *B*) to smoothly influence surrounding vertices when moving points, which is especially useful when refining forms or relaxing the topology.
7. As you build the mesh, use the main **Quad Draw** controls to edit and refine it:
   - Hold *Shift* and drag over the surface to smooth and relax the vertices.
   - To extend the topology, hold *Tab* and drag from an edge to extrude new polygons and continue your edge flow.
   - To delete geometry, hold *Ctrl* + *Shift* and click on an edge, or double-click an edge loop and delete it to remove the entire loop.

Continue practicing these basic operations until you feel comfortable controlling the mesh. Once you understand how to place, move, extend, and clean topology, you are ready to focus on building proper edge flow for deformation.

Building edge flow for deformation

Follow these steps to build clean edge flow that supports natural deformation during animation:

1. Start by focusing on the main deformation zones, where clean edge flow is essential for animation. Before adding complexity, always build a solid low-poly foundation. The goal is to establish the main loops with as few polygons as possible, focusing on structure and flow rather than density. Once the base topology is working correctly, you can gradually add more subdivisions and supporting loops to refine the shape and make everything resolve cleanly.
2. Around the *shoulder*, build circular edge loops that wrap around the deltoid area, separating the arm from the torso. These loops should flow smoothly from the chest into the upper arm, allowing the shoulder to rotate without creating pinching or volume loss.

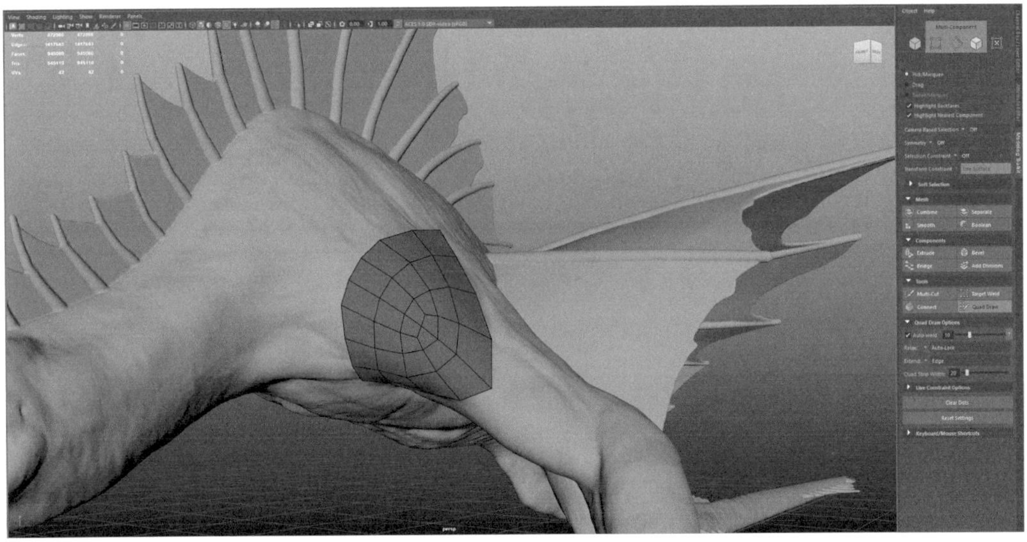

Figure 4.13 – Shoulder topology showing circular loops wrapping around the deltoid and connecting the chest to the arm

3. Around the *hips and upper leg*, build circular loops that wrap around the femur, defining the transition between the pelvis and the thigh. These loops should follow the natural insertion of the leg into the body, allowing the hip joint to rotate correctly while preserving volume in the glute and upper thigh.

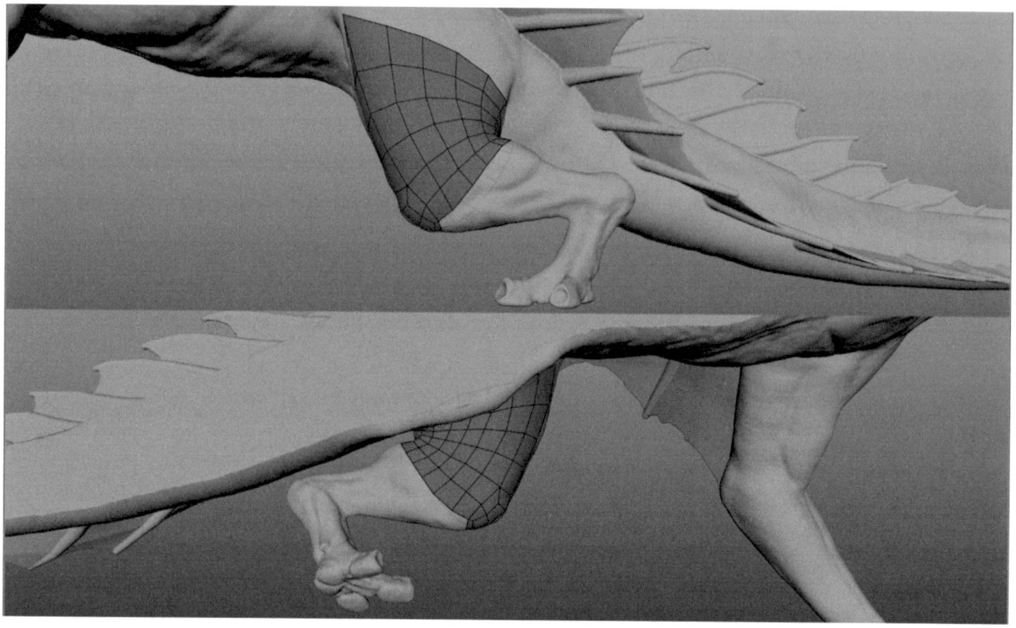

Figure 4.14 – Legs topology showing circular loops wrapping around the leg insertion

When working on articulation areas such as *knees*, *elbows*, and *heels*, it is essential to add proper support loops to preserve volume during deformation. These areas are subject to compression and stretching, and without adequate topology, they will quickly collapse or produce visible artifacts when animated.

A reliable approach is to start from a simple 4 x 4 grid structure, then build a clean loop that wraps entirely around the joint. This circular loop acts as a deformation buffer, allowing the mesh to bend smoothly while maintaining volume.

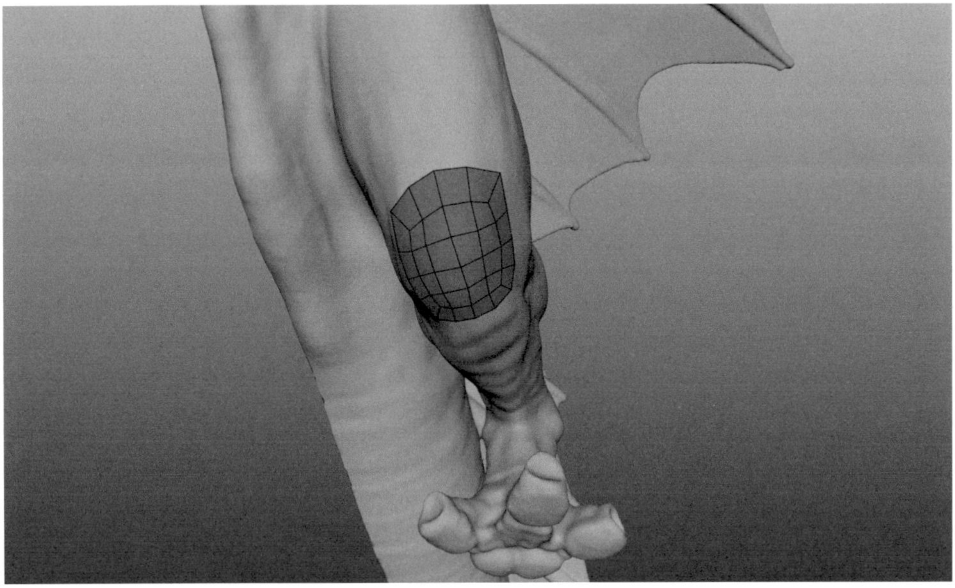

Figure 4.15 – Example of a 4x4 grid-based topology with a continuous loop wrapping around a joint area

4. Continue around the *jawline and mouth*, building concentric loops that define the lips and surrounding muscles. These loops are critical for facial deformation, as they control stretching, compression, and lip movement during speaking or roaring.

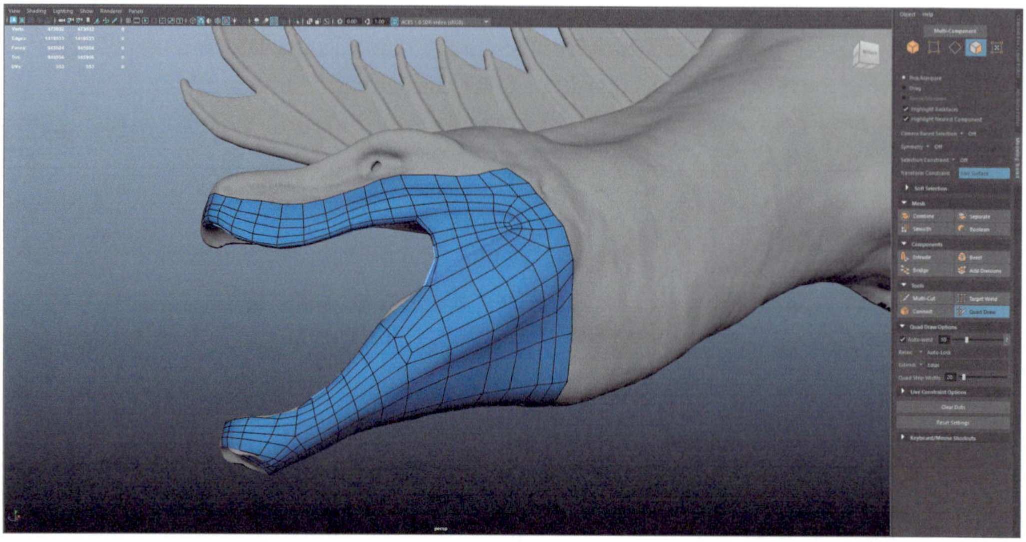

Figure 4.16 – Mouth topology with concentric loops defining lip structure and deformation zones

5. For the *eyes*, start with a clean circular loop around the eyelids. This loop should follow the natural shape of the eye socket and allow consistent deformation when blinking or squinting, avoiding sharp pinching in the corners.

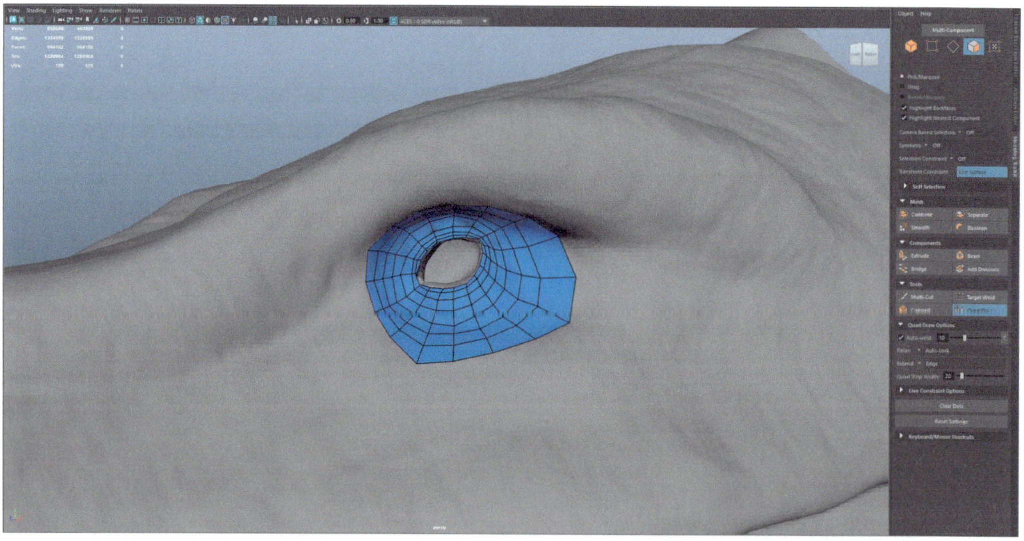

Figure 4.17 – Eye topology showing circular loops around the eyelids for clean blinking deformation

Handling topology in complex structures

After establishing the main deformation loops, it is important to focus on more complex structures such as **membranes**, **wings**, and **crest spikes**. These elements require a slightly different approach, as they combine thin surfaces with directional flow and localized detail.

1. When building topology for *membranes*, the most important rule is to *wrap the edge flow around each individual structure*. Every membrane, whether it is part of a wing, a lateral flap, or a crest extension, must be clearly defined by surrounding edge loops that follow its shape and direction.

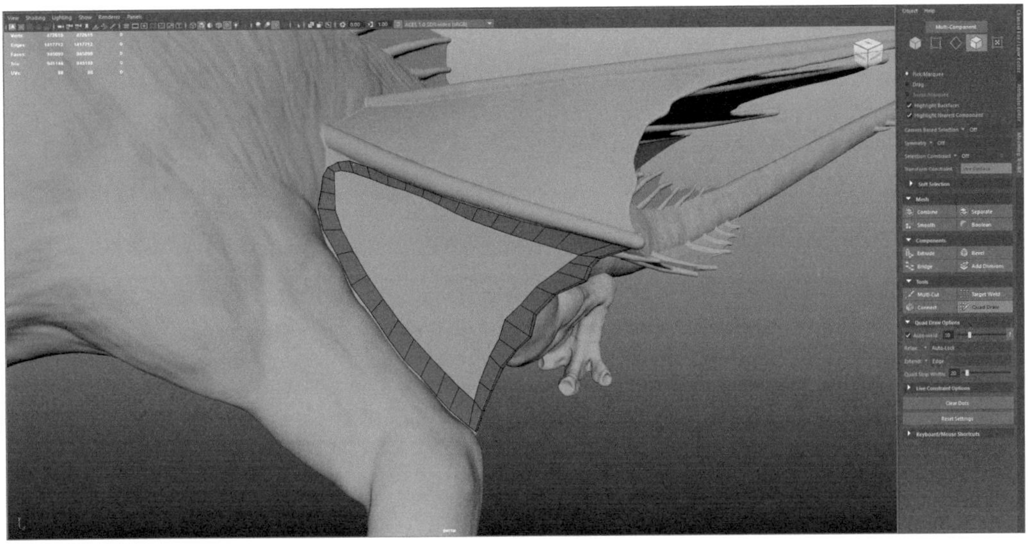

Figure 4.18 – Membrane topology showing edge loops wrapping around each structure and defining clean deformation areas

2. A key principle is that each membrane should contain a central supporting loop that runs along its middle. This loop acts as a structural guide, helping maintain thickness, control deformation, and avoid collapsing when the surface bends.

Note

It is strongly recommended to keep the topology on the *upper* and *lower* sides of the membrane as consistent as possible. Matching edge flow and similar polygon density on both sides ensures predictable deformation, prevents twisting, and maintains even thickness across the surface.

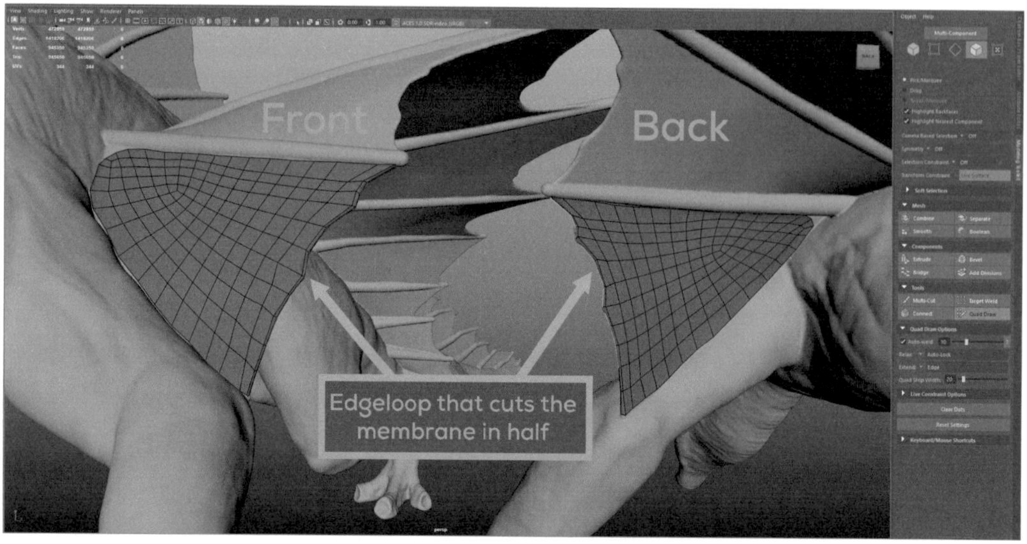

Figure 4.19 – Central supporting loop running through the middle of the membrane for structural stability

3. In addition to membranes, *crest spikes* must also be carefully structured. Each spike should be treated as its own volume, with loops wrapping around its base and gradually flowing into the surrounding topology. Avoid merging spikes directly into flat surfaces without proper loop support, as this will create shading artifacts and unstable deformation.

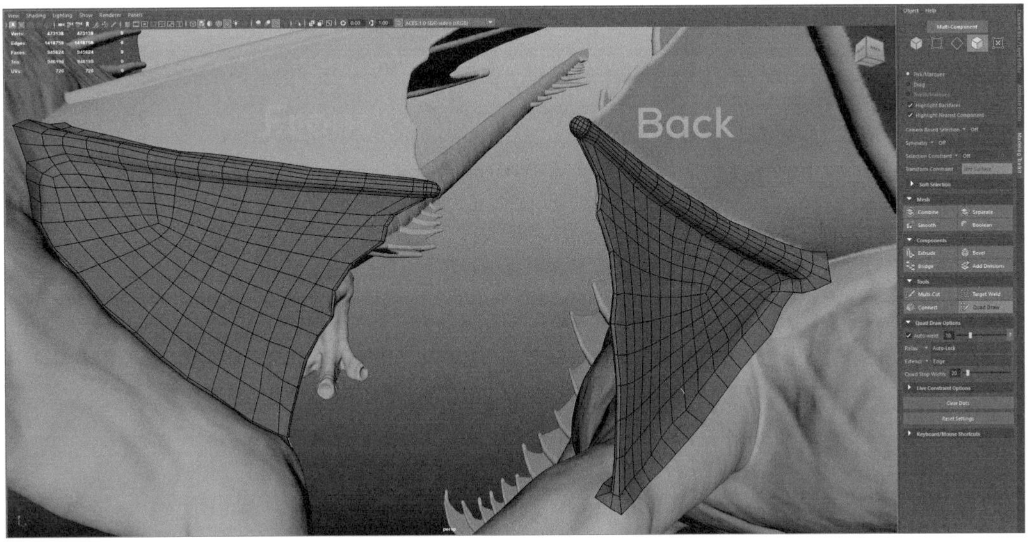

Figure 4.20 – Front and back membrane topology showing controlled edge-loop distribution and central support

Note

When building topology around anatomical features such as eyes, fingers, limbs, spines, or teeth, it is good practice to start from a very low-resolution base, often a single polygon, and progressively subdivide it.

By doing this, you naturally move from 4 sides to 8, then to 16, maintaining a structure based on multiples of four. While this is not a strict rule that must always be followed, it helps create clean topology with predictable connections between different anatomical areas.

Structuring the retopology process

Before moving forward, it's important to understand that the following phases represent a general retopology strategy applied to the entire creature, not just the previous membrane example. The images below will show the full topology from different angles (body, limbs, head, and membranes), helping you understand what each phase should look like once completed.

Build the topology progressively in phases, as follows:

1. **Phase 1**: Roughly block the main structure with the minimum number of quads necessary to capture the silhouette. At this stage, use the **Quad Draw** tool to place points and generate simple polygons, focusing only on primary forms and large volumes. Avoid adding unnecessary density and keep the topology as simple as possible.
   You should clearly recognize the overall shape of the creature, even with a very low polygon count.

Figure 4.21 – Low-density blocking of the main forms. The topology focuses on primary volumes using a minimal number of quads, defining the silhouette without unnecessary detail

2. **Phase 2**: Continue working with the Quad Draw tool to extend your topology and bridge separate polygon patches where needed. Begin connecting different areas, such as limbs to the torso, the head to the neck, and the membranes to the body. Focus on maintaining a continuous edge flow that follows the anatomy and avoids abrupt changes in direction.

The mesh should be fully connected, with no isolated patches, and the edge flow should start to follow the main anatomical directions.

Figure 4.22 – Topology connection and flow development. Separate mesh sections are connected using Extend and Bridge, establishing a continuous edge flow across the body, limbs, and membranes

3. **Phase 3**: Add support edges or denser loops only where surface tension or deformation requires them. Refine critical areas such as joints, face, and membranes by introducing additional loops to support deformation and preserve volume, without overloading the mesh.

   If you notice that the topology becomes too dense or contains more loops than necessary, apply loop reduction techniques such as the **diamond pattern** (which reduces four edge loops into two) or the **trapezoid pattern** (which reduces three loops into one). These methods help maintain a clean and efficient topology while preserving surface continuity. *Figures 4.23* to *4.27* illustrate how these techniques are applied across different parts of the model.

   > **Tip**
   >
   > Make sure to follow the rules discussed in the *Identifying and fixing N-gons, poles, and triangles* recipe earlier in the chapter, ensuring that all reductions preserve a clean quad-based structure.

In *Figure 4.23*, diamond and trapezoid patterns are used to reduce edge loops while maintaining clean topology flow:

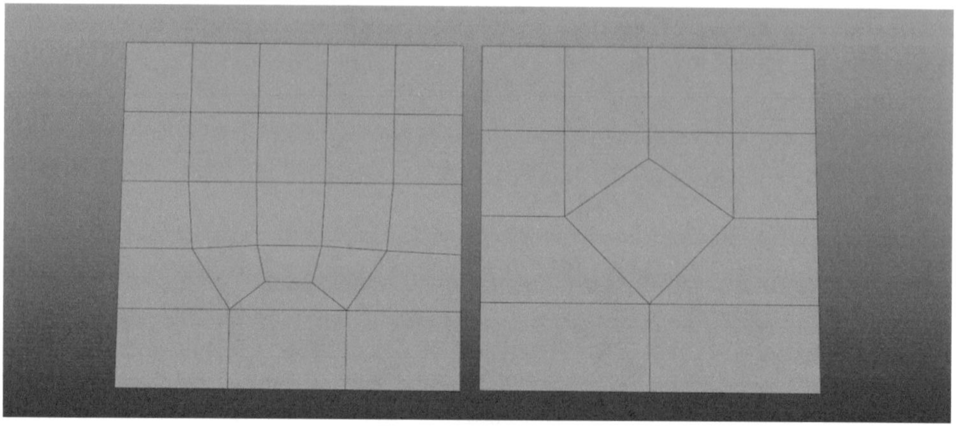

Figure 4.23 – Loop reduction techniques

Next, *Figure 4.24* shows how a clean quad distribution supports facial deformation and finger articulation, with loops flowing naturally around the eyes, mouth, and joints:

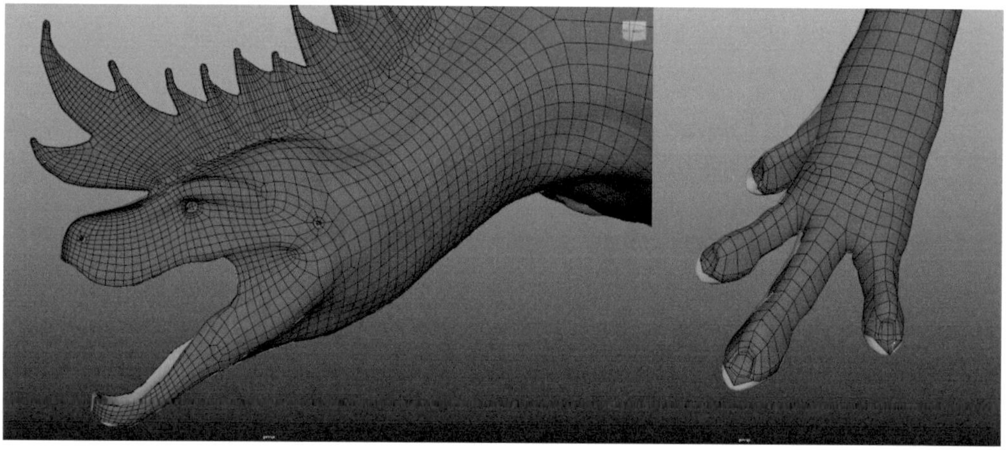

Figure 4.24 – Detailed topology on head and digits

Then, in *Figure 4.25*, the image highlights how clean edge flow supports deformation in the hind leg, while each membrane and spike is structured with controlled loops and central support lines:

Figure 4.25 – Rear leg and dorsal crest topology

The next image focuses on transitions between complex surfaces. Clean edge flow supports thin surfaces, while loops in the mouth and chest ensure stable deformation and smooth transitions:

Figure 4.26 – Membrane, inner mouth, and chest topology

Finally, the complete retopology demonstrates how all elements come together into a cohesive, production-ready mesh. The mesh shows consistent edge flow across the entire creature, with loops organized for deformation, volume preservation, and clean subdivision:

Figure 4.27 – Full retopology overview

Tip

After completing each section, use the **Relax** function in the **Modeling Toolkit** to even out your quads while preserving surface curvature. It's an excellent way to smooth tension without distorting the mesh.

Before exporting the mesh back to ZBrush, always check the vertex count. ZBrush's subdivision system performs best with a base mesh of around 24,000 vertices, which allows reaching approximately 99 million points at subdivision level 7.

Tip

While working on your retopology, enable Maya's **Heads Up Display** to monitor the vertex count in real time. Go to **Display** | **Heads Up Display** | **Poly Count** and keep an eye on the **Vertices** value as your topology grows. Checking the count regularly is much easier than reducing the mesh later, and it helps you stay close to the recommended base mesh target before exporting back to ZBrush.

At this stage, your retopology should be clean, fully connected, and optimized for subdivision. This ensures that once re-imported into ZBrush, the model will subdivide predictably and support high-frequency detailing without artifacts.

> **Note**
>
> If your base mesh exceeds 24,000 vertices, ZBrush will not reach its maximum resolution level, which limits tertiary sculpting and the precision of displacement maps. Keeping the vertex count balanced ensures that your detailing workflow remains efficient and technically stable.

How it works...

The workflow described in this section is built around a fundamental principle of production retopology: *topology is about controlling deformation, readability, and subdivision behavior.*

Preparing and projecting the sculpt

Starting with a decimated mesh directly affects how accurately you can project and read forms inside Maya. A dense sculpt introduces visual noise and slows down interaction, while a properly decimated version preserves the essential volumes and allows you to focus on structure instead of detail.

The use of **Make Live** combined with **Quad Draw** transforms the sculpt into a projection surface. This is critical because it removes the need to manually align vertices in 3D space. Every point you place is automatically constrained to the surface, allowing you to think in terms of flow and structure rather than positioning.

Building topology in phases

The retopology process is structured around three main phases: blocking, connecting, and refining.

The reason you begin with a low-density **blocking** phase is to establish hierarchy. At this stage, you are defining where topology needs to exist, and not solving topology everywhere. By keeping the mesh simple, you can quickly adjust proportions, redirect loops, and correct anatomical flow without being locked into unnecessary density. This is why the checkpoint focuses on silhouette recognition rather than detail accuracy.

When moving into the **connecting phase** using **Extend** and **Bridge**, the goal shifts from placement to continuity. Separate patches are integrated through a continuous edge flow that follows anatomical directions. This is what transforms disconnected pieces into a functional mesh. If this step is done incorrectly, no amount of refinement later will fix the underlying deformation issues.

The third phase of **refining** introduces supporting loops only where needed, and this is where mistakes are commonly made. Adding loops everywhere increases density but does not improve deformation. Instead, loops must be placed strategically in areas of compression and stretching, such as joints, membranes, and facial features. These loops act as buffers that preserve volume during subdivision and animation.

In production, areas of compression and stretching are not limited to major joints. Supporting loops must also follow muscle direction and structural transitions. For example, the biceps area requires loops aligned with the muscle flow to support twisting and flexing. The knee and heel need clearly defined loops to manage compression and weight distribution. Without these structures, deformation quickly breaks down.

Beyond the phase-based workflow, it is important to understand how topology controls deformation and optimization in production.

Controlling deformation through edge flow

Similarly, complex surfaces such as membranes and crests require dedicated loop structures. A loop that runs across the membrane acts as a structural guide, while additional loops wrapping around the base of crests or spikes ensure a smooth integration with the main body and prevent shading artifacts.

For example, circular loops around shoulders, hips, and eyes are not arbitrary patterns. They replicate the way real deformation behaves, allowing rotation and compression to distribute evenly across the surface. Without them, the mesh collapses or creates visible artifacts when animated.

Membranes follow a slightly different logic. Unlike solid volumes, they require a balance between *directional flow* and *structural support*. The central supporting loop running through each membrane acts as a stabilizing spine, maintaining thickness and preventing the surface from collapsing when bent. Keeping similar topology on both sides ensures predictable behavior and avoids twisting during deformation.

Loop reduction techniques such as the **diamond and trapezoid patterns** are not optimization tricks, but structural decisions. They allow you to reduce density while preserving edge flow continuity. This is essential to maintain a clean quad-based topology, especially when transitioning between high-density and low-density areas.

A clean edge flow also has a direct impact on the rigging stage. During weight painting, evenly distributed edge loops produce smoother weight interpolation, making joints easier to paint and reducing the amount of manual cleanup required. As a result, rigging artists can achieve more stable deformations with less effort, improving both the quality of the final animation and the efficiency of the production pipeline.

Optimizing topology for subdivision

The vertex count check is not just a technical constraint. It directly impacts how far you can push subdivision in ZBrush. A controlled base mesh ensures that you can reach high levels of detail without breaking performance or introducing artifacts, maintaining a predictable and efficient workflow from retopology to final sculpt.

In production, this entire process is not linear but iterative. You constantly move between blocking, connecting, and refining. However, thinking in these phases helps you maintain control over complexity, ensuring that every polygon added has a clear purpose.

Note

Across different industries, retopology follows similar principles but leads to different density targets depending on the final use of the asset.

To make this difference clearer, I created a simple visual comparison showing how the same type of model can be approached in three common production contexts.

As shown in the image:

- **Left**: Game-oriented mesh, lower density with visible triangle usage
- **Center**: Animation mesh, medium density with cleaner quad distribution
- **Right**: VFX base mesh, higher density even at the "low poly" stage

This is not a strict rule, but a practical visual guide to understanding how topology density scales across different pipelines.

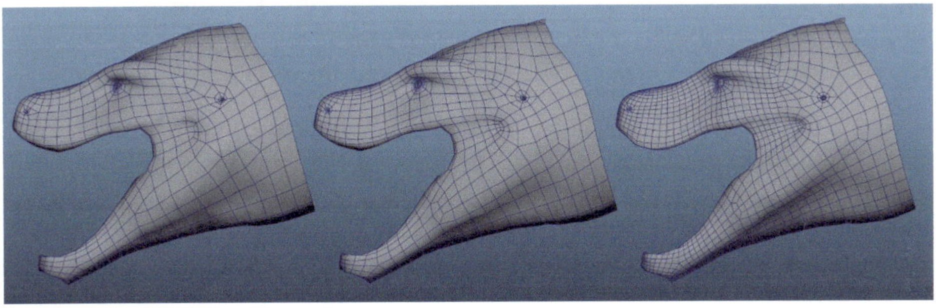

Figure 4.28 – Comparison of topology density across different production contexts

There's more...

While building your topology, it is highly recommended to frequently toggle **Smooth Preview** (press *3* in Maya) to evaluate how your mesh behaves under subdivision. This gives you immediate feedback on shading continuity, surface tension, and potential pinching before it becomes a problem.

Always ensure that all vertices are properly merged. Unmerged points can create cracks, shading artifacts, or unexpected behavior during subdivision and deformation.

Be especially careful when using relax or smoothing tools. Over-smoothing can unintentionally collapse vertices into each other, breaking the topology structure. For this reason, always apply these operations in a controlled and precise way, and treat them as precise adjustments rather than broad fixes.

Handling topology in complex areas: eyes, eyelids, ears and nose, claws and teeth, as well as tongue and gums

Certain anatomical regions in a creature or character, such as eyelids, nostrils, ears, tongue, and gums, require more attention during topology because they are heavily involved in deformation. These areas are constantly stretching and compressing, so the edge flow must be clean, predictable, and well-controlled.

In contrast, elements such as teeth and claws are structurally much simpler. They behave more like hard-surface forms, where deformation is limited, and the main goal is to maintain clean and readable topology.

The tongue and gums sit somewhere in between. They do deform, but their structure is relatively simple compared to areas like the eyelids. Here, the goal is to keep the topology clean and consistent, especially in the transition between the teeth, tongue, gums, and the main mesh.

When working on the eye region, it is important to separate geometry from deformation. The eyeball itself is made of simple elements such as the pupil, iris, and cornea, which do not require complex topology. However, the quality of deformation depends entirely on the eyelids, which drive the edge flow and control how the area behaves during blinking.

In this recipe, we will focus exclusively on topology, ensuring that each element, including the tongue and gums, is properly integrated into the mesh and that the edge flow remains consistent and functional.

Getting ready

Follow these steps to ensure your environment is ready before following the recipe:

1. Make sure your decimated or **DynaMesh** version of the sculpt is already imported into Maya and ready to be used as a projection surface for retopology.
2. In this recipe, we will work directly on this mesh using the **Quad Draw** tool, so ensure that your scene is clean and responsive, and that the main volumes of the model are clearly readable.
   If you are not familiar with the **Quad Draw** workflow or its basic controls, refer to the *Using the Quad Draw tool for manual retopology* recipe before proceeding.
3. At this stage, it is important to work on a separate **DynaMesh** version of the head. So, if needed, refer back to the *Sculpting the head from a sphere* recipe in *Chapter 2* to understand how the head was originally structured and separated during the sculpting phase.

How to do it...

In the following steps, you will build topology for complex anatomical areas, adapting your approach based on their structure and deformation needs:

1. Start by establishing a clean circular structure of eight quads (see **1** in *Figure 4.29*) around each opening area, such as the eyelids, nostrils, and ear canal. This first loop defines the primary boundary of the structure and must remain simple and evenly distributed.
2. Begin by placing 16 points around the opening using **Quad Draw**, then create the first closed loop. Keep the spacing uniform and avoid stretching polygons.
3. Fill the center by creating a single polygon and *subdivide it twice*, generating a simple internal structure that will act as the base for further refinement (see **2** in *Figure 4.29*). This creates a stable starting point without introducing unnecessary complexity.
4. Connect the inner area to the first loop by creating quads between the central geometry and the surrounding ring.
5. Fill the space evenly, making sure each face remains a clean quad and the edge flow stays radial around the opening.

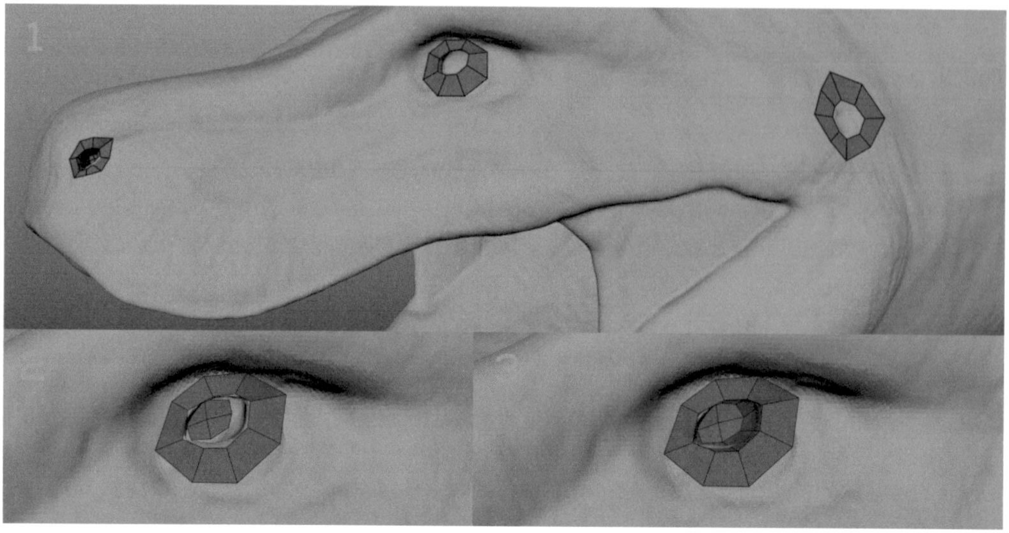

Figure 4.29 – Building the base topology for eyelids, nostrils, and ear openings

6. Add supporting loops where needed to increase density and better define the shape. Focus on areas that require more curvature or deformation support, such as the eyelids or the inner edge of the opening (see **3** in *Figure 4.29*).
   For the eyelids, ensure that the topology includes *one loop running across the full thickness of the eyelid* and at least *three loops defining the structure* to properly support volume and deformation during blinking.

   As a general guideline, aim for around 16 edges circulating the eyelids, while 8 edges are usually sufficient for nostrils and ear openings, reflecting their lower deformation complexity.

   If some vertices do not properly conform to the surface, reposition them using **Quad Draw** to ensure they sit correctly on the sculpt and maintain a clean, even edge flow.

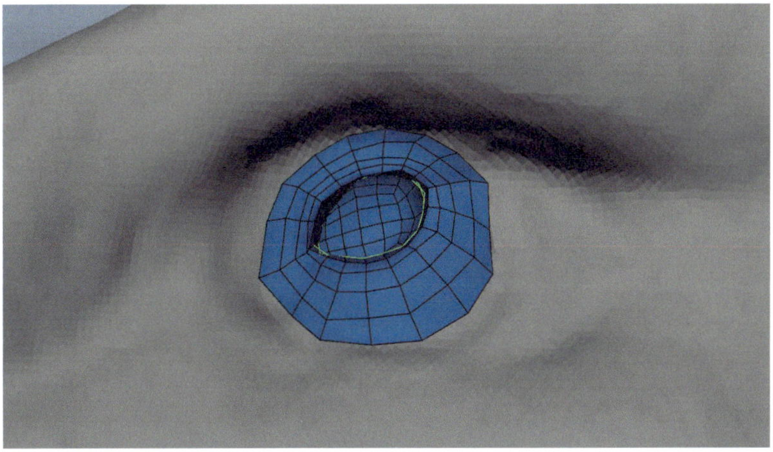

Figure 4.30 – Eyelid topology with supporting loops defining thickness and curvature

The structure should read as a clean circular topology with evenly spaced quads. When previewing with **Smooth Preview** (press *3*), the surface should appear stable, without collapsing or creating visible artifacts around the opening.

Building the eye geometry

Now we move on to building the eye geometry. In this section of the workflow, we will create the basic structures of the eye, starting from a simple sphere, which will be used to define the main components, such as the cornea, iris, and pupil:

1. Start by creating a **Polygon Sphere** in the center of the Maya scene using **Create** | **Polygon Primitives** | **Sphere**.
2. Set the sphere to 16 subdivisions on both axes (16 × 16) to achieve a clean and evenly distributed topology.
   If you need to adjust the subdivision values, go to the **Channel Box** | **INPUTS** | **polySphere1** and modify the settings directly from there. Do not modify the position or scale of the sphere. Only rotate it 90 degrees on the *X* axis so that the pole, or "tip" of the topology, faces the *Z* axis (front view). This ensures a clean and consistent orientation for the eye setup.
3. Create a second **Polygon Sphere** in the center of the Maya scene using the same process as in *step 1*.
4. Set the sphere to 128 subdivisions on both axes (128 × 128) to achieve a higher level of detail.

5. Keep it rotated 90 degrees on the *X* axis and do not modify its position or scale, so it remains perfectly aligned with the first sphere.

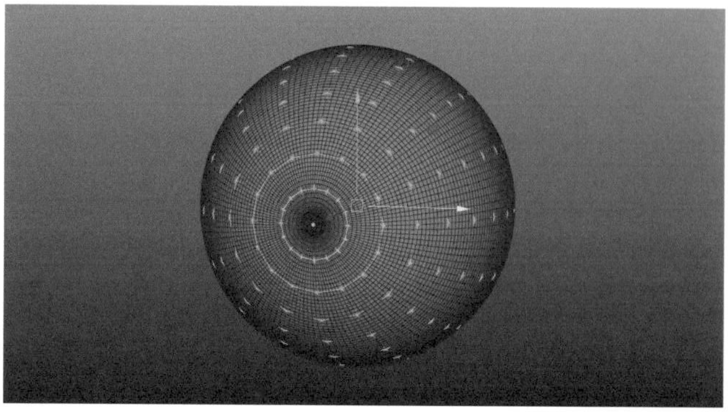

Figure 4.31 – The low-density sphere positioned inside the high-resolution 128 × 128 sphere, used as a projection surface for building the eye geometry

6. Select the low-resolution sphere and choose the edge loops you want to remove. Press *Ctrl* + *Delete* to remove the selected edges without leaving extra vertices.
   Keep only the loops needed to define a clean circular structure, ensuring the mesh remains evenly distributed and easy to control for the next steps.

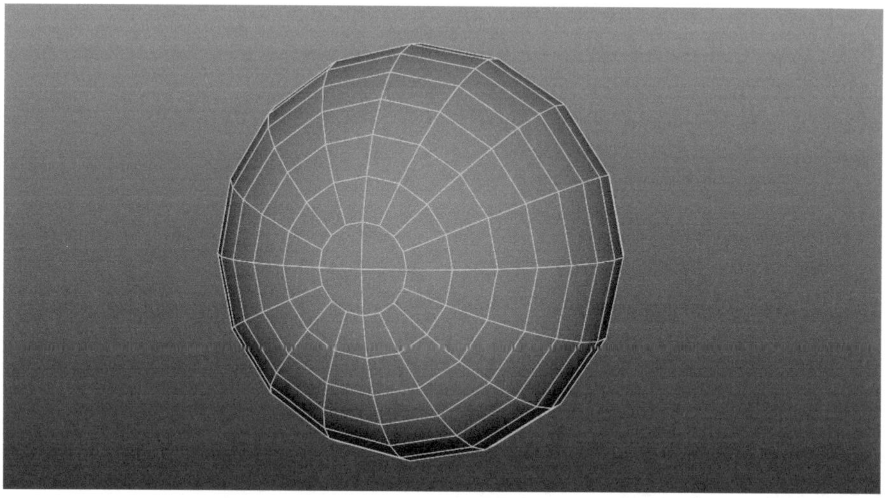

Figure 4.32 – Removing unnecessary edge loops on the low-resolution sphere using Ctrl + Delete to clean the topology

7. Select the inner vertices and use the **Multi-Cut** tool to connect them, creating a clean grid that follows the existing topology. Make sure the connections are evenly spaced and aligned with the surrounding edge flow to maintain a consistent quad structure.

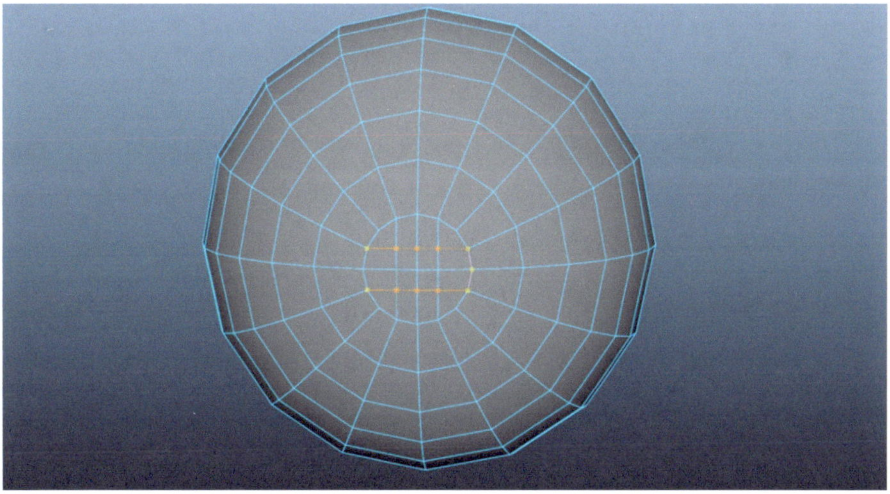

Figure 4.33 – Connecting inner vertices with Multi-Cut to establish a clean quad grid

8. Once the topology is correctly structured, subdivide the low-resolution sphere once to increase the density.
9. Then set the 128 × 128 sphere to **Make Live** and use **Quad Draw** to reposition the vertices so they snap accurately onto the surface.
10. After that, hold *Shift* while **Quad Draw** is active to apply a uniform **Relax/Smooth** across the entire low-resolution sphere. This evenly relaxes the topology while keeping the vertices snapped to the live surface. The result should be a clean and consistent quad structure that conforms perfectly to the spherical shape. This object will be the **cornea**.

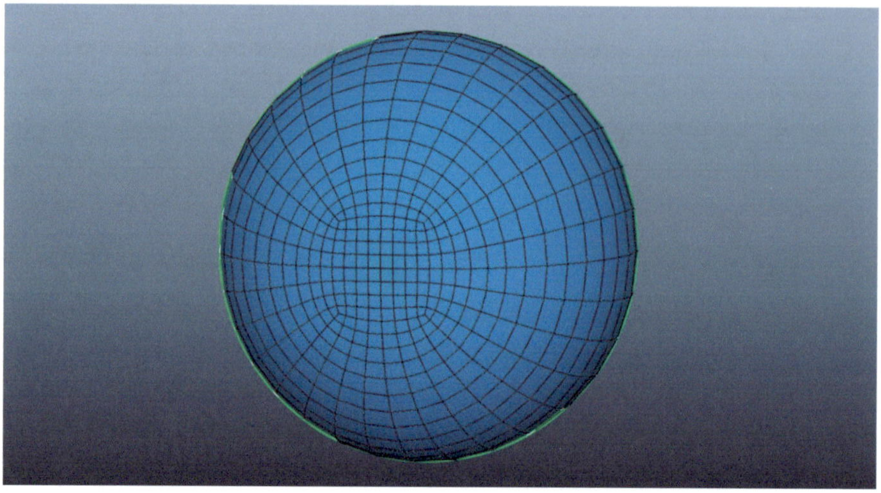

Figure 4.34 – Final smoothed topology evenly distributed across the sphere after subdivision and projection

11. Now, we'll create a sphere that will be used as the **iris**. Create a new **Polygon Sphere** with 32 × 32 subdivisions, rotate it 90 degrees on the *X* axis, and slightly scale it down.
12. Delete the front-facing polygons, then adjust the remaining geometry by moving the pivot and using **Soft Selection** to shape it.
13. Refine the loops until they match the curvature of the eye and achieve the result shown in *Figure 4.35*:

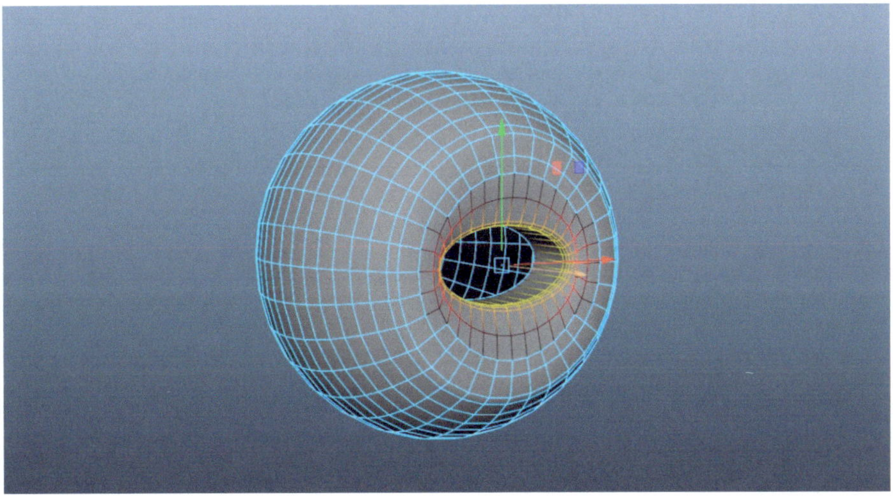

Figure 4.35 – Iris geometry created from a 32 × 32 sphere, with front faces removed and reshaped using Soft Selection

14. Next, to build the **pupil**, we'll create a new **Polygon Sphere** with 16 × 16 subdivisions. Leave its default orientation unchanged.
15. First, scale the sphere down uniformly to fit inside the iris, then scale it on the *Z* axis to flatten it slightly. Position it inside the iris, keeping it centered and aligned with the existing geometry.
16. Select all the eye components and group them, renaming the group `L_eye_GRP`. Once grouped, position the entire eye setup exactly where you originally placed the base sphere that was used to simulate the eye, then rotate it as needed to match the socket correctly.

Figure 4.36 shows the final eye setup:

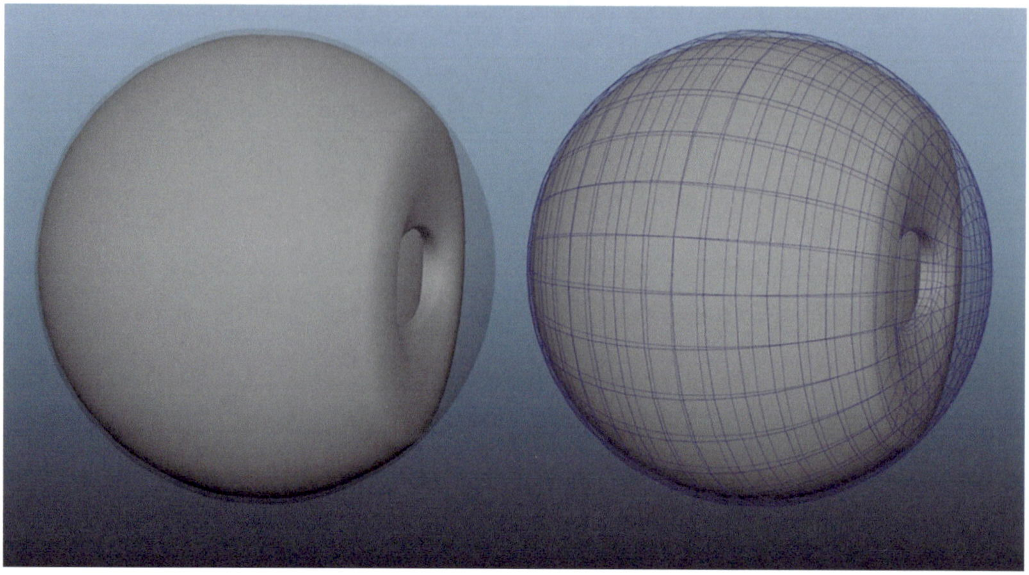

Figure 4.36 – Final eye setup integrated into the head, showing clean topology flow and properly aligned eye geometry

Building topology for claws and teeth

Now we move to claws, which follow the same logic as teeth. The topology approach is identical, since both are simple, rigid forms with minimal deformation. In this section, the process will be demonstrated on a *single claw*, but the same technique can be consistently applied to all claws and teeth across the model.

1. Set the claw **DynaMesh** as a **Make Live** surface so it can be used as a reference for retopology without modifying the original sculpt. This allows you to rebuild the structure directly on top of the high-resolution form.
2. Using **Mesh Tools | Quad Draw**, begin building a very low-resolution mesh on the surface. Keep the topology extremely simple, defining a slightly squared section to better control the volume and establish clean edge flow from the start.
3. Add *one loop along the length of the claw* and *one across it* to define the main curvature. Do not add any additional loops.
4. Then use **Edit Mesh | Smooth** to increase the topology density uniformly instead of manually inserting more loops.

Figure 4.37 – From left: Initial low-poly cage, loop refinement following the curvature, and the completed topology ready for subdivision

The same approach used for the mouth and jaw loops described earlier in this recipe (see *Figure 4.16*) also applies to the gums and tongue. Since these areas follow the same structural logic, the retopology process does not introduce new techniques.

Start by preparing the surface for retopology:

1. Start by taking the **DynaMesh** of the gums and tongue and setting them as **Make Live**.
2. Then use **Mesh Tools** | **Quad Draw** to rebuild the topology directly on the surface.

Since this process follows the same core retopology principles demonstrated earlier, only the final result is shown in *Figure 4.38*. The goal is to maintain a clean edge flow that follows the curvature of the gums and tongue, integrating smoothly with the surrounding topology.

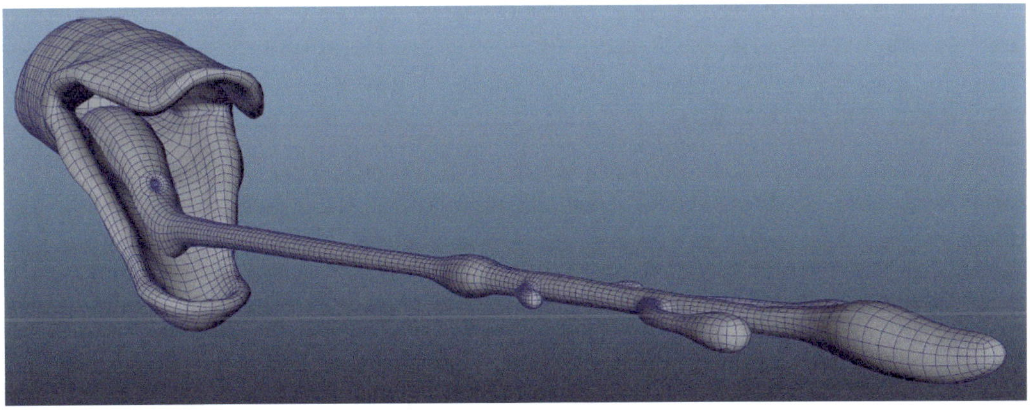

Figure 4.38 – Final retopology of gums and tongue, showing clean edge flow and consistent quad distribution across connected soft tissue forms

How it works...

This workflow is built around a fundamental principle of production topology: *separating complexity into controllable systems while preserving clean edge flow*. Each step is designed to progressively organize geometry, starting from simple structures and refining them only when necessary.

At the core of this approach is the idea of starting simple and adding density only where it is needed. When building areas such as the eyes, instead of beginning with a dense mesh, we construct a low-resolution structure that defines the main edge flow. This ensures that the topology remains readable and predictable, avoiding unnecessary complexity from the beginning.

The use of a high-resolution sphere as a projection surface is key to maintaining accuracy. By snapping the low-resolution topology onto a perfectly smooth reference, we remove irregularities introduced during manual construction. This guarantees that the final surface conforms to an ideal spherical shape, which is essential for elements like the cornea.

Another important concept is **topological hierarchy**. The eye is not treated as a single mesh but as a combination of elements with different roles: cornea, iris, and pupil. Each component is built separately with the appropriate level of complexity. This separation allows for better control in downstream departments such as shading and rigging, where each part may require different materials or behaviors.

For deforming areas like *eyelids*, the topology is driven by deformation rather than shape alone. The loops are arranged to follow the natural motion of the skin, ensuring that compression and stretching behave in a stable way. This is why multiple loops are required across the thickness of the eyelid, while fewer loops are sufficient for less dynamic areas such as nostrils or ears.

In contrast, elements like claws and teeth follow a different logic. These are structurally rigid forms, so the topology does not need to support complex deformation. Instead of building dense geometry, we define a very simple, low-resolution cage and then rely on subdivision to generate smoothness. This approach keeps the topology clean while maintaining full control over the silhouette.

The same reasoning applies to gums and tongue, which sit between rigid and highly deformable structures. Here, the topology must be clean and continuous, especially in transition areas where different surfaces meet.

Finally, the consistent use of tools like **Quad Draw**, **Multi-Cut**, and **Smooth** is intentional for the following reasons:

- **Quad Draw** allows precise control over surface reconstruction

- **Multi-Cut** helps define directional flow
- **Smooth** is used to redistribute topology evenly without breaking the structure

Together, they create a balanced workflow where control and automation are combined.

If this process is followed correctly, the result is a mesh that is clean, efficient, and production-ready, with predictable deformation behavior and a clear logical structure that can be easily understood and modified by other artists in the pipeline.

There's more...

When creating the cornea and snapping the low-resolution sphere onto the high-resolution one using **Smooth** and **Quad Draw**, we used a fast and practical approach directly inside Maya. However, other projection methods, such as Maya's **ShrinkWrap** deformer, can provide greater accuracy when needed.

In this book, we'll use ZBrush because it offers a reliable projection workflow that integrates naturally with the creature pipeline covered throughout the previous chapters. Instead of relying on smoothing to conform the low-poly sphere, both the low-resolution and high-resolution spheres can be exported to ZBrush. Once imported, project the low-resolution sphere onto the high-resolution one using **Project All**, then subdivide it once and repeat the projection.

This extra step addresses a subtle but important issue. When smoothing a low-poly sphere in Maya, the geometry tends to shrink slightly and lose volume. Because the sphere is built with a limited number of edge loops, such as 16 by 16, the polygon distribution is not perfectly uniform. After subdivision, the shape becomes slightly oval, which can affect shading, reflections, and overall accuracy, especially for elements like the cornea where precision is critical.

By projecting in ZBrush, the volume is preserved, and the surface remains perfectly spherical even after subdivision. The corrected geometry can then be exported back to Maya, resulting in a cleaner and more physically accurate model.

Relying only on smoothing for spherical shapes often leads to subtle volume loss that may only become visible under proper lighting or close-up renders. Whenever precision matters, projection workflows remain the safer choice.

5

UV Mapping with UDIMs: Fixing Distortions and Optimizing Workflow

In this chapter, you will build a production-ready UDIM UV layout for `dragonCrest`, focusing on solving real distortion issues that appear on complex organic surfaces.

Instead of relying on automatic tools, you will learn how to manually plan UV seams based on anatomy, muscle flow, and deformation needs. Special attention will be given to critical areas such as the face, membranes, and joints, where stretching can easily break texture quality.

A **UDIM (U-Dimension and V-Dimension)** is a multi-tile UV mapping system that allows a single model to use multiple UV tiles instead of being limited to a single 0-1 UV space. This approach provides significantly higher texture resolution and allows artists to store much more texture information while keeping the asset organized and scalable for production.

You will validate your UVs using directional and pixel-density checkers, ensuring consistent texel density across UDIMs. Here, **texel density** defines how many texture pixels are assigned to a given surface area of a 3D model. Keeping it consistent ensures that texture details have the same visual resolution across the entire asset, avoiding noticeable differences in quality.

The workflow integrates Maya and ZBrush, using tools such as **Unfold3D** and **PolyRaven** to achieve clean and controllable results. PolyRaven is a commercial plugin for Autodesk Maya that extends its native UV tools with advanced workflow utilities. It can be purchased from the official PolyRaven website: `https://www.polyraven.com/`.

By the end of this chapter, you will have a structured and scalable UDIM layout for `dragonCrest`, ready for texturing in production, with a clear understanding of how to fix distortion and optimize UV space where it matters most. You will also learn how to manage a large number of UDIMs efficiently to push texture resolution where needed, following the same production approach I used while working on large-scale creatures such as the dragons in *House of the Dragon* (first released in 2022) and the albino T-Rex in *Love, Death & Robots: Season 4* (2025).

In particular, the following recipes will be covered in this chapter:

- Planning multi-UDIMs and the half-character UV workflow
- Packing and ordering multi-UDIMs: Substance 3D Painter versus Mari
- UVs for secondary elements: eyes, claws, teeth, gums, tongue
- Fixing or updating UDIMs without losing work in ZBrush

Figure 5.1 shows the overall UV seam strategy used for `dragonCrest`, highlighting how the cuts are planned around anatomical flow, deformation zones, and membrane structures before the actual unwrapping process begins:

Figure 5.1 – UV seam layout for dragonCrest

Technical requirements

To follow this chapter effectively, you will need the following setup. As mentioned in previous chapters, make sure your scene is correctly configured in terms of scale and project structure.

Required software

- **ZBrush 2024 or later** for UV validation and re-import checks

- **Maya 2024 or later** for primary UV unwrapping and UDIM organization
- **Unfold3D** integrated in Maya or as a standalone solution for precise unwrapping
- **PolyRaven** or an equivalent UV packing tool for optimized multi-UDIM layouts

Recommended tools and resources

Refer to the *Technical requirements* section in *Chapter 4* for the required software, companion files, and download instructions. The same assets are used throughout this chapter, including the production-ready retopology with the complete UV layout and the directional UV checker texture.

You can download the example project files for this book by following the instructions in the *Download the example code/resource files* section in the *Preface* of this book.

This chapter's code/resource files are included in the downloadable code/resource bundle.

Asset scale and layout

- Work in meters, as explained in previous chapters, to maintain consistency across the pipeline.
- For high-end cinematic assets, a texel density between 30 and 55 px/cm is commonly used, depending on the importance of the region and the production requirements. If you are working on a less powerful workstation, consider using a lower texel density, around 10 to 20 px/cm, together with 4K UDIMs, to reduce texture memory usage, painting overhead, and map export times.
- Expect between `20–40` UDIM tiles depending on asset size and membrane complexity.

Hardware requirements (recommended)

For hardware specifications, refer to the *Technical requirements* section in *Chapter 1*, where system requirements and performance optimization are covered in detail.

Planning multi-UDIMs and the half-character UV workflow

When preparing UVs for `dragonCrest`, and more generally for complex creatures with elongated anatomy and membranes, proper planning is as important as the unwrapping itself. Without a clear UDIM strategy, you will quickly run into inconsistent texel density, visible seams, and inefficient use of texture space, especially across the membranes and tail.

For this asset, we will adopt a half-character workflow. We will unwrap only one side of the model, focusing on clean seam placement, balanced texel density, and a logical UDIM distribution between the head, body, limbs, and membranes. Once validated, the UVs will be mirrored to ensure perfect symmetry and technical consistency.

This approach allows us to maintain control over critical areas such as the face and membranes, which require higher resolution compared to less visible regions. By the end of this recipe, you will have a structured UDIM layout for `dragonCrest`, designed to support efficient texturing and predictable results in production.

Getting ready

This recipe is performed entirely inside Autodesk Maya, without requiring any operations in ZBrush. Before starting the UV layout, make sure you are working on a clean half of the `dragonCrest` model. Only one side of the character should be present, with the geometry properly cut along the centerline.

It is essential that the central edge loop is perfectly aligned on the world axis, with all vertex positions set to $X = 0$. This ensures that the UVs can be mirrored later without any offset or distortion. This is essential to guarantee a clean and accurate mirror when rebuilding the full model.

Check that the cut is clean and continuous across the entire model, especially along the head, torso, and tail, where alignment issues are more likely to appear. This setup is critical to guarantee symmetry and consistency when duplicating and mirroring the UV layout.

How to do it...

In this workflow, we will start from the half version of `dragonCrest`, as prepared in *Chapter 4*. Working on half of the model allows us to speed up the process, since the other side will be mirrored later. We will work specifically on the left side of the model.

Preparing the UV workspace

Let's begin by preparing the Maya workspace and establishing a visual understanding of how the geometry is currently distributed in UV space:

1. Start by opening the **UV Editor** from **UV** | **UV Editor**. At this stage, the goal is not to unwrap yet, but to clearly visualize how the model will be translated into UV space. Make sure you can see both the 3D model and the **UV Editor** at the same time. This will allow you to immediately understand how every change on the geometry affects the UV layout. Before proceeding, take a moment to inspect the current state of the mesh in the **UV Editor**, even if it is still unorganized, to get a first reading of how the geometry is distributed.

Tip

If you are working on creature or character assets, using two monitors can significantly improve your workflow. Keep the perspective view on one screen and the **UV Editor** on the other to constantly compare geometry and UV layout.

If you only have one monitor, split the Maya interface into two panels, placing the perspective Viewport on one side and the **UV Editor** on the other, as shown in *Figure 5.2*.

Figure 5.2 – Overview of the suggested Viewport layout in Maya

2. With the **UV Editor** open, start by selecting only the body of `dragonCrest`. We will begin from this main section and then move step by step to the other parts of the creature.
3. In the **UV Toolkit**, go to **Create | Normal-Based** and apply the projection only to the body.
4. Once applied, check the result in the **UV Editor**, but do not clean or reorganize anything yet, and verify that the entire body UV layout is contained within the first UDIM tile **U1V1 (1001)**.

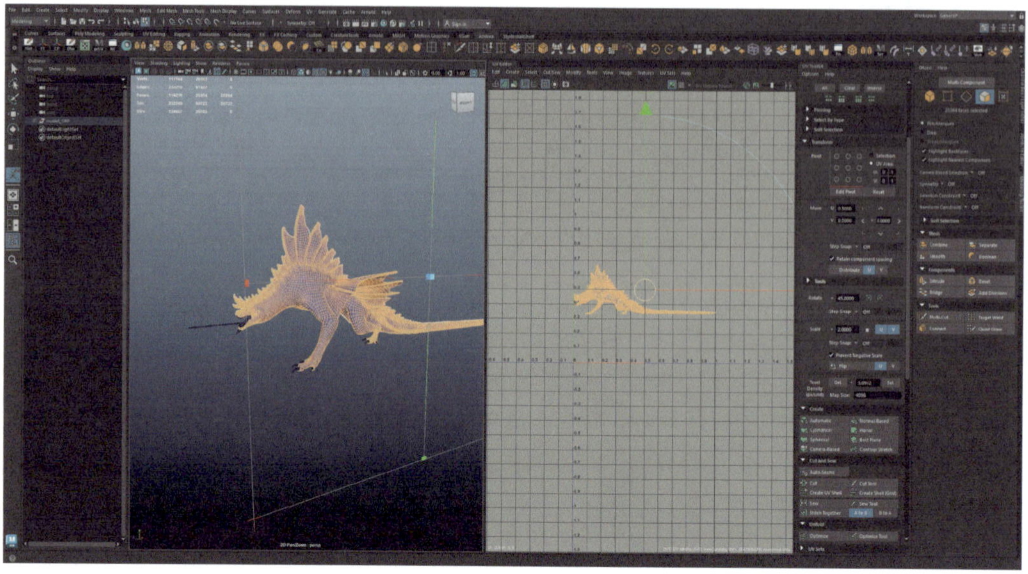

Figure 5.3 – Normal-Based projection applied only to the body section of the model

5. To display the UDIM numbering in the **UV Editor**, enable the **UDIM tile display** using the dedicated button in the **UV Editor** toolbar, located near the display and image controls.
6. Once enabled, and with the UVs selected, the **UV Editor** will display the UDIM numbering of the tiles currently in use. This allows you to clearly see in which UDIM tile (**1001**, **1002**, and so on) each UV shell is placed.
   Make sure that the body UV shells are clearly visible inside tile **1001** and use this numbering as a reference while organizing your layout in the next steps.

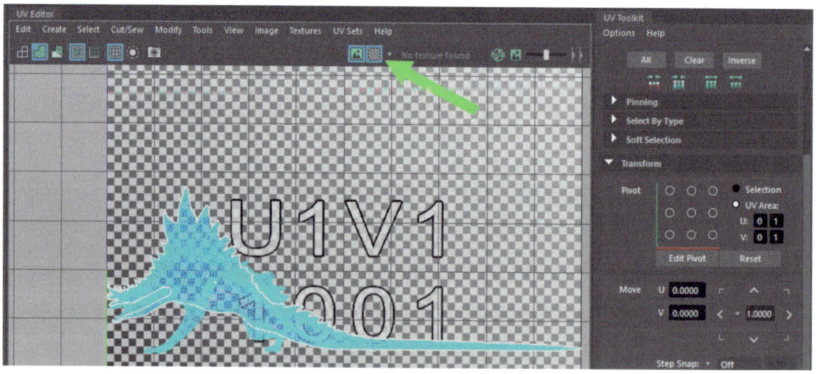

Figure 5.4 – UDIM numbering enabled in the UV Editor, showing UV shells distributed inside tile 1001

Note

You can also enable UV distortion display from the **UV Editor** by going to **View** | **UV Distortion**. This provides quick visual feedback on how the UVs are distributed.

In general, *blue* areas indicate compression; *red* areas indicate stretching; *neutral* tones indicate a more even distribution. Keep in mind that this visualization is only an approximation and may vary depending on the distortion mode. It should be used as a quick check, not as a final validation.

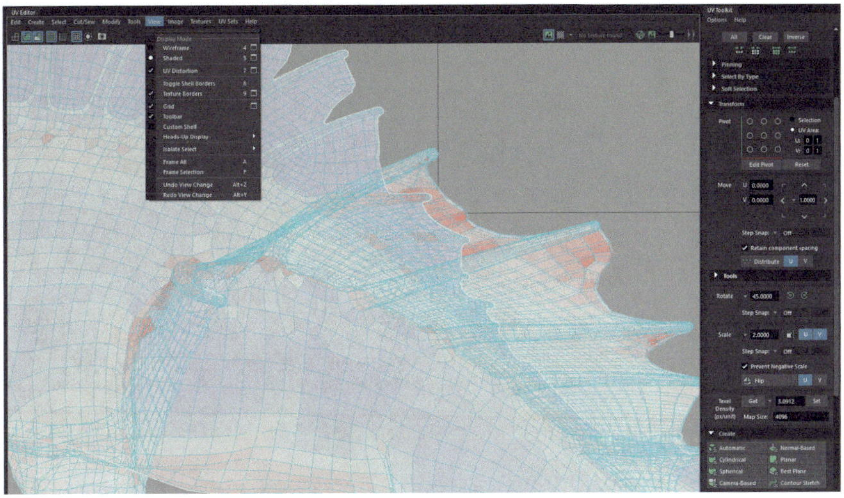

Figure 5.5 – UV distortion visualization enabled in the UV Editor

7. To better evaluate the UV layout, make sure the **UV Editor** is using the default UV display shader. This will allow you to clearly identify overlapping shells and orientation issues.

8. Inspect the UVs and look for problematic areas. Pay attention to the color feedback:
    - *Blue tones* indicate UVs with a positive orientation
    - *Red tones* indicate UVs with a negative (flipped) orientation
    - *Purple areas* indicate overlapping UVs

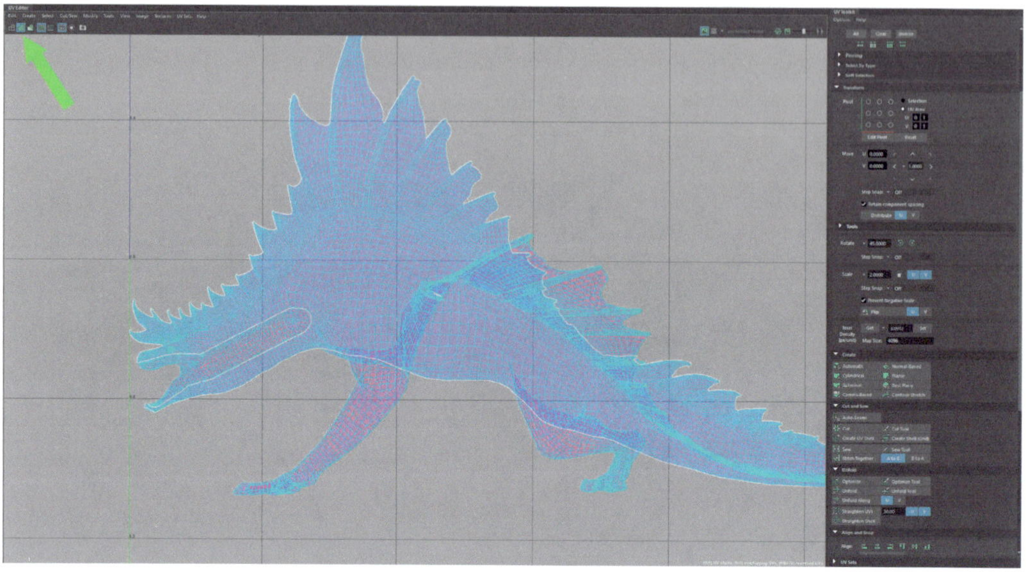

Figure 5.6 – UV display showing overlapping areas highlighted in purple across the body and limbs

9. Select all the current UV shells of the body and temporarily move them into the negative UV space. This will free up the main UDIM tile **(1001)** so you can start organizing and separating the first anatomical regions more clearly.
   Do not worry about placement or layout at this stage. The goal is simply to clear the working space and begin isolating key areas, such as the torso, back, and main body mass, before rebuilding the UV structure.

Figure 5.7 shows the difference between **positive space** (UDIM tiles starting from **1001**) and **negative space**, used as a temporary working area for organizing UV shells:

Figure 5.7 – UV space overview

Blocking the main anatomical regions

With the workspace prepared, the next stage is to establish the primary anatomical separations that will define the overall UV structure of `dragonCrest`.

1. Start separating the main anatomical regions of the body by selecting edge loops and cutting them using the **UV Toolkit**. Focus on broad, readable areas rather than small details.
2. Select the edge loops that define the main sections of `dragonCrest`, such as the side membranes, the dorsal crest, the central body mass, the tail fins, and the legs around the shoulder area.

3. Once selected, apply the cut using **UV Toolkit | Cut and Sew | Cut**. At this stage, the cuts do not need to be perfect. The goal is to quickly block out the primary regions and create a clear separation between the main anatomical parts of the model.

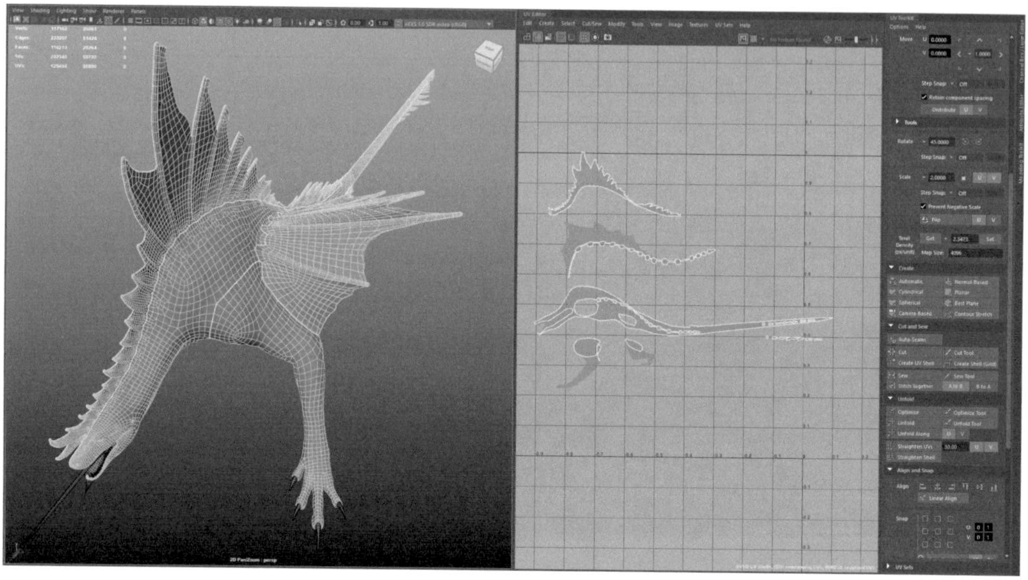

Figure 5.8 – Initial edge loop selection and UV cuts applied to separate major anatomical regions

Before continuing with the UV separation, it is important to understand that **Cut** and **Sew** will be used throughout this workflow. These tools allow you to break and reconnect UV shells. **Cut** is used to separate parts of the mesh by creating seams, while **Sew** is used to stitch UV shells back together when needed. These operations will be used continuously in the next steps to shape and control the UV layout.

Another important piece of information worth mentioning is how to quickly switch between different UV component selections inside the **UV Editor**. By right-clicking in the **UV Editor**, you can choose between UVs, edges, vertices, faces, and UV shells. This allows you to precisely control how you select and cut your UVs. In particular, edge selection will be used to define seams, while shell selection will help you organize and move UV islands more efficiently.

4. Continue separating the UVs by focusing on the head first, as it is the most important area for resolution and readability.
5. Start by isolating the main components: separate the lower jaw from the upper jaw, and isolate the internal parts such as eyes, nostrils, and ears.

6. Once separated, move and organize all these elements inside the **1001** UDIM tile, keeping them straight and aligned according to the UV space orientation.
7. After each separation, apply an initial unfold to the selected shells to relax the UVs. You can find this tool in **UV Toolkit | Unfold | Unfold**.
   Do not try to fully finalize the layout at this stage. The goal is to establish a clean and readable structure starting from the most critical area of the asset.

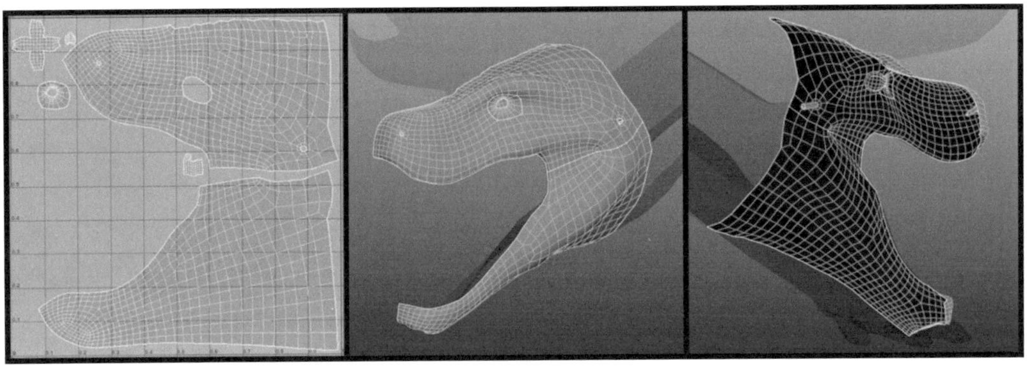

Figure 5.9 – Head UVs separated into main components and relaxed using Unfold inside UDIM 1001

Establishing texel density and UV flow

Once the major UV regions are separated and readable, the layout can be standardized by defining texel density and validating directional UV flow across the surface:

1. Once the head UVs are organized, define your texel density reference from this area. In the **UV Toolkit**, under the **Transform section | Tools**, set the **Map Size** to `4096`. Then select one of the head UV shells and press **Get** under **Texel Density**. The value obtained will be used as the reference for the entire UV set.
   Do not modify the value. This number represents the density that will be applied consistently across all other regions of the model.
2. To better control the orientation of your UVs, you can use **PolyRaven UV Tools**, a plugin available from its official website: `https://www.polyraven.com/uv/`. Once installed, open the **PolyRaven UV Tools** panel and locate the **Checker and Flow Material** section. Click **Create/Update** to generate the utility materials inside the **Hypershade**. These materials are designed to help visualize UV direction and distribution, and will be used in the next steps to align the UV flow correctly.

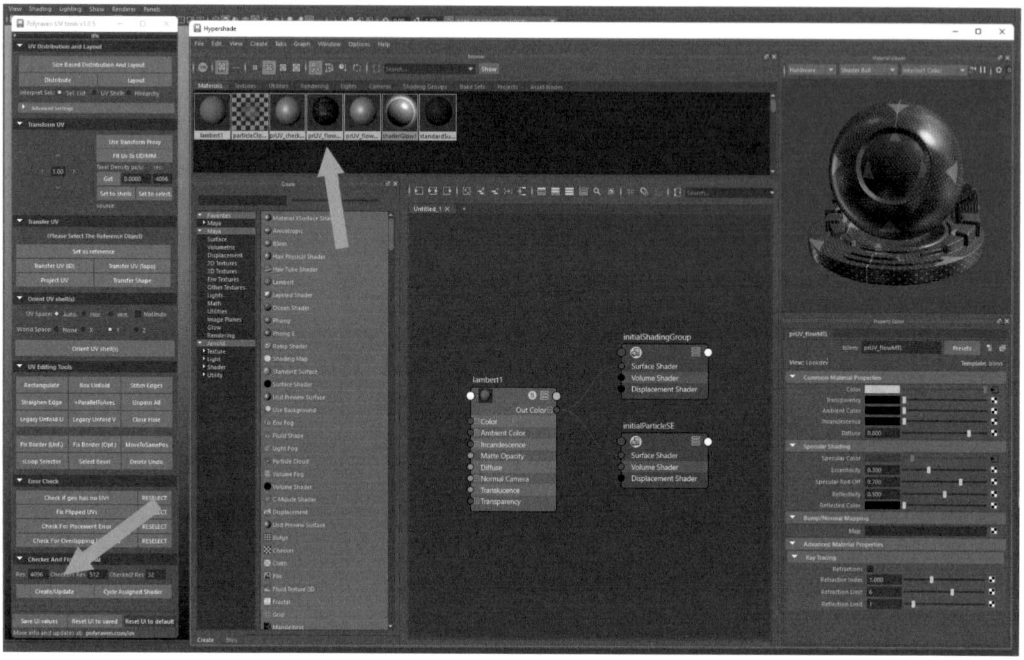

Figure 5.10 – Overview of the PolyRaven UV Tools panel showing the Checker and Flow Material section

3. Open the **Hypershade** and locate the material named `prUV_flowMTL`. Assign this material to your model. To apply it, select the mesh in the Viewport, then right-click on the material in **Hypershade** and choose **Assign Material to Selection**.

Tip

Alternatively, if you do not have access to PolyRaven, you can create your own directional checker texture or download the `checker_uv` provided in the `Chapter04_05` folder in the accompanying GitHub repository (see the *Technical requirements* section for access).

If you do not have PolyRaven UV Tools, follow these steps to create an equivalent shader manually:

1. Open **Window | Rendering Editors | Hypershade**, then create a Lambert material from **Create | Maya | Surface | Lambert.**
2. Rename the material to something descriptive, such as `UV_Checker_MAT`, so it can be easily identified later.
3. Select the material and click the **checker** icon next to **Color**.

4. In the **Create Render Node** window, choose **2D Textures | File**. In the **File** attributes, click the **folder** icon next to **Image Name** and select the downloaded checker texture.
5. Next, select the model, right-click the Lambert material in the **Hypershade**, and select **Assign Material to Selection.**

Finally, enable texture display in the Viewport by selecting **Shading | Textured** or pressing 6. This setup allows you to evaluate UV direction and identify flipped shells or inconsistent UV flow.

Figure 5.11 – Example of a directional checker texture used to evaluate UV flow without external tools

4. Use the flow material to evaluate and correct the direction of your UV shells. The arrows displayed on the surface represent the UV flow direction. Adjust and rotate your UV shells so that the arrows follow a consistent and logical anatomical direction across the model.
5. If needed, you can use the **Orient Shells** tool to quickly align multiple UV shells. This tool can be found in **UV Toolkit | Arrange and Layout | Orient Shells**.
   Keep in mind that consistency does not always mean identical direction. In some areas, such as membranes, the flow may need to be reversed on one side to maintain a coherent directional flow across the surface.

Figure 5.12 – UV flow visualization showing consistent directional flow across different anatomical regions

Organizing the Multi-UDIM layout

After the UV shells have been validated and aligned, the layout can now be distributed across multiple UDIM tiles following a structured anatomical hierarchy:

1. Start distributing the UV shells across multiple UDIM tiles, beginning with the most important areas and expanding progressively across the model.

Figure 5.13 – Side view of the dragon showing the main UV cuts used to separate anatomical regions

2. Move the mouth interior into the **1002** UDIM tile, keeping it separate from the head. Continue isolating and placing regions step by step, organizing the UVs in a logical anatomical order.

   A practical approach is to distribute UDIMs starting from **1001** and moving forward following the anatomy of the creature, for example: head, mouth interior, neck, back, shoulders, front limbs, belly, hind legs, crest, membranes, and tail.

   This is not a strict rule, but maintaining a consistent and logical order will make your UV layout much easier to manage, especially when working with a large number of UDIMs.

   Figure 5.14 shows the UV layout after assigning a different Lambert material to the geometry associated with each UDIM row. This color coding provides a quick visual reference for identifying UDIM groups and verifying that related anatomical regions are organized consistently before continuing the workflow. Each row is assigned a different colored Lambert material to visually identify UDIM ranges (for example, 1001–1010, 1011–1020, and so on).

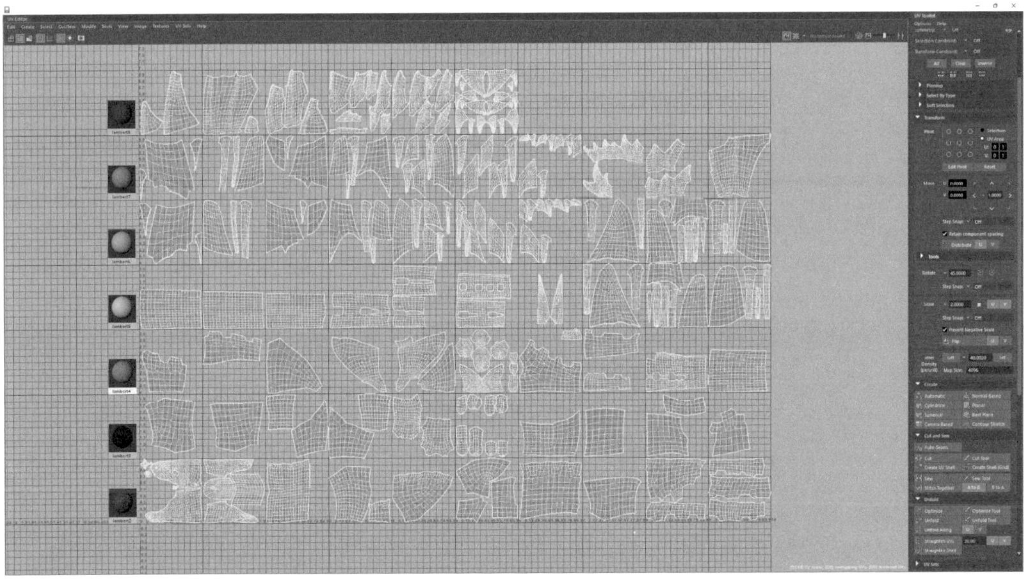

Figure 5.14 – UV layout organized across UDIMs, with regions grouped and aligned per row

To better visualize how the anatomical regions correspond to the UV layout, you can temporarily assign color-coded materials to different sections of the model, as shown in *Figure 5.15*:

Figure 5.15 – Color-coded model showing how each anatomical region is distributed across the UV layout

3. At this stage, take a moment to review some of the most critical seam areas across the model. Instead of focusing only on the global layout, zoom in on complex regions where UV decisions directly affect texture quality and deformation:
    - **Membranes**: Use the central edge loop that runs across the membrane as your primary separation line. This loop naturally divides the surface into two clean areas and should always be exploited to maintain a predictable and clean UV layout. Additionally, separate the spikes from the membrane surface. This allows you to isolate them easily during texturing, giving you more control when assigning materials, masks, or variations between hard and soft surfaces.

Figure 5.16 – Membrane UVs showing central loop separation

- **Mouth and lips:** Around the mouth, maintain a continuous edge loop along the lips to clearly separate the external skin from the inner mouth. This separation is essential to avoid stretching and to preserve clean transitions during texturing.

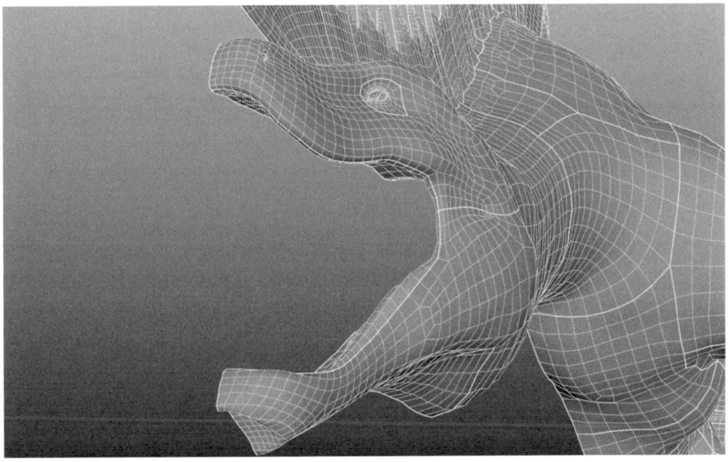

Figure 5.17 – Mouth UVs showing lip loop separation

- **Limbs and fingers:** Treat each finger as an individual element. Separate each finger into its own UV shell, and clearly divide the inner side of the palm from the outer side. Additionally, split each finger into top and bottom sections. This allows the UVs to unfold more evenly, reducing stretching on cylindrical forms and improving texture consistency across bending areas. This approach ensures better control during unfolding and results in cleaner, more predictable UV layouts, especially in deformation-heavy regions.

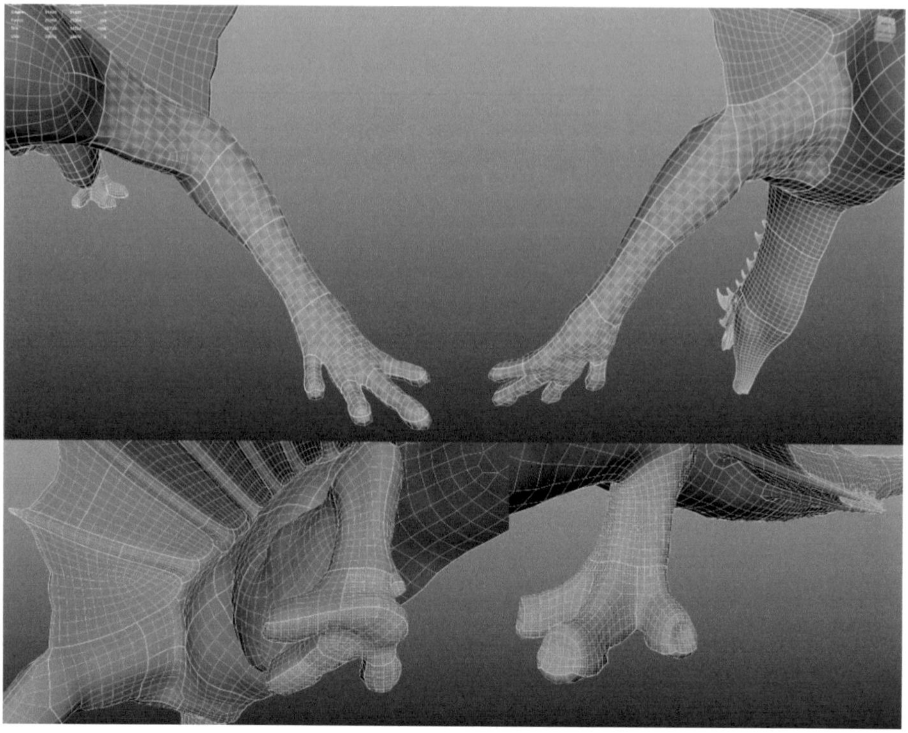

Figure 5.18 – Hand UVs with separated fingers and palm regions

These regions require more attention compared to broader surfaces, as mistakes here are much more visible in final renders.

> **Tip**
>
> If you are working on a machine with limited performance, try to keep your UV layout manageable. As a guideline, aim for around 8–10 UDIM tiles for half of the creature during the initial stages. In full production environments, the number of UDIMs can increase significantly depending on the level of detail required. For example, high-end cinematic assets may use dozens or even over a hundred UDIMs to achieve maximum texture resolution. The key is how efficiently you distribute them based on the importance of each area.

How it works...

In this workflow, the UV layout is built as a structured system rather than a simple flattening process. Every decision, from the initial cuts to the final UDIM distribution, is driven by the need to balance readability, deformation behavior, and production efficiency.

At the beginning of the process, we work only on half of the character. This is a standard production approach that allows us to speed up the workflow while maintaining perfect symmetry. By focusing on one side, we reduce the amount of work by half and ensure that all UV decisions remain consistent when the model is mirrored later.

Starting from the head is not accidental. The head contains the highest density of visual information and is typically the focal point of the asset. By extracting the texel density from this area, we establish a consistent reference that propagates across the entire UV set. In this case, `dragonCrest` was calibrated around a value of approximately 40, which already represents a high-quality result. In cinematic production, hero assets often reach values around 55, although this depends on multiple factors such as camera distance, shading requirements, and rendering constraints.

The use of **Cut** and **Sew** is fundamental to controlling how the surface behaves once unfolded. **Cut** defines where the mesh is allowed to relax, while **Sew**, literally "stitch," restores continuity between UV shells where needed. These operations are tools to manage tension across the UV layout. Incorrect cuts lead to stretching, while excessive continuity results in compression and unpredictable distortion.

As the UVs are separated, the process shifts from geometry to logic. Organizing the layout using an anatomical order allows the UVs to reflect the structure of the creature itself. This is important when working with multiple UDIM tiles, where a clear and predictable distribution simplifies not just the layout process, but also downstream tasks such as texturing, shading, and look development.

When distributing UVs across UDIM tiles, it is vital to understand that the logic differs depending on the type of asset. In hard surface or mechanical models, it is common to pack many small UV shells tightly into a single UDIM to maximize space efficiency. In contrast, when working on large organic creatures, each UDIM is often dedicated to fewer but significantly larger regions. This is because surface continuity, texture readability, and deformation quality take priority over packing density.

For creatures like `dragonCrest`, the goal is to assign space based on anatomical importance. Larger and more visible regions naturally occupy more UV space, even if this results in fewer shells per tile. A perfectly packed UV is not always a production-ready UV. In many cases, clarity and control are far more important than maximizing space usage, especially when dealing with high-resolution multi-UDIM assets.

Orientation plays a critical role in maintaining visual consistency. Directional checkers or flow-based materials allow you to evaluate how textures will behave across the surface. However, in this case, consistency does not mean uniformity — in areas such as membranes, the UV direction may need to be reversed on one side to preserve a continuous visual flow. Without this consideration, textures can appear broken or inconsistent during rendering.

The separation of critical regions such as membranes, mouth, and limbs is driven by both deformation and shading requirements. Membranes benefit from a central loop cut that allows the surface to unfold evenly, while separating the spikes provides greater flexibility during texturing and material assignment. Around the mouth, maintaining a clean loop along the lips ensures a clear distinction between inner and outer surfaces, preventing stretching and preserving sharp transitions.

Limbs and fingers require additional attention due to their cylindrical structure and deformation behavior. Each finger should be treated as an independent element, with a clear separation between the inner and outer sides of the hand. Splitting each finger into top and bottom sections allows the UVs to unfold more evenly, reducing twisting and ensuring better texture consistency in bending areas.

Although not mandatory, the introduction of **PolyRaven** highlights an important concept. Visualizing UV direction through flow-based materials provides immediate feedback on orientation issues that are otherwise difficult to detect. Even when using a simple directional checker, the goal remains the same: to ensure that UVs follow a coherent and predictable flow across the entire model.

Finally, the number of UDIMs is a direct consequence of the level of detail required. In high-end cinematic production, assets can reach very high UDIM counts to support extreme resolution. However, efficiency is determined by how UDIMs are organized and distributed. A well-structured layout will always outperform a dense but poorly organized one, avoiding unnecessary complexity and excessive computation times.

If you come from a game art background, this workflow may seem unusual. In real-time production, UVs are often packed as efficiently as possible to maximize texture usage and reduce memory consumption. Overlapping symmetrical parts, reusing UV space, and minimizing the number of texture sets are common optimization techniques. While these methods are highly effective for games, they are generally avoided in high-end VFX, where each anatomical region benefits from having its own unique texture space for maximum flexibility during texturing and look development.

Note

Avoid relying entirely on automatic layout tools for large projects. **Auto-packing** often breaks the logical organization of your UVs, making the layout harder to read and manage. Manual placement helps maintain a clear structure and keeps the UV layout predictable across multiple iterations.

Packing and ordering multi-UDIMs: Substance 3D Painter versus Mari

Once the UVs are unwrapped, the next step is to complete the model and prepare the UV layout for texturing. In this stage, we mirror the geometry to rebuild the full `dragonCrest`. After duplicating and mirroring the mesh, make sure to correctly merge the central vertices along the symmetry axis to avoid shading or UV inconsistencies. At this point, the UV layout must be adapted depending on the texturing software used in the pipeline.

Mari is a high-end 3D painting application widely used in VFX for texturing complex assets with large numbers of UDIMs. **Substance 3D Painter** is one of the most widely used texturing applications across games, animation, and VFX.

Mari supports both positive and negative UDIM space. This means that mirrored UV shells can remain flipped in negative space, allowing you to keep a clean separation between left and right sides while preserving identical UV topology and texel density. Substance 3D Painter, on the other hand, only supports positive UDIM space. Because of this, mirrored UVs cannot remain in negative space and must be repositioned into the positive grid. This often results in overlapping or mirrored shells occupying the same UDIM tile.

The purpose of this recipe is to understand how the same layout behaves differently depending on the software. You will complete the geometry, mirror the UVs, and observe two possible configurations: one optimized for Mari, with mirrored UVs kept in negative space, and one adapted for Substance 3D Painter, where all UVs are reorganized into the positive UDIM space.

Figure 5.19 shows a side-by-side comparison of the Mari UV layout with negative space and the Substance 3D Painter layout with mirrored positive UVs:

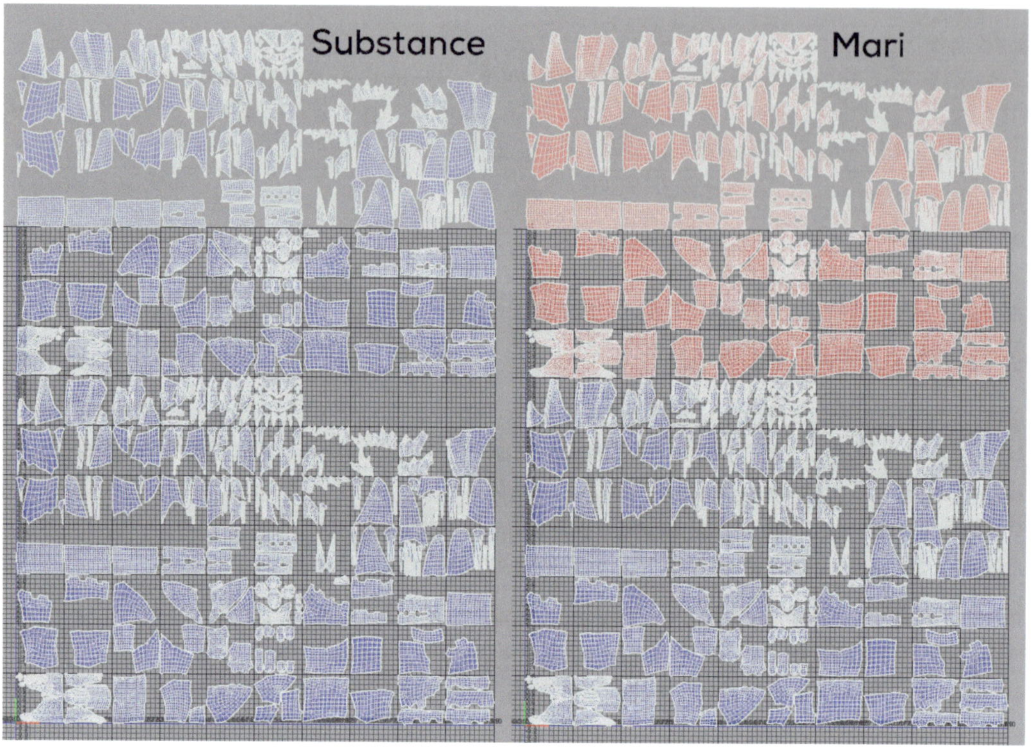

Figure 5.19 – Side-by-side comparison of the Mari and Substance 3D Painter layouts

Getting ready

Before starting, make sure you have access to the `dragonCrest` asset prepared for this recipe. You can find the `dragonCrest_retopology_uvset_v001` file provided in the `Chapter04_05` folder in the book's repository. To access the repository link, follow the steps in the *Download the example code/resource files* section in the *Preface*. Then, check the following:

- Ensure that the half `dragonCrest` model created in the previous recipe is set up correctly for mirroring.
- Verify that the central edge loop of the model is perfectly aligned, with all its vertices positioned at *X = 0*. This is essential to guarantee a clean and predictable symmetry when duplicating and merging the mesh.
- At this stage, make sure that only one half of the model is present in the scene.

- Confirm that the UVs on the left side are already fully unwrapped, organized, and validated, with a consistent texel density across all regions.
- Finally, make sure that the pivot of the asset is correctly positioned at the center of the Maya scene. This will allow you to mirror the geometry accurately without introducing offsets or misalignments.

How to do it...

In this recipe, we will complete the UV layout by mirroring the character and adapting it for different texturing workflows. We will start with the **Substance 3D Painter** setup, which is the most straightforward approach, and then expand the process to handle other cases.

Mirroring the character for the Substance 3D Painter workflow

The first stage focuses on rebuilding the full character using Maya's **Mirror** workflow while preparing the UV layout for Substance 3D Painter compatibility:

1. Start by selecting the main geometry of your asset. In this case, the *body* of `dragonCrest`. At this stage, make sure you are working with the half-character prepared in the previous steps, with clean UVs already organized on one side.
2. Once selected, go to **Mesh** | **Mirror** to duplicate the geometry across the central axis.

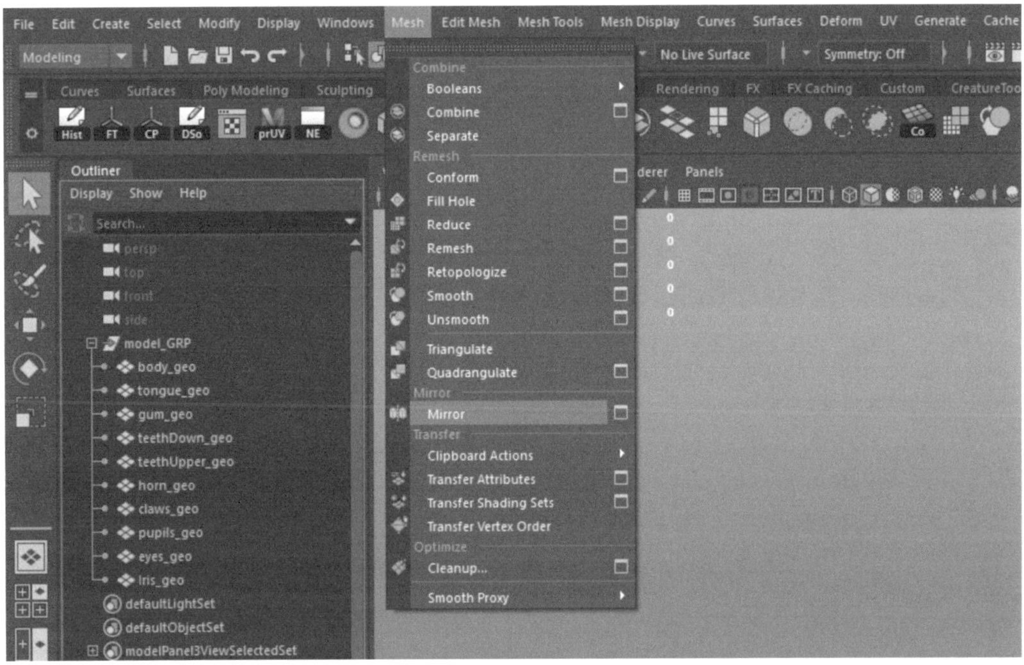

Figure 5.20 – Mirror tool accessed from the Mesh menu in Maya

3. After applying the **Mirror** operation, Maya will automatically generate a small option panel for the **polyMirror** node directly in the Viewport.
   If you accessed the **Mirror** tool without opening the option box, this panel must be adjusted manually.
4. Set the **Merge Threshold** to `0.001` to ensure that the vertices along the centerline are properly welded without creating gaps or overlaps. Then, set **Flip UVs** to **World U**. This is essential for the Substance 3D Painter workflow, as it preserves the correct UV orientation, ensuring that the UV normals remain correct (*blue*). The remaining settings should not require changes, but make sure they match the values shown here to avoid inconsistencies during mirroring.

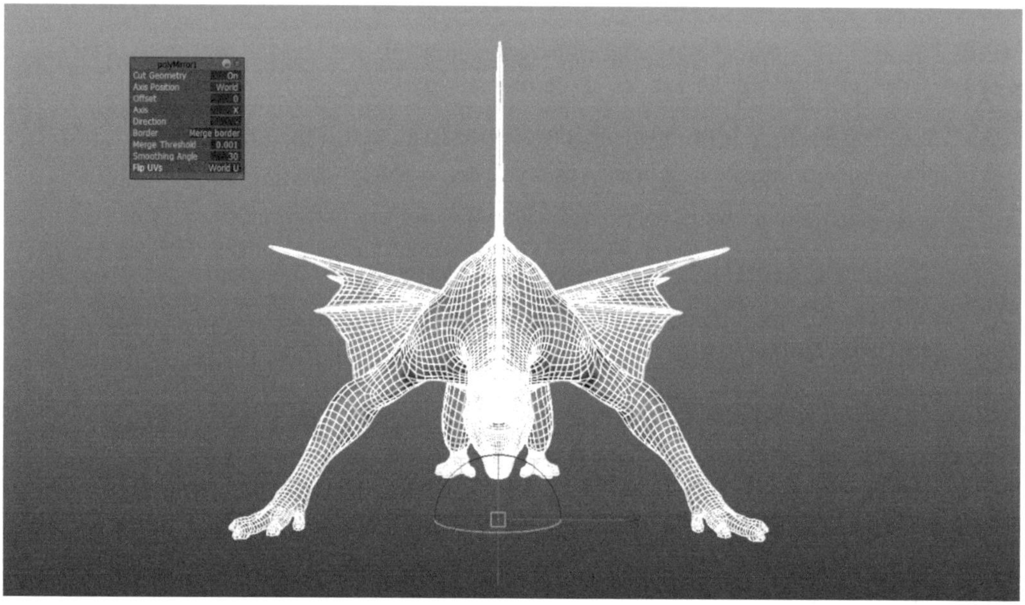

Figure 5.21 – polyMirror node settings showing Merge Threshold and Flip UVs configuration

5. After applying **Mirror** and merging the center vertices, your model should now be fully symmetrical. At this stage, take a moment to verify that the central seam is correctly welded by inspecting the geometry along the middle line. There should be no visible gaps or overlapping vertices.
6. Open the **UV Editor** to check the result. You should now see a perfectly mirrored UV layout: one side corresponds to the original UVs you created, while the mirrored side appears in the negative space along the *U* axis. This behavior is expected and confirms that the UVs have been correctly mirrored according to the current setup.

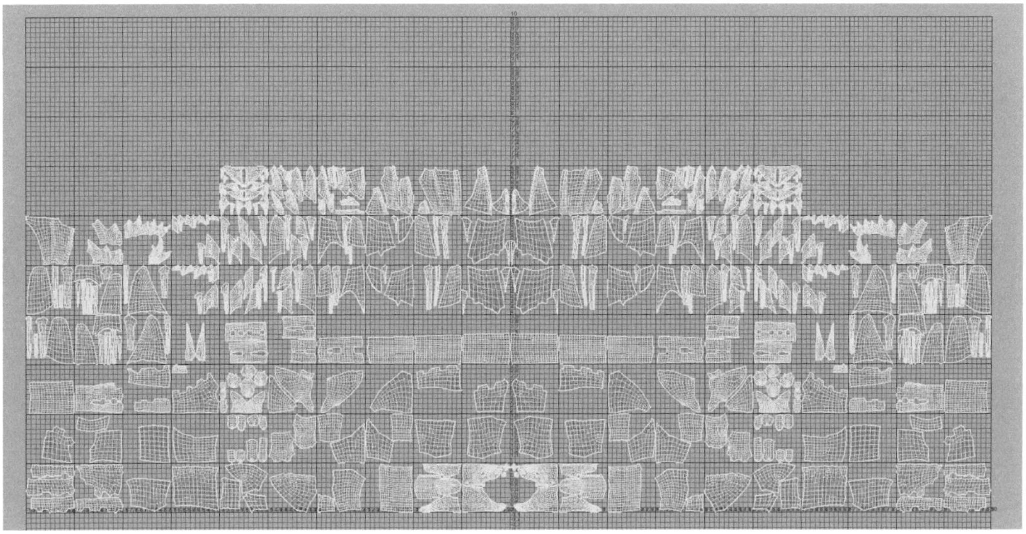

Figure 5.22 – Mirrored UV layout showing original shells and mirrored shells in negative U space

Tip

At this stage, you may notice that the mirrored UV shells remain separated along the center seam. For assets using a relatively small number of UDIMs, for example around 10 to 15 tiles, artists often sew this seam to create a continuous UV shell. On large VFX assets with many UDIMs, however, it is common practice to keep the seam open, making the layout easier to organize and individual anatomical regions easier to manage during texturing.

Reorganizing UVs into positive UDIM space

Once the mirrored UVs have been generated, the next step is to reposition the negative-space shells into the positive UDIM grid required by Substance 3D Painter:

1. In the **UV Editor**, select the entire column of UV shells located in the negative space along the *U* axis (U-1). This corresponds to the mirrored side of the model generated during the **Mirror** operation.
2. Use a **drag selection** to select all the UV shells on the negative side. Be careful to include the entire vertical column while avoiding any shells in the positive space. Pay close attention to your selection and make sure you are selecting *only the UDIMs in the U-1 space*, without accidentally including tiles from the positive range. This step is

critical to avoid breaking the UV layout in the next operation. This selection will be used in the next step to reorganize the layout for the Substance 3D Painter workflow.

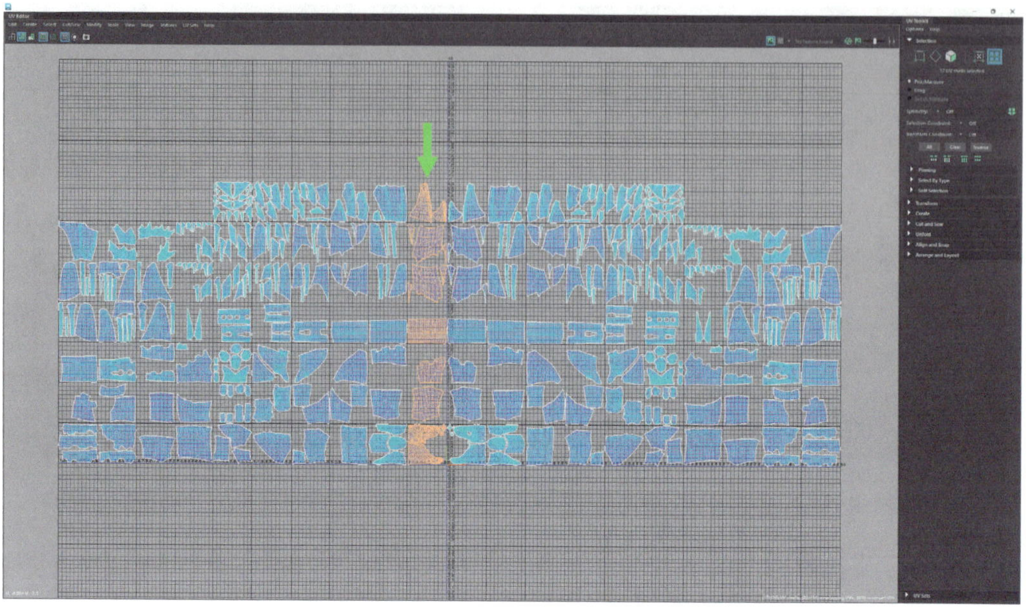

Figure 5.23 – Selection of UV shells in the negative U-1 space representing the mirrored side of the model

3. With the negative U-1 column still selected, move the entire set of UV shells into the positive space. Translate the selection along the *U* axis and position it in the **U+1** column, aligning it with the corresponding shells from the original side. To do this, go to the **UV Editor** and locate the **UV Toolkit** panel on the right side.
4. Inside the **UV Toolkit**, open the **Transform** section, where you can directly control the translation values. You can move the UVs either by manually adjusting the **Transform** values or by using the *arrow* buttons, which act as a quick shortcut for incremental movement.

Before moving the UVs, make sure that the increment value is set to `1.0000`. The increment value is set to `1.0000` to ensure precise movement of one tile at a time when repositioning UVs from negative to positive space.

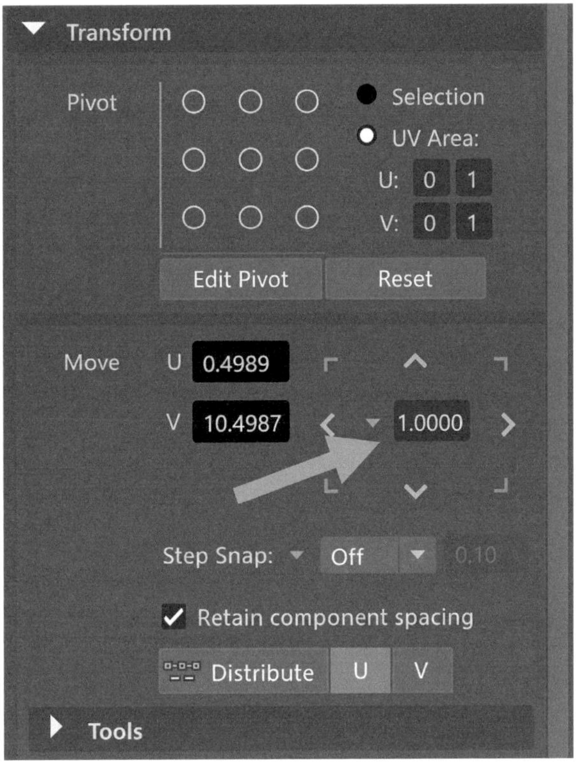

Figure 5.24 – UV Toolkit Transform used to translate UV shells across UDIM tiles

This value is often set to **0.1** by default, which is not suitable for UDIM-based workflows. Setting it to 1 ensures that each step moves the UV shells exactly one tile, allowing precise placement from negative to positive space.

5. Move the UV shells along the *U* axis until they are perfectly aligned with the original layout, maintaining continuity across the surface.

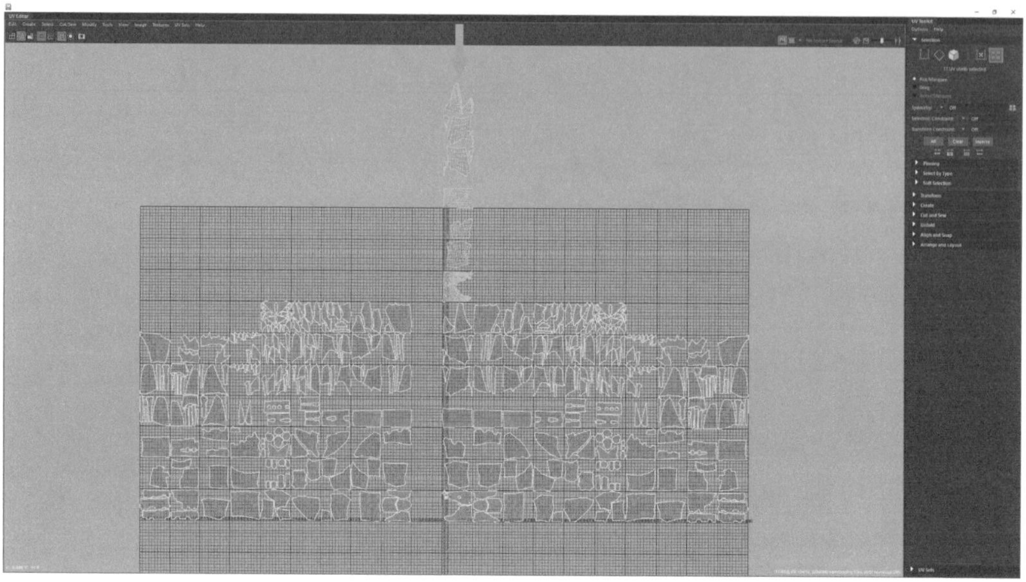

Figure 5.25 – UV shells moved from U-1 to U+1, aligned with the original layout

6. Once the first UV column has been moved from negative to positive space, repeat the same operation across all remaining columns. Follow a consistent rule: each negative column must be moved to its corresponding positive tile, for example U-2 to U+2, U-3 to U+3, and so on.

   Work progressively from the center outward, selecting one column at a time and making sure you isolate only the correct UDIM range. Maintain alignment and spacing with the original layout to preserve continuity across the surface.

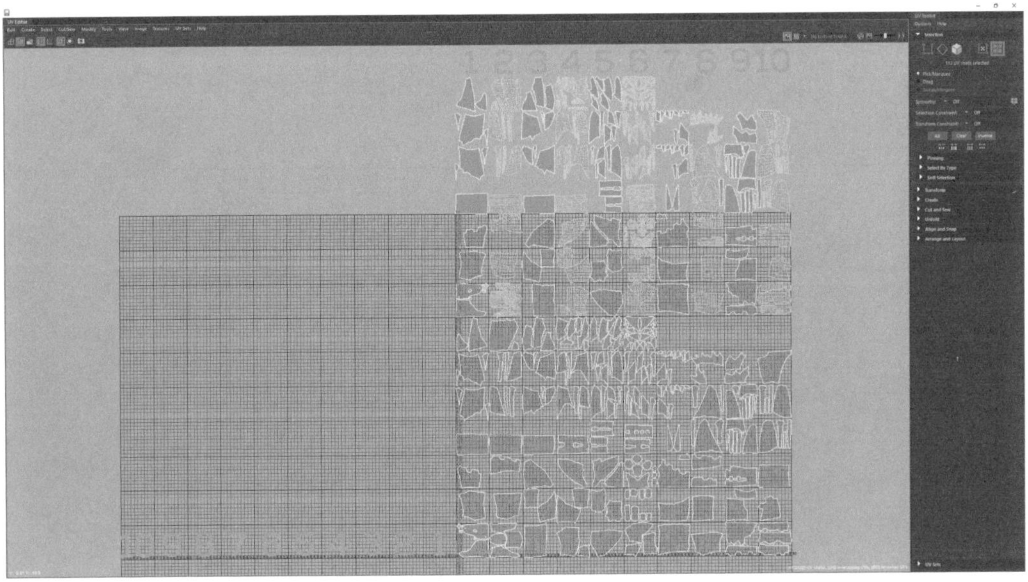

Figure 5.26 – UV layout diagram showing the repositioning of negative UDIM columns into their corresponding positive tiles

Building the Mari-compatible UV layout

Unlike Substance 3D Painter, Mari supports negative UDIM space, allowing mirrored UVs to remain separated rather than overlapping inside the same tiles:

1. Repeat the same process described in *step 1* of the *Mirroring the character for the Substance 3D Painter* section, starting again from the clean half-character version of the asset, making sure the central edge loop is perfectly aligned at *X = 0*. This time, instead of using **Mirror**, go to **Edit | Duplicate Special** and open the option box using the small square next to the command.
2. In the settings, set the first value of the **Scale** to `-1` to mirror the geometry along the *X* axis.
3. Finally, press **Apply** to create the mirrored side of the model.

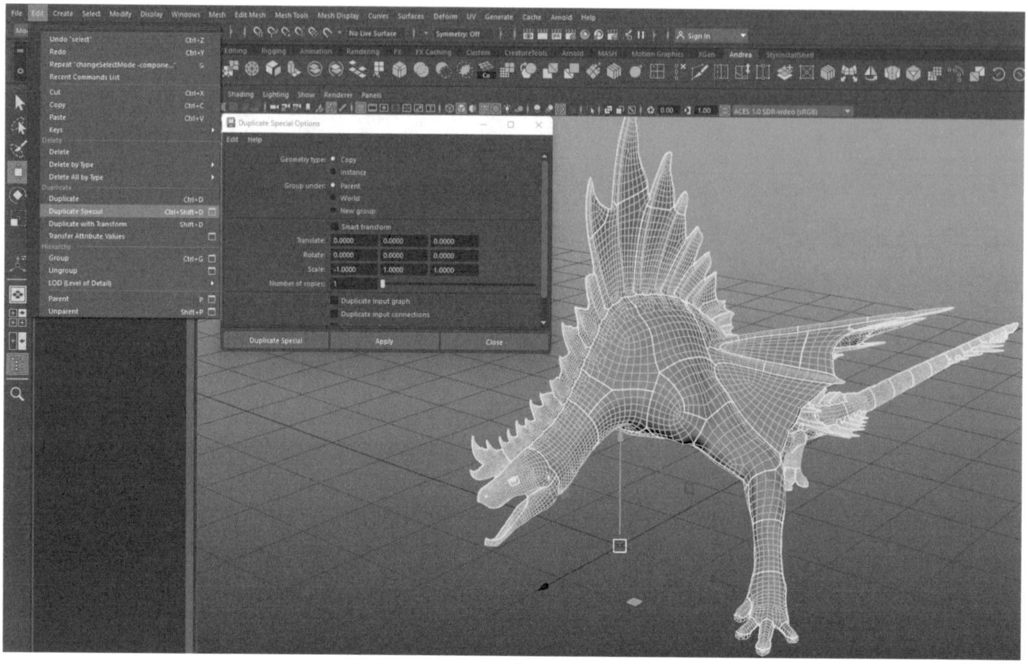

Figure 5.27 – Duplicate Special options used to mirror the geometry along the X axis

4. After creating the mirrored side, select the duplicated half of the model and clean the geometry before proceeding. Go to **Edit** | **Delete by Type** | **History** to remove the construction history.
   This ensures that no unnecessary nodes remain in the scene, keeping the file clean and stable.

5. Then go to **Modify** | **Freeze Transformations** to reset all transform values while preserving the current position of the geometry. This step is essential to avoid issues later in the pipeline, especially when exporting or working with other departments.
6. With this, the UVs of the duplicated half remain in the same position but become flipped, showing a negative UV orientation. Select all the UV shells of this duplicated side, then prepare to reposition them into a clean and organized area of the UV layout. Before moving them, take a moment to inspect the original half and identify where the current UDIM layout ends. This will help you understand which row is free and safe to use. Once identified, move the selected UV shells into an empty UDIM row above the existing layout, keeping the structure clean and avoiding overlaps.

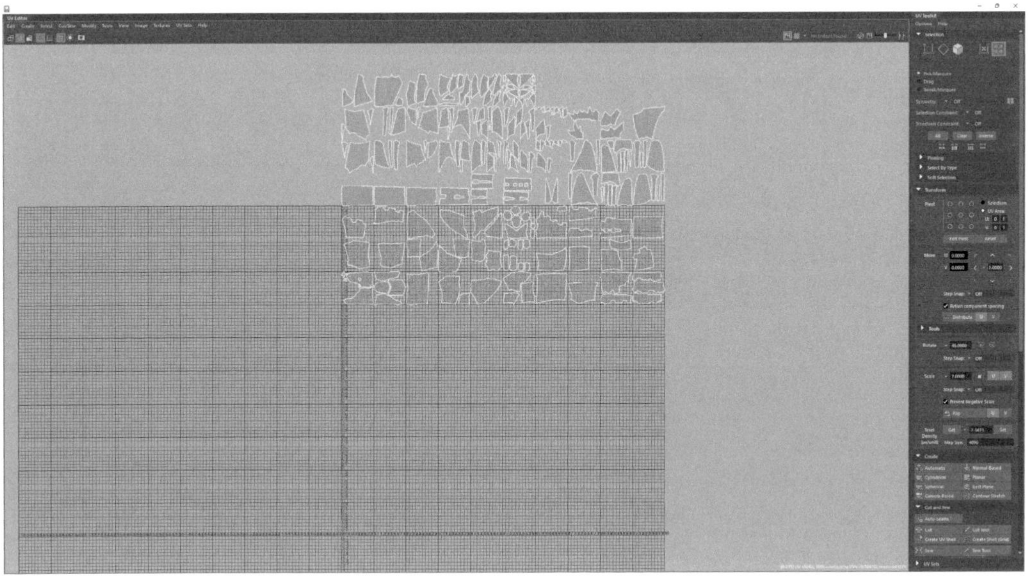

Figure 5.28 – Mirrored UV shells moved into a new UDIM row above the original layout

7. Now, select both halves of the model and combine them into a single object. Go to **Mesh** | **Combine** to merge the selected meshes into one unified geometry.
8. Once combined, merge the vertices along the central seam. Go to **Edit Mesh** | **Merge** to open the merge options. In the settings, set the **Distance Threshold** value to `0.0001`, then press *Enter*. This ensures that only the vertices along the centerline are welded together without affecting other parts of the mesh.
9. After merging, clean the geometry by going to **Edit** | **Delete by Type** | **History**, then apply **Modify** | **Freeze Transformations** to reset all transform values. Finally, reposition the pivot to the center of the Maya world.
10. At this stage, you should now have a fully combined asset with a clean and consistent UV layout ready for Mari. Open the **UV Editor** and carefully inspect the entire layout. Make sure that all UV shells are correctly positioned, with no overlaps or misaligned areas, and that both sides of the model are clearly separated across positive and negative UDIM space.

    Take a moment to verify that the layout remains readable and logically organized, as this will directly impact the efficiency of the texturing process.

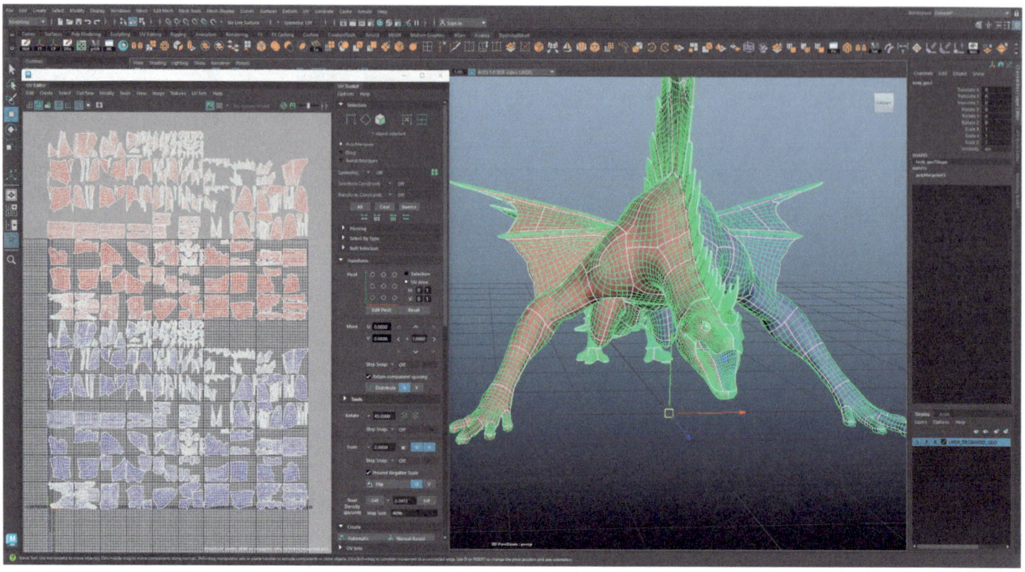

Figure 5.29 – Final UV layout prepared for Mari

Tip

Sometimes, after combining multiple meshes, you may encounter an issue where some or all UV coordinates are lost. This can happen due to inconsistencies in the mesh data or vertex order.

If this occurs, a reliable workaround is to export each object individually as an OBJ file, then reimport them into Maya and repeat the combine operation.

If the issue still persists, export the meshes again as OBJ, open them in another software such as ZBrush, and re-export them once more as OBJ. Then import them back into Maya and repeat the process.

This extra step usually rebuilds the mesh data correctly and prevents UVs from disappearing after the geometry is combined.

How it works...

This workflow is built around a key production principle: working on half of the character allows you to maintain full control over topology, UVs, and symmetry while reducing complexity during the most critical stages of the process. By keeping the central edge loop perfectly aligned at $X = 0$, you ensure that every operation performed on one side can be mirrored or duplicated in a predictable and clean way when rebuilding the full model.

The difference between the Substance 3D Painter and Mari workflows starts from how symmetry is handled. In the Substance 3D Painter approach, the mesh is mirrored directly using the **Mirror** tool, which rebuilds the full model while keeping everything inside positive UV space. This is necessary because Substance 3D Painter only reads positive UDIM coordinates. As a result, both sides of the model occupy the same UDIM tiles, and one side appears flipped. This is not an error, but an expected behavior required to maintain compatibility with the software.

In contrast, the Mari workflow gives you more flexibility. Instead of relying on a direct mirror, the model is duplicated using **Duplicate Special** with a negative scale on the *X* axis. This allows you to rebuild the second half of the model while preserving UV separation. The mirrored side initially exists in negative UV space, which is fully supported by Mari. This approach keeps both halves visually separated and avoids overlapping shells, making the layout easier to read and debug in complex assets.

The process of moving UVs from negative to positive space is not just a technical requirement, but a way to maintain a clear and logical UDIM structure. By reorganizing each column step by step, from negative to positive values, you ensure that every UDIM tile follows a consistent order. This becomes essential when working on large creatures, where the number of UDIMs can grow significantly and visual clarity directly impacts production efficiency.

Unlike hard surface assets or smaller props, where packing efficiency is often the priority, organic creatures require a different mindset. In this case, UVs are not only about optimizing space, but about maintaining a readable structure that follows the anatomy of the model. Each region is placed intentionally, even if it means leaving unused space. This is because the goal is to simplify texturing, look development, and debugging later in the pipeline.

This workflow demonstrates how UV layout decisions are not only technical, but also driven by the requirements of the target pipeline. By controlling symmetry, UDIM distribution, and UV orientation manually, you ensure that the asset remains clean, predictable, and adaptable across different texturing workflows. Maintaining a logical structure in your UVs allows you to scale the asset efficiently, especially when dealing with complex creatures where clarity and control are more important than pure space optimization.

UVs for secondary elements: eyes, claws, teeth, gums, tongue

These elements do not require rebuilding the full workflow used for the main body. The same tools are used, but the approach is simplified and driven by the type of geometry.

For hard surface-like elements such as claws and teeth, the goal is to keep clean cuts and readable shapes. In most cases, a single strategic cut is enough to unfold the geometry correctly while minimizing distortion. When organizing these elements in the UV layout, you can either place them manually in a clean and logical order or use tools such as **PolyRaven** to help align and distribute them more efficiently. Keeping a clear order is important to maintain readability, especially when dealing with multiple small pieces.

For softer elements like gums and tongue, the approach remains closer to organic surfaces, but without the same level of complexity required for the main body. The focus is on maintaining clean transitions and avoiding stretching in deformation areas. The eyes follow a simpler logic, where the geometry is typically split into two main parts, separating the visible front area from the rest of the structure to ensure predictable shading and texture projection.

Finally, all these secondary elements are placed sequentially after the last UDIM used for the main body, or organized in a new row directly above it, maintaining a consistent and easy-to-read structure across the entire UV layout. This is shown in *Figure 5.30* as follows:

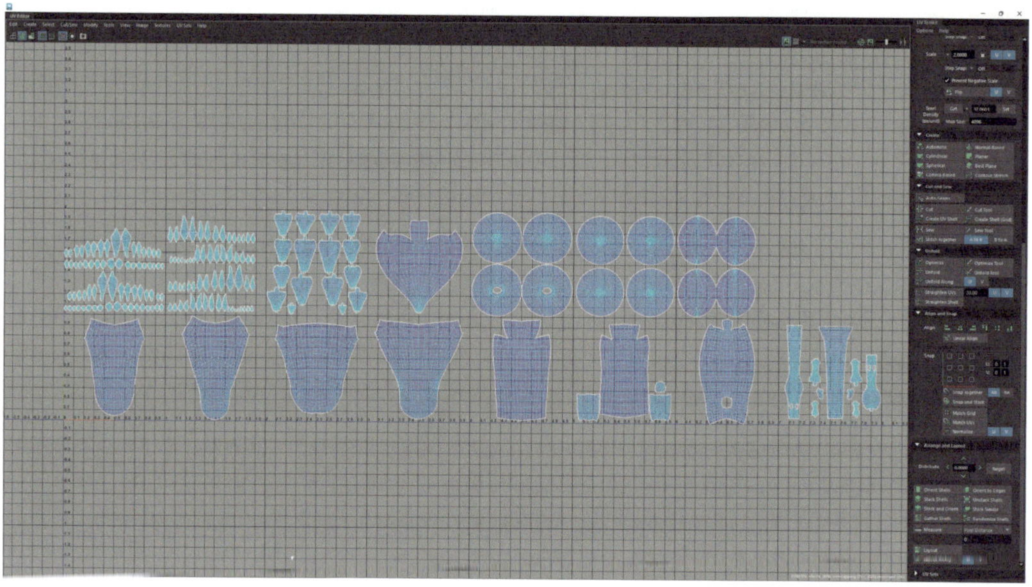

Figure 5.30 – Final UV layout showing secondary elements organized after the main UDIM sequence

Getting ready

This setup follows the same logic described in the *Packing and ordering multi-UDIMs: Substance 3D Painter versus Mari* recipe. So you can refer back to the *Getting ready* section of that recipe for a complete explanation of symmetry preparation and pivot alignment.

How to do it...

The tongue is a relatively simple organic element, but it still requires careful UV planning to avoid stretching, especially in thin areas and branching shapes. The goal is to create a clean and predictable layout that preserves volume and supports smooth texture projection.

Unlike harder elements, here we focus more on deformation and surface continuity rather than strict geometric separation.

1. Start by selecting the tongue geometry and analyzing where stretching is most likely to occur. Focus on areas where the shape changes direction or thickness, such as thin tips, branching extensions, and transition zones between larger and smaller volumes. These regions tend to compress or expand during the **Unfold** process.

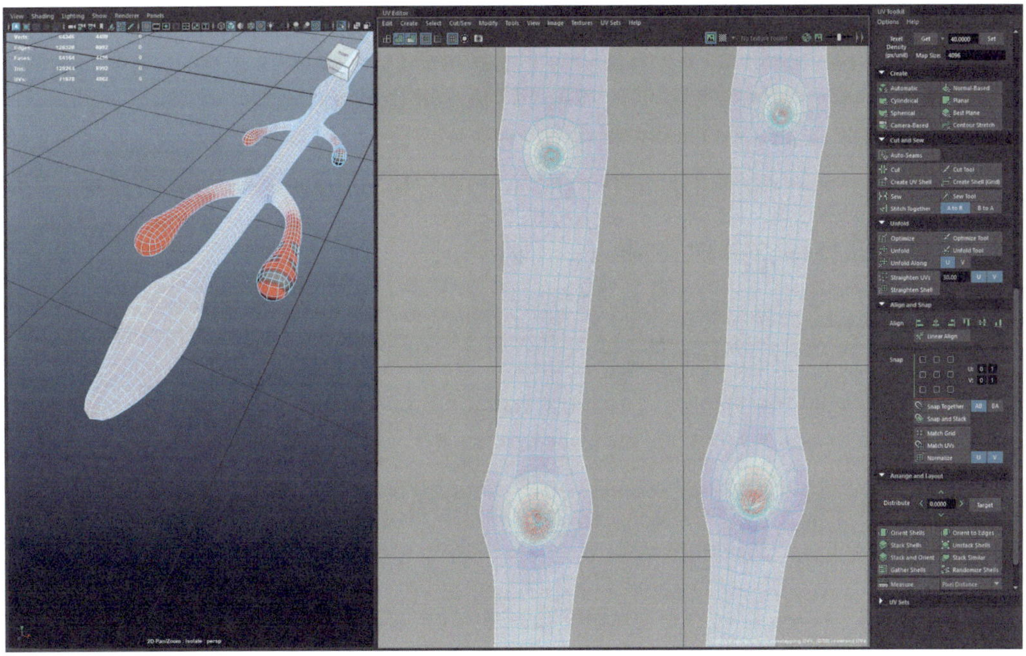

Figure 5.31 – Example of an intentionally incorrect UV layout on the tongue, visualized using UV distortion. The highlighted areas reveal stretching and compression, helping identify where additional cuts and better UV distribution are required

2. To make this analysis more reliable, apply a temporary checker texture in the Viewport. Distorted or elongated squares clearly indicate where UV stretching will happen, helping you decide where to place your cuts more accurately.

> **Tip**
>
> For more standard tongue shapes, the process is usually much simpler. In most cases, you can select the central edge loop that separates the upper and lower parts of the tongue and use it to split the geometry into two shells. After that, apply an **Unfold** and place both shells vertically in the UV space. This approach keeps the layout clean, predictable, and easy to manage, especially for simpler anatomical structures.

3. As discussed earlier in the recipe, start by selecting the tongue and creating a base UV layout using either **UV Toolkit** | **Unfold** | **Unfold (Normal Based)** or a simple **Planar** projection to establish an initial distribution.
4. Once you have a readable starting point, move to the **UV Toolkit**, open the **Texel Density** section, and use **Get** to sample the texel density from an existing part of the creature. Then apply it to the tongue using **Set**.

   This step allows you to quickly estimate how much UV space the tongue will require and how many UDIMs might be needed. It is important that the texel density value remains consistent with the rest of the creature, or at least very close, to ensure uniform texture resolution across the asset. Slight variations are acceptable, but large differences will result in visible inconsistencies during texturing and rendering.

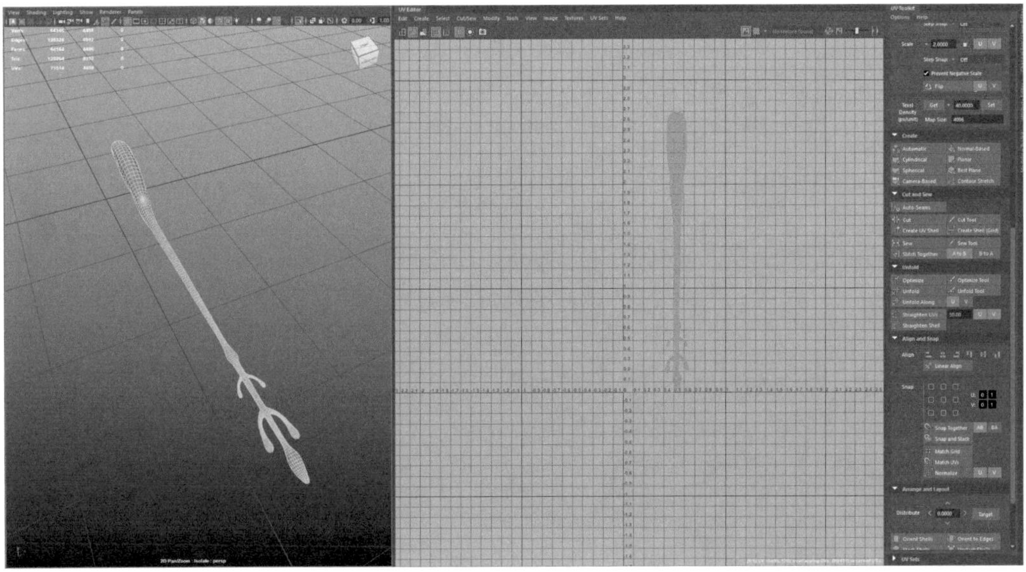

Figure 5.32 – Initial UV projection applied to the tongue, showing a first distribution used to evaluate texel density and estimate UDIM space before refining the layout

5. In this case, divide the tongue horizontally into three main sections using **Cut** inside the **UV Editor**. Select the edges where you want to separate the geometry, then apply **UV Toolkit** | **Cut and Sew** | **Cut** to create clean UV splits.
   This approach allows you to better distribute the UVs and ensures higher resolution during the texturing and rendering stages. By breaking the geometry into controlled segments, you reduce stretching and gain more control over how details will be painted across the surface.

6. Once the UV shells are properly unfolded, start organizing them in a clean and precise way inside the UDIM. Try to maintain a logical orientation across all pieces. In this case, the layout is arranged from top to bottom, following a consistent directional flow that makes the UVs easier to read and manage.
   While placing the shells, aim to keep them as symmetrical as possible within the UDIM when it makes sense. This helps maintain visual consistency and can simplify texture painting later on. To improve alignment, you can use grid snapping by holding *X* while moving the shells and adjust their position using the pivot to place them accurately.

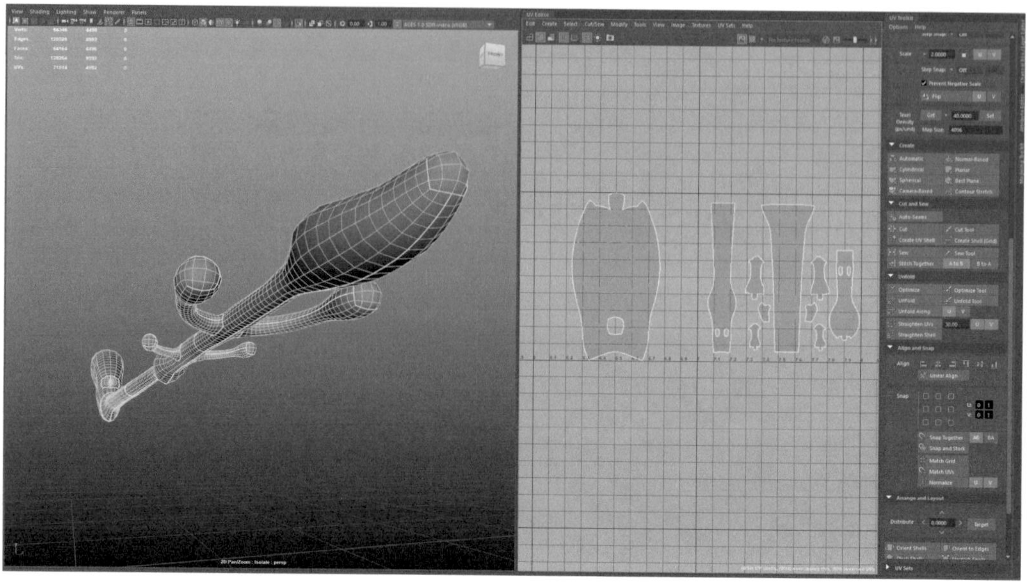

Figure 5.33 – Seam placement on the tongue geometry, showing cuts positioned in low-visibility areas to maximize UV opening while minimizing distortion during the unfold process

7. Apply the same logic to the gums, focusing on clean cuts, minimal distortion, and a readable UV layout. Since the structure is simpler, the goal is to keep the shells as open and organized as possible without overcomplicating the process.
   While at this stage, identify areas of the gums that will never be visible in the final render, especially regions deeply hidden inside the mouth. For these parts, you have different options depending on your production needs. You can delete the faces entirely to optimize the geometry, or remove their UVs if they are not needed for texturing. A more flexible approach is to keep them and scale their UV shells down significantly, moving them into an unused area of the UDIM. This allows you to preserve the geometry for potential future use, such as breakdowns or close-up shots, while minimizing their impact on UV space and texture resolution.

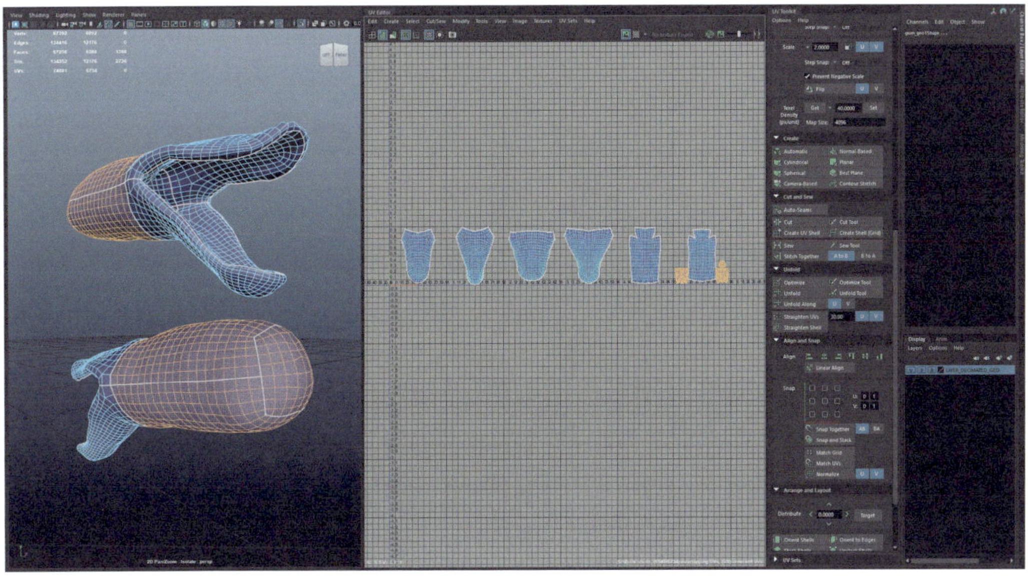

Figure 5.34 – Identification of hidden gum areas and corresponding UV shells, highlighting regions that can be optimized by scaling down or relocating to unused UDIM space without affecting the final render

8. Apply the same logic to the eyes. Start by creating a central cut along the main diameter loop to properly open the UV shell, then use **Unfold** from the **UV Toolkit** to relax the geometry.

   A critical aspect at this stage is the orientation of the UVs. When working with circular or spherical shapes, the unfold process often breaks the original spatial correspondence between the 3D model and the UV layout. As a result, the top area in UV space may no longer match the top area in 3D space. To correct this, manually identify *one or two reference polygons* in the 3D view and locate their corresponding position in the **UV Editor**. Then rotate the UV shell until the orientation matches the original 3D space. Once aligned, organize the shells cleanly and consistently within the UDIM.

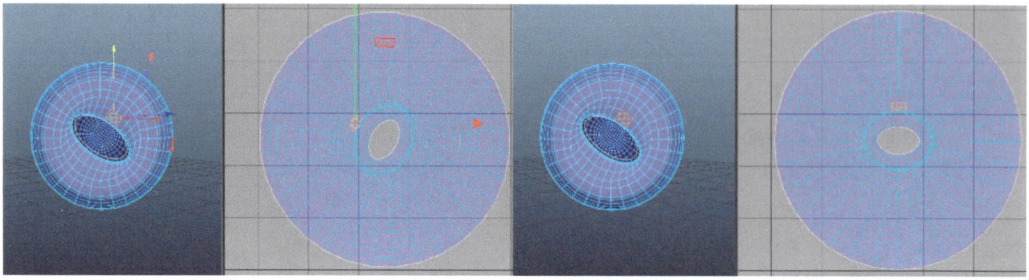

Figure 5.35 – Eye UV orientation before and after correction, showing how the initial unfold breaks the spatial alignment and how manual rotation restores a coherent correspondence with the 3D model

9. Once all the UVs are properly unwrapped and validated, you can mirror the model to complete the full geometry. Follow the same approach explained in the previous recipe, *Packing and ordering multi-UDIMs: Substance 3D Painter versus Mari*. Select the geometry and use **Edit | Duplicate Special**.
10. Open the option box and set the **Scale X** value to `-1`, then press **Apply** to generate the mirrored side. This ensures a perfectly symmetrical result while preserving the UV layout built on one half of the model.
11. After mirroring, you may notice that the UVs of the duplicated side are placed in negative space and appear flipped. If needed, you can correct their orientation directly in the **UV Editor**. Select the UV shells and use **UV Toolkit | Transform | Flip U** to invert them along the *U* axis and restore a consistent orientation.

Figure 5.36 – UV Toolkit Transform panel showing the Flip U option used to correct the orientation of mirrored UV shells by inverting them along the U axis

12. For the iris, eye, and pupil, a different approach can be used. Since these are smaller elements but extremely important for the final result, you can significantly increase their texel density. The human eye is naturally drawn to the eyes of a character, so it is

worth dedicating more texture resolution to these areas. Instead of following a strict texel density value, you can take advantage of the available UDIM space and scale these UV shells to occupy as much space as needed. This allows you to achieve sharper details and better control during texturing, especially for close-up shots where the eye becomes the focal point.

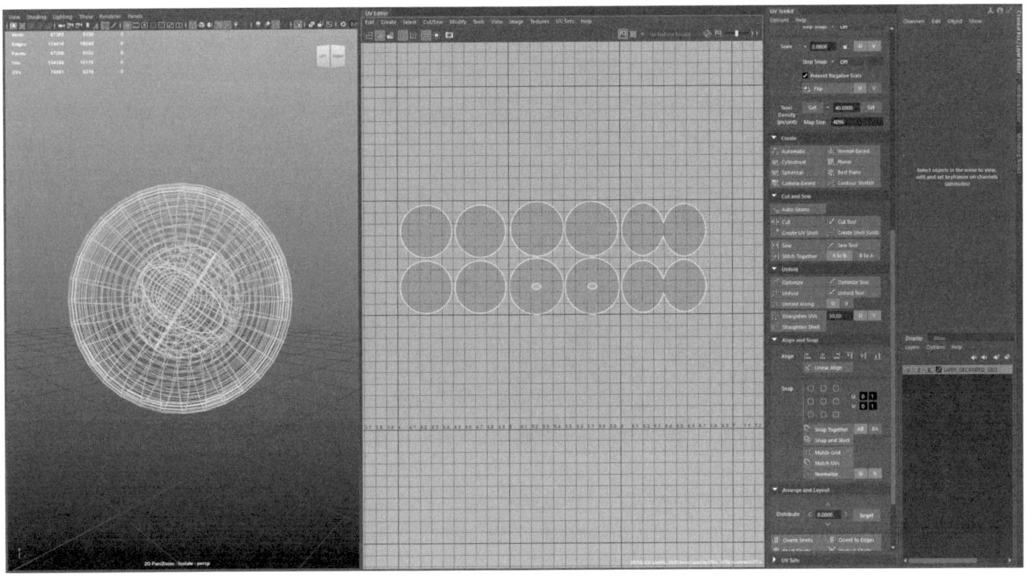

Figure 5.37 – UV layout showing increased texel density for iris, eye, and pupil by maximizing UDIM space

13. For teeth and claws, there are two valid approaches to create clean UVs (explained below). In this example, both methods are shown, but you are free to choose the one that best fits your asset and topology:

    - The *first approach*, used for the two teeth on the left, is to split the geometry in half. This is done by creating a central cut, then unfolding the two sides separately and placing them next to each other in a straight and readable layout. This method is simple and works well for most organic shapes.
    - The *second approach*, used for the claw, relies on a more structured topology. Since the shape behaves similarly to a simplified box, you can create a single UV shell by cutting along the underside and opening the geometry across three sides, leaving the two end caps connected. This allows you to keep the UV in one piece while minimizing seams and distortion.

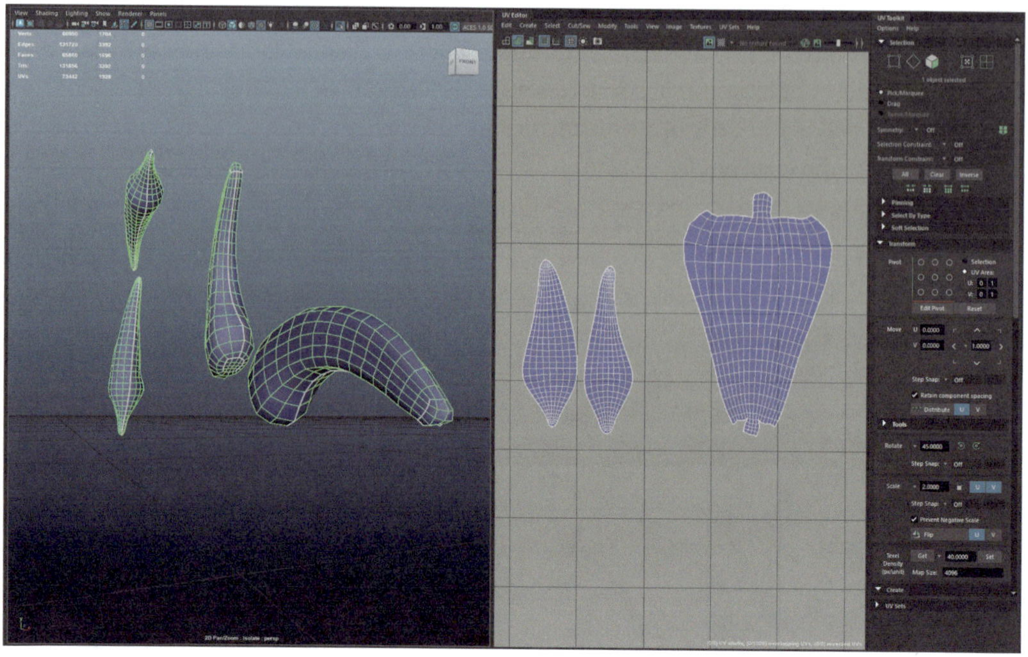

Figure 5.38 – Comparison between two UV approaches for teeth and claws: split shells versus single-piece unfolding based on topology

14. Finally, organize all teeth and claws inside the UV space cleanly and consistently. In this case, the layout follows a production-driven logic: start from the molars and progressively place each tooth next to the previous one, moving from left to right. This creates a clear visual sequence that mirrors the natural order of the teeth. While not strictly required, this approach becomes extremely useful in production, as it allows texture artists to quickly identify and isolate each element, making painting, masking, and lookdev adjustments faster and more predictable.

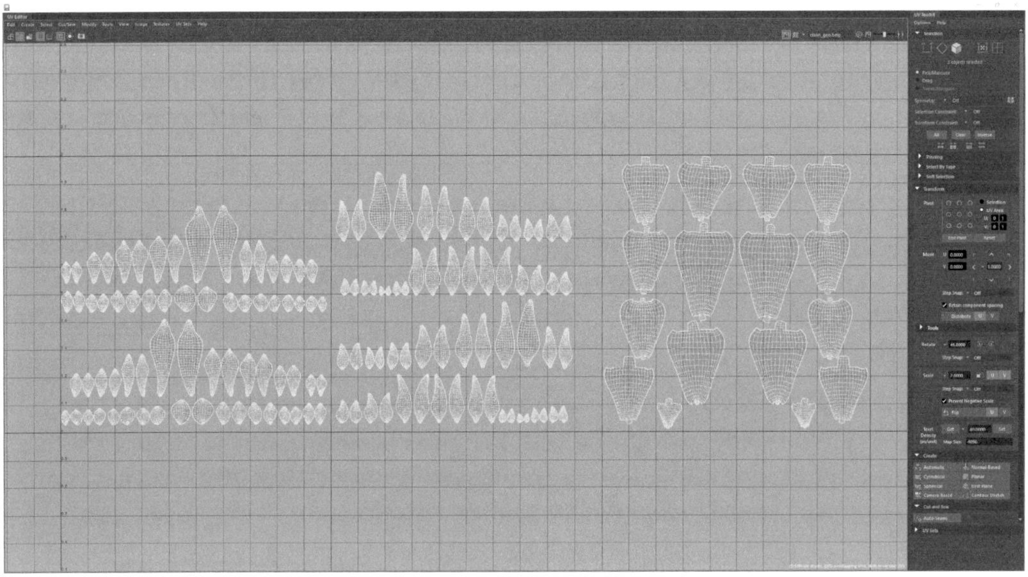

Figure 5.39 – Teeth and claws UVs arranged from molars to smaller teeth, ordered left to right to create a clear and production-friendly layout

How it works...

In this exercise, the UV workflow is driven more by practical readability and control rather than strict uniform rules. The goal is not to enforce perfect consistency, but to adapt the layout based on the importance and behavior of each element.

The first key concept is identifying and controlling stretching. In the process of intentionally creating a distorted UV layout and analyzing it with the UV distortion visualization, it becomes clear where the geometry fails to unfold correctly. Thin tips, branching areas, and transition zones tend to stretch or compress, and these are the areas where seams must be placed more carefully. This approach shifts the workflow from guessing to visually driven decisions.

For organic elements such as the tongue and gums, the priority is to keep the UV shells as clean and continuous as possible. Instead of overcutting the geometry, strategic seams are used to allow the surface to open naturally while preserving volume. At the same time, hidden areas inside the mouth can be optimized by reducing their UV size or moving them away, allowing more space for visible regions.

Circular elements like the eye introduce a different type of problem. When unfolded, they lose their original spatial orientation. This is why manual correction is necessary. By selecting reference polygons in 3D space and matching them in the **UV Editor**, the shell can be rotated back into a coherent orientation. This ensures that what is "up" in 3D remains consistent in UV space, which is essential for predictable texturing.

Another important aspect in this workflow is the flexible use of UV space. Instead of strictly matching texel density across all elements, smaller but visually important parts such as the eyes, teeth, and claws are intentionally scaled to occupy more UDIM space. This allows for sharper details and better control during texturing, especially in areas that naturally draw the viewer's attention.

The mirroring process follows a production-friendly approach. By working on half of the model and using **Edit | Duplicate Special** with a negative **Scale X** value, the geometry is duplicated while preserving the UV layout. Any flipped UVs generated in negative space can then be corrected using **Flip U** inside the **UV Toolkit**, restoring a consistent orientation.

Finally, the organization of UV shells is based on production logic rather than technical necessity. Elements such as teeth are arranged in a clear sequence starting from the molars and progressively moving to smaller teeth. This structured layout does not impact rendering directly, but greatly improves usability, allowing texture artists to quickly identify, isolate, and work on specific parts of the asset.

Fixing or updating UDIMs without losing work in ZBrush

In production, it is very common to discover UV issues after most of the sculpting and detailing work is already completed. A misplaced UDIM tile, flipped UV shells, or an inconsistent layout can affect displacement maps, texture projection, and overall shading quality. Even though these situations are common, many artists are not fully confident about how to handle them once the model is already structured with subdivision levels and sculpted details.

Figure 5.40 shows an example of UV overlapping, which is one of the most common issues in production. In this, multiple parts of the mesh share the same UV space, causing repeated or incorrect texture projection:

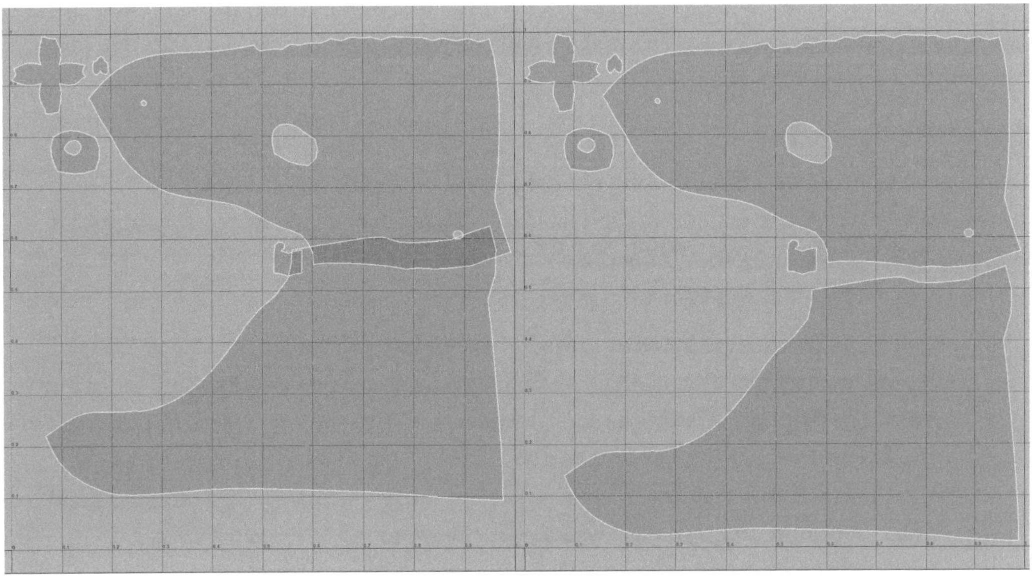

Figure 5.40 – Example of UV overlapping

The goal of this recipe is to show a clear and reliable workflow to update UVs in Maya and re-import them into ZBrush while keeping full consistency with the existing sculpt. The focus is on understanding how to approach these changes in a controlled and predictable way.

In this recipe, we will use the main body SubTool of the dragon, where a UDIM layout needs to be adjusted when the sculpt is already in an advanced stage. Even though the example focuses on the body SubTool, the same workflow can be applied to any part of the asset. You will learn how to maintain vertex order during export and import, how to reproject details when needed, and how to validate the updated UDIM layout before moving forward to texturing.

By understanding this process, you gain the confidence to perform late-stage UV changes in a clean and structured way. This is a critical production skill, especially when working under tight deadlines and iterative feedback.

Getting ready

For this recipe, make sure you are using the `dragonCrest` model after completing the retopology recipes in *Chapter 4* and the detailing recipes in *Chapter 6*.

At the same time, open the corresponding Maya file of the same asset, which will be used to inspect and update the UV layout. This recipe assumes that both files are aligned and represent the same version of the model.

If you have not completed these chapters yet, I recommend doing so before continuing, as this recipe assumes the model already contains a finished retopology, multiple subdivision levels, and the final sculpted details.

How to do it...

To repair or update UVs without losing sculpted detail, you will work between ZBrush and Maya, making sure vertex order remains consistent during export and import. This process allows you to rebuild or correct UDIMs safely while keeping every subdivision and fine sculpt intact. Now, follow these steps:

1. Start in ZBrush and go to the lowest subdivision level of your sculpt. From the **Tool | Export** menu, export the mesh as an OBJ. If you want to preserve SubTool grouping, enable the **Grp** option before export. If you export with the **Grp** option enabled, make sure to import the OBJ into Maya as a single mesh. Otherwise, the model may be imported as multiple separate meshes, making the UV editing process more difficult. This low-resolution mesh will serve as your reference for UV repair in Maya.

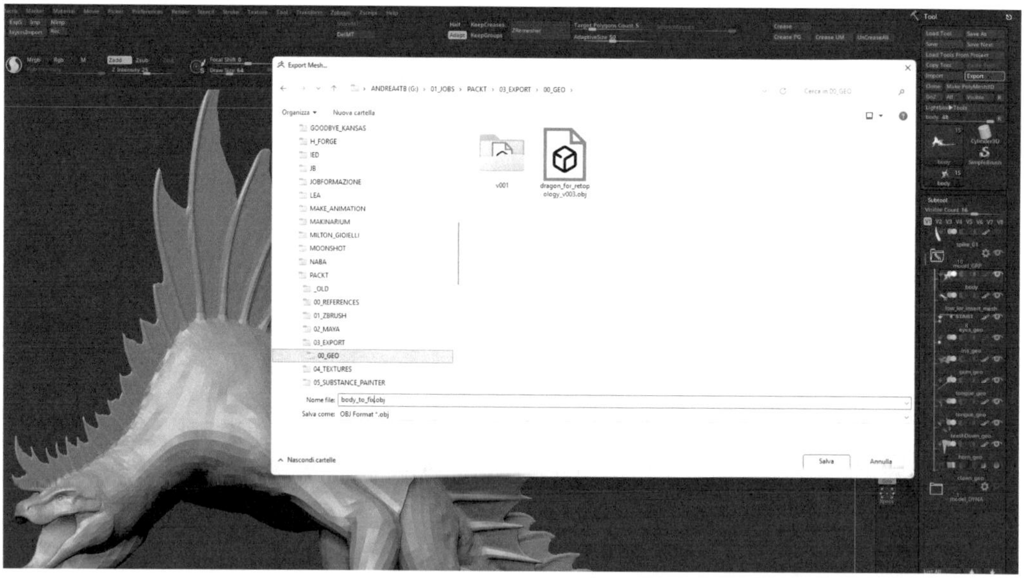

Figure 5.41 – ZBrush export settings window with lowest subdivision selected

2. Import the exported mesh into Maya and open the **UV Editor**. Identify any issues such as overlapping UVs, visible stretching, flipped shells, or areas that need to be re-unfolded after sculpting changes.

3. Use a checker map or **PolyRaven**'s directional checker to quickly visualize problems, then fix them by moving, rotating, scaling, or re-cutting the UV shells as needed.
4. After fixing the problem, re-export the mesh using OBJ instead of FBX. FBX can often cause scale mismatches and incorrect positioning, so OBJ remains the most stable option for this workflow.
5. Return to ZBrush and select your original sculpt. At the lowest subdivision level, open **Tool | Import** and load the corrected OBJ. If the vertex order has not changed, ZBrush will automatically update the UVs while keeping all sculpted detail and subdivisions intact.

> **Tip**
>
> Always keep both the original sculpt and the fixed UV mesh backed up before importing. If an issue appears during import, you can revert immediately without losing any work.

6. If the vertex order has changed due to topology fixes, ZBrush will not recognize the updated mesh. In this case, follow these steps:
    1. Import the corrected model as a new Tool. Before importing, add a simple primitive such as a **Sphere** and use **SubTool | Insert** to load the updated OBJ, replacing the primitive with your corrected mesh.
    2. Once imported, subdivide the new geometry until it matches the resolution of the original sculpt.
    3. Then use **Tool | SubTool | Project | Project All** to transfer the details from the old mesh to the new one, working progressively subdivision by subdivision (for example, level 1 to level 1, level 2 to level 2, and so on). This approach is especially useful when fixing real production issues, such as topology errors on elements like the horn, as it allows you to rebuild clean geometry while preserving all the sculpted detail.

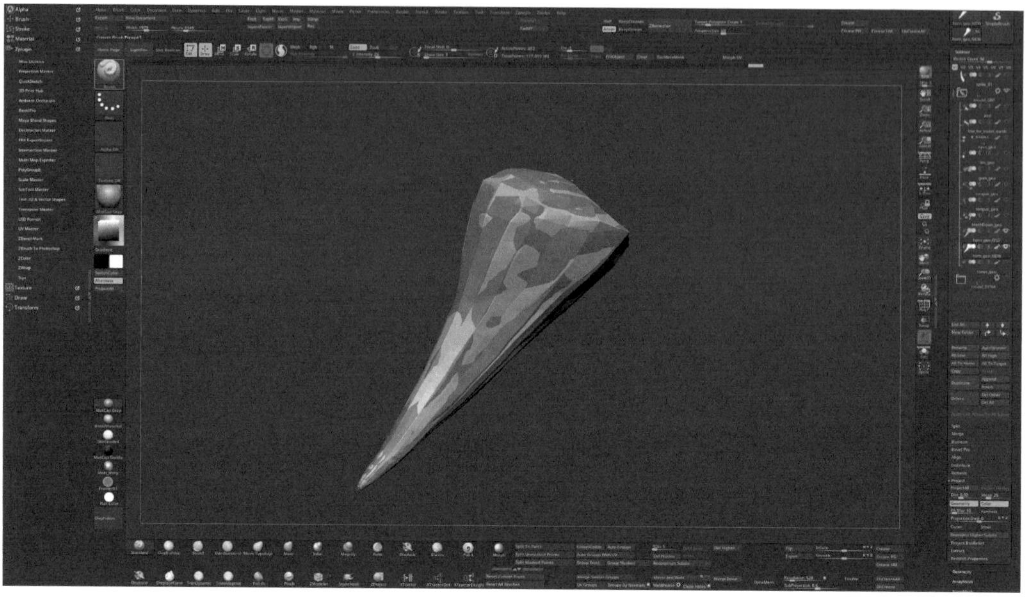

Figure 5.42 – Old and updated horn meshes displayed as separate SubTools in ZBrush, with the Projection panel visible, ready to transfer sculpted details from the original model to the corrected topology

> **Note**
>
> Avoid modifying the topology when fixing UVs if you want to preserve your existing subdivision levels. Adding or removing vertices changes the vertex order, forcing you to reproject all sculpted details onto a new mesh. While reprojection is a valid workflow, it introduces additional complexity and can generate artifacts, especially in dense or highly detailed areas. For this reason, it should be approached carefully and only when necessary. Whenever possible, limit your changes to UV shells, seams, and UDIM placement to maintain a safe and predictable round-trip between Maya and ZBrush.

7. Finally, verify that the projection has been applied correctly. Compare the original and the updated mesh to ensure that all sculpted details match across the entire surface.

Check for any loss of volume, projection artifacts, or areas where details may not have transferred properly.

8. If needed, adjust the projection settings or repeat the **Project All** process on specific subdivision levels to refine the result. Once everything matches correctly, you can safely continue working with the updated model.

Figure 5.43 – Comparison between original and updated mesh after projection, confirming that sculpted details have been transferred correctly

How it works...

This workflow is built around a simple but critical principle: maintaining the relationship between geometry and sculpted detail while updating UVs.

When the vertex order is preserved, ZBrush can update UVs directly without affecting subdivision levels. This is the safest and most efficient scenario, because all sculpted information remains perfectly aligned with the mesh. However, in real production, this condition is not always guaranteed.

In this recipe, the horn example represents a common situation where topology needs to be fixed. As soon as vertices are added, removed, or reordered, ZBrush can no longer match the updated mesh with the original one. At this point, the workflow shifts from a simple UV update to a detail transfer process.

ZBrush projection works by comparing two meshes with similar shapes and transferring surface information from one to the other. By subdividing the corrected mesh to match the original sculpt and projecting details progressively, subdivision by subdivision, the result becomes more stable and predictable. This step-by-step approach reduces projection errors and helps maintain surface fidelity.

Projection, however, is not a perfect operation. On complex areas such as sharp tips or tight curvature transitions, artifacts may appear. This is why it is important to verify the result at each subdivision level instead of relying on a single projection pass.

Another key aspect is the use of **Insert** instead of **Import** when bringing the corrected mesh into ZBrush. This allows you to keep both the original and updated meshes as separate SubTools, making it easier to compare them and validate the projection.

Lastly, validation is a crucial step. Comparing the original and updated meshes ensures that volume, surface quality, and fine details are preserved. Any mismatch usually indicates issues with projection distance, subdivision levels, or topology differences, and should be corrected before moving forward.

This workflow reflects a production mindset: instead of restarting from scratch, you fix problems while preserving as much work as possible, maintaining both efficiency and quality.

There's more...

In production, fixing UVs after sculpting is not an unusual task but part of the normal workflow. Layout errors, flipped UV shells, or missing UDIMs often appear late in the pipeline, especially during the review stage for texturing or rendering. The key is learning how to correct these issues safely, without ever modifying topology. Once you understand this process, you can make UV updates confidently, even during final production stages, without the risk of losing sculpted detail.

A professional habit is to keep a reference OBJ of the last approved UV layout for every asset. If a later change introduces a problem, you can quickly compare the new version against the reference to check vertex count, tile placement, and scale. This small but reliable step can prevent costly mistakes, especially when multiple artists work on the same model.

To build confidence in this workflow, try small controlled exercises on test meshes before applying the method to production assets. Re-UV a model in **Maya**, export it, and re-import it into **ZBrush** using **Import with the same vertex order** to confirm that the sculpted details remain untouched. Then push it further: modify topology by adding an edge loop and use **Project All** to transfer detail from the old sculpt to the new mesh. Observe how projection behaves around areas with fine geometry such as the eyes or mouth, and how it reacts to slight topology changes. These small experiments will train your eye and make you faster when handling real production assets.

When using **Project All**, subdivide gradually and project at each level to avoid shrinkage or artifacts. This layered approach ensures that even delicate surface details project smoothly.

Note

Avoid auto-smoothing, triangulation, or mesh optimization tools when preparing UV fixes. These can change vertex order, making ZBrush unable to recognize the updated mesh and forcing you to redo the entire projection process.

6

Using Layers in ZBrush: Correct Workflow for Primary, Secondary, and Tertiary Details

Throughout my production experience, I've found that artists are often tempted to focus too early on pores, scales, and other surface details. In most cases, stronger results come from first establishing solid primary forms and clear anatomical structure. This chapter focuses on how to properly structure your sculpt through the three levels of detail: **Primary forms, Secondary forms**, and **Tertiary details**, ensuring clarity and control at every stage.

Instead of jumping directly into pores or fine surface noise, we will first reinforce the importance of strong primary forms and silhouette, then build up secondary structures such as folds, wrinkles, and muscle transitions. Only after that will we approach tertiary details, including pores, scales, and surface breakup, with a clear understanding of how they support the underlying forms.

One of the most important mindset shifts for improving as an artist is understanding that these three levels are not just separate steps, but layered systems of information. In production, I personally push this concept further by subdividing each level into smaller stages. Instead of thinking only in terms of primary, secondary, and tertiary, I approach the sculpt as a sequence of progressive refinements:

1. Start with large primary forms
2. Then build medium structures inside those forms
3. And only later introduce smaller variations on top

This logic is repeated at every level, creating a consistent and controlled workflow.

A key tool that supports this workflow is **Morph Target**. Once properly understood, it becomes much more than a corrective tool. It allows you to safely push details, test variations, blend transitions between different surface types, and preserve information before making risky changes. In a production environment, this means working faster while maintaining full control over the sculpt.

By the end of this chapter, you will be able to structure your sculpt in a production-friendly way, maintaining readability while progressively increasing detail. More importantly, you will develop a workflow that allows you to make decisions at the right time, reducing unnecessary rework and avoiding the common trap of over-detailing too early.

In this chapter, we are going to cover the following main recipes:

- Reprojecting and validating primary forms on the clean retopologized mesh
- Sculpting secondary forms: wrinkles and medium shapes
- Sculpting tertiary forms: using Surface Noise for global skin details
- Sculpting tertiary forms: sculpting with XYZ Textures

Figure 6.1 shows the primary, secondary, and tertiary detail progression, where primary defines silhouette, secondary adds anatomical forms, and tertiary introduces microdetails:

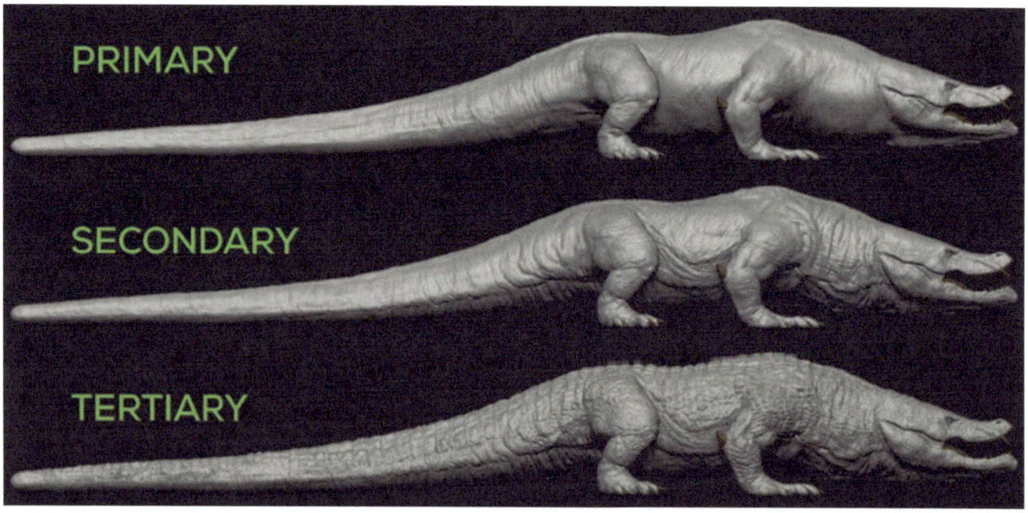

Figure 6.1 – Example of primary, secondary, and tertiary detail progression on a creature model

Technical requirements

To complete this chapter, you will need **ZBrush 2024** or later and **Adobe Photoshop 2024** or later. As mentioned in previous chapters, make sure your scene is correctly configured in terms of scale and project structure.

For the minimum hardware and software requirements recommended for this book, please refer to the *Technical requirements* section in *Chapter 1*. This chapter focuses on high-resolution sculpting and layer-based workflows, so your system should be able to handle dense geometry and multiple subdivision levels without performance issues.

Ensure you have the following assets:

- High-resolution creature sculpt in **DynaMesh**, with primary forms and blocking already established (as explained in *Chapter 2*)
- The same creature with a clean low-poly topology, created through retopology (as explained in *Chapter 3*)
- **XYZ Textures Maps** – High-resolution displacement maps captured from real-world surfaces and widely used in film, VFX, and creature production to create realistic pores, scales, wrinkles, and skin variation.
  For artists looking to achieve a professional level of surface detailing, I highly recommend investing in the **XYZ Texture library**, which can be found here: `https://texturing.xyz/collections/animals`.

  > **Note**
  >
  > Note that these commercial assets are not included with the downloadable files accompanying this book and must be obtained separately.

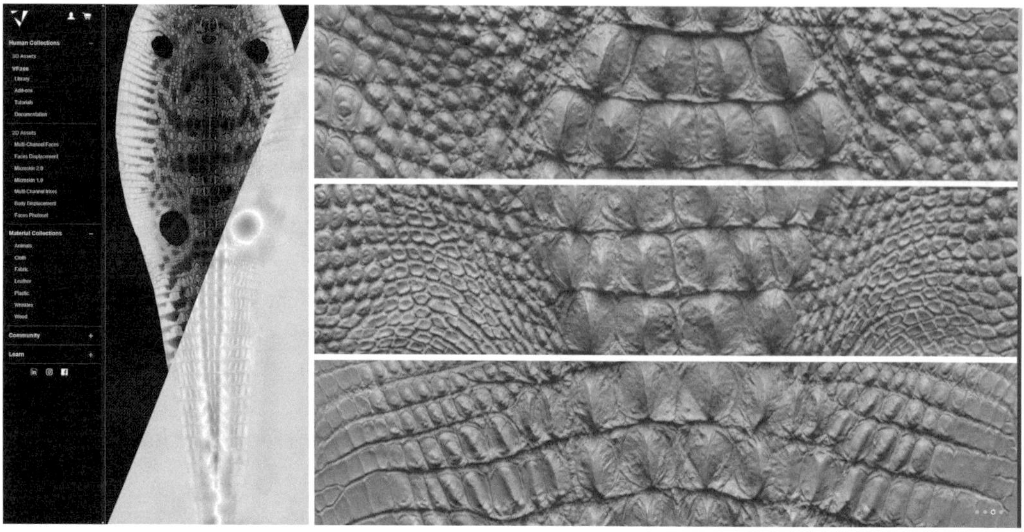

Figure 6.2 – The XYZ Textures website showing available displacement maps

- In addition to XYZ Textures, this chapter uses custom alphas and noise maps. The alpha provided with this book was personally created for educational purposes and will be included with the downloadable assets. It is intended as a starting point for generating surface breakup and noise variation rather than as a direct replacement for professional XYZ Texture assets.

  While custom alphas can be extremely useful for creating scales, skin breakup, and tertiary details, XYZ Texture Maps remain a unique production resource because of their exceptional resolution, realism, and the vast amount of real-world surface information they contain.

The `Chapter06_07` folder in the GitHub repository includes the following assets:

- `aldabraGiantTortoise_alpha_TX.png`: A procedural skin texture created specifically for this book, with the assistance of AI, to generate large-scale surface breakup and natural skin variation. It is intended as a practical starting point for creating procedural skin details.
- `dragonCrest_body_primary_dec_v001.obj`: A decimated version of the creature containing the completed primary forms used as the starting point for the workflows in this chapter.

- `dragonCrest_body_secondary_dec_v001.obj`: A decimated version of the creature with the secondary details already sculpted, used for the secondary detailing workflows.
- `dragonCrest_body_tertiary_dec_v001.obj`: A decimated version of the creature with the tertiary details already completed, allowing you to follow the high-frequency detailing workflows demonstrated in this chapter.

You can download the example project files for this book by following the instructions in the *Download the example code/resource files* section in the *Preface* of this book.

This chapter's code/resource files are included in the downloadable code/resource bundle.

Reprojecting and validating primary forms on the clean retopologized mesh

By this stage, the primary forms have already been established during the blocking phase. After completing retopology and UVs, the focus shifts to transferring that work onto a clean, production-ready mesh.

This is also the point where we begin working with Layers in ZBrush, which are essential for maintaining control over the sculpt. **Layers** allow you to separate different levels of detail, adjust their intensity, and make non-destructive changes. In a production environment, this becomes crucial to test variations and manage complex surfaces without affecting the underlying forms.

Instead of rebuilding the sculpt, we import the new mesh as a SubTool and use a projection workflow to transfer all the existing information onto the new topology. This process has already been introduced in the *Fixing or updating UDIMs without losing work in ZBrush* recipe in *Chapter 5*, so here we will focus on applying it in a more structured and controlled way.

The goal of this recipe is to move from a sculpting mesh to a topologically correct asset with proper UVs, ready for further detailing and integration into the production pipeline. At the same time, it is important to verify that the primary volumes remain consistent and readable across subdivision levels, as any deformation introduced at this stage will propagate through the rest of the sculpt.

The following overlay compares the original DynaMesh sculpt with the clean retopologized mesh used throughout this workflow:

Figure 6.3 – Overlay between the DynaMesh sculpt and the retopologized mesh used to validate volume matching before projection

Getting ready

Before starting, make sure you have both versions of your creature ready: a high-resolution DynaMesh sculpt with established primary forms and a clean low-poly mesh created through retopology and UVs.

If you are jumping directly into this recipe, make sure you have completed the workflows covered in the following chapters:

- *Chapter 2, Blocking with DynaMesh and ZSpheres: Establishing Primary Shapes*
- *Chapter 3, Blocking Complex Areas: Hands, Mouth, and Functional Structures*
- *Chapter 4, Retopology in Maya: Understanding Topology Theory and Creating Clean Geometry for Animation*
- *Chapter 5, UV Mapping with UDIMs: Fixing Distortions and Optimizing Workflow*

These chapters provide the sculpt, topology, and UV assets required for the workflow presented in this recipe.

How to do it...

In this workflow, we transfer the existing sculpt from the DynaMesh model to the clean retopologized mesh. The process is performed progressively across subdivision levels to preserve the original forms without introducing artifacts or distortions. Follow these steps:

1. Select the clean retopologized mesh SubTool and start subdividing it using **Tool** | **Geometry** | **Divide** or use the *Ctrl* + *D* shortcut.
2. Before proceeding, store a **Morph Target** using **Tool** | **Morph Target** | **StoreMT**. This will allow you to recover or blend details later if needed.
3. Increase the subdivision levels gradually until the mesh can support the level of detail of the original sculpt, avoiding jumping directly to the highest resolution.

Figure 6.4 – Subdivision levels increasing with Morph Target stored and ready to be used for later corrections

4. Before starting the projection, create a new layer using **Tool** | **Layers** | **New** and rename it to `Primary` or `Muscles`. Activate this layer before continuing, so that all subsequent changes are recorded.

Tip

Layers depend on topology

Once you create a Layer in ZBrush, avoid making any changes that modify the mesh topology. For example, if you export the lowest subdivision level to Maya to edit the topology, remove edge loops or vertices, perform a **ZRemesher** pass, or make any other topological changes, the Layers will no longer work correctly after reimporting the mesh. In most cases, the subdivision levels will also no longer match. Any topological modification invalidates the stored Layer information.

Although Layer intensity can be increased beyond 1, do so carefully. Values above 1 simply amplify the stored sculpt and, depending on the type of detail recorded, may produce exaggerated or unpredictable results. In production, I generally recommend keeping most Layers between 0 and 1, using higher values only after carefully evaluating the result.

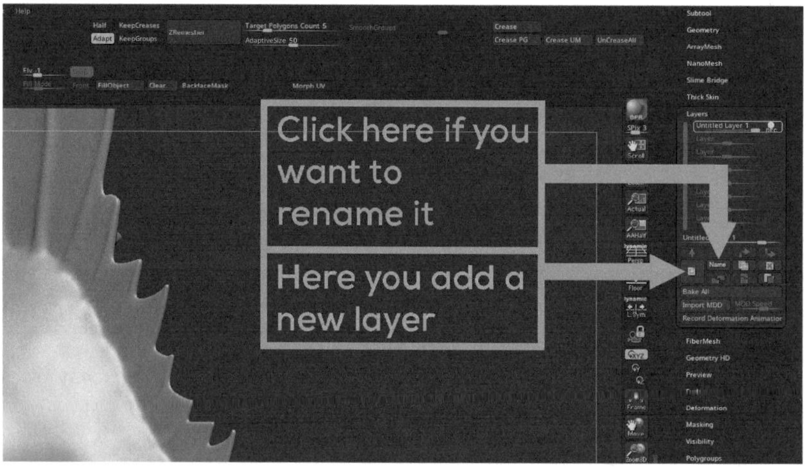

Figure 6.5 – Creating and naming a new Layer before starting the projection workflow

5. Once you reach the highest subdivision level, move back to the lowest level using *Shift + D*. At this stage, make sure only the necessary SubTools are visible, keeping the DynaMesh sculpt as the source for projection.
6. With the clean mesh selected, start the projection using **Tool** | **SubTool** | **Project** | **Project All**. Set the **Dist** value between `0.01` and `0.02` to avoid projection errors and unwanted intersections.

7. Move to the next subdivision level using the *D* shortcut, which increases the active subdivision level, and repeat the projection process. Continue this step progressively, projecting details level by level to maintain clean surface transitions and preserve the original volumes.

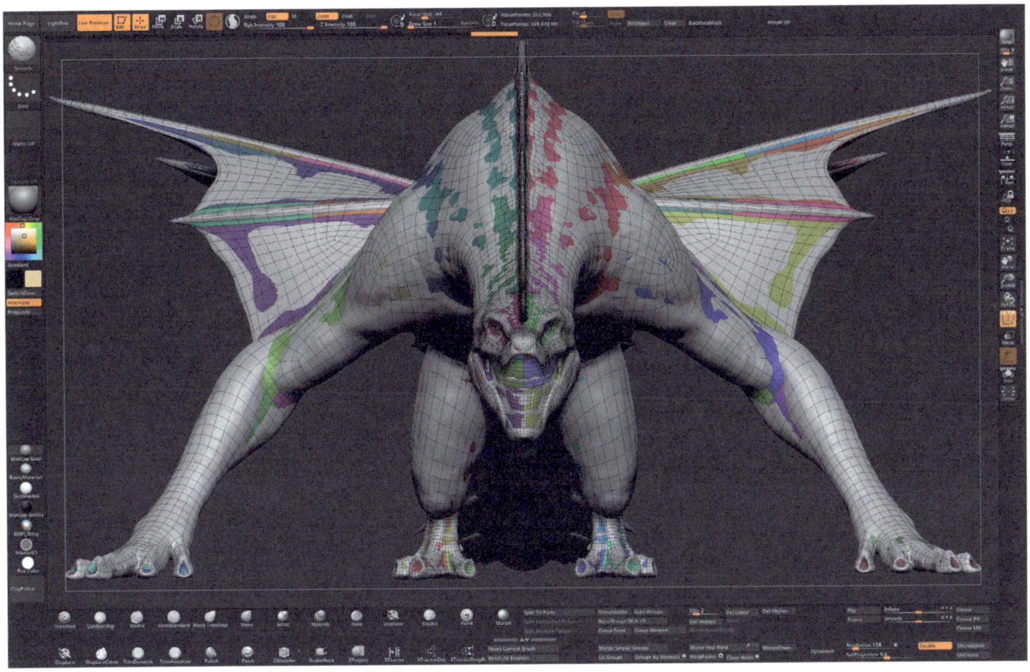

Figure 6.6 – Subdivision level 2 before projection, showing the clean mesh without transferred detail

As shown in *Figures 6.6* and *6.7*, subdividing the retopologized mesh with **Tool** | **Geometry** | **Smt** enabled (the button located next to **Divide**) causes ZBrush to smooth the surface between subdivision levels. This process can slightly shrink or soften the original DynaMesh volumes.

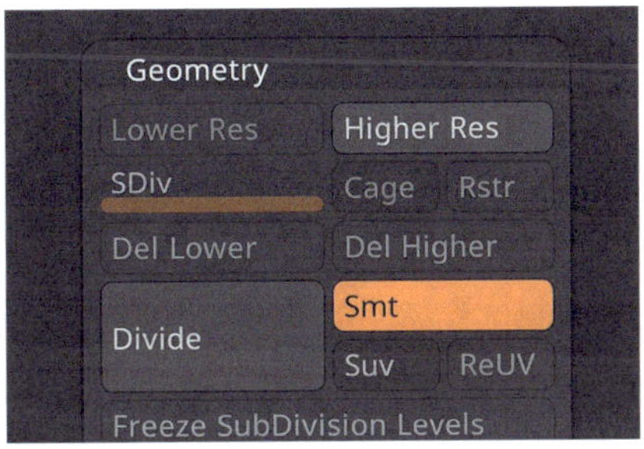

Figure 6.7 – The Smt option controls whether ZBrush smooths the mesh during subdivision

When **Smt** is disabled, ZBrush creates new subdivision levels without modifying the original shape, which can be useful when preserving the exact geometry is critical. This approach is commonly used in hard-surface workflows but can also be valuable for organic models in specific situations.

After projection, the retopologized mesh recovers the original silhouette and primary forms, allowing it to closely match the source sculpt while maintaining clean production-ready topology.

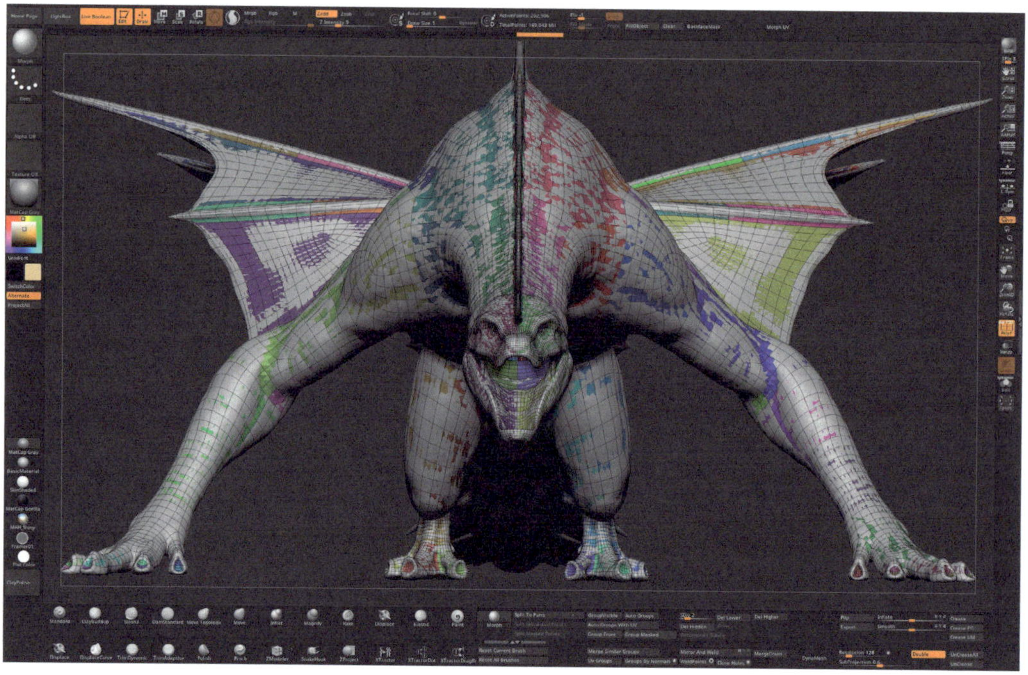

Figure 6.8 – Subdivision level 2 after projection, where the mesh conforms to the original DynaMesh and matches its volumes

8. Continue subdividing and projecting until the clean mesh reaches a vertex count that matches or slightly exceeds the original DynaMesh. As a practical benchmark, a creature body blocked in **DynaMesh** often ranges between *1 and 2 million vertices*, while the head may contain approximately *2 to 3 million vertices*. Once the projected mesh reaches a similar or slightly higher density, it is usually capable of capturing all available primary forms and surface information. Beyond this point, further subdivision is unnecessary, as the mesh is already capable of capturing all the available detail.

9. At the highest subdivision level, inspect the mesh for projection artifacts, especially in critical areas, such as membranes, thin surfaces, or overlapping geometry, where errors are more likely to occur.

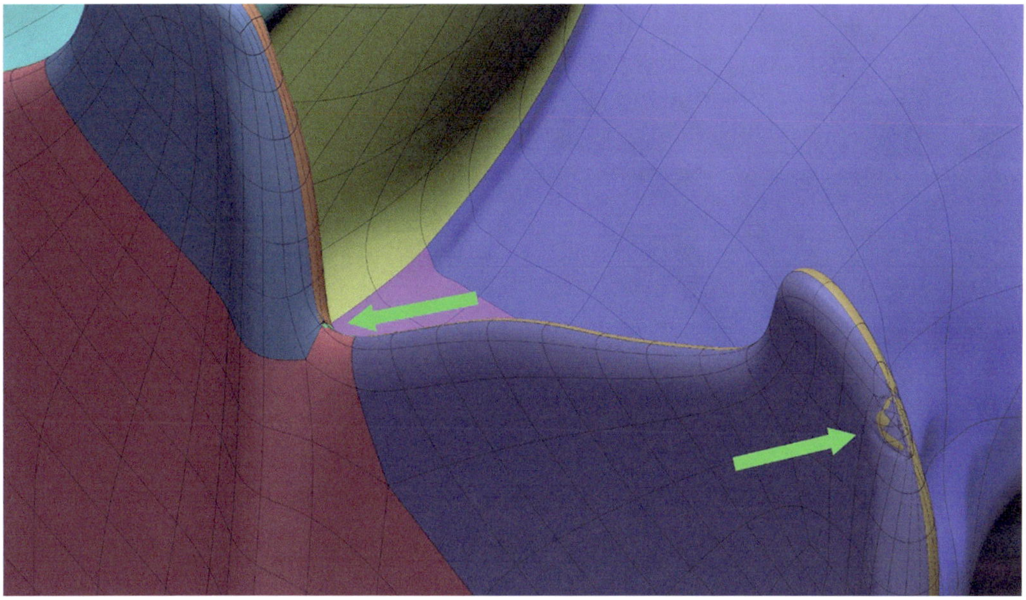

Figure 6.9 – Projection artifacts appearing in thin, overlapping areas of the mesh

> **Note**
>
> A **projection artifact** is an unwanted surface error introduced during the projection process. These artifacts often appear as spikes, pinching, stretched polygons, collapsed volumes, or surface distortions caused by nearby or overlapping geometry. Thin membranes, intersecting surfaces, and tightly packed areas are particularly susceptible to these issues. Always inspect the model carefully at the highest subdivision level before proceeding, as small projection errors can become much more visible once secondary and tertiary details are added.

10. To fix these areas, use the **Morph** Brush, available in **Brush** | **Morph**. Gently paint over the problematic regions to restore the original stored state. Keep the **ZIntensity** low, typically between 5 and 15, to maintain full control and avoid abrupt transitions.
11. If needed, apply a very subtle **Smooth** with low intensity to improve the transition between projected and restored areas, being careful not to soften the underlying forms.

Figure 6.10 shows the result after using the **Morph Brush**, with restored surface continuity and stable volumes in critical areas:

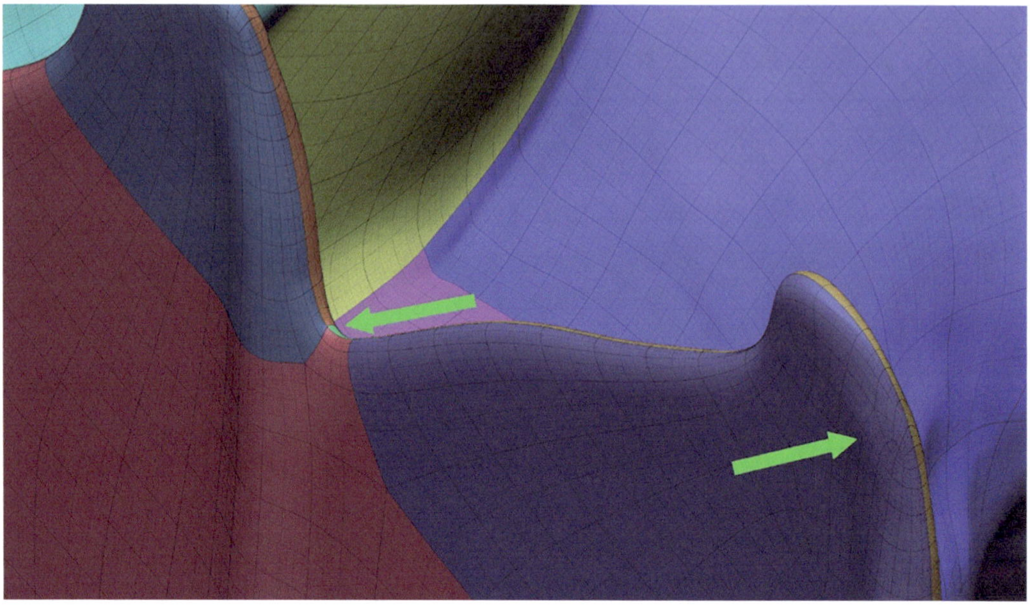

Figure 6.10 – Cleaned result after fixing projection artifacts using the Morph Brush

> **Tip**
>
> Use the **Morph Brush** subtly and build corrections gradually. Small adjustments give better control than strong strokes.

How it works...

The projection workflow described in this recipe is based on this principle: *detail can only be transferred correctly if the target mesh has enough resolution to capture it*. This is why the clean mesh is subdivided progressively until it reaches a vertex count comparable to the original DynaMesh.

Working from the lowest subdivision level upward ensures that primary forms are transferred first, creating a stable foundation for higher-frequency detail. If projection is performed only at high resolution, the mesh tends to capture noise without properly reconstructing the underlying volumes, resulting in unstable surfaces.

In this context, the **Morph Target** stored in *step 2* is not used as a sculpting variation tool, but as a reliable backup of the clean mesh. Since this mesh originates from a controlled low-poly retopology and is subdivided without introducing distortion, it represents a stable and predictable state of the model. By using the **Morph** Brush in *step 10*, you are effectively blending between two states: the projected result and the original clean surface, allowing you to remove artifacts locally while preserving the overall structure.

At the same time, **Layers**, introduced in *step 4,* provide an additional level of control over the process. When a layer is created and the **Record** button is active, ZBrush stores all the changes performed on that layer, including projection and sculpting operations. This means that the modifications are not permanently baked into the mesh and can be adjusted later.

Each layer can be toggled on or off to evaluate its contribution, allowing you to compare the projected result with the underlying base state. The intensity slider normally ranges from **-1** to **+1**, which controls how strongly the stored deformation is applied:

- At **0,** the layer has no effect
- At **1**, the stored deformation is fully applied
- Negative values invert the deformation, which makes it possible to push the sculpt in the opposite direction and evaluate alternative results

A key control in the **Layers** palette, the **Layer Intensity Value** (highlighted in *Figure 6.11* by the arrow labeled **+5 to -5**), allows this range to be extended up to +5 and -5. This is useful when you want to exaggerate the stored deformation far beyond its original value, either to test stronger shape variations or to better evaluate how much influence the layer has on the surface.

The following image highlights the main Layer controls:

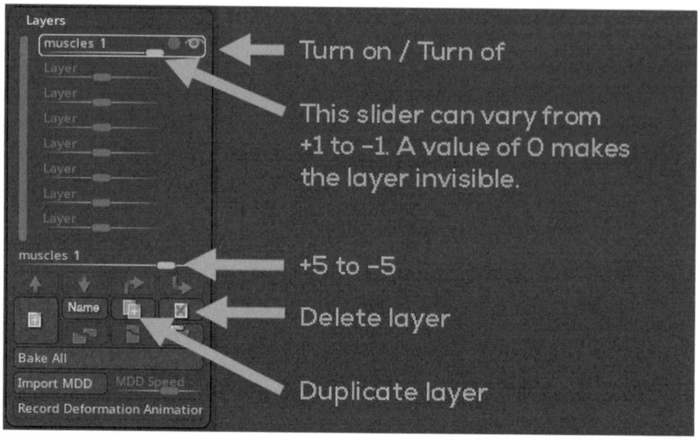

Figure 6.11 – Overview of the ZBrush Layers interface and its main controls

In practice, the **Layer Intensity Value** should be used carefully, because amplifying a layer too much can easily break the original forms and create unnatural transitions. The layer stack can also be reorganized using the arrow controls (see *Figure 6.11*), allowing you to move layers up or down. This affects how changes are evaluated in sequence and gives you more flexibility when managing complex modifications across multiple sculpting stages.

In this workflow, the layer acts as a controlled recording of the projection process, while the **Morph Target** provides a stable fallback. Together, they allow you to work in a non-destructive way, giving you the ability to fix issues, test variations, and refine the result without losing the integrity of the original forms.

Sculpting secondary forms: wrinkles and medium shapes

Now we'll focus on building secondary forms, with particular attention to wrinkles and soft tissue areas. These elements are essential to describe how the skin reacts to underlying structures, adding weight, tension, and believability to the creature.

Before starting, it is important to rely on a focused set of references. Secondary forms are derived from observing how skin behaves under tension, compression, and gravity across different species. Studying reptiles, mammals, and large animals helps identify recurring patterns that can be translated into your sculpt.

Before sculpting individual wrinkles, it's important to understand the logic behind their direction. Skin folds are not random. They are guided by the underlying anatomy, the tension generated by movement, and the interaction between different skin folds. Thinking in terms of flow rather than isolated wrinkles will help you create more believable secondary forms on any creature.

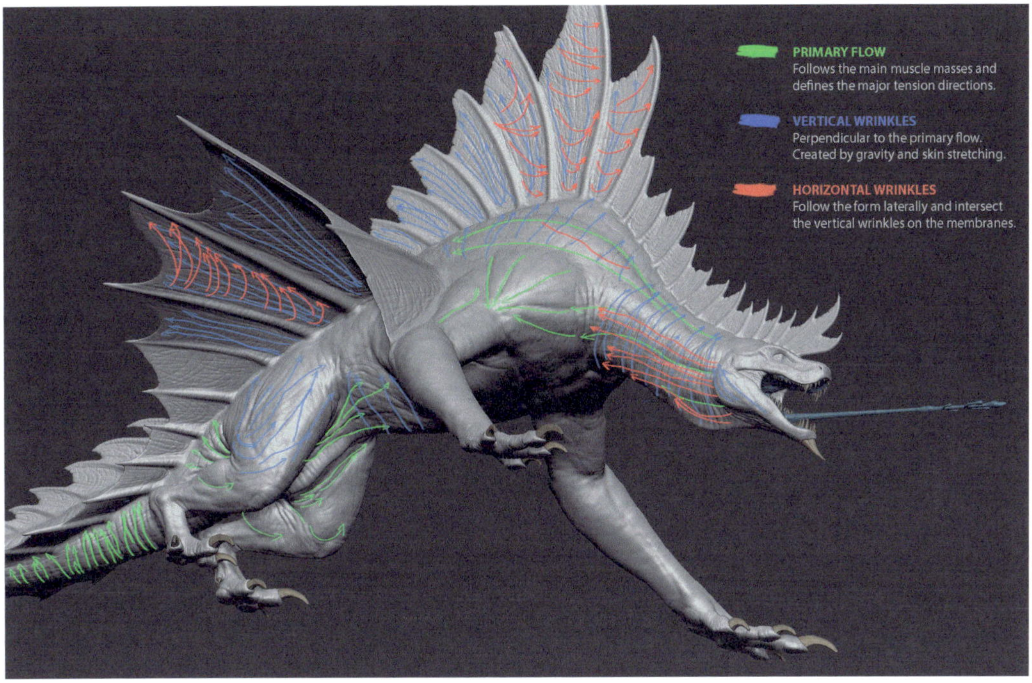

Figure 6.12 – Wrinkle flow guide showing the primary anatomical flow together with the main wrinkle directions generated by tension and compression

Rather than working across the entire model at once, it is more effective to isolate a specific area and develop a clear methodology. In this recipe, we will focus on the neck, a region where compression, stretching, and overlapping forms naturally occur. This makes it an ideal area to understand how wrinkles are constructed and how fat volumes behave under deformation. The goal is to establish a solid and repeatable workflow; once understood, the same logic can be applied consistently across the rest of the character.

Figure 6.13 shows the type of secondary form development we will build throughout this workflow:

Figure 6.13 – Secondary forms applied across the character to establish skin flow and anatomical tension

Getting ready

Before starting this recipe, make sure the following elements are prepared:

- A clean retopologized mesh with well-established primary forms. If you are joining this workflow directly, complete the previous recipe, *Reprojecting and validating primary forms on the clean retopologized mesh*, before proceeding. The silhouette and major anatomical volumes should already be clearly defined, as secondary details rely on this structure to read correctly.
- Prepare a focused reference board that highlights wrinkles, skin behavior, and soft tissue deformation across different species. I recommend organizing your references in **PureRef** (`https://www.pureref.com/`) and gathering material from sources such as **Pinterest** (`https://in.pinterest.com/`), **ArtStation** (`https://www.artstation.com/?sort_by=community&dimension=all`), wildlife photography websites, and documentary footage. These references will guide your decisions and help you avoid arbitrary or repetitive patterns.

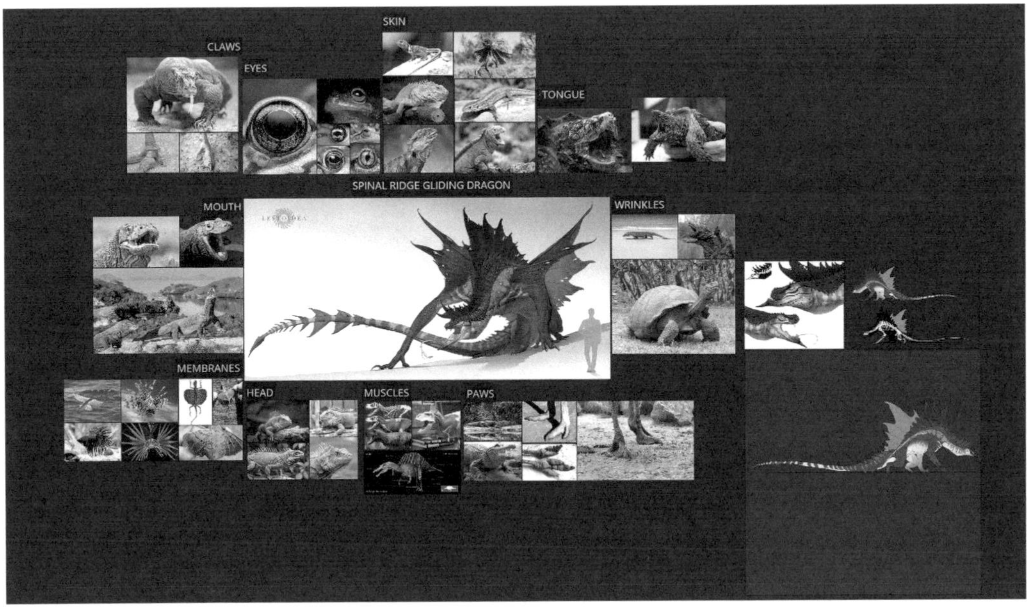

Figure 6.14 – Reference board used to study secondary and tertiary forms across different species

- Work at a subdivision level that provides enough resolution to sculpt smooth transitions without introducing unnecessary density, typically one or two subdivision levels below the highest subdivision level. At this stage, the model should be stable and ready to support medium-level deformation without breaking the underlying forms.

How to do it...

In this workflow, we will start by setting up a clean and controllable layer before sculpting any secondary forms. This step is essential to keep the sculpt non-destructive and allow adjustments later without affecting the base geometry. Working with Layers from the beginning reflects a production mindset, where flexibility and iteration are key, especially when dealing with art direction changes or feedback. Now, let's get started.

1. Before sculpting any wrinkles, create a new layer dedicated to the neck area. This will allow you to control the intensity of the deformation and refine it at any stage of the process. Go to **Tool** | **Layers** and click on **New** to create a new layer. Immediately rename it to something clear and production-friendly, such as `wrinkles_neck`.

Tip

In a production environment, it is common to organize Layers by region and type of detail. For example, use clear and readable naming, such as `SEC_wrinkles_neck`, `SEC_wrinkles_chest`, or `SEC_wrinkles_head`. This approach makes it easier to isolate and adjust specific areas during reviews or art direction changes. However, if you are working on a less powerful machine, consider keeping a simplified structure with only a few Layers, such as muscles, wrinkles, and skin, to maintain better performance and avoid unnecessary overhead.

2. Select the **Slash3** Brush and set the **ZIntensity** between `15` and `30`. Use a medium to small **Draw Size** and zoom in on the neck to maintain control over each stroke.

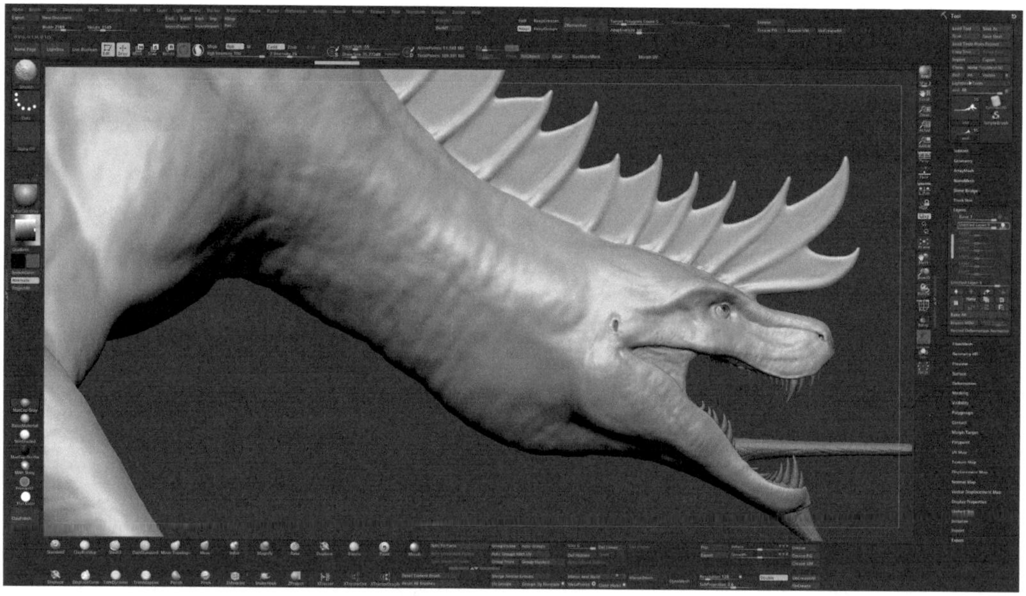

Figure 6.15 – A new layer created and activated for the neck, with the Slash3 Brush settings and working area prepared

3. Start carving large vertical wrinkles that follow the natural direction of tension. These first cuts should define how the skin stretches and compresses, creating a sense of volume and weight rather than surface detail. Focus on long, confident strokes that describe the structure of the neck.

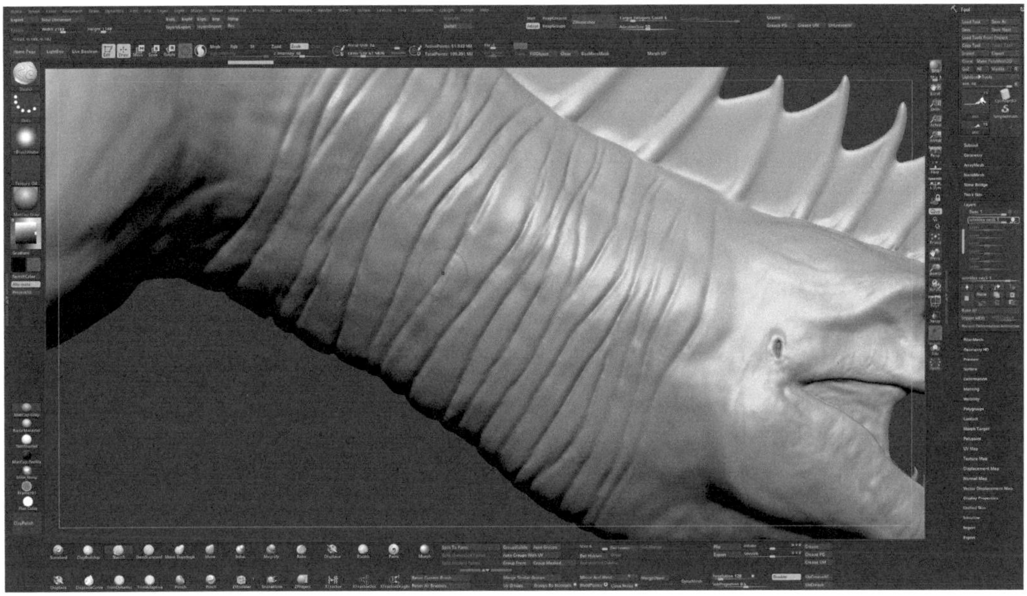

Figure 6.16 – Primary vertical wrinkles defining volume, direction and brush size

4. Avoid creating parallel, evenly spaced lines. This is one of the most common mistakes and immediately makes the surface feel artificial. Uniform spacing and identical wrinkles will break realism very quickly. Always introduce variation in size, spacing, and direction to avoid repetitive patterns. For example, a large fold followed by a medium one, then smaller ones, and back to a larger structure. This variation creates a more natural and believable pattern.

> **Tip**
>
> Think of these wrinkles as sculptural forms, not surface details. If the neck reads well with only a few large folds, you are building a strong foundation for the next steps.

5. If you want to increase the sculptural weight of the wrinkles, you can reinforce them using the **Standard** Brush, or alternatively, **Magnify** or **Inflate**.
   The **Magnify** and **Inflate** brushes expand the surface outward, almost like inflating a balloon, which can quickly add volume but may become harder to control. For this reason, I generally prefer the **Standard** Brush, using a **ZIntensity** between `10` and `20`, to selectively strengthen the wrinkles that need more visual weight and realism, depending on the type of creature.

6. Work by following the direction of each individual wrinkle, gradually building up the volume along its length rather than applying it uniformly. For better control, perform this step *two or three subdivision levels below the maximum resolution*, where the forms remain readable and easier to manage.
   Keep in mind that this specific creature is not ideal for pushing this technique too far, as the skin is relatively tight. Over-accentuating the wrinkles here can quickly break believability, so use this approach with moderation and only where the anatomy supports it.

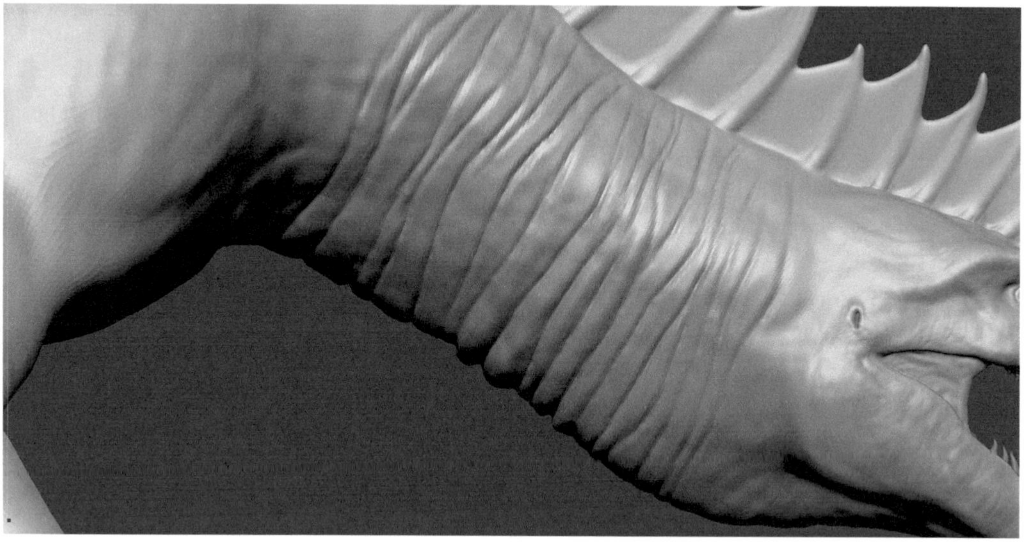

Figure 6.17 – Primary wrinkles refined to strengthen volume and improve skin flow

7. At this stage, assume that the primary and secondary forms are established, meaning the larger wrinkles already define the main flow and deformation of the neck.

8. The next step is to introduce a *second pass of medium secondary details* to break uniformity and add variation. Using the same directional logic, start layering smaller wrinkles between the larger ones, slightly shifting their direction based on compression and stretching areas.
9. Avoid filling every space evenly. Instead, focus on creating rhythm and hierarchy, where medium wrinkles support and enrich the larger forms without flattening them. This step is essential to move from a structured sculpt to a more natural and believable surface.

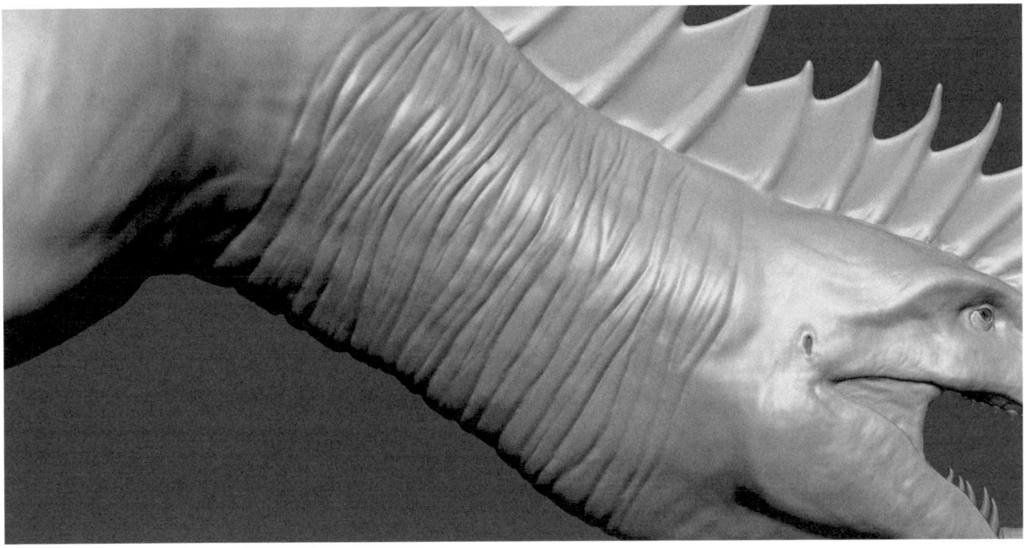

Figure 6.18 – Medium secondary wrinkles introducing variation

10. Finally, add the *smallest secondary details and subtle horizontal wrinkles* to break the overall regularity of the surface.
    These details should be introduced selectively, only where the anatomy and deformation require them, such as compression zones or transition areas. Use a lighter touch and keep the intensity low, allowing these finer wrinkles to support the existing structure without overpowering it.

    The goal is to enrich the surface with micro-variation while preserving the clarity and readability of the primary and medium forms.

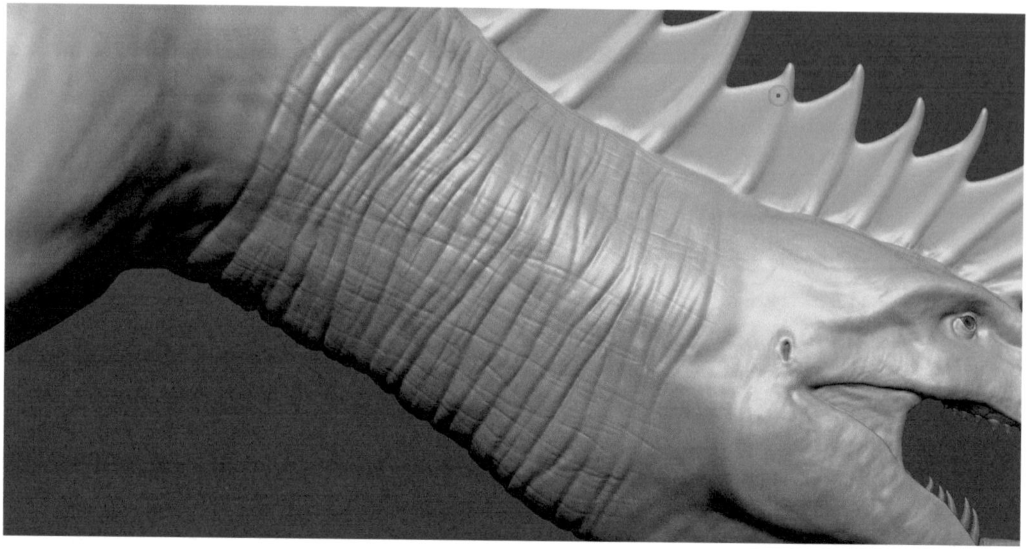

Figure 6.19 – Initial secondary wrinkle pass defining the main skin flow

When sculpting smaller secondary and horizontal wrinkles, avoid drawing continuous, straight lines across the surface. Instead, break your strokes into short, slightly offset segments, following the local curvature of the form. This helps create a more organic and less artificial result. Work with a low **ZIntensity** and build the effect gradually, layering strokes rather than trying to define the wrinkle in a single pass. Let the horizontal wrinkles interact with the vertical ones instead of sitting on top of them, so the surface feels integrated rather than patterned.

How it works...

Another important decision made during this workflow is building wrinkles hierarchically rather than sculpting every fold at the same time. As demonstrated in the previous steps, you first established the primary wrinkle flow using the **Slash3** Brush, then progressively introduced medium and smaller wrinkles only after the larger forms were clearly readable.

This sequence creates a natural hierarchy across the surface. Areas under tension should remain cleaner, while compressed regions naturally accumulate overlapping folds. This progression creates a believable rhythm across the surface and prevents the sculpt from looking noisy or uniformly detailed.

If you are still building confidence with this process, you can temporarily separate these wrinkle passes into different Layers, for example one for the larger secondary wrinkles, one for the medium forms, and another for the smallest details. This makes it easier to evaluate how each level contributes to the final sculpt, adjust their intensity independently, and receive production feedback without affecting the entire surface. In production, however, this approach is usually simplified to a smaller number of Layers to keep the sculpt organized and easy to manage.

This layered approach keeps the sculpt readable throughout the detailing process while allowing continuous adjustments as new wrinkles are introduced. Whether you are refining the sculpt yourself or responding to supervisor feedback, preserving this hierarchy makes it much easier to iterate without compromising the overall skin structure.

Combined with a controlled use of Layers, this workflow allows you to refine, compare, or even disable individual wrinkle passes at any stage of production without affecting the underlying sculpt or losing the flexibility to refine the surface later in production.

Common mistakes

Even with a solid workflow, secondary forms can quickly lose credibility if a few key principles are ignored. Most mistakes do not come from lack of skill, but from applying the right tools in the wrong way or at the wrong stage:

- One of the most common issues is pushing the **Slash3** Brush too far. When the intensity is too high, the result stops reading as compression and starts to feel like a cut. Instead of soft, organic folds, the surface becomes sharp and artificial. Keeping the intensity controlled allows the wrinkles to remain believable and integrated into the form.
- Another frequent problem is overcrowding the surface with too many folds. When every area is filled with detail, the sculpt loses rhythm and readability. Real skin always alternates between areas of tension and areas of rest. Without this contrast, the surface becomes noisy and difficult to read, even if each individual wrinkle is technically correct.
- A more subtle but equally important mistake is ignoring the underlying anatomy. Wrinkles are not decorative elements. They are a direct consequence of how the skin reacts to structure and movement. When folds are placed randomly, without following the direction of the masses, they fail to communicate weight and deformation, making the sculpt feel disconnected.

There's more...

In some cases, especially on complex creatures, you may end up with a large number of Layers managing different levels of secondary detail. While this provides maximum control during sculpting, it can quickly increase file size and impact performance.

If you reach a point where you are confident with the result and no longer need to adjust individual Layers, it is a good practice to consolidate them into a single clean layer. The following workflow shows how to safely consolidate multiple wrinkle Layers into a single clean layer once the sculpt is approved:

1. Before starting, always save a backup of your file, as this process is destructive and cannot be reversed.
2. To merge your secondary detail Layers into one, first make sure that all the Layers you want to combine are visible and active. Then go to **Tool** | **Morph Target** and click on **StoreMT** to store the current state of the sculpt.
3. If the **StoreMT** button is not available, it means a **Morph Target** is already stored. In this case, click on **DelMT** to delete the existing one, and then store a new **Morph Target** before proceeding.
4. Once the **Morph Target** is stored, delete the Layers you no longer need. At this point, create a new clean layer and rename it appropriately, for example, `wrinkles`.
5. Now select the **Morph** Brush, set a large **Draw Size**, and increase the **ZIntensity** to `100`. Gently brush across the entire area of the model where the details were present. This will restore the stored **Morph Target** onto the new layer, effectively baking all the visible detail into a single layer.

By doing this, you simplify the layer structure and significantly reduce file complexity, while preserving the visual result.

Sculpting tertiary forms: using Surface Noise for global skin details

ZBrush **Surface Noise** is an extremely useful tool for quickly covering large areas of a creature with consistent skin breakup and surface variation. In this case, we will use it mainly on the membranes, where repetitive detail helps create a believable skin texture without requiring every area to be sculpted entirely by hand.

This technique is particularly effective on broad or repetitive surfaces, where manually sculpting every detail would be unnecessarily time-consuming. The most important part of the process is choosing the correct alpha or noise pattern, as this will define the overall character of the skin.

Another important aspect to understand before using **Surface Noise** is how the projection itself works, as shown in *Figure 6.20*. In ZBrush, noise can be applied using different methods. The **NoisePlug** system is mainly designed for hard surface workflows and procedural mechanical patterns, so it will not be covered in this chapter.

Figure 6.20 – Surface Noise projection modes: UV, NoisePlug, and 3D

For organic creatures, the two most useful options are applying the noise through **UVs** or using the **3D** projection mode. When using **UVs**, the pattern follows the UV layout of the model, making it ideal for clean and controlled distribution across the surface.

The **3D** option works differently. Instead of relying on UVs, ZBrush projects the noise based on the current orientation of the model inside the Viewport, effectively creating a planar projection directly onto the geometry. This can be extremely useful when the UV layout is not suitable for the desired effect or when you need a fast way to apply breakup across complex surfaces such as membranes or overlapping organic forms.

However, **Surface Noise** should never fully replace hand sculpting in a production workflow. Procedural noise alone often looks too uniform and artificial. For this reason, the generated detail should always be refined manually where needed, adding variation, directional changes, and localized adjustments to avoid a repetitive result.

When used correctly, **Surface Noise** becomes a fast way to establish a believable base layer of tertiary breakup that can later be enhanced with more specific sculpted details. *Figure 6.21* shows the membrane detailing result we will build throughout this workflow:

Figure 6.21 – Surface Noise applied to the dragonCrest membranes, adding subtle skin breakup and tertiary variation

Getting ready

Before applying **Surface Noise**, ensure the following:

1. Use the clean retopologized version of your creature with the final UDIM UV layout already completed. **Surface Noise** in UV mode relies on a properly unwrapped mesh to distribute the pattern consistently across the model.
2. Prepare a clean version of the model by temporarily disabling the secondary wrinkle Layers. This makes it easier to evaluate the breakup generated by the noise without interference from existing medium forms.
3. Make sure the model is displayed at the highest subdivision level, so the geometry can properly support the tertiary detail generated by the noise.
4. Choose the correct alpha or noise pattern. At this stage, this is essential as it will define the overall skin language of the membranes and large repetitive areas. For this recipe, we will focus on subtle organic skin variation rather than aggressive or highly stylized patterns.

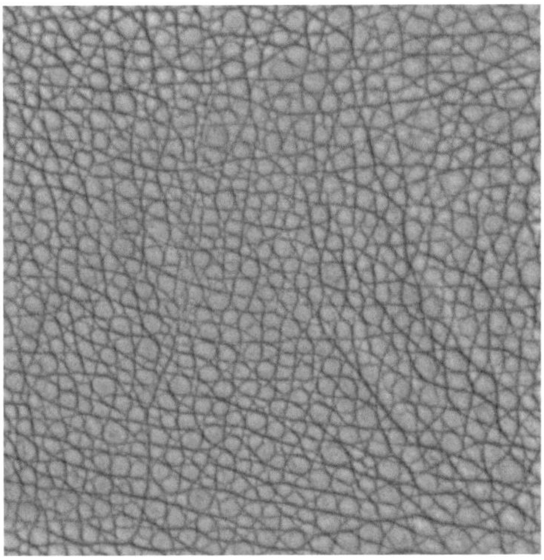

Figure 6.22 – Alpha used to create organic surface breakup on the membranes

5. Keep real-world visual references nearby, especially references showing how skin is subdivided and compressed on reptiles, amphibians, or leathery surfaces, to guide your decisions and avoid procedural-looking results.

How to do it...

In this recipe, we will use ZBrush **Surface Noise** to quickly establish a global layer of skin breakup across the membranes of the dragon. The goal is to create subtle tertiary variation that helps the surface react more naturally to light while keeping the sculpt flexible and non-destructive. By combining Layers and **Morph Target**, the effect can be adjusted, refined, or removed at any stage of the workflow.

One important thing to know before starting is that the **NoiseMaker** window uses its own navigation system, which behaves differently from the standard ZBrush Viewport. Spending a few moments testing the navigation and preview controls will make the adjustment process much easier.

1. Begin by pushing the model to its highest useful subdivision level. Go to **Tool** | **Geometry** and activate the maximum **SDiv** level so the mesh contains enough resolution to support fine tertiary detail without creating pixelated breakup.
2. Disable all the secondary wrinkle Layers and keep visible only the primary forms of the sculpt. This makes it easier to evaluate the procedural breakup generated by the **Surface Noise** without interference from medium wrinkles or existing tertiary detail.
3. Once the secondary Layers are disabled, go to **Tool** | **Morph Target** | **StoreMT** and store a new **Morph Target** using only the primary forms active. This will allow you to

later soften or remove the procedural noise selectively using the **Morph** Brush, especially in cleaner areas such as membrane edges, claws, or eyelids.

4. Create a new layer inside the **Tool | Layers** palette and rename it something production-friendly, such as `TER_noise_membranes`.
5. Activate the layer by enabling **Record** before applying any procedural detail. Working inside a dedicated recording layer keeps the **Surface Noise** completely non-destructive, allowing you to adjust its intensity, blend it with other details, or disable it later without affecting the underlying sculpt.
6. Go to **Tool | Surface** and activate **Noise** to preview the procedural breakup directly on the model.
7. Once enabled, click on **Edit** to open the **NoiseMaker** window, where you can control the alpha, scale, strength, UV projection, and overall behavior of the procedural skin detail.

Figure 6.23 – Surface Noise activated with the NoiseMaker panel ready for procedural skin detail adjustments

8. Once the **NoiseMaker** window is open, load the alpha you want to use for the skin breakup. In the bottom-left section of the **NoiseMaker** panel, click on the area labeled **Alpha On/Off** and select the tileable alpha that best matches the type of skin detail you want to achieve on the membranes.

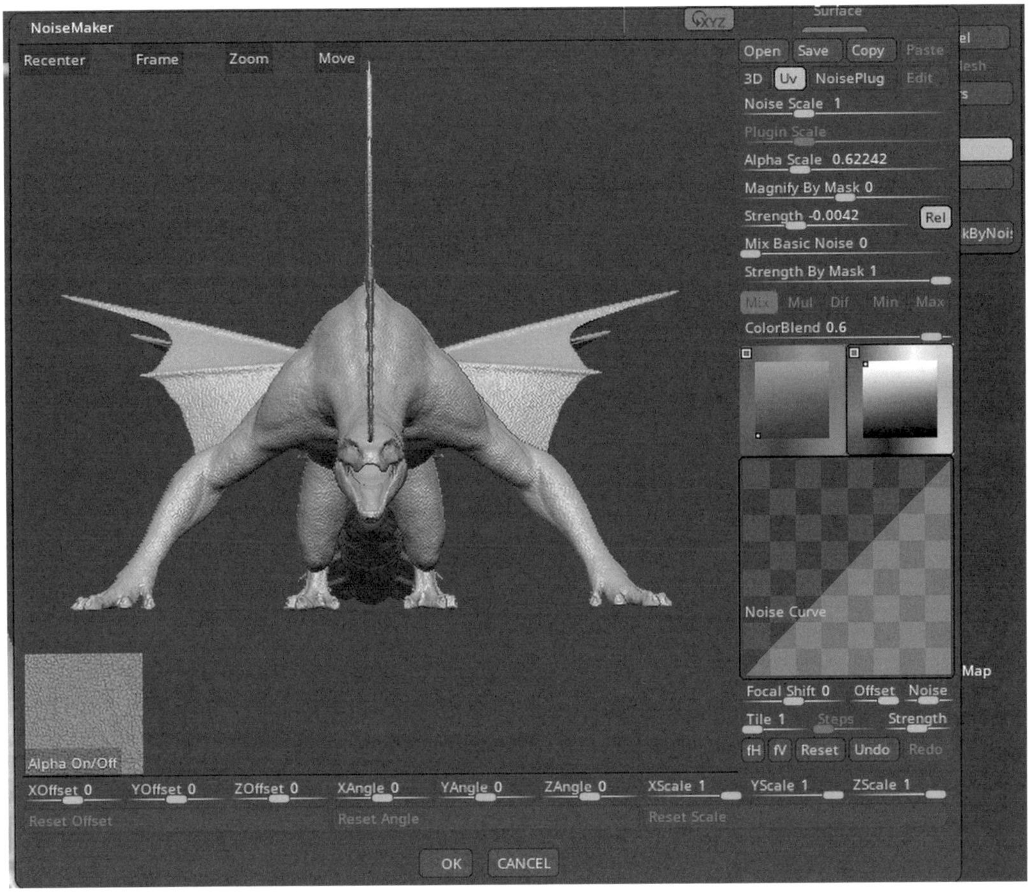

Figure 6.24 – NoiseMaker panel with a custom skin alpha loaded through the Alpha On/Off slot

9. Enable the **UV** option inside the **NoiseMaker** panel so the procedural detail follows the UV layout of the model instead of being projected in 3D space. This allows the skin pattern to remain stable and consistent across the membranes and prevents stretching caused by Viewport-based projection. As explained in *Chapter 5*, this workflow only works correctly if the model already has a clean and properly organized UV layout.

10. The first important adjustment in the **NoiseMaker** panel is setting **Mix Basic Noise** to `0`. This parameter blends your custom alpha with ZBrush's default procedural noise. By reducing it to `0`, only your selected alpha will affect the surface detail.

    Once this value is set to `0`, the **Noise Scale** parameter becomes irrelevant, since it only controls the scale of ZBrush's internal default noise pattern and no longer influences the custom alpha projection.

11. Start adjusting the **Alpha Scale** value to control the size of the procedural skin breakup across the membranes. This parameter defines how large or small the alpha pattern appears on the surface. For this dragon, I set the **Alpha Scale** to `0.6`, which creates a fine leathery skin variation without making the detail feel oversized or repetitive.
12. Once the **Alpha Scale** feels correct, the next step is controlling how strongly the noise affects the surface. This is managed through the **Strength** value, which determines how much the procedural pattern is pushed inward or outward on the mesh. Positive values inflate the detail, while negative values carve it into the surface. For skin breakup like this, it is usually better to keep the effect subtle, allowing the noise to support the sculpt rather than overpower it.

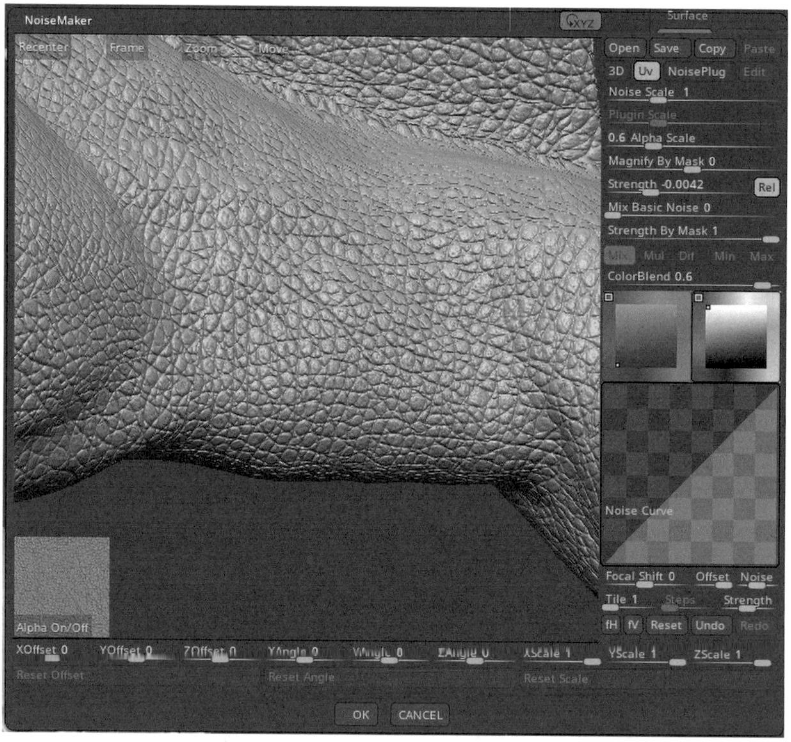

Figure 6.25 – NoiseMaker panel showing Strength set to -0.0042 for subtle recessed skin breakup

13. Once you are satisfied with the preview, press **OK** to confirm the **NoiseMaker** settings.

At this stage, there are two possible workflows depending on the result you want to achieve. The first option is using **Mask By Noise**, which generates a mask based on the procedural pattern across the entire model. This mask can then be used to manually sculpt selected areas or combined with tools such as **Tool** | **Deformation** | **Inflate** to push the masked regions outward and create additional surface depth.

The second option, which we will use in this recipe, is pressing **Apply to Mesh**. This permanently applies the procedural noise to the geometry while still recording the effect inside the active layer, keeping the workflow non-destructive and fully adjustable through the layer intensity. This is the option we'll go with for the next phase of the recipe.

After applying the noise to the mesh, the next step is cleaning all the areas where this tertiary detail is not needed. Select the **Morph** Brush using the *B, M, O* keys and begin removing the procedural breakup from regions that should remain clean or smooth.

This is especially important around areas such as claws, gums, eyelids, sharp skin transitions, or any zone where the noise would interfere with the readability of the sculpt. Since the **Morph Target** was stored before applying the **Surface Noise**, the **Morph** Brush allows you to locally restore the original clean surface while preserving the rest of the procedural detail.

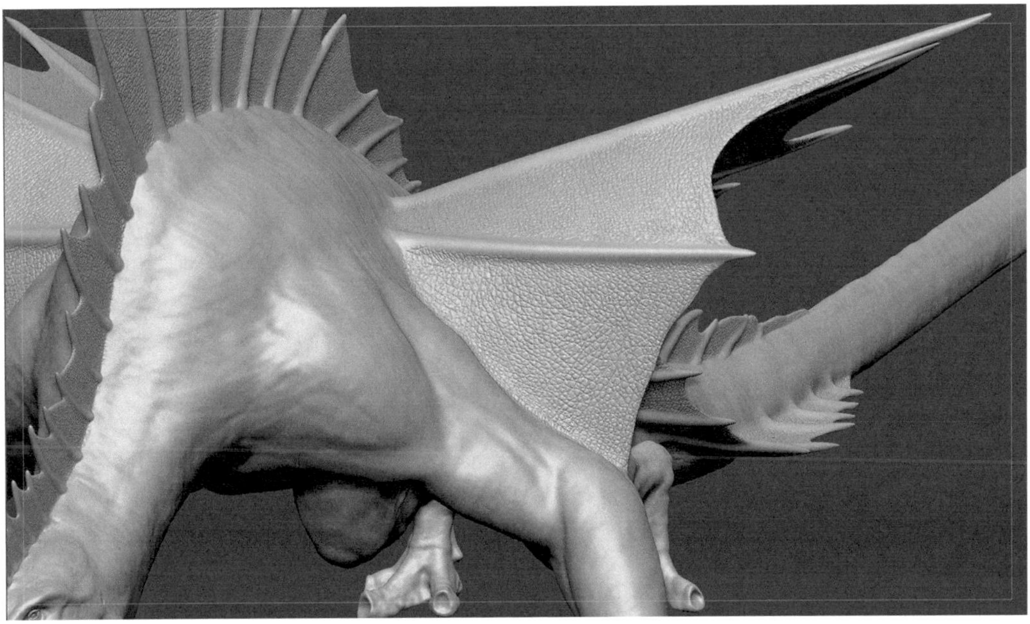

Figure 6.26 – Morph Brush used to selectively clean Surface Noise from unwanted areas of the model

Tip

Creating two or three variations of the same alpha at slightly different sizes can greatly improve the realism of the skin breakup. Smaller anatomical areas usually require finer detail, while broader surfaces benefit from larger and more open patterns. Adapting the scale of the noise to the size of the anatomical region helps avoid repetitive results and creates a more believable skin distribution across the creature.

How it works...

Surface Noise is most effective when applied over simplified and readable forms. For this reason, tertiary detail is usually created with most secondary wrinkle layers temporarily disabled. Removing medium wrinkle information makes the surface feel more stretched and visually cleaner, allowing the procedural breakup to project more evenly across the model. This not only improves the readability of the noise itself but also avoids distortions and overlapping patterns caused by complex secondary forms.

Using a dedicated layer together with **Morph Target** keeps the workflow completely non-destructive. This allows artists to test different alpha scales, strengths, and projection methods without permanently damaging the sculpt. If certain areas become too noisy or distracting, the **Morph** Brush can quickly restore the original clean surface while preserving the rest of the procedural detail.

Scale variation also plays a major role in making the result believable. Real skin does not maintain the same pore density across the entire body. Smaller anatomical areas usually require finer detail, while broader surfaces benefit from larger and more open breakup patterns. Creating multiple variations of the same alpha at different scales helps avoid repetition and gives the membranes a more organic distribution of detail.

Once the tertiary breakup is established, try re-enabling the secondary wrinkle Layers and evaluate how the different levels of detail interact together. This is an important stage because it allows you to understand whether the tertiary noise is supporting the medium forms correctly or if certain areas have become too busy or visually confusing. Often, the best results come from subtle adjustments after seeing all detail Layers combined together under neutral lighting.

Figure 6.27 – Surface Noise integrated with the secondary wrinkle Layers, creating a more natural interaction between medium and tertiary skin detail

Sculpting tertiary forms: sculpting with XYZ Textures

XYZ Textures are one of the fastest and most production-proven methods for adding realistic tertiary skin detail to a creature. Unlike procedural **Surface Noise**, XYZ maps contain real scanned skin information, making them extremely useful for introducing believable pores, compression patterns, and natural skin breakup that would be very time-consuming to sculpt entirely by hand.

In production, these textures are rarely used as a final result on their own. Instead, they work as a foundation that artists refine and adapt manually depending on the anatomy and the type of creature. The goal is not to "stamp" detail everywhere, but to use the projection as a starting point that supports the sculpt while preserving artistic control.

For this recipe, we will focus only on the neck area of the dragon to demonstrate the workflow in a clean and readable way. The neck is an excellent region for testing XYZ projection because it contains stretched skin, compression zones, and layered secondary wrinkles that react well to tertiary breakup.

As with the previous **Surface Noise** workflow, it is usually better to temporarily disable most secondary wrinkle Layers before projecting XYZ details. Simpler and more stretched forms allow the projection to sit more cleanly on the surface, avoiding distortion and helping the skin information integrate more naturally with the anatomy.

Once the projection is applied, we will manually refine the result using sculpting brushes to break symmetry, introduce variation, and adapt the detail to the directional flow of the neck folds. This combination of scan information and hand sculpting is what gives the final surface a believable production-quality result.

Figure 6.28 shows the XYZ detailing result we will build in this workflow:

Figure 6.28 – XYZ tertiary detailing applied to the dragon and refined manually to integrate with the existing wrinkle structure

Note

This recipe assumes familiarity with core ZBrush concepts such as masking, alpha manipulation, subdivision levels, **Morph Target**, **Layers**, and projection-based workflows. While each step is explained throughout the recipe, a basic understanding of these tools will help you focus on the artistic decisions rather than the mechanics of the software.

Getting ready

For this recipe, you'll need your creature sculpt at the highest practical subdivision level, ideally around **50–100** million points if your hardware allows. This ensures enough vertex density for accurate XYZ projection without visible pixelation. Before starting, ensure the following:

- Deactivate all secondary Layers and keep only the primary forms visible to preserve readability during projection.
- Load the XYZ bump map you want to use as an alpha inside the **Alpha** palette. If necessary, you can prepare and crop the texture in Photoshop, isolating only the specific skin area you are interested in projecting. This helps keep the projection cleaner, more focused, and easier to control during the sculpting process.

If you want to create custom alphas from interesting skin images found online, import the texture using **Texture** | **Import** and convert it into an alpha with **Texture** | **Make Alpha**.

When choosing reference images, avoid textures with extremely strong contrast between dark and bright areas. In projection workflows, very dark values often translate into flatter or less readable detail rather than deeper skin information. Textures with balanced grayscale values usually produce cleaner and more believable results once projected onto the sculpt.

If necessary, rebalance the image beforehand in Photoshop using **Image** | **Adjustments** | **Levels** or **Curves** to soften extreme contrast and create more even grayscale transitions.

How to do it...

In this recipe, we will project XYZ tertiary skin information onto the neck of the dragon to create more realistic pores, skin tension, and natural surface breakup. Rather than relying only on procedural noise, this workflow uses real scanned skin information combined with manual sculpting adjustments to achieve a more believable production-quality result. As with the previous workflows, the goal is to integrate the tertiary information with the existing anatomy and wrinkle flow of the creature. Let's begin:

1. Before starting the XYZ projection, create a new layer inside **Tool** | **Layers** and rename it using a production-friendly name, such as `TER_skin_neck` or `skin_neck`.
2. Activate the layer in **Record** mode so every projected and sculpted detail will be stored non-destructively. This allows you to control the intensity of the projection later, blend it with other Layers, or completely disable it if needed during look development or art direction changes.
3. Before continuing, store a new **Morph Target** using **Tool** | **Morph Target** | **StoreMT**. This will be extremely useful later to selectively clean, soften, or completely restore

specific areas of the projection using the **Morph** Brush, helping you avoid destroying important sculpted details while keeping full control over the tertiary surface breakup.

4. Import your XYZ bump map inside the **Alpha** palette. Then, hold *Ctrl* and, while keeping it pressed, select the imported XYZ bump map from the **Alpha** palette. This assigns the selected alpha to the **Mask** brush. Release *Ctrl*, then go to **Stroke** | **Rect** and select the **Rect** stroke type instead of **Dots**. Finally, hold *Ctrl* again and drag on the model to project the alpha as a mask.

   Using *Ctrl* + *drag* with the **Rect** stroke allows you to project the alpha as a mask directly onto the surface with full control over scale, rotation, and placement. This is especially useful for aligning the skin detail with the anatomical direction of the neck and avoiding repetitive projections.

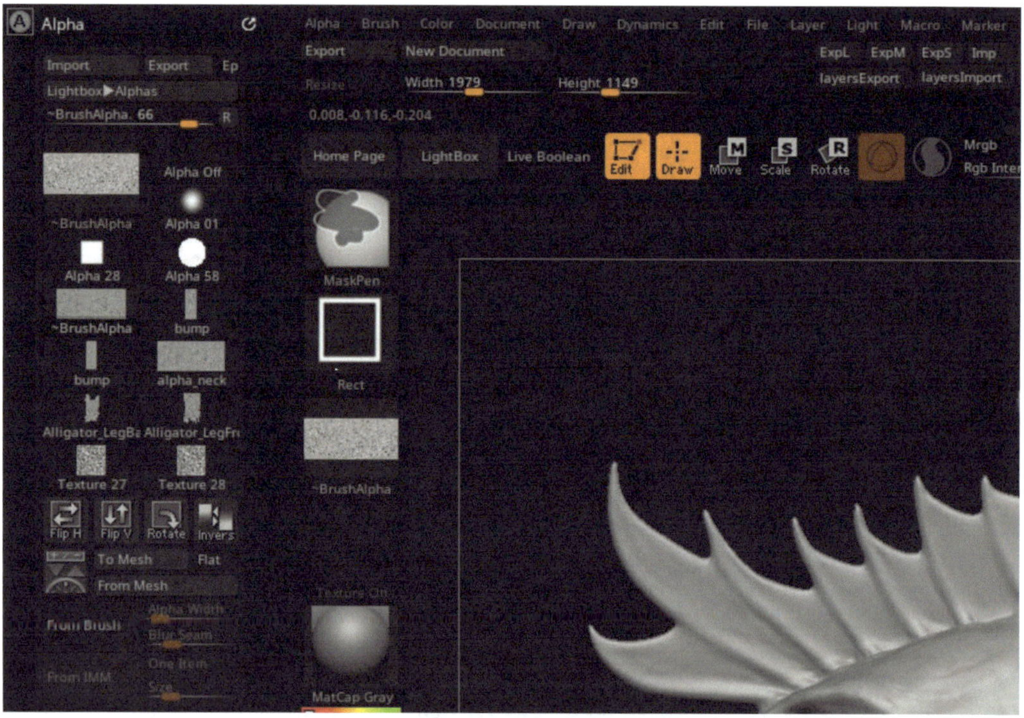

Figure 6.29 – XYZ bump alpha loaded with Rect stroke active for controlled tertiary projection

5. Move to a **Side** view of the neck before starting the projection. In this case, the dragon's neck naturally bends downward, while the XYZ texture flows horizontally. Instead of rotating the alpha itself, rotate the camera relative to the character so the texture direction follows the anatomical flow more naturally.
   To do this in ZBrush, press and hold *Shift* first, then click and drag with the left mouse button, or with the pen on your tablet. Once the camera snapping starts, you can release *Shift* and continue rotating freely while maintaining the aligned view. This technique is extremely useful for matching directional skin textures to curved anatomical areas without distorting the projection.

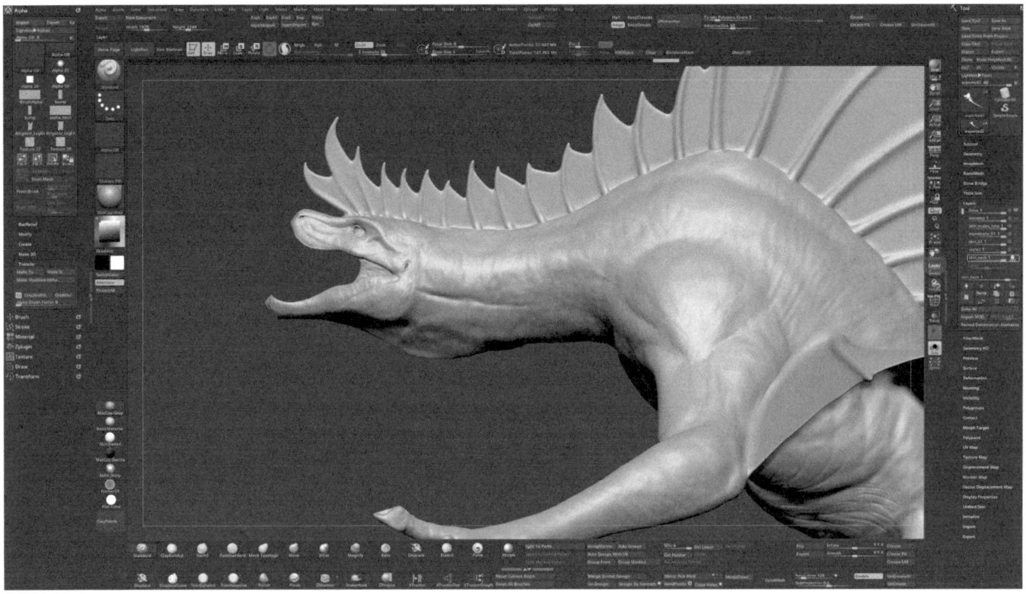

Figure 6.30 – Side view rotated to align the horizontal XYZ texture with the downward anatomical flow of the neck

Note

A note on mask projection

Before continuing with the next step, it is important to understand how mask projection behaves while working in **Symmetry** mode. During this stage, keeping the sculpt symmetrical is extremely useful because it allows the tertiary skin information to remain consistent across both sides of the neck.

When working in orthographic views such as **Top**, **Bottom**, **Left**, or **Right**, mask projection usually behaves correctly because the projection direction remains clean and predictable. However, problems often appear when moving into 3/4 views. Since the alpha is projected from the camera direction, the mask can accidentally intersect both sides of the mesh at the same time, creating overlapping projections and unwanted skin detail on the opposite side of the character.

For this reason, it is very important to carefully control how the camera is rotated before projecting the mask.

If a specific projection angle is necessary and overlapping cannot be avoided, a safer workflow is to temporarily disable symmetry and project the detail only on one side of the character. Once the projection and sculpting adjustments are complete, duplicate the SubTool, mirror it, and project the detail back onto the opposite side while masking the already finished regions to avoid destroying the previous work.

6. With **Symmetry** activated and the camera correctly aligned, begin projecting the XYZ alpha onto the neck by holding *Ctrl* and dragging on the surface using the **Rect** stroke.

7. Position the projection carefully so the skin flow follows the anatomical direction of the folds and stretched areas of the neck.

   At this stage, focus on creating a believable distribution of skin information rather than covering the entire surface perfectly. Slight variations in placement and orientation will help the final result feel more natural and less procedural.

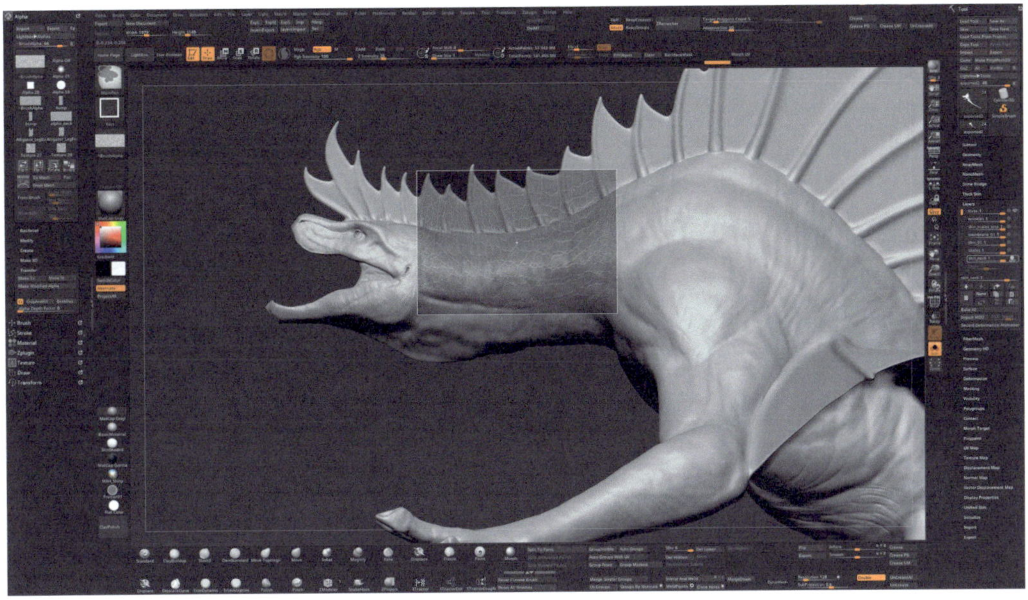

Figure 6.31 – XYZ mask projection applied on the neck using Ctrl + drag with Rect stroke active

8. Once the projection is positioned correctly, invert the mask so the protected and affected areas are swapped. This allows the projected skin information to become the active region that will receive the sculpting adjustments in the next step.

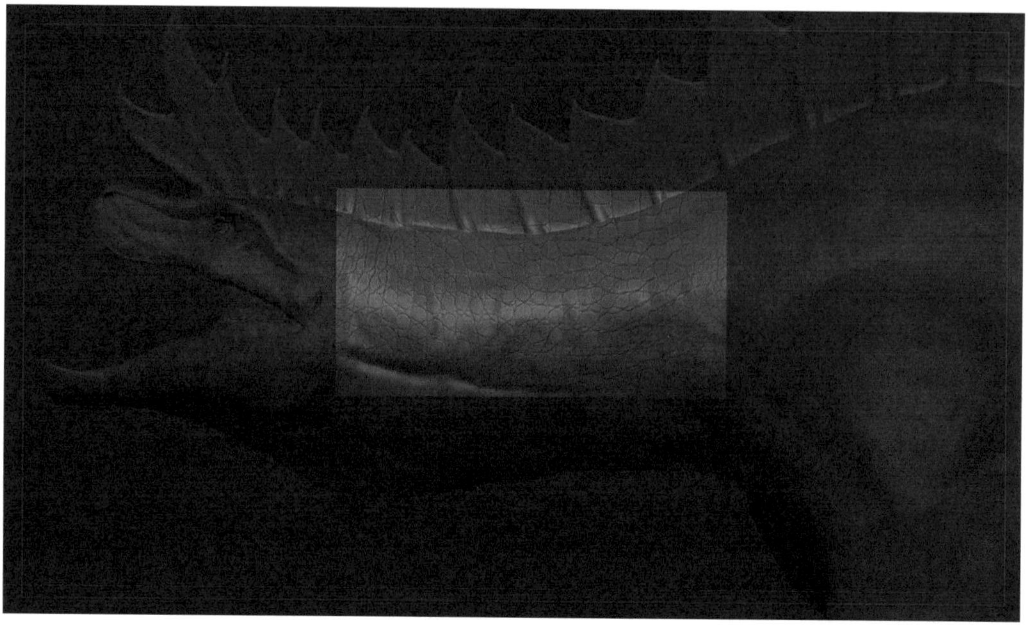

Figure 6.32 – Inverted XYZ mask ready for tertiary sculpting adjustments

9. With the mask inverted, you can now start pushing the tertiary detail into the surface. One option is using **Tool** | **Deformation** | **Inflate** to globally expand the masked skin information.

   For more controlled and organic results, it is usually better to sculpt manually over the mask using brushes such as **Standard**, **ClayBuildup** with the rounded **Alpha 06**, or the **Elastic** Brush to soften and blend the forms more naturally into the anatomy.

10. Keep the brush intensity very low during this stage, usually between `1` and `7`, to maintain maximum control over the tertiary breakup. For the **Elastic** Brush, slightly higher values around `30` generally work better for soft skin transitions and subtle organic inflation.

11. If you decide to use **Tool** | **Deformation** | **Inflate** instead of manual sculpting, keep the values very subtle. In this scene, I used an **Inflate** value of `1`, which was already enough to create a believable amount of skin extrusion without making the tertiary detail feel too swollen or artificial. Small values generally provide much better control and preserve the natural tension of the surface.

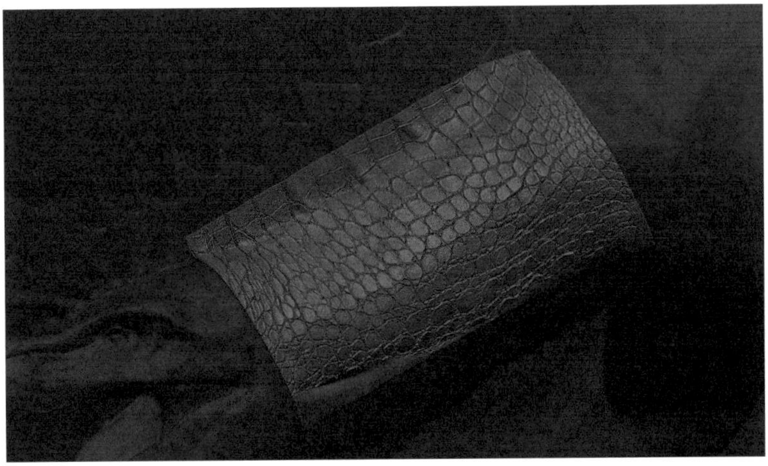

Figure 6.33 – Inflate deformation applied subtly to enhance the projected XYZ tertiary detail

12. Once the tertiary detail is applied, switch to the **Morph** Brush using *B, M, O* and begin cleaning all the areas where the XYZ projection is not needed.
13. Focus especially on cleaner anatomical regions such as membrane borders, sharp transitions, claws, gums, or any area where excessive tertiary breakup could reduce readability.
14. Use a soft brush and low intensity to gradually restore the original surface stored inside the **Morph Target** while preserving the projected detail only where it supports the anatomy.

Figure 6.34 – Morph Brush used to selectively clean and restore unwanted XYZ projection areas

At this stage, begin sculpting manually over the projected XYZ detail to personalize and integrate the surface with the rest of the creature. In this case, the projected scales are still relatively flat, so the goal is to increase their volume and improve the variation between the different skin elements.

For this type of work, I usually prefer using the following brushes:

- **Elastic Brush**: It allows the forms to expand naturally without destroying the smaller tertiary information already projected on the surface.
- **Inflate Brush**: Alongside brushes such as **Standard** and **ClayBuildup**, the **Inflate** Brush is used at a low intensity of around 7 to gently push selected scales outward and create more depth variation.
- **Magnify Brush**: For sharper and more localized volume accents, this brush works very well at an intensity of `20`.
- **Slash3 Brush**: To sharpen wrinkles, cuts, or scale separations, I use this brush at a very low intensity, usually around `10-20`. In some sharper regions, especially along the borders of the scales, using **Slash3** in **ZAdd** mode helps create a cleaner and more defined edge without making the sculpt feel too mechanical.

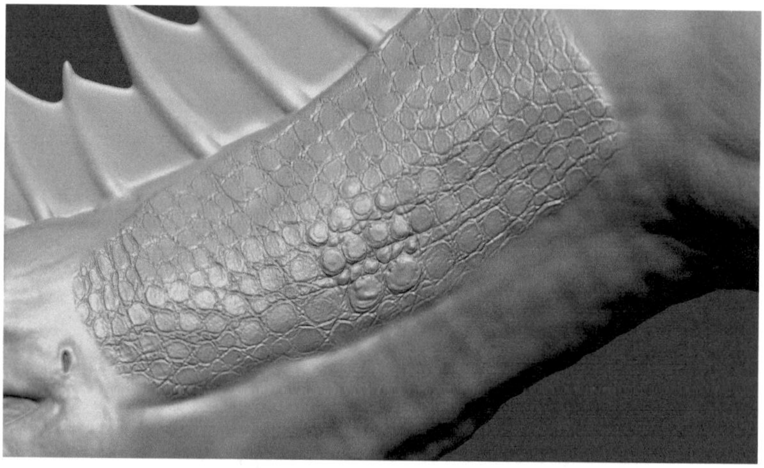

Figure 6.35 – Manual sculpting pass over the XYZ projection using the Elastic, Standard, and Slash3 brushes to increase scale volume and sharpen surface transitions

How it works...

This workflow combines the precision of real scanned skin information with the flexibility of manual sculpting. Unlike procedural **Surface Noise**, XYZ projections contain directional and organic breakup captured from real surfaces, which immediately adds a more believable skin quality to the creature. However, the projection alone is never enough. The real strength of this technique comes from how the projected information is integrated and sculpted into the anatomy afterward.

One of the most important aspects of this process is working with only the primary forms visible while all secondary wrinkle Layers remain disabled. Keeping the surface cleaner and less compressed makes the projection easier to read and prevents the tertiary detail from becoming visually chaotic. Broad anatomical surfaces also allow the alpha to project more evenly, especially in stretched areas such as the neck membranes and skin folds.

Using the **Rect** stroke together with *Ctrl* projection gives full control over scale, direction, and placement of the skin detail. Instead of stamping the texture randomly, the projection should always follow the anatomical flow of the creature. In this example, rotating the camera instead of rotating the alpha allowed the horizontal skin texture to naturally follow the downward direction of the dragon's neck, producing a much more believable result.

The XYZ textures and other projected alpha workflows are fundamentally camera-dependent. Unlike procedural noise, the projected detail is captured from a specific viewing angle, which means the quality of the result depends heavily on how accurately the projection direction matches the underlying forms. Understanding this relationship helps prevent distortion, overlapping projection data, and unnecessary cleanup work later in the process.

After the mask is inverted, the projected information becomes a guide rather than a final result. Using **Inflate**, **Elastic**, **Standard**, **ClayBuildup**, **Magnify**, and **Slash3** brushes allows you to reinterpret the scanned information instead of simply copying it. This stage is where the sculpt starts feeling alive, because the tertiary forms begin adapting to the underlying anatomy rather than remaining a flat texture projection.

The **Morph Target** workflow is equally important because it provides complete control over cleanup and readability. Restoring cleaner areas around membranes, sharp transitions, or anatomical landmarks prevents the surface from becoming noisy everywhere. In production, believable skin usually comes from balancing highly detailed regions with calmer resting areas.

Finally, once the tertiary projection feels integrated correctly, try reactivating the secondary wrinkle Layers to evaluate the final interaction between primary, secondary, and tertiary forms. This is usually the moment when the skin starts feeling cohesive and production-ready, with the larger wrinkle flow supporting the smaller surface breakup naturally.

7

Creating Custom Brushes and Insert Meshes for Creature Tertiary Details

In this chapter, you'll learn how to create reusable detailing tools and production-friendly workflows for adding tertiary information to creatures in ZBrush. Instead of sculpting every scale, spike, or horn manually, you'll build custom brushes and Insert Mesh workflows that allow you to distribute complex details quickly while maintaining consistency across the entire character.

You'll start by creating custom scale brushes and understanding how to repeat surface elements efficiently on organic forms. Then, you'll explore how **Insert Mesh brushes** can be used to add spikes, horns, and secondary protrusions in a controlled and non-destructive way. The goal is not only to improve sculpting speed but also to create reusable detailing systems that can be adapted to different creatures and production scenarios.

Finally, you'll use Morph Targets to blend and adjust tertiary surface information, learning how to mix different skin patterns and textures while keeping full artistic control over the sculpt. This approach is especially useful when combining multiple surface materials and avoiding destructive edits during the detailing phase.

In this chapter, we'll cover the following recipes:

- Creating custom brushes for scales
- Using Insert Mesh brushes to add spikes, scales, and horns
- Using Morph Targets for better control and adjustments

By the end of this chapter, you'll understand how to build efficient tertiary detailing workflows that can be reused across different creature projects, improving both sculpting speed and production consistency.

Figure 7.1 shows the type of result we'll be working toward as we create custom scale brushes, Insert Mesh elements, and controlled tertiary skin variations:

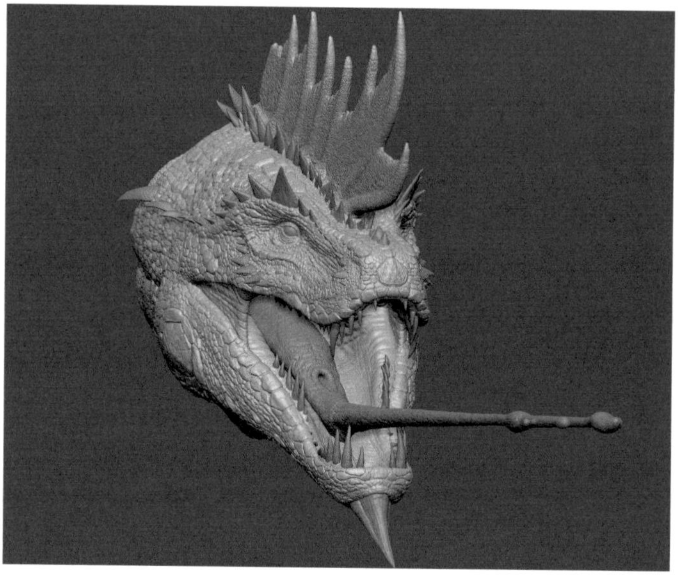

Figure 7.1 – dragonCrest head showing custom scales and Insert Mesh details

Technical requirements

To complete this chapter, you'll need **ZBrush 2024** or later, **Maya**, and **Unfold3D** for topology and UV preparation workflows related to Insert Mesh creation and reusable detailing assets.

For hardware specifications and recommended system configurations, please refer to the *Technical requirements* section in *Chapter 1*.

For the required software, companion files, and download instructions, refer to the *Technical requirements* section in *Chapter 6*.

In addition, the `Chapter06_07` folder in the GitHub repository includes the following custom brushes created specifically for this book:

- `InsertMesh_scales_001.zbp`: A custom **InsertMesh** Brush containing reusable scales that can be quickly placed and customized to enrich creature surfaces.
- `MAB_scales_001.zbp`: A custom **MultiAlpha** Brush designed to create layered skin breakup and scale variations while maintaining a fast, non-destructive sculpting workflow.

You can download the example project files for this book by following the instructions in the *Download the example code/resource files* section in the *Preface* of this book.

This chapter's code/resource files are included in the downloadable code/resource bundle.

Creating custom brushes for scales

In creature production, **custom brushes** are one of the fastest and most efficient ways to create believable skin patterns while maintaining consistency across large surfaces. Instead of sculpting every single scale manually, building a personalized alpha brush allows you to stamp complex forms repeatedly while still keeping artistic control over variation and silhouette.

In this recipe, we will create a custom scale brush directly inside ZBrush by sculpting the pattern on a plane and converting it into a reusable **Alpha 3D** Brush. This workflow is useful for creature artists because it allows you to generate complex scale structures that already contain depth, layering, and organic transitions before applying them across the model.

The scales will follow a reptilian structure inspired by iguanas, tortoises, and large lizards, focusing on readable forms that work correctly under production lighting and displacement rendering.

By the end of this recipe, you will have a custom reusable brush that can be applied across different body regions while maintaining consistent detail quality and sculpting speed. *Figure 7.2* shows the final scale sculpt that we will create before generating the brush:

Figure 7.2 – The custom scale Alpha 3D Brush used throughout this recipe

Getting ready

Before creating the custom scale brush, we first need to ensure the following:

1. Prepare a clean sculpting surface that will be used to build the scale pattern. In this workflow, we will use a simple **Plane3D** inside ZBrush as the base geometry for sculpting the scales that will later become a reusable **Alpha 3D** Brush.
2. Start by selecting **Tool** | **Plane3D** and convert it into editable geometry using **Tool** | **Make PolyMesh3D**. This step is essential because primitive objects inside ZBrush cannot be sculpted until they are converted into a PolyMesh3D object.

Other than this, no complex setup is required at this stage. The purpose of this preparation is simply to create a neutral sculpting surface where the scale forms can be developed cleanly before generating the final brush.

How to do it...

We will start by preparing the plane so it can hold enough geometry for sculpting the scale pattern. Before adding subdivisions, it is important to disable smoothing; otherwise, ZBrush will soften the borders of the plane and slightly shrink the surface during subdivision. Follow these steps:

1. With the **Plane3D** already converted into a **PolyMesh3D** and visible on the canvas, open **Tool** | **Geometry** and switch off **Smt** before subdividing the mesh. This keeps the plane flat and preserves its original borders while we increase the resolution for sculpting.

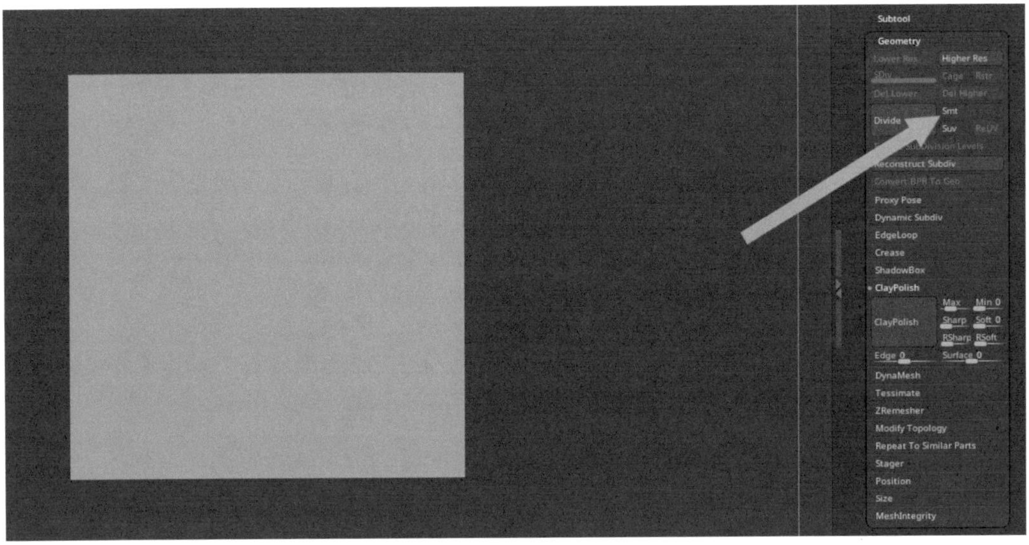

Figure 7.3 – The Smt option disabled before subdividing the Plane3D

2. After disabling **Smt**, continue subdividing the plane using **Tool | Geometry | Divide** until you reach approximately **7** to **8** subdivision levels. This amount of geometry is usually more than enough to sculpt detailed scale information while keeping the workflow responsive and easy to manage.
   At this stage, the goal is simply to create a dense and stable sculpting surface capable of holding tertiary detail without visible pixelation or stretched forms.
3. Activate **Symmetry** on the *X* axis by pressing *X* on the keyboard. At this stage, we will begin defining the main silhouette of the scale using a simple mask as a visual guide for the sculpting process.
4. Using *Ctrl* to paint a mask directly on the plane, sketch the overall perimeter of the scale shape. Do not focus too much on precision at this stage. The goal is simply to establish a readable primary shape that will later be refined and enriched with tertiary information. This initial mask acts as a foundation for the entire brush and helps maintain consistency and symmetry while sculpting the scale structure.

Figure 7.4 – Initial masked silhouette used to define the primary shape of the scale

> **Note**
>
> While sculpting the scale, avoid pushing any part of the surface below the original plane level. The untouched plane must always remain the *zero height value* for the future **Alpha 3D** Brush. If parts of the sculpt go into negative depth, ZBrush may interpret a different height as the new reference level when generating the brush. This often causes the surrounding square plane to be sculpted as well once the alpha is applied to another surface. To avoid this issue, always build the scale outward from the plane instead of carving inward.

5. Once the primary silhouette of the scale has been established, invert the mask by holding *Ctrl* and clicking on the canvas background. This allows you to protect the surrounding plane while sculpting only the scale itself.
6. Start building the main volume using brushes such as **Brush** | **ClayBuildup** and **Brush** | **Standard** to establish thickness, surface tension, and the primary anatomical direction of the scale. Focus first on creating large, readable forms before moving into smaller surface information.

7. After the primary structure is working correctly, refine the secondary details using brushes such as **Brush | Slash3** or **Brush | DamStandard** to define sharper separations, directional cuts, and smaller surface transitions. At this stage, avoid over-detailing the sculpt. We simply need to create a versatile brush capable of being reused across multiple areas of the creature.

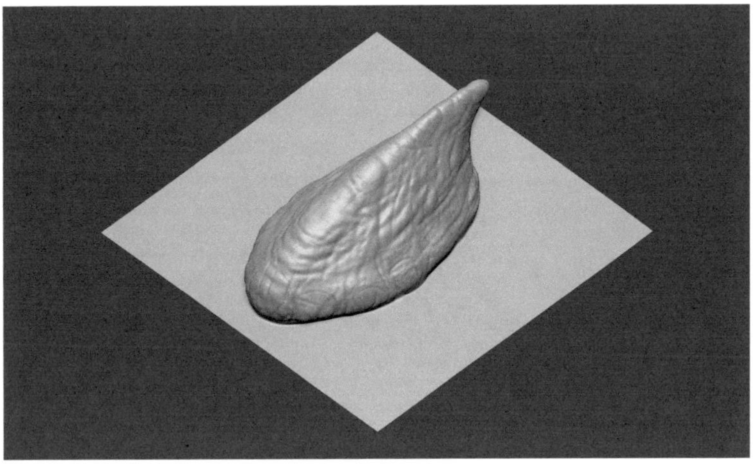

Figure 7.5 – Scale sculpt refined using ClayBuildup, Standard, Slash3, and DamStandard brushes

8. Once the scale sculpt is completed, switch to a perfectly frontal orthographic view so the scale is viewed directly from the top relative to the plane surface. Since the Plane3D is positioned vertically in the scene, the camera must face the sculpt straight on before generating the alpha.

   This step is *very important* because the **GrabDoc** process (a function that captures the visible depth information from the current camera view and converts it into an alpha) captures depth information based entirely on the camera angle relative to the mesh. If the camera is slightly rotated or positioned in perspective, the generated alpha can become distorted, stretched, or produce incorrect depth information once converted into a **MultiAlpha** Brush.

To avoid projection errors, make sure the scale fills the canvas correctly and that the camera is perfectly aligned before continuing.

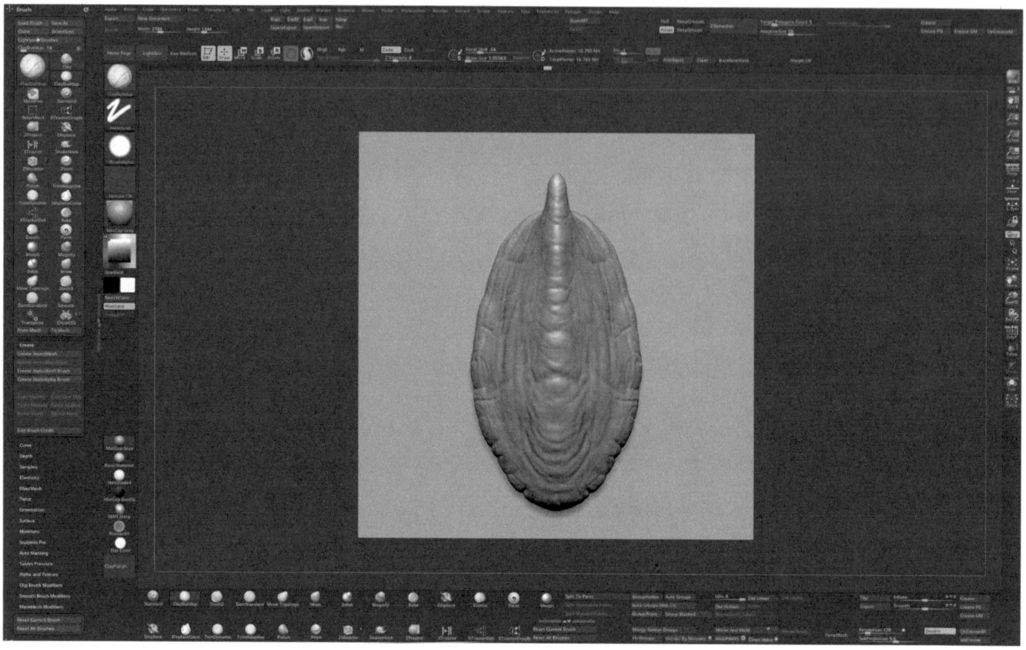

Figure 7.6 – Frontal orthographic view used before generating the GrabDoc alpha

9. After positioning the sculpt in a perfectly aligned frontal view, select **Brush | Chisel3D**. This brush already supports the MultiAlpha workflow and provides an excellent base for generating reusable sculpting brushes with volumetric depth information.

Note

In this recipe, the **MultiAlpha Brush system** is used to convert the sculpted scale into a reusable **Alpha 3D** Brush. The technical advantages of this workflow are explained later in the *How it works...* section.

10. Once the brush is selected, go to **Brush | Create | Create MultiAlpha Brush**. ZBrush will automatically generate a new custom brush using the depth information captured from the sculpted scale. The resulting brush can now be reused across the creature surface to stamp consistent tertiary scale details while preserving the original sculpted volume. At this point, it is recommended to test the brush on a separate plane or sphere to verify that the depth and silhouette behave correctly during sculpting.

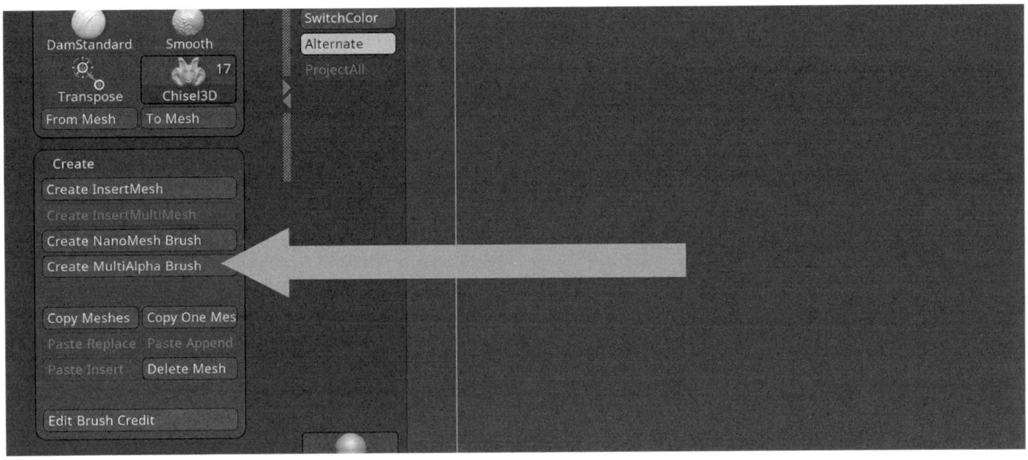

Figure 7.7 – The MultiAlpha Brush button used to generate the custom 3D scale brush from the sculpted plane

Now that we have generated our custom **MultiAlpha** Brush, we can create a personalized icon to make the brush easier to identify and organize inside the ZBrush interface, especially when working with large custom brush libraries during production.

1. Start by selecting a simple **Sphere3D** from the **Tool** palette and convert it into editable geometry using **Tool | Make PolyMesh3D**. This sphere will be used as the preview object for generating the final brush icon.
2. After converting the sphere into a PolyMesh object, increase the resolution using **Tool | Geometry | Divide** until the surface has enough geometry to display the scale details correctly. A few subdivision levels are usually sufficient for this purpose.

3. Once the sphere is subdivided, select your newly created custom scale brush and begin applying the scales across the sphere surface. Try to distribute the details evenly while rotating the model to create a readable and visually appealing preview of the brush behavior. At this stage, the goal is to create a clean and recognizable representation of the brush before capturing the final icon.

Figure 7.8 – Custom scale brush applied on a subdivided sphere for icon generation

4. Once the preview sphere has been detailed with the custom scales, position the model at a clean, readable angle inside the canvas. This view will become the visual representation of the brush inside the **Brush** palette. Go to **Brush | SelectIcon** located at the top of the interface. ZBrush will capture the current Viewport and assign it as the new custom icon for the brush, making it easier to identify during future sculpting sessions and production workflows.

Figure 7.9 – Using Brush | SelectIcon to generate the custom brush icon

5. After generating the custom icon, the final step is to permanently save the brush so it can be reused in future projects and production workflows. Go to **Brush** | **Save As** and save the new **MultiAlpha** Brush inside your custom brush library.
   At this stage, it is recommended to use a clean naming convention that clearly identifies both the asset and the brush purpose. For example:

   `MAB_scales_001.zbp` (as in our GitHub folder), `MAB_dragonCrest_scales_v001.zbp`, or `MAB_scales_v001.zbp`

   In this case, the prefix `MAB` stands for `MultiAlpha Brush`, making it immediately clear which type of brush is being used inside the production library. Using structured naming conventions becomes important when managing large collections of custom brushes shared across multiple creature projects.

Now that the custom **MultiAlpha** Brush is ready, my recommendation is to apply it to the `dragonCrest` creature using a dedicated sculpting layer while temporarily disabling all existing secondary and tertiary detail layers.

This approach makes it much easier to evaluate the scale pattern clearly without visual noise coming from wrinkles, pores, skin breakup, or additional surface information already present on the creature. Working on an isolated layer also gives you full control over intensity, blending, and adjustments later in the sculpting process.

In production, this workflow is useful because it allows artists to test multiple scale patterns non-destructively while keeping the base sculpt clean and fully editable. Once the scale distribution is working correctly, the layer intensity can be adjusted or combined with the remaining detailing passes.

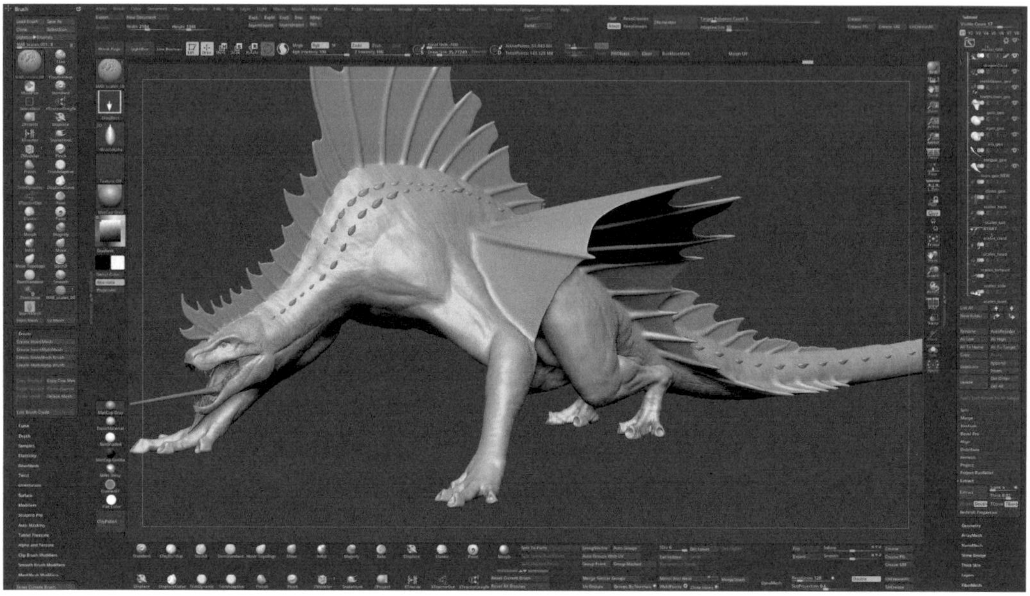

Figure 7.10 – Custom scale brush applied on the dragonCrest creature using a dedicated sculpting layer

How it works...

This workflow is based on a very important concept in creature detailing. Instead of relying on standard grayscale alphas, we are generating a custom **MultiAlpha Brush**, which is capable of preserving much more volumetric information during sculpting.

A traditional alpha usually affects the surface mostly along the surface normal direction, creating height variation that primarily pushes information outward along the local depth axis. While this works well for pores, wrinkles, and surface breakup, it becomes more limited when dealing with layered reptilian scales or forms that require stronger silhouette variation.

By sculpting the scale manually on a subdivided plane and generating the brush through **GrabDoc** and **Brush | Create | Create MultiAlpha Brush**, we are effectively capturing real volumetric depth information directly from the sculpt. This allows the brush to preserve not only height variation, but also the lateral shape transitions and directional forms visible in the original sculpted scale.

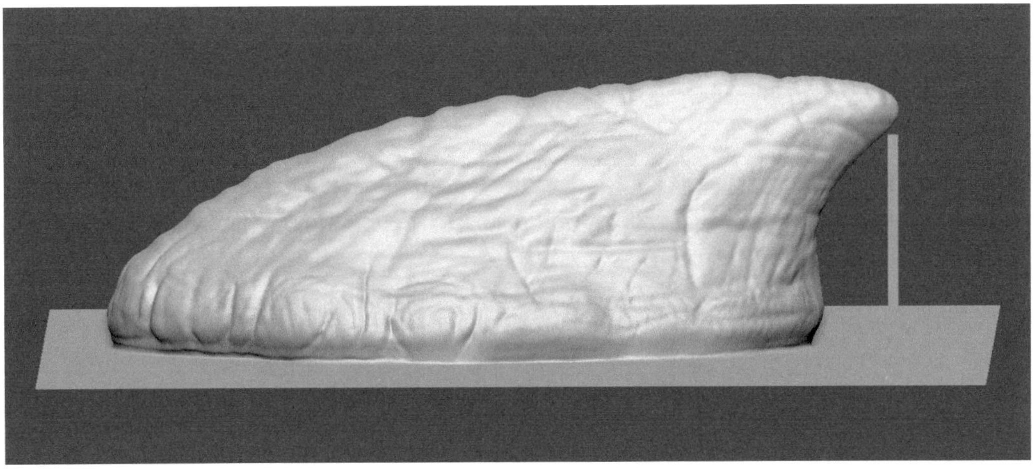

Figure 7.11 – Example of volumetric scale depth preserved by the MultiAlpha Brush

The real strength of the **MultiAlpha** Brush workflow appears when multiple scale variations are sculpted on separate SubTools. During brush creation, ZBrush can use these individual SubTools as separate brush elements, allowing a single brush to contain multiple scale designs instead of repeating the same shape everywhere.

From a production perspective, this reduces visible repetition, creates more natural surface variation, and allows artists to build reusable libraries of scales that can be shared across multiple creature projects.

Using Insert Mesh brushes to add spikes, scales, and horns

In this recipe, we will explore how to create and use custom **InsertMultiMesh (IMM)** brushes to efficiently place spikes, scales, horns, and secondary creature elements across the `dragonCrest` model. An **IMM Brush** is a special type of Insert Mesh brush that can contain multiple mesh variations inside a single brush, allowing artists to quickly cycle through or randomly place different elements during sculpting. Unlike standard sculpting workflows, where each element is manually rebuilt, Insert Mesh brushes allow artists to rapidly distribute reusable geometry while preserving consistency, silhouette quality, and production speed.

One of the most important aspects of this workflow is that the meshes used for the Insert Mesh brushes will already contain clean topology and production-ready UVs. This means the inserted elements can immediately integrate into downstream workflows such as texturing, lookdev, displacement generation, and rendering without requiring additional reconstruction later in production.

For this reason, the workflow shown in this recipe has been specifically designed around clean retopology and organized UV preparation rather than simple concept sculpting. The goal is not only to create visually appealing secondary elements, but also to build reusable assets ready for a professional VFX or animation pipeline.

By the end of this recipe, you'll be able to distribute custom Insert Mesh spikes and scales across the `dragonCrest` creature while preserving clean topology and organized UVs, as shown in *Figure 7.12*:

Figure 7.12 – Insert Mesh spikes and secondary elements distributed across the dragonCrest creature using clean topology and production-ready UVs

> **Note**
>
> If you have not read them yet, it is highly recommended to review the *Handling topology in complex areas: eyes, eyelids, ears and nose, claws and teeth, as well as tongue and gums* recipe in *Chapter 4*, together with the *UVs for secondary elements: eyes, claws, teeth, gums, tongue* recipe in *Chapter 5*, as these workflows directly support the techniques explained in this recipe.

Getting ready

Before starting this workflow, complete the following preparation steps:

1. Open the latest version of the `dragonCrest` creature and temporarily disable only the tertiary skin detailing layers, such as fine scale noise, micro skin breakup, and small tertiary surface patterns. The secondary forms and wrinkle layers should remain

visible, since they are extremely important for understanding where spikes, horns, and secondary elements should be integrated anatomically across the creature.

2. Keep the wrinkle information active to help evaluate skin compression, tension areas, and natural directional flow, allowing the Insert Mesh elements to feel properly embedded into the anatomy rather than randomly placed on top of the surface.
3. Leave the tertiary skin information intentionally disabled because, once the horns or spikes are inserted, the surrounding integration area will usually need to be resculpted to blend the new geometry correctly into the existing skin forms.
4. Create a simple **Sphere3D**, which will later be transformed into the base geometry for the Insert Mesh workflow.

As explained in previous chapters, make sure the project scale and scene organization remain consistent throughout the workflow.

> **Note**
>
> This workflow is intentionally designed around production-ready assets rather than sculpt-only details. The spikes, horns, scales, and other anatomical elements created in this recipe are built with clean topology and organized UVs from the beginning. This allows them to be reused across multiple creatures while remaining ready for downstream tasks such as rigging, texturing, displacement generation, and rendering without requiring additional reconstruction work later in production.

How to do it...

In this workflow, we will create a custom scale element starting from a simple sphere and transform it into reusable geometry for the Insert Mesh workflow. Unlike the previous recipe focused on **MultiAlpha** Brushes, this technique produces real geometry with clean silhouette information, making it ideal for spikes, horns, large scales, and secondary creature elements intended for production use. The workflow is divided into the subsections that follow.

Sculpting the base scale element

The main goal of this stage is to sculpt a believable scale with strong primary and secondary forms while keeping the topology flexible enough for future retopology and UV preparation.

Let's begin:

1. Start by selecting the previously created **Sphere3D** and convert it into editable geometry using **Tool | Make PolyMesh3D**.

2. Once converted, in **Tool | Geometry | DynaMesh**, set **Resolution** to approximately 512, then click **DynaMesh**. This value provides enough density to sculpt clean forms while still remaining responsive during the blocking phase.
3. Begin sculpting the scale using the same primary and secondary form-building workflow introduced in the *Sculpting the claws* section of the *Blocking hands and fingers for creatures* recipe in *Chapter 3*. Focus on creating a clean, readable silhouette and a strong anatomical structure that can be reused efficiently across the creature. Avoid spending time on tertiary details or micro surface noise at this stage.

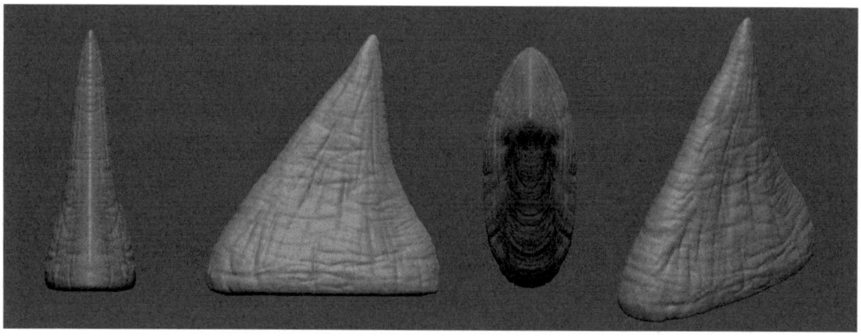

Figure 7.13 – Sculpting the base scale using DynaMesh and the Move, ClayBuildup, and Slash3 brushes

Retopologizing and preparing production geometry

Once the scale sculpt is completed, export the geometry as an OBJ file and bring it into **Maya** to begin the retopology and UV preparation process. Now the goal is to transform the sculpted concept geometry into a clean, production-ready asset suitable for Insert Mesh workflows. The retopology should focus on creating clean edge flow and a manageable polygon density while preserving the original silhouette of the sculpt. After completing the topology, proceed with the UV layout preparation so the scale is immediately ready for texturing and downstream production tasks once inserted on the creature.

For the complete retopology and UV workflow demonstrated in this recipe, please refer to the *Handling topology in complex areas: eyes, eyelids, ears and nose, claws and teeth, as well as tongue and gums* recipe in *Chapter 4*, together with the *UVs for secondary elements: eyes, claws, teeth, gums, tongue* recipe in *Chapter 5*.

These chapters explain the exact workflow used to prepare clean secondary geometry for production integration.

1. Once the retopology and UV preparation are completed in Maya, export the cleaned geometry as an **OBJ** file and return to ZBrush.

2. Before importing the new mesh, insert a temporary primitive inside the current Tool using **Tool | Append**. This step is important because ZBrush requires an existing SubTool before replacing geometry through the import process.
3. After appending the primitive, select it and go to **Tool | Import**, then import the newly exported OBJ containing the clean topology and UVs. If the workflow has been performed correctly, the new retopologized scale should appear perfectly aligned with the original DynaMesh sculpt while preserving the updated topology and UV information.

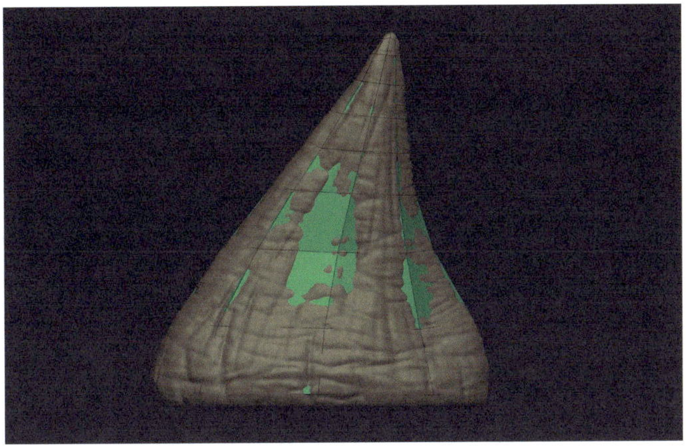

Figure 7.14 – Retopologized scale imported back into ZBrush and aligned with the original DynaMesh sculpt

4. Increase the subdivision levels (usually between 6 and 7 subdivision levels) of the new mesh with the clean topology to prepare it for detail projection from the original DynaMesh sculpt.
5. Once the mesh has enough subdivisions to support the transferred information, proceed with the projection workflow to recover the sculpted scale details. For this step, please refer to the *Reprojecting and validating primary forms on the clean retopologized mesh* recipe in *Chapter 6*, starting from *step 5* onward, where the subdivision setup, projection workflow, and validation process are covered in detail.

Note

Since these elements will often be repeated many times across the creature surface, it is recommended to keep the final geometry reasonably optimized whenever possible. A range between approximately 50,000 and 150,000 polygons is usually more than sufficient for most secondary assets such as scales, spikes, and horns. Using excessively dense geometry for repeated Insert Mesh elements can quickly make the ZBrush file unnecessarily heavy and difficult to manage during production.

Figure 7.15 shows the result of the projection workflow, where the sculpted detail from the original DynaMesh scale has been transferred onto the clean, subdivided topology while preserving the optimized mesh structure:

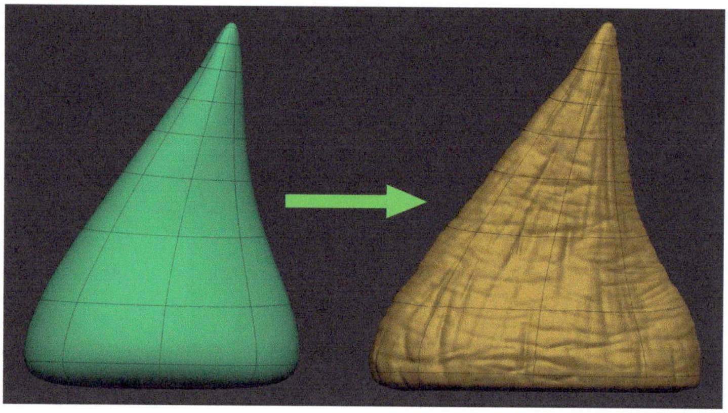

Figure 7.15 – Detail projection from the original DynaMesh sculpt onto the clean retopologized mesh

Creating the Insert Mesh Brush

The next step is to convert the scale into a reusable Insert Mesh element that can be distributed efficiently across the creature:

1. Once the projection process is completed and the details have been successfully transferred, keep the model at the highest subdivision level and use **Tool** | **Geometry** | **Del Lower** to remove all lower subdivision levels from the mesh.
   Our focus is to preserve only the final production-ready geometry that will later be converted into an Insert Mesh element. Removing the lower subdivision levels also helps simplify the workflow before generating the final **InsertMultiMesh (IMM)** Brush.

Figure 7.16 – Deleting lower subdivision levels after the detail projection process

2. Before generating the **InsertMesh** Brush, switch the camera to a perfect **Top** view. This step is important because the orientation of the camera directly affects the insertion direction and alignment of the future IMM element inside ZBrush.
3. Once the model is correctly aligned in **Top** view, go to **Brush** | **Create** | **Create InsertMesh** to generate the new **InsertMesh** Brush from the selected geometry. Before creating the **InsertMesh** Brush, make sure the mesh no longer contains subdivision levels. Insert Mesh creation only works correctly on meshes with a single subdivision level, whether the geometry comes from a clean production topology or from a DynaMesh workflow. This is why the **Del Lower** operation performed in *step 1* is essential before generating the IMM element.

If the camera orientation is incorrect during creation, the inserted element may appear rotated or misaligned when used on the creature surface, making placement and sculpting much more difficult later in the workflow.

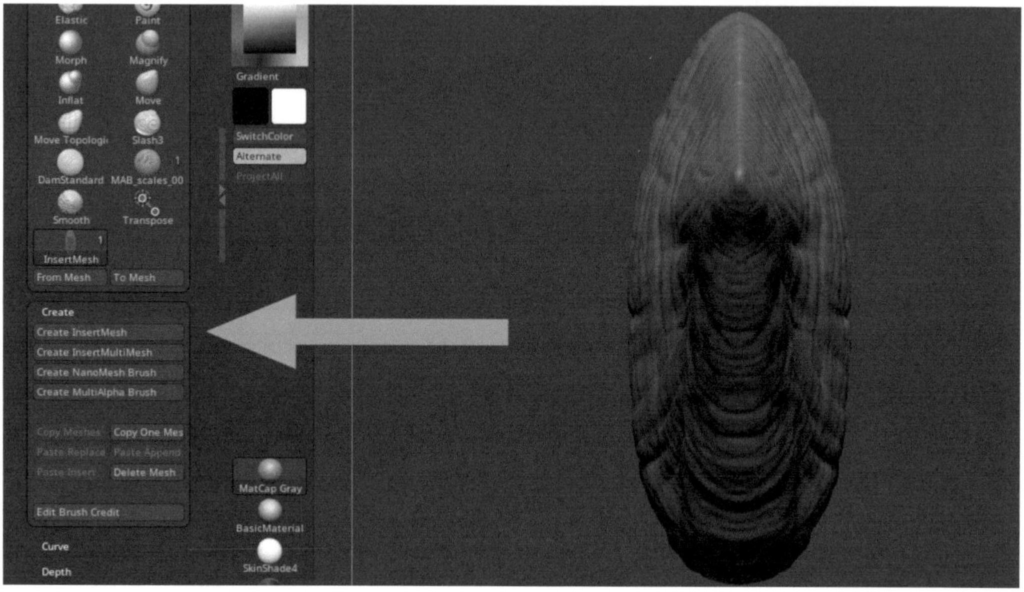

Figure 7.17 – Creating the Insert Mesh Brush from the scale geometry using a perfect Top view

Tip

If you want to create multiple Insert Mesh variations inside the same brush, simply keep all the necessary SubTools visible and use **Brush** | **Create** | **Create InsertMultiMesh**. ZBrush will automatically generate an **IMM** Brush containing all the visible meshes.

Preparing the creature for IMM placement

Before placing the Insert Mesh elements, we'll create a dedicated working version of the creature optimized for placement and integration:

1. Since Insert Mesh brushes only work correctly on meshes without subdivision levels, my recommendation is to duplicate the current version of the `dragonCrest` creature containing the primary and secondary details before starting the IMM placement process.

2. Select the creature SubTool and use **Tool** | **SubTool** | **Duplicate** to create a copy of the model.
3. Once duplicated, rename the new version to `dragonCrest_INSERTMESH` so it can be easily identified inside the project while keeping the original sculpt untouched.
4. This duplicated version will be used specifically for Insert Mesh integration, allowing you to freely insert spikes, horns, and secondary geometry without affecting the original high-subdivision production file.

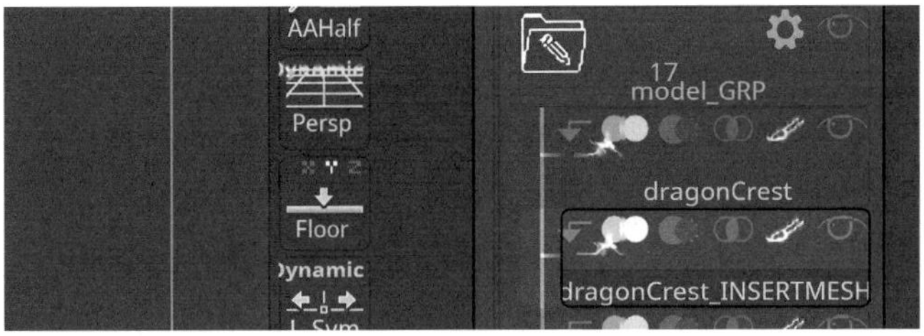

Figure 7.18 – Duplicated dragonCrest SubTool renamed to dragonCrest_INSERTMESH

5. Before starting the Insert Mesh placement process, bake all active layers on the duplicated creature to permanently preserve the primary and secondary sculpted information.
6. Once the layers have been baked, move the model to an intermediate subdivision level, in this case approximately **subdivision level 3 (SDiv 3)**, which provides a good balance between readable anatomical detail and manageable polygon density for IMM integration.
7. Remove both the higher and lower subdivision levels using **Tool** | **Geometry** | **Del Higher** followed by **Tool** | **Geometry** | **Del Lower**. The result should be a clean working mesh containing only a single subdivision level suitable for Insert Mesh workflows.

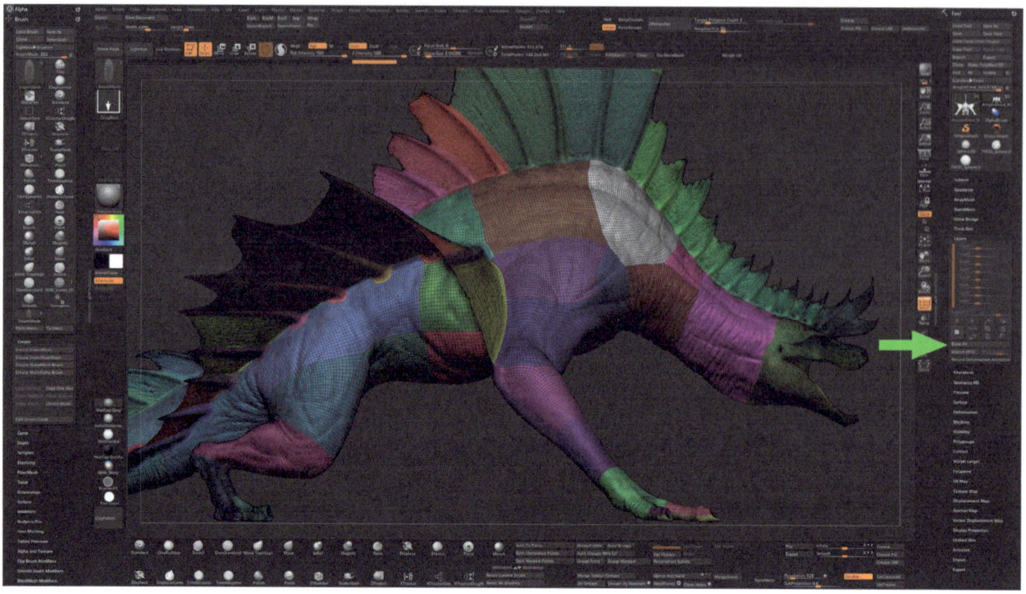

Figure 7.19 – dragonCrest_INSERTMESH prepared at an intermediate subdivision level after baking layers and deleting subdivision history

Placing and distributing Insert Mesh elements

Now, we'll distribute the custom spikes and scales across the creature while maintaining anatomical flow, silhouette quality, and visual variation:

1. Start inserting your custom Insert Mesh elements across the creature surface, following the anatomical flow and silhouette language established by the original concept design. In my case, I will create and use *three different variations of spikes and secondary scales* to avoid repetition and generate a more natural distribution across the `dragonCrest` creature.
2. To insert a mesh element, click and drag on the creature surface using the **InsertMesh** Brush. Dragging toward the *right* increases the overall size of the inserted element, while dragging back toward the *left* modifies the base width and proportions of the mesh rather than simply changing its height. This behavior is useful for creating natural variation from the same Insert Mesh element without constantly switching between different brushes.
3. Focus on varying scale size, orientation, spacing, and directional flow depending on the anatomical region. Larger elements can help reinforce major silhouette breaks, while smaller secondary spikes can enrich transition areas and improve the overall visual rhythm of the creature.

At this point, focus not only on distributing the Insert Mesh elements but also on evaluating how they affect the character's overall readability, silhouette, and personality.

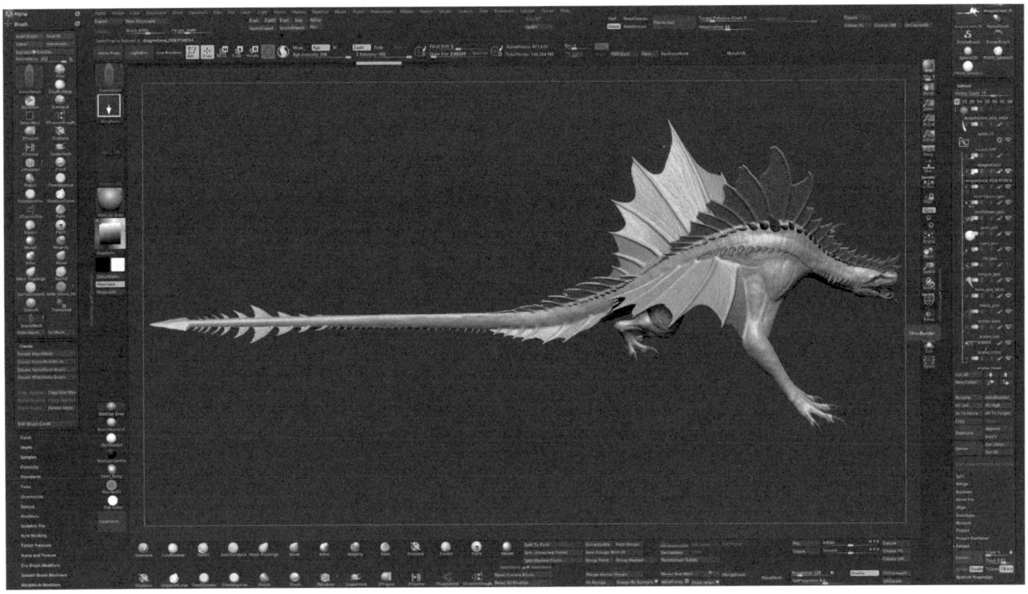

Figure 7.20 – Final distribution of the custom Insert Mesh spikes and scales across the dragonCrest creature

Tip

While placing the Insert Mesh scales and spikes, it is usually faster and cleaner to work only on the left half of the creature first. Once the distribution is completed, use the mirroring workflow to transfer the elements to the opposite side of the model. After the mirrored result is approved, manually place the central scales and spikes where needed to break symmetry and create more natural transitions along the spine and main anatomical areas.

Once the distribution is complete, use **Tool** | **Geometry** | **Modify Topology** | **Mirror And Weld** to transfer the scales and spikes to the opposite side of the creature. After checking the mirrored result, manually add the central scales and spikes where needed to break symmetry and create more natural transitions along the spine and other key anatomical areas.

Reorganizing UVs after IMM placement

The final stage is to reorganize the resulting UVs so the asset is ready for texturing, displacement, and rendering workflows:

1. After all the spikes and secondary scales have been placed – and once the mesh satisfies the requirements for **Reconstruct Subdiv** – reconstruct the subdivision levels using **Tool** | **Geometry** | **Reconstruct Subdiv** until the mesh regains the original subdivision structure used before the Insert Mesh workflow started.
2. After reconstructing the subdivisions, export the updated asset at subdivision level 1 as an OBJ file and bring it back into Maya.
3. Reorganize the UVs of all inserted spikes and scales, since the UVs generated from the Insert Mesh workflow may initially overlap. This UV cleanup phase is crucial to prepare the asset correctly for texturing, lookdev, displacement generation, and final rendering workflows.

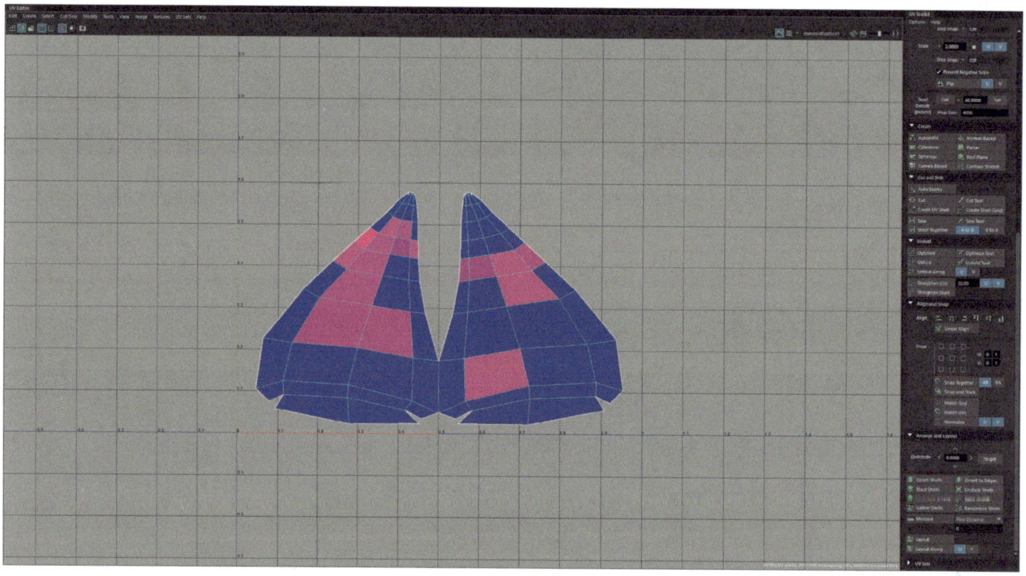

Figure 7.21 – Overlapping mirrored UVs generated after the Insert Mesh workflow, showing both positive and negative mirrored shells before UV cleanup and reorganization

When the UV cleanup process is complete, the spikes and scales can be organized into a production-ready layout suitable for texturing and displacement workflows. *Figure 7.22* shows the final UV arrangement after reorganization:

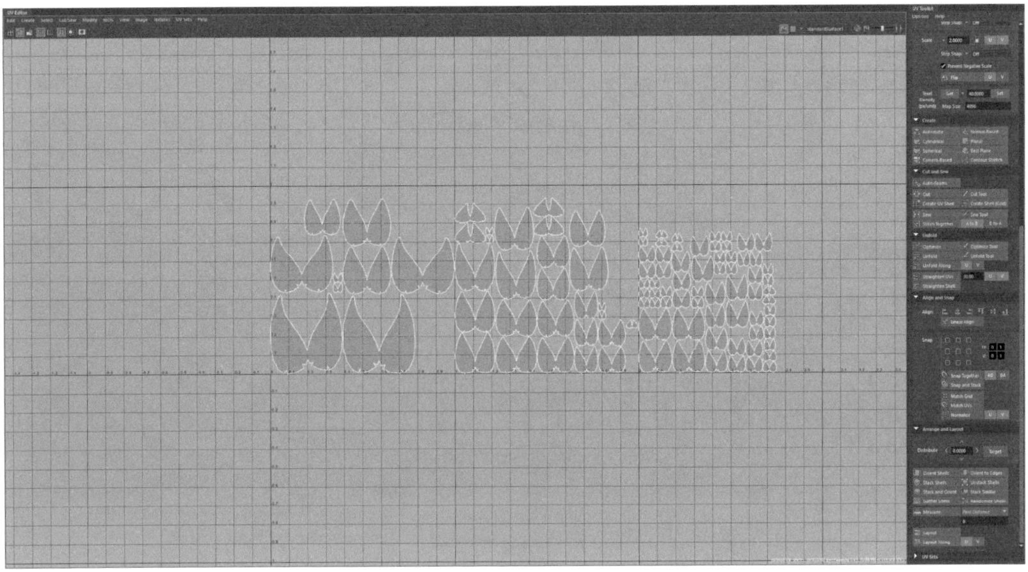

Figure 7.22 – Reorganized UV layout with optimized shell distribution and consistent texel density ready for production

Note

In game production workflows, overlapping UVs on repeated elements such as spikes or scales are often considered completely acceptable and highly efficient for optimization purposes, since multiple meshes can share the same texture space and reduce memory usage. However, for high-end animation and VFX workflows, it is generally recommended that each spike or scale have its own dedicated UV space to support unique displacement, texture variation, close-up rendering quality, and advanced surfacing workflows, except in specific optimization cases.

4. Once the UV layout has been finalized in Maya, export the updated asset again as an **OBJ** file and return to ZBrush.
5. At **subdivision level 1 (SDiv 1)**, import the updated low-poly mesh into the corresponding SubTool. Provided that its vertex order has not changed, ZBrush will update the UVs across the subdivision hierarchy while preserving the existing sculpted and projected details. The spikes and scales will now contain fully updated production-ready UVs correctly integrated into the creature workflow. *Figure 7.23* shows the PolyGroup organization generated from the final UDIM layout:

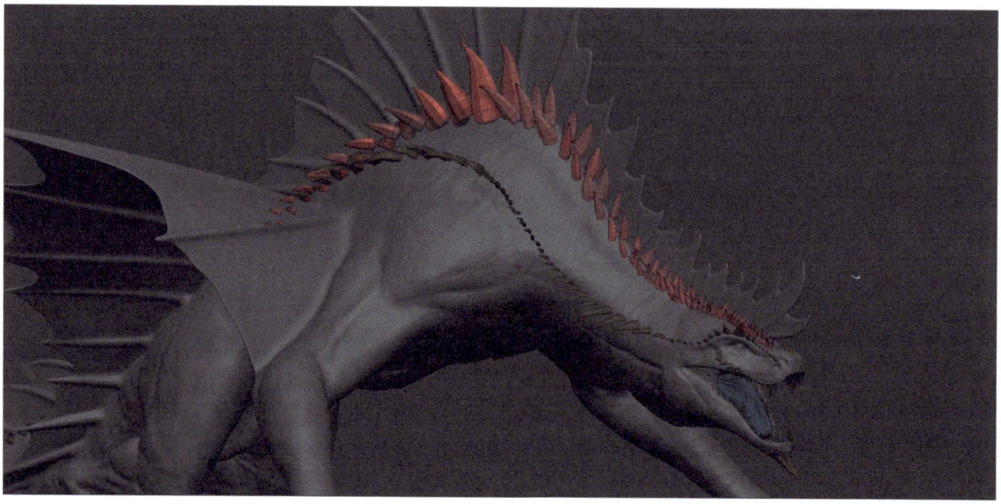

Figure 7.23 – PolyGroups generated from the final UDIM layout

How it works...

This workflow combines several production techniques into a single non-destructive pipeline designed for creating reusable secondary assets such as spikes, horns, and large scales directly inside ZBrush. Unlike standard sculpting workflows, where details are permanently integrated into the main surface from the beginning, Insert Mesh Brushes allow you to place, iterate, replace, and reorganize secondary elements while maintaining full control over the creature structure. This approach requires additional preparation at the beginning but greatly reduces repetitive sculpting work later in production.

The first important concept is that the sculpted scale is not created directly as an IMM element. Instead, the process starts from a DynaMesh sculpt because **DynaMesh** provides complete freedom during the blocking phase. This allows you to focus entirely on silhouette, volume language, and anatomical readability without being constrained by topology.

Once the sculpt is approved, the workflow shifts into a production preparation stage. Retopology and UV creation are essential because the final Insert Mesh element is intended to become reusable geometry rather than a temporary sculpted detail. Clean topology improves deformation, subdivision reconstruction, UV management, projection stability, and overall scene performance.

One of the biggest advantages of reusable geometry is that the asset only needs to be built, retopologized, and UV-mapped once. After it is added to an **InsertMultiMesh** Brush, the same production-ready asset can be distributed across multiple areas of the creature or even reused on future creatures without rebuilding the geometry from scratch (only requiring UV reordering when needed, as discussed in the UV chapters).

The projection stage ensures that the visual quality of the original DynaMesh sculpt is preserved after the asset has been converted to clean production topology. This allows the final Insert Mesh asset to preserve the visual quality of the original sculpt while remaining lightweight and technically optimized.

This balance between sculptural quality and technical optimization is one of the main reasons IMM workflows are widely used in creature, character, and asset production. The final asset remains visually consistent while still being efficient to manage across large projects.

From a look development perspective, IMM assets make it possible to test different scale distributions, densities, and silhouette variations very quickly. Artists can explore multiple visual directions while continuing to work from the same approved source asset, reducing production time without introducing visual discrepancies across the creature.

See also

- The *Handling topology in complex areas: eyes, eyelids, ears and nose, claws and teeth, as well as tongue and gums* recipe in *Chapter 4*
- The *UVs for secondary elements: eyes, claws, teeth, gums, tongue* recipe in *Chapter 5*

Using Morph Targets for better control and adjustments

In this recipe, we will use Morph Targets inside ZBrush to integrate two different skin approaches on the `dragonCrest` creature. In this example, the head contains manually sculpted skin information designed to support the primary anatomical forms, while the neck uses a procedural noise-based treatment to generate faster tertiary surface variation.

The challenge is that these two approaches often create visible seams, abrupt changes in detail density, or surface transitions that feel disconnected from the underlying anatomy. This recipe uses Morph Targets to selectively restore portions of the sculpted information, allowing manually sculpted skin and procedural surface detail to blend in a more natural and controlled way.

This workflow is particularly useful when combining hand-sculpted regions with procedural detail passes. Instead of manually re-sculpting every transition area, the **Morph** Brush provides a fast and flexible way to control how the different skin patterns interact while maintaining the original sculpt information underneath.

In production, this approach is valuable because creature surfaces rarely use a single uniform skin language across the entire body. Different anatomical regions often require different detail densities and sculpting techniques, and Morph Targets provide an efficient way to art direct those transitions without permanently damaging the existing layers.

At the end of this recipe, the `dragonCrest` creature will have cleaner, more believable transitions between manually sculpted skin and procedural tertiary detail, resulting in a cohesive production-ready surface treatment.

Figure 7.24 – Transition area between manually sculpted skin and procedural noise-based skin before Morph Target blending

Getting ready

Before starting this recipe, complete the following steps:

1. Open the latest version of the `dragonCrest` creature containing completed primary forms, secondary forms, retopology, UVs, and subdivision levels suitable for tertiary detailing. This asset is the result of the workflows covered throughout *Chapters 4, 5,* and *6*. A lightweight low-poly version (`dragonCrest_approved.fbx`) is available in the GitHub repository (see the *Technical requirements* section for access instructions) accompanying this book.
2. For this workflow, we will specifically work with two tertiary skin layers:
   - `skin_head`: Contains the manually sculpted skin information used on the head area.
   - `skin_neck`: Contains the procedural or noise-based tertiary skin breakup used on the neck region.

The goal of this recipe is to integrate these two different skin treatments using Morph Targets while maintaining believable anatomical transitions and preserving the strongest characteristics of both surface patterns.

How to do it...

In this workflow, we will progressively integrate two different tertiary skin treatments using Morph Targets and the **Morph** Brush. Rather than manually re-sculpting the transition areas from scratch, this technique allows us to blend multiple surface approaches together while maintaining the original sculpt information underneath. Follow these steps:

1. Start by temporarily disabling all tertiary detail layers except for the `skin_neck` layer containing the procedural noise-based skin treatment. Go to **Tool** | **Layers** and click the visibility **eye** icon to keep only the `skin_neck` layer visible. The neck surface should display only the procedural tertiary breakup while the manually sculpted head skin remains hidden.

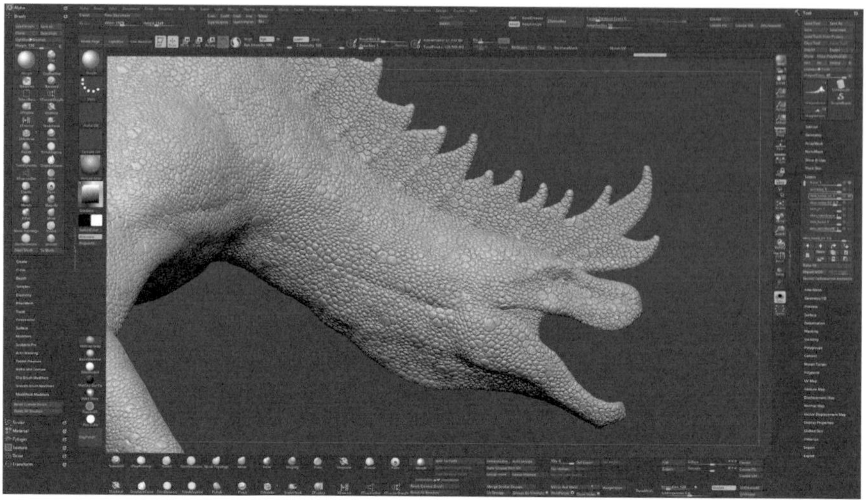

Figure 7.25 – Procedural neck skin layer isolated before starting the Morph Target blending workflow

2. Once only the `skin_neck` layer is visible, store the current state of the creature as a **Morph Target**. Go to **Tool** | **Morph Target** and select **StoreMT**. This operation captures the current visible surface information and saves it as the reference state that will later be recovered using the **Morph** Brush.

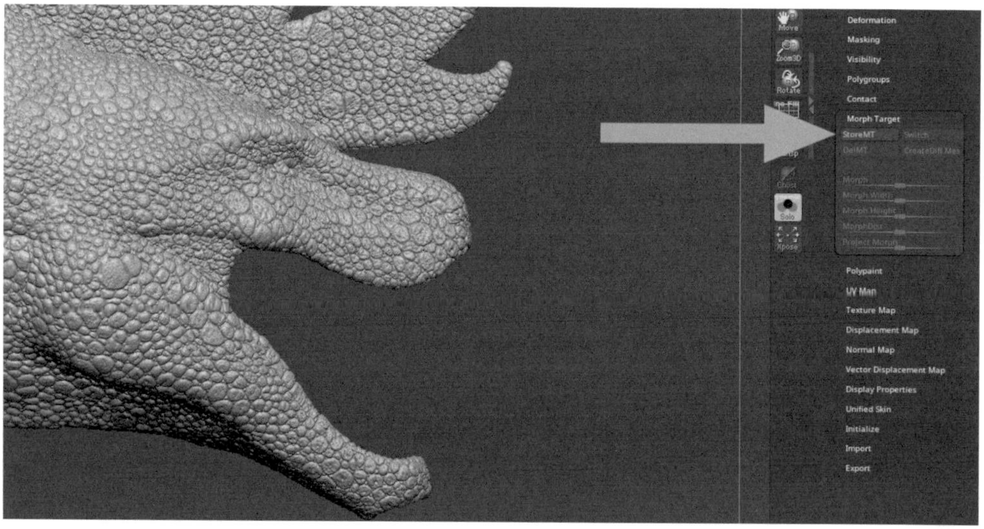

Figure 7.26 – Storing the current tertiary skin state before starting the Morph Brush blending and transition workflow

3. After storing the **Morph Target**, disable the `skin_neck` layer and make the `skin_head` layer visible, containing the manually sculpted skin details of the head area. At this stage, the creature will display only the hand-sculpted skin treatment while the procedural neck breakup remains stored internally inside the **Morph Target**.
   For artists who want a safer and more flexible workflow, this is also a good moment to create a new dedicated sculpt layer for the transition process. This allows all **Morph** Brush adjustments and blending operations to remain isolated on a separate layer, making the integration easier to tweak or reduce later without affecting the original skin passes.

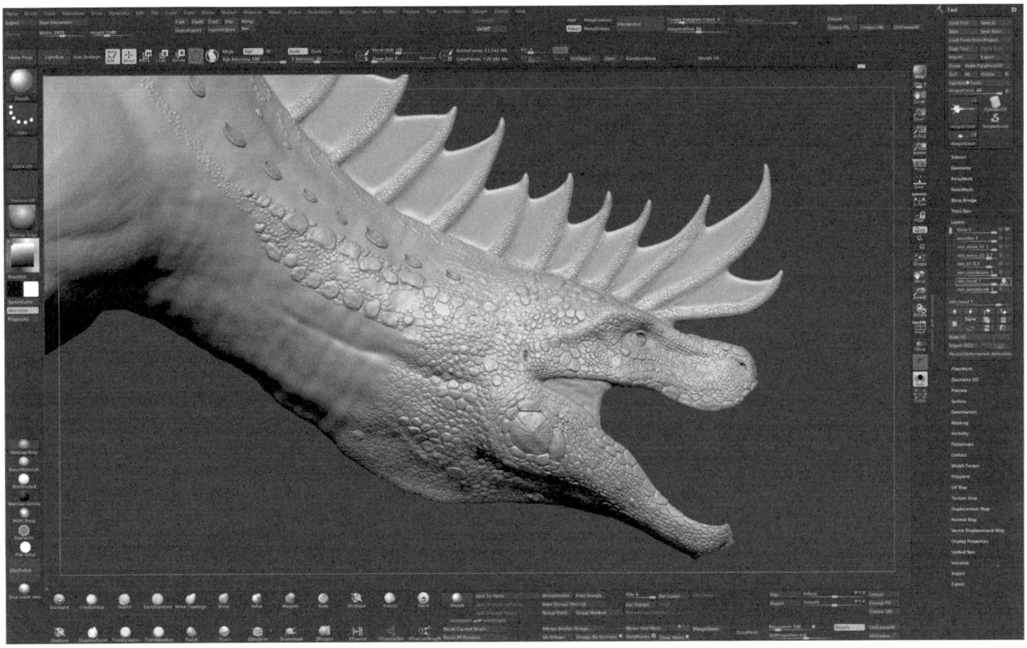

Figure 7.27 – Switching from the procedural neck skin layer to the manually sculpted head skin layer before Morph Target blending

4. Select the **Morph** Brush and begin sculpting directly over the transition area where the manually sculpted head skin meets the procedural neck skin. As you paint with the **Morph** Brush, ZBrush will progressively recover the stored **Morph Target** information, allowing the procedural neck breakup to blend naturally into the hand-sculpted skin.
   The most important recommendation during this phase is to avoid using the **Morph** Brush at full intensity. Instead of working at **Z Intensity** `100`, use much softer values, usually between `5` and `10`, to maintain precise control over the blending process. Lower intensities allow the transition to build progressively and help create smoother

integrations between the two skin treatments without producing abrupt surface changes.

5. Work slowly across the border areas and focus on breaking the visible separation between the two detail patterns rather than completely replacing one skin type with the other.

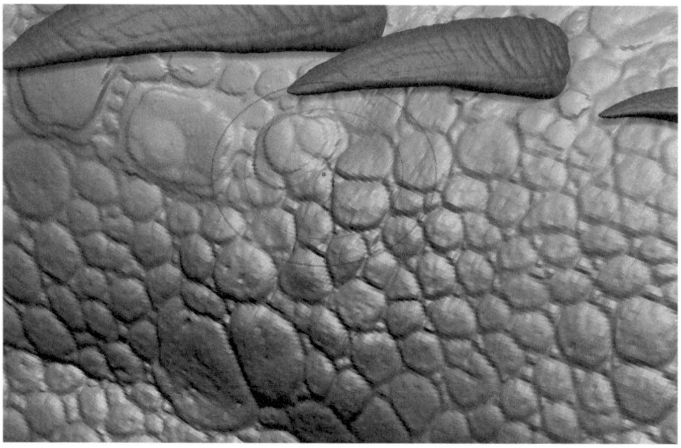

Figure 7.28 – Using the Morph Brush at low intensity to progressively blend the procedural neck skin into the manually sculpted head details

6. Once the transition area has been integrated and softened correctly, you can temporarily increase the **Morph** Brush intensity up to `100` in areas where the procedural skin treatment already works correctly and does not require gradual blending. This allows you to fully recover the stored **Morph Target** information in a much faster and cleaner way.
   Here, the goal is no longer to create soft transitions, but to quickly restore the correct skin treatment in broader regions where the noise-based breakup already fits the anatomy and visual language of the creature. Use the lower intensity workflow only near the transition zones, while stronger values can help speed up the process in more stable surface areas.

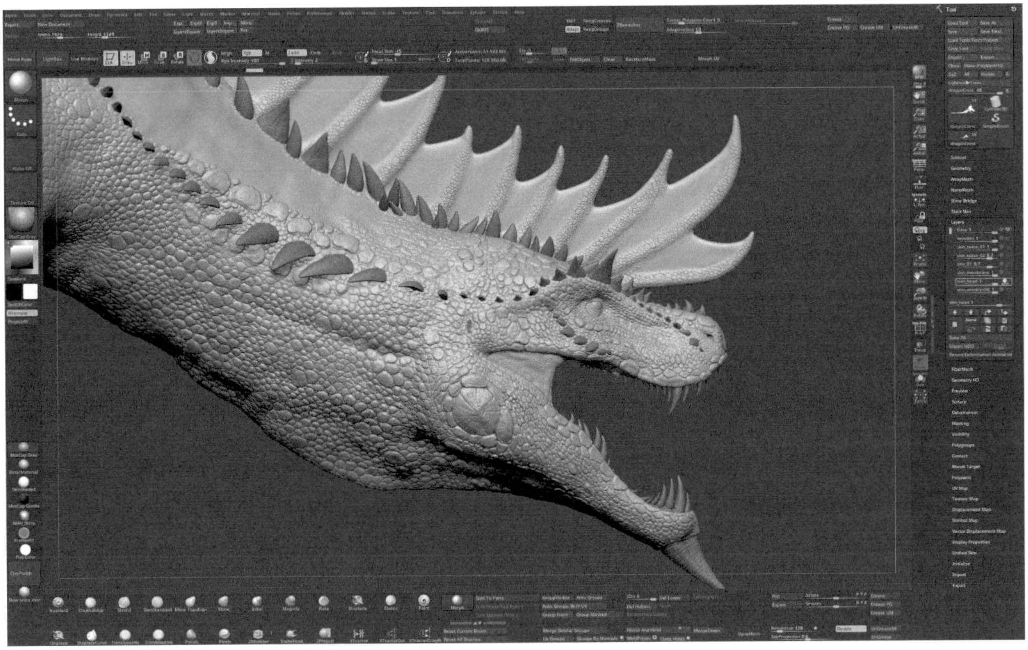

Figure 7.29 – Using the Morph Brush at full intensity to quickly restore the procedural skin treatment in stable surface regions

7. Once the **Morph Target** integration is completed, manually refine the transition areas wherever additional cleanup or surface adjustments are needed. At this point, small sculpting corrections can help improve the continuity between the two skin treatments and remove any remaining visible separation or repetitive patterns if the result still feels inconsistent.

   Use this final pass to reinforce the natural directional flow of the skin and improve the overall readability of the surface integration.

Figure 7.30 – Final manual refinement pass applied after the Morph Target blending process

Note

Performing a **final manual sculpting pass** is almost always a good practice, but the amount of refinement depends heavily on the importance of the area and how visible that region will be in the final creature shots. Secondary areas visible only in wide shots may require minimal cleanup, while hero regions intended for close-up rendering usually benefit from additional hand-sculpted refinement.

Here we are entering the final phase of tertiary detailing, and this is the perfect moment to introduce asymmetry into the sculpt:

1. Create a dedicated layer, disable **Symmetry** on the *X* axis, and focus on the areas that naturally draw the viewer's attention, such as the face, chest, and the central line of the creature's body.
2. Even subtle variations can make a significant difference. Adjust the size and distribution of scales, slightly alter wrinkle patterns, break repetitive shapes, and introduce small imperfections that make the surface feel more organic and believable.

This sculpting pass, combined with the texturing stage, where textures should also avoid being perfectly mirrored, is one of the most effective ways to push a creature toward a realistic and production-ready result. Nature is never perfectly symmetrical, and neither should your creature be! As I always say, *"In our work, as in life, perfection emerges from imperfection."*

How it works...

This workflow works because Morph Targets in ZBrush allow us to store a precise snapshot of the surface state and later selectively recover that information using the **Morph** Brush. Instead of manually re-sculpting every transition area between two different skin treatments, we can blend multiple tertiary detail passes together while preserving all the original sculpted information underneath.

The **Morph** Brush does not simply smooth or blur details. Instead, it restores the previously stored surface state directly on the mesh. This is why the brush becomes extremely powerful for integrating different skin approaches together.

This technique is particularly useful because tertiary skin detail often changes depending on the anatomical region of the creature. Large neck areas may benefit from procedural noise-based breakup to quickly generate believable organic variation, while hero facial regions usually require more artistic control through hand-sculpted skin patterns. The **Morph Target** workflow allows both approaches to coexist without permanently destroying or replacing one another.

Another important advantage is that Morph Targets recover information rather than forcing artists to recreate it manually. In production, manually rebuilding every transition area between different skin treatments is both time-consuming and difficult to keep consistent. Morph Targets dramatically reduce this workload while preserving the original sculpt quality.

The final manual cleanup pass remains important because even a successful **Morph Target** integration can still produce repetitive transitions or surface rhythms that feel too procedural. Morph Targets should therefore be considered a blending tool rather than a complete solution.

They are effective at merging different skin treatments, but the final level of realism usually comes from additional hand sculpting.

Once the transition has been softened and integrated using the **Morph** Brush, manual sculpting is often required to restore anatomical flow, introduce variation, and reinforce the visual hierarchy of the surface. Small hand-sculpted adjustments can then improve skin directionality and create more natural variation between the primary, secondary, and tertiary forms.

From a production perspective, this workflow is crucial because it remains fully non-destructive. Since the different skin treatments are stored inside separate layers and Morph Targets, artists can continuously iterate, reduce, or completely redesign transition areas without losing the original sculpt passes. This makes the technique highly flexible for cinematic creatures where skin treatments often evolve during look development, surfacing validation, or final lighting reviews.

There's more...

Before reviewing the final sculpt, make sure to enable all the previously created layers so the creature displays the complete combination of primary anatomical forms, secondary sculpting information, and tertiary surface detailing. Viewing the asset with all layers active is vital because it allows you to evaluate how the different sculpting passes interact together across the entire creature surface.

This validation stage helps confirm that the transitions between large anatomical forms, wrinkles, skin breakup, Insert Mesh elements, and manually sculpted details remain visually cohesive and production-ready from every camera angle.

At this stage, the `dragonCrest` creature already contains the full combination of workflows explored throughout this chapter. The final sculpt integrates primary anatomical forms, secondary wrinkles, procedural and hand-sculpted tertiary skin details, custom IMM spikes and scales, **Morph Target** blending techniques, and manually refined surface transitions.

The views in *Figure 7.31* help evaluate how all these layers work together across the entire creature silhouette and anatomy from multiple camera angles. Studying the model from different perspectives is important during production because some areas may read correctly in a single shot but lose clarity or balance once viewed in motion or from alternative camera positions.

Figure 7.31 – Final validation views of the completed dragonCrest creature

These final validation views are useful before moving into later production stages, such as posing, displacement extraction, texturing, look development, and final rendering. Checking the sculpt from every major angle helps identify repetitive patterns, weak silhouette areas, inconsistent tertiary breakup, or anatomical regions that may still require manual refinement before the asset is considered production-ready.

8

Dividing the Model to Maximize Resolution

This chapter focuses on one of the most important workflows used in high-end creature production when a unified sculpt can no longer support the level of detail required for cinematic-quality surface work.

The amount of subdivision resolution required on a creature always depends on multiple factors, such as shot distance, rendering requirements, topology quality, and the type of detail needed on the surface. A creature intended only for medium or distant shots may never require this type of workflow, while hero assets used in close-up cinematic shots often need significantly more local sculpting resolution.

One of the most important factors for maximizing subdivision efficiency is starting from a clean and optimized low-resolution topology. In production, a creature prepared correctly for high-resolution sculpting will often stay around approximately 20,000 to 24,000 polygons at subdivision level 1. Maintaining a lightweight base mesh allows the subdivision hierarchy to generate significantly more usable geometry density at higher levels.

In the case of our `dragonCrest` creature, the topology is considerably heavier because of the complex membrane structures and overall anatomical construction of the asset. This resulted in the creature reaching only around six subdivision levels before the unified mesh already contained nearly 52 million polygons.

Even though the sculpt quality remains stable, the model no longer has enough local geometry density in some areas to continue refining the smaller scales with additional precision. The problem is simply the inability to further define and refine the scale shapes due to the lack of additional subdivision resolution available on the unified mesh.

Even at nearly 52 million polygons, smaller scales begin losing definition because the mesh no longer contains enough geometry to support additional sculpt refinement.

To solve this problem, in this chapter's recipes, you'll learn how to divide the creature into multiple production sections based on logical anatomical regions and UDIM organization. By splitting the model strategically, each section can gain additional subdivision levels independently, allowing much higher local sculpting resolution while maintaining production stability. Therefore, we'll divide the `dragonCrest` creature into two main sections:

- Head, neck, half torso, part of the crest, front legs, and forelimbs
- The remaining part of the torso and crest, the lateral membranes, the hind legs, and the tail

This simplified example makes the workflow easier to understand, but in real production environments, it is very common to divide creatures into three, four, or even more sections depending on the complexity of the anatomy, the subdivision requirements, and the level of sculpted detail needed for the final shots.

In this chapter, we will explore the following recipes:

- Dividing the model into UDIM sections
- Updating the Maya mesh while preserving vertex order

The following example shows a common resolution limitation encountered on a unified creature mesh:

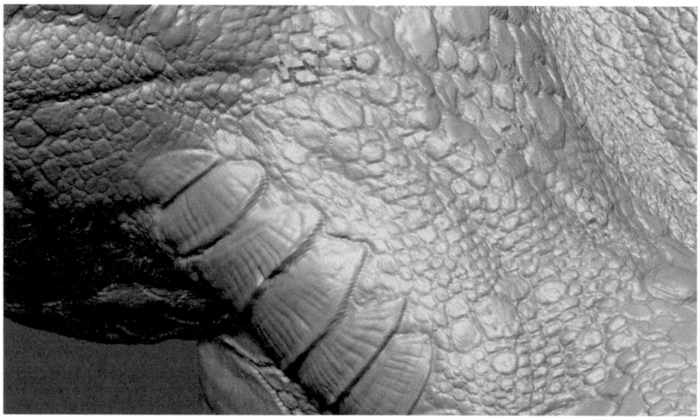

Figure 8.1 – Loss of scale definition due to insufficient local geometry density

Technical requirements

For the minimum hardware and software requirements recommended for this book, please refer to the *Technical requirements* section in *Chapter 1*.

For this chapter, you will need the fully sculpted `dragonCrest` creature containing the finalized primary, secondary, and especially tertiary sculpted information developed throughout *Chapters 4, 5,* and *6*. The creature should already include all the skin detailing, scale refinement, membrane detailing, and tertiary surface breakup necessary for cinematic-quality sculpting workflows.

You will also need the completed UDIM layout organization (see the *Planning multi-UDIMs and the half-character UV workflow* and *Packing and ordering multi-UDIMs: Substance 3D Painter versus Mari* recipes in *Chapter 5*), since the mesh separation process demonstrated in this chapter will be based directly on the existing UDIM distribution and PolyGroup organization.

For the workflows demonstrated in this chapter, ensure you are using:

- **ZBrush 2024** or later
- **Maya 2024** or later

You can download the example project files for this book by following the instructions in the *Download the example code/resource files* section in the *Preface* of this book.

This chapter's code/resource files are included in the downloadable code/resource bundle.

Dividing the model into UDIM sections

In this recipe, we'll divide the `dragonCrest` creature into two main UDIM-based sections in order to increase the available subdivision resolution and continue refining the sculpted scales with more precision.

The goal of this recipe is not to change the creature topology, but simply to separate the model into multiple production sections so that each part can support additional subdivision levels independently. For this example, the creature is divided into two main sections, giving priority to the head, neck, half torso, part of the crest, front legs, and forelimbs, where the highest concentration of sculpted details is located.

Strictly speaking, this dragon would also benefit from separating the tail into an additional production section, as its length and surface area can quickly consume the available subdivision budget. However, to keep the workflow easier to follow and focus on the core technique, this recipe intentionally uses only two sections.

In a real production asset, the separation strategy always depends on the character and the distribution of sculpted detail. When defining separation boundaries, avoid splitting the model at arbitrary locations. Instead, place the cuts along natural anatomical transitions, such as the base of the neck, the shoulder region, the base of the tail, or other areas where the separation can be hidden more easily. This preserves the visual continuity of the sculpt while making each production section easier to manage.

Figure 8.2 shows the final PolyGroup organization used for the subdivision splitting workflow:

Figure 8.2 – dragonCrest creature divided into two main production sections using UDIM-based PolyGroups

Getting ready

Before starting the mesh separation workflow, follow these steps:

1. Open the final sculpted version of the `dragonCrest` creature inside ZBrush. The model should already contain all the approved primary, secondary, and tertiary sculpted information completed in the previous chapters.
2. To avoid damaging the original production sculpt, duplicate the main creature SubTool before starting the separation process. Go to **Tool** | **SubTool** | **Duplicate** and create a working copy that will be used for the subdivision splitting workflow.
3. After duplicating the SubTool, activate all the approved sculpting Layers and bake them into the geometry. This step is important because the topology will soon change during the mesh separation process, making the original Layers incompatible with the new topology structure.

4. Once the Layers are baked, switch the model to the lowest subdivision level. Working at the lowest subdivision is essential because the PolyGroup generation process only requires the base topology and UV layout information.
5. Finally, go to **Tool | Polygroups | UV Groups**. This operation automatically generates separate PolyGroups based on the existing UDIM layout of the creature, allowing the model to be visually divided into logical production sections.

How to do it...

In this workflow, we will isolate specific UDIM regions and reorganize them into larger production PolyGroups that will later be separated into independent subdivision sections. The goal is to create cleaner, high-resolution sculpting regions while maintaining logical anatomical continuity across the creature. Now, follow these steps:

1. Start by activating the **SelectLasso** Brush and entering **PolyGroups** selection mode using *Ctrl* + *Shift*. Hold *Ctrl* + *Shift* and click directly inside one of the polygons belonging to the UDIM section you want to isolate. Since the model was previously organized using UV Groups, ZBrush will automatically select the entire UDIM region associated with that PolyGroup.

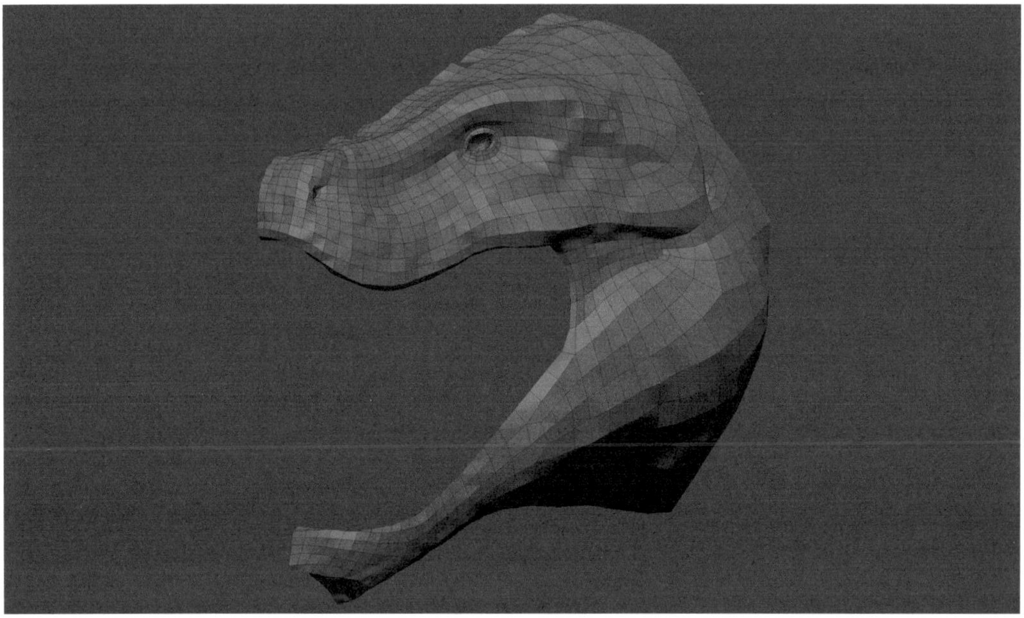

Figure 8.3 – Selecting a complete UDIM PolyGroup using Ctrl + Shift and click inside the polygon area (UDIM 1001)

2. Once the first UDIM section is selected, invert the visibility by holding *Ctrl* + *Shift* and dragging once on the empty canvas area. This operation hides the currently selected section and reveals the rest of the creature. From this stage onward, continue selecting all the UDIM regions that should belong to the same future subdivision section.

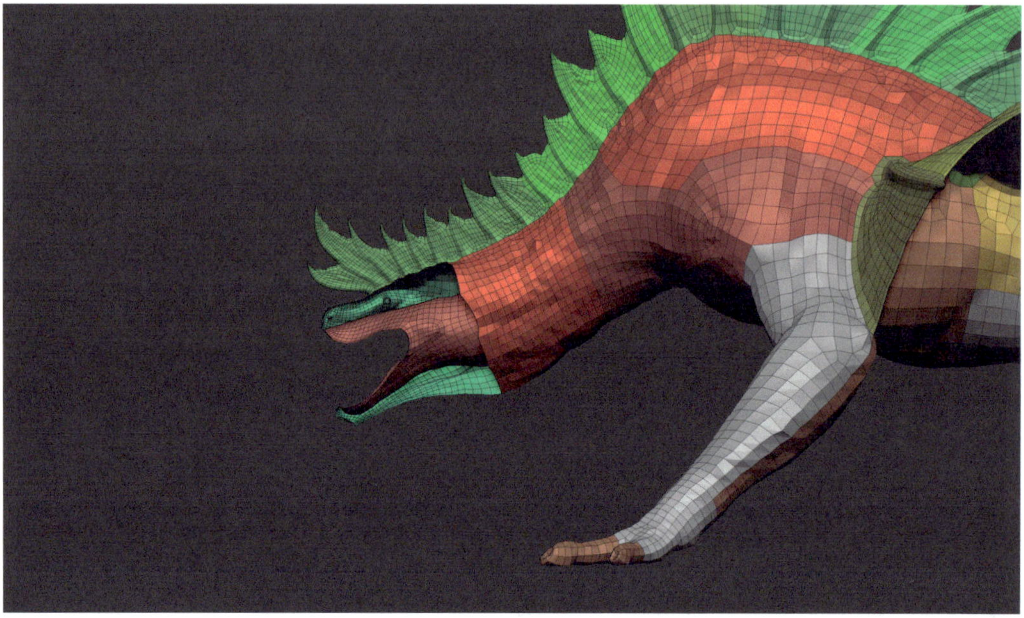

Figure 8.4 – Inverting the current selection to continue isolating the UDIM regions that will belong to the same subdivision section

3. Continue using *Ctrl* + *Shift* and click to select additional UDIM PolyGroups until all the desired regions are isolated together. In this example, the head, neck, front legs, and half crest sections are grouped into the same future subdivision region.
4. Once all the required UDIM sections are selected, hold *Ctrl* + *Shift* and drag again on the canvas to reveal the hidden geometry. At this point, only the intended regions should remain selected together.

5. Finally, press *Ctrl* + *W* to assign a completely new PolyGroup to the selected regions. This creates a clean production separation that will later be used to split the creature into independent high-resolution sculpting sections.

Figure 8.5 – Creating a new unified PolyGroup from the selected UDIM sections using Ctrl + W

6. After creating the first PolyGroup section, invert the selection once again using *Ctrl* + *Shift* and drag on the empty canvas. This will reveal the remaining hidden UDIM regions belonging to the torso, tail, membranes, and remaining body sections. Once these regions are visible and isolated together, press *Ctrl* + *W* again to assign them to a second unified PolyGroup.

At the end of this process, the creature will be cleanly divided into two large production PolyGroups corresponding to the two future high-resolution subdivision sections.

Figure 8.6 – Inverting the visibility again to isolate the remaining body UDIMs before assigning the second production PolyGroup

Once the two main production PolyGroups are created, follow these steps next:

1. Duplicate the creature SubTool one more time by going to **Tool | SubTool | Duplicate**. The objective is to create two independent working versions of the same creature, each one dedicated to a specific subdivision section.
   In the *first duplicated SubTool*, only the head, neck, and front-leg PolyGroup section will remain visible. In the *second duplicated SubTool*, only the torso, tail, and membrane section will remain active. This separation will allow each region to gain additional subdivision levels independently without affecting the rest of the creature.

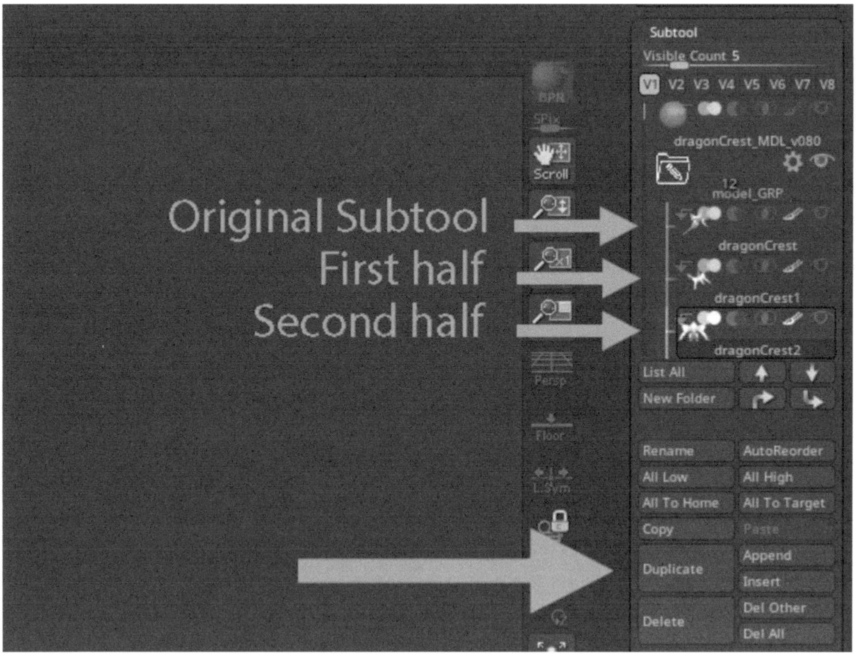

Figure 8.7 – Duplicating the SubTool again in preparation for separating the creature into two independent high-resolution sculpting sections

2. After duplicating the SubTool, isolate only the PolyGroup corresponding to the head, neck, front legs, and crest section. To create a safer production margin between the future separated meshes, progressively expand the visible region by going to **Tool** | **Visibility** | **Grow**.

   Repeat the **Grow** operation about three times. Although the exact amount depends on the project, I generally recommend creating an overlap of three to four edge loops. This provides a small "buffer zone" that is usually sufficient for projecting details and blending the transition without unnecessarily increasing the overlap area.

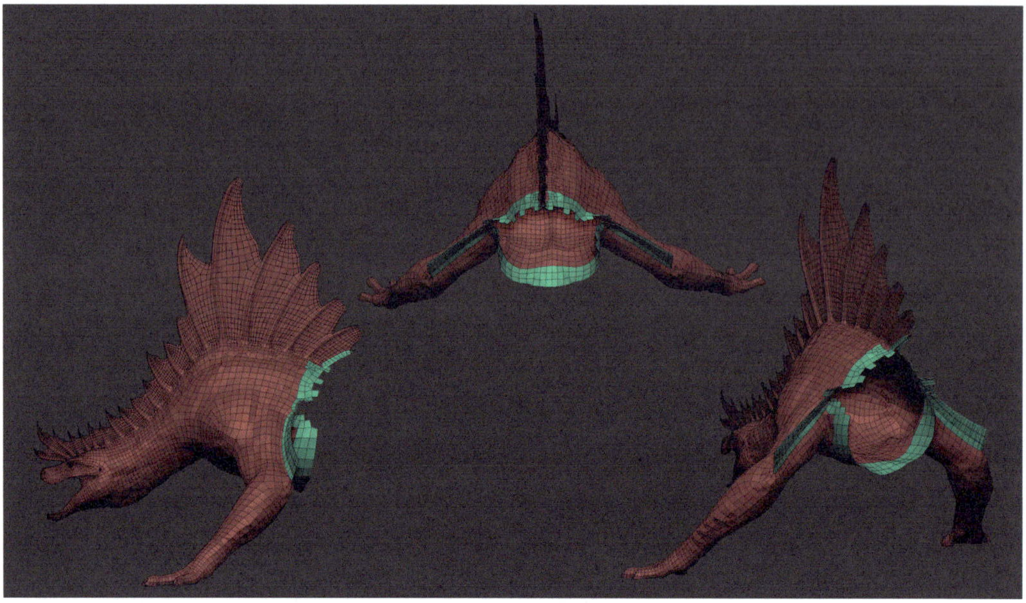

Figure 8.8 – Expanded PolyGroup overlap before mesh separation

3. Once the visible section contains both the main anatomical region and the additional three overlap loops, increase the subdivision levels back to the highest available resolution. These extra loops will later act as a projection transition area, allowing both separated sections to maintain perfectly coherent sculpted details across the border.
4. After restoring the maximum subdivision level, first remove all lower subdivision levels by going to **Tool** | **Geometry** | **Del Lower**. Then, permanently remove the hidden geometry by going to **Tool** | **Geometry** | **Modify Topology** | **Del Hidden**. This creates an independent high-resolution sculpting section containing only the visible anatomical region plus the additional overlap margin required for the later reprojection and blending process.

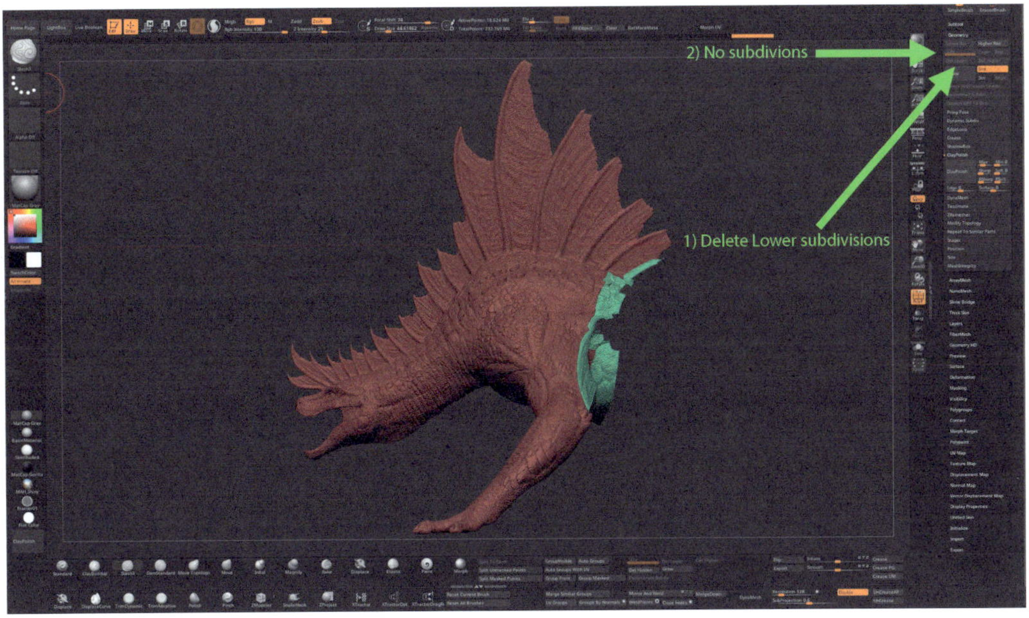

Figure 8.9 – Removing the lower subdivision levels and deleting the hidden geometry to create the first independent high-resolution sculpting section

5. After creating the first independent sculpting section, reconstruct the subdivision hierarchy by going to **Tool** | **Geometry** | **Reconstruct Subdiv**.
6. Repeat the operation until ZBrush rebuilds all the lower subdivision levels possible for the new separated mesh.
7. Once the subdivision hierarchy has been reconstructed, return to the highest subdivision level and add an additional subdivision step using **Divide** or simply pressing *Ctrl* + *D*.

Because the mesh now contains significantly less geometry overall, the new subdivision level can provide much higher local polygon density for refining smaller scales and tertiary sculpted forms. This is where the workflow starts becoming extremely powerful, since the separated section now supports a level of sculpting precision that was no longer possible on the original unified creature mesh.

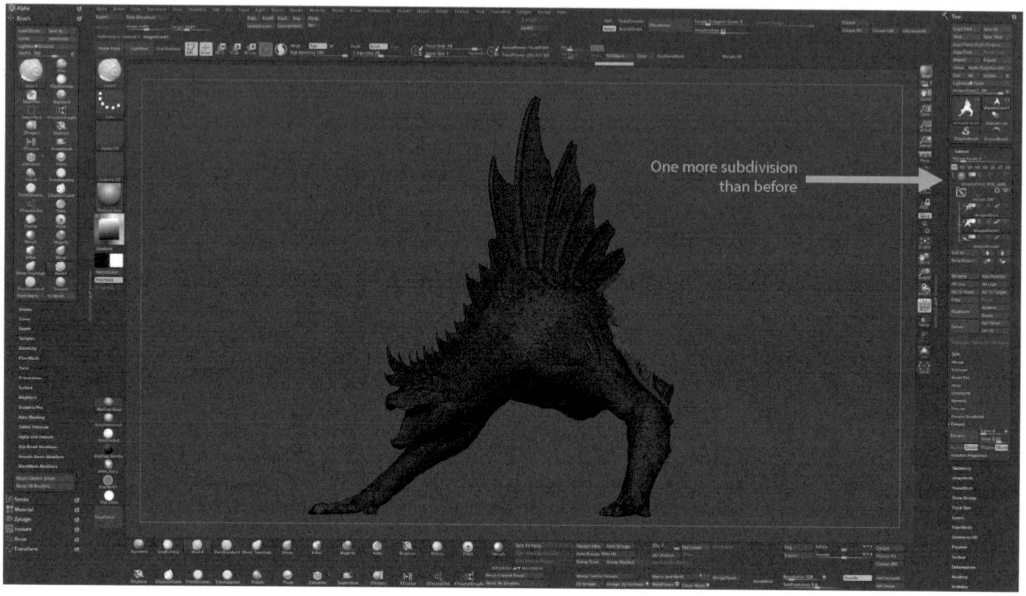

Figure 8.10 – Reconstructing the subdivision hierarchy and adding an additional subdivision level to increase local sculpting resolution

8. Repeat the same workflow on the second duplicated SubTool, but this time isolate the torso, tail, and membrane PolyGroup section. Follow the same steps used previously to create the overlap margin, delete the hidden geometry, reconstruct the subdivision hierarchy, and add another subdivision level.

Figure 8.11 – Repeating the subdivision separation workflow on the torso, tail, and membrane section of the creature

From this stage onward, both sections now contain an additional subdivision level, allowing you to further refine smaller scales, tertiary transitions, and surface details with much higher precision.

Once the first section is fully sculpted and approved, use the projection workflow demonstrated in the *Reprojecting and validating primary forms on the clean retopologized mesh* recipe, in *Chapter 6*, to transfer the updated overlap details onto the torso and tail section. As a quick reminder, project the details progressively across each subdivision level using **Project All**, adjusting the **Dist** value according to your model to capture the sculpted details while avoiding projection artifacts. This allows you to continue sculpting the second area while maintaining full sculptural continuity across the creature.

How it works...

This workflow works because the `dragonCrest` creature is no longer forced to use the same subdivision density across the entire unified mesh. The original sculpt had already reached nearly 52 million polygons, but the available resolution was still not enough to refine some of the smaller scales with the level of definition needed for a cinematic asset.

By dividing the creature into two production sections, each mesh becomes lighter and can receive one additional subdivision level independently. This gives us more local geometry where we need it, especially in areas where the scales were losing definition on the original unified model.

The PolyGroup selection based on UDIMs is important because it allows the split to follow an already organized production structure. Instead of cutting the creature randomly, we use the UDIM layout to create logical sections that still make sense for sculpting, displacement generation, and later updates in Maya.

One of the biggest advantages of this workflow becomes apparent later in the pipeline. If the overlap projection is performed correctly, the transition between the separated sections remains virtually invisible when generating the final displacement and normal maps. Although minor projection artifacts can occasionally appear along the transition area, they are usually negligible and can be easily refined during the texturing stage in Mari or Substance 3D Painter. This makes the workflow robust enough for production while preserving the additional sculpting resolution where it is needed most.

Separating the creature into independent meshes allows each section to use its own subdivision hierarchy instead of sharing a single polygon budget across the entire character. As a result, every additional subdivision level is concentrated only on the active production section, dramatically increasing the available local geometric density. This extra geometry can then be used to sculpt finer scales, sharper transitions, and more complex tertiary details that would not be possible on the original unified mesh.

After the section has been separated, **Reconstruct Subdiv** is used to rebuild the lower subdivision levels from the new mesh. This is important because we still need a usable low-poly version of each separated section. That low-poly will later be exported and updated in Maya, both to keep the asset compatible with the rigging workflow and to support proper displacement map extraction.

Once both sections are prepared, the projection step helps maintain sculptural continuity between them. After refining one section, the overlap area can be projected onto the other section, so the sculpt continues naturally from head and neck into the body, tail, and membrane area.

This approach keeps the workflow practical: we gain more resolution for sculpting, preserve continuity between the separated pieces, and still maintain a low-poly structure that can be updated in Maya for rigging, surfacing, and map export.

There's more...

For this recipe, the workflow was intentionally simplified by baking all the sculpting Layers and consolidating the approved primary, secondary, and tertiary information into a single final sculpt before separating the mesh. In this example, all the sculpted forms had already been approved, and the only remaining goal was to increase the available subdivision resolution to add finer surface detail. Under these conditions, this approach is faster, easier to manage, and more than sufficient for most production assets.

In high-end VFX productions, however, the workflow often depends on the requirements of the Look Development department rather than on sculpting alone. If the look development pipeline uses separate displacement and normal maps for primary forms, secondary forms, and tertiary details, each sculpting stage must remain independent throughout production. In this case, every detail level is projected separately onto the production meshes, allowing each map to be updated individually without affecting the others.

This approach requires additional organization, more projection passes, and more careful version management, but it provides maximum flexibility when late production changes are required.

For example, if only the tertiary skin breakup needs to be refined after look development has started, only the tertiary sculpt and its corresponding maps need to be updated, leaving all previously approved primary and secondary information untouched.

The layered projection workflow is generally reserved for hero creatures and high-priority assets, where the additional production complexity is justified by the need for maximum flexibility throughout the VFX pipeline. When the sculpt is already approved and the remaining work is limited to adding finer detail, consolidating the sculpt before separating the mesh is usually the most efficient production choice.

Updating the Maya mesh while preserving vertex order

Now that the `dragonCrest` creature has been separated into two independent sculpting sections and both areas contain additional subdivision resolution, the unified production mesh also needs to be updated correctly.

Technically, the workflow could still continue using the old unified mesh extracted before the subdivision split process. However, this would no longer represent the most accurate or production-correct version of the asset because the newly refined sculpted details now exist only inside the updated, separated sections.

For this reason, the geometry must be rebuilt and updated properly inside Maya, so the final production mesh reflects the latest sculpted information generated during the subdivision splitting workflow.

Note that this step is very important because the updated low-resolution geometry will later become the version used for rigging, displacement extraction, surfacing, rendering, and final production delivery. Maintaining a clean and consistent low-poly structure also guarantees that the asset remains stable and predictable during downstream workflows.

In real production environments, this type of geometry update is common whenever a creature continues evolving after rigging or look development has already started. Updating the mesh correctly while preserving the original topology structure is essential for keeping the entire production pipeline stable and compatible.

Figure 8.12 shows the updated sculpting sections imported into Maya before rebuilding the final production mesh:

Figure 8.12 – The two updated creature sections imported and aligned inside Maya

Getting ready

Before starting this workflow, complete these preparation steps:

1. Open Maya and make sure that the two separate `dragonCrest` sculpting sections are finalized and approved in ZBrush. At this stage, both sections should already contain the updated high-resolution sculpted details created after the subdivision-splitting process.
2. Locate the original unified low-poly mesh extracted from the untouched `dragonCrest` SubTool. This is one of the main reasons why the original creature mesh was intentionally preserved during the previous workflow instead of being modified directly.
3. Verify that the original unified low-poly mesh still contains the original production vertex order used during the rigging and skinning process. This will allow us to correctly rebuild and update the final geometry inside Maya while preserving compatibility with the existing rigging workflow.

How to do it...

In this workflow, we will rebuild the updated production mesh by using the original unified SubTool as the vertex order reference and the two separated sculpting sections as the updated geometry source. The goal is to bring everything back into a clean Maya workflow without losing compatibility with the existing rigging and skinning pipeline.

Exporting the source geometry from ZBrush

We will start in ZBrush by preparing the original unified mesh and the two separated pieces, then export the necessary low-resolution geometry so it can be rebuilt correctly in Maya. Follow these steps:

1. Start by selecting the original unified `dragonCrest` SubTool.
2. Before exporting the mesh, make sure all the approved sculpting Layers are visible and active so the exported geometry contains the latest approved primary, secondary, and tertiary sculpted information.
3. Once the approved Layers are active, export the unified mesh as an OBJ file using a clean production name such as `dragonCrest.obj`.
4. Select the separated front section of the dragon by isolating only the main production PolyGroup without the additional overlap geometry used for the projection transition. Make sure the **SelectLasso** Brush is active, then hold *Ctrl* + *Shift* and click directly on the PolyGroup to visually isolate only the section you want to export.

5. Once isolated, export the mesh by going to **Tool | Export** and save it as an OBJ file named `dragonCrest_part_01.obj`.
6. Repeat this process on the torso and tail section, exporting the second mesh through **Tool | Export** as `dragonCrest_part_02.obj`.

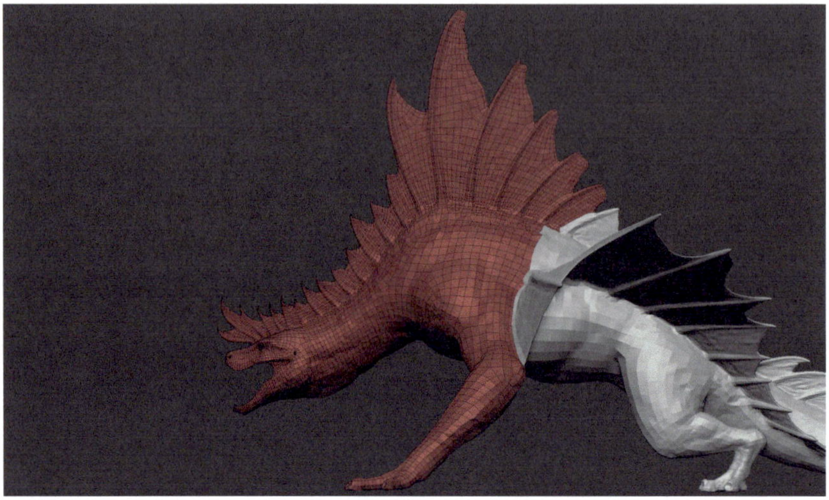

Figure 8.13 – Clean production section isolated without the additional overlap margin before exporting the separated mesh as an OBJ file

Rebuilding the production mesh in Maya

With the source meshes exported, we can now rebuild the updated production mesh while preserving the original topology structure and vertex order required by the rigging pipeline:

1. Open Maya and import the three exported OBJ files by going to **File | Import**. Import the original unified mesh `dragonCrest.obj` together with the two updated, separated sections: `dragonCrest_part_01.obj` and `dragonCrest_part_02.obj`.
2. After importing the three meshes inside Maya, duplicate the original unified `dragonCrest` mesh using *Ctrl* + *D* and rename the duplicated version `dragonCrest_new_01`.

   This duplicated mesh will become the new updated production geometry, while the original `dragonCrest` mesh will remain untouched as the reference mesh containing the original production vertex order required for the rigging and skinning workflow.

Keeping the original mesh intact is extremely important because it allows you to safely preserve the original production geometry while the updated version is rebuilt separately.

3. Hide all the meshes except `dragonCrest_new_01` and `dragonCrest_part_01`, then select `dragonCrest_part_01` and move it slightly along the *X*-axis. This offset is only used to improve visibility and make the mesh selection easier before performing the attribute transfer workflow.

Figure 8.14 – Offsetting dragonCrest_part_01 along the X-axis to improve visibility and simplify the upcoming attribute transfer workflow

4. Select `dragonCrest_part_01` first, followed by `dragonCrest_new_01` as the target mesh. With both meshes selected in the correct order, go to **Mesh | Transfer Attributes**, then open the command options by clicking the small square option box next to **Transfer Attributes**.

Figure 8.15 – Opening the Transfer Attributes options after selecting the updated sculpted section and the duplicated production mesh

5. Inside the **Transfer Attributes Options**, start from the default settings and then disable all unnecessary attributes by setting them to **Off**. The only attribute that should remain enabled is **Vertex position** because we only want to transfer the updated vertex positions from the sculpted section onto the duplicated production mesh.

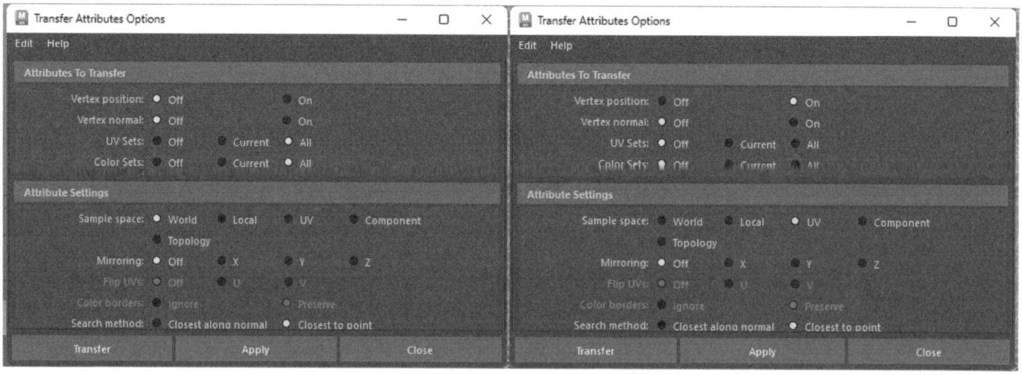

Figure 8.16 – Default Transfer Attributes configuration before isolating the vertex position transfer workflow

6. Next, set the **Sample space** to **UV**. By using the UV sample space, Maya will use the shared UV layout between the two meshes to identify the corresponding vertex regions and transfer only the updated vertex positions from `dragonCrest_part_01` onto `dragonCrest_new_01`.

   This workflow is powerful because it allows the geometry shape to be updated while preserving the original topology structure and production vertex order required for rigging and skinning.

Figure 8.17 – Transfer Attributes configured to transfer only vertex positions based on the shared UV layout

7. Once the settings are configured correctly, press **Apply**.

8. After applying the transfer, the mesh may initially appear visually broken or exploded outside the updated region. This is completely normal and does not mean the workflow failed.

    > **Note**
    >
    > Don't panic if the mesh suddenly appears exploded after applying **Transfer Attributes**. This temporary result is expected. Because part of the mesh was removed, some vertices no longer have a valid positional correspondence on the source mesh. Maya temporarily collapses these vertices onto incorrect locations while preserving the original topology. The mesh will be fully reconstructed during the blend shape restoration in the next steps.

    This happens because `dragonCrest_part_01` contains only a partial section of the creature. Maya transfers the updated vertex positions only across the UV regions shared by `dragonCrest_part_01` and `dragonCrest_new_01`.

    Since the remaining areas of the unified mesh do not exist inside the source geometry, Maya attempts to relocate those unmatched vertices using the closest UV information it can still identify, producing the temporary exploded result visible in the Viewport.

9. Rename the original unified reference mesh from `dragonCrest` to `dragonCrest_BS`. This mesh will now be used as the blend shape source responsible for transferring the updated sculpted deformation onto the rebuilt production geometry.

10. Next, select `dragonCrest_BS` first and then select `dragonCrest_new_01` as the target mesh. Once both meshes are selected in the correct order, go to **Deform | Blend Shape**. The blend shape connects the rebuilt production mesh to the preserved unified reference mesh, allowing the unmatched regions to be restored non-destructively.

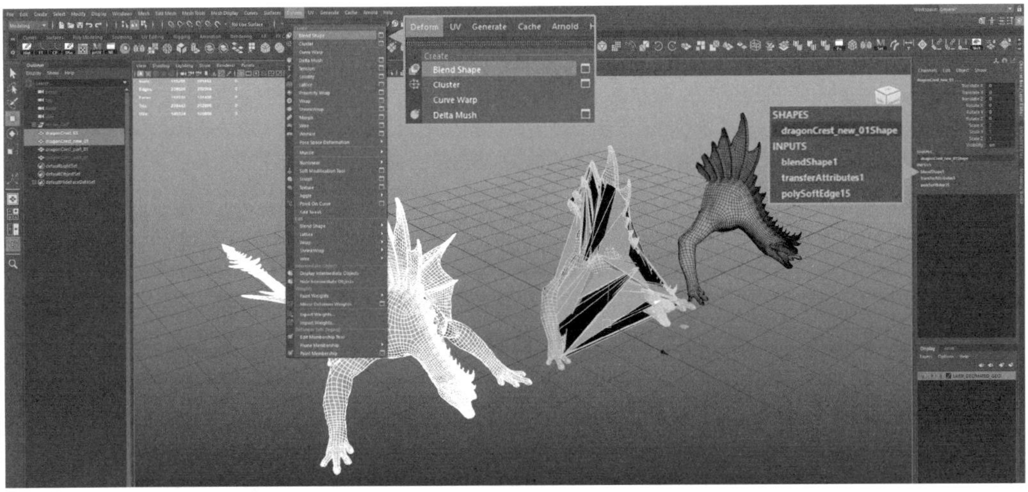

Figure 8.18 – Creating the blendShape node and verifying it in the Maya INPUTS stack

11. Inside the Maya **INPUTS** stack of `dragonCrest_new_01`, open the newly created **blendShape** node. Since the original reference mesh was renamed earlier, the **blendShape** channel will now appear as `dragonCrest_BS` with a default value set to `0`.
12. If you increase this value to `1`, Maya will reconstruct the original unified creature shape using the stored blend shape deformation information coming from `dragonCrest_BS`. This step is useful because it automatically restores the collapsed or incorrectly transferred vertices generated during the partial **Transfer Attributes** workflow. Since the blend shape still preserves the original production topology relationship, Maya can correctly rebuild the missing regions while maintaining the updated sculpted information already transferred from the separated section.

Figure 8.19 – dragonCrest_BS blend shape value set to 0, showing the temporary exploded geometry generated after the partial Transfer Attributes operation

Figure 8.20 – dragonCrest_BS blend shape value set to 1, reconstructing the original unified creature shape and restoring the collapsed vertex regions while preserving the updated sculpted section

> **Tip**
>
> At this stage, do not apply **Delete History** and do not freeze the transformations on any of the meshes for any reason. The workflow still depends on the active **Transfer Attributes** and **blendShape** nodes, so cleaning the history too early would remove the connections needed to rebuild the geometry correctly.
>
> You can still move the meshes in the Maya scene for visibility and selection purposes, but avoid applying **Freeze Transformations** or **Delete History** until the workflow is completed and the final mesh has been properly validated.

Isolating the updated sculpted region

This stage focuses on identifying and isolating the exact vertex region that contains the newly transferred sculpted information. At this point, we want to preserve the updated vertex positions generated by the previous transfer when the `dragonCrest_BS` value is set to `0`, because this state contains the newly transferred sculpted information.

At the same time, the remaining parts of the creature will need to be reconstructed using the original deformation stored inside the **blendShape**.

Since the blend shape relationship has already been created correctly, we can now also hide the `dragonCrest_BS` mesh by pressing *H* to keep the Maya scene cleaner and easier to manage visually during the next operations.

To achieve this, the next step is to create a precise blend shape vertex selection using the same UV shell regions shared with `dragonCrest_part_01`.

1. Select the `dragonCrest_part_01` mesh and go to **Deform** | **Paint Weights** | **Blend Shape** and click on the small square option box next to the command to open the **Paint Blend Shape Weights Tool Settings** and activate the Paint Blend Shape Weights workflow.

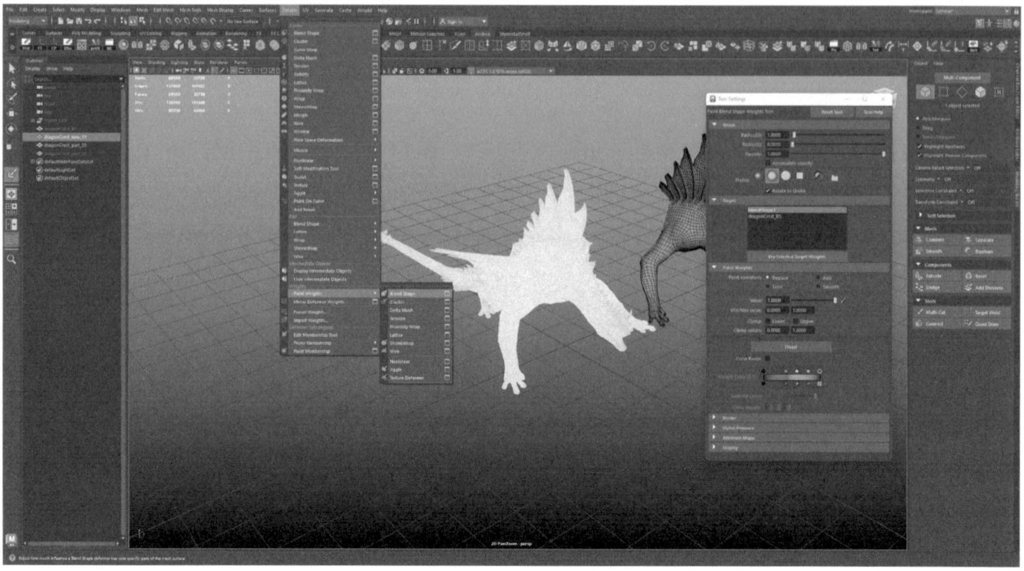

Figure 8.21 – Accessing the Blend Shape Paint Weights workflow to isolate the updated sculpted vertex regions from the reconstructed creature deformation

By painting the blend shape weights, we can precisely control which vertices should preserve the updated vertex positions generated from the **Transfer Attributes** workflow and which vertices should instead use the reconstructed shape coming from the original `dragonCrest_BS` deformation.

Since the UV shells perfectly match the same regions used by `dragonCrest_part_01`, this allows us to isolate the exact updated sculpted area while keeping the rest of the creature reconstructed from the original unified production mesh.

In practice, the selected region will receive a blend shape weight of **0**, preserving the transferred vertex positions, while the remaining vertices retain a weight of **1** and use the reconstructed deformation from `dragonCrest_BS`.

In the next steps, we will paint and isolate these vertex regions to preserve the transferred sculpted information while allowing the blend shape to reconstruct the remaining areas of the creature.

2. Once the **Paint Blend Shape Weights** tool is active, the entire mesh should appear *white*. This indicates that the blend shape currently has a weight value of `1` across the entire surface.
3. Open the **UV Editor** and select `dragonCrest_part_01`. Identify all the UDIM tiles and UV shells belonging to the separated sculpted section.
4. Next, select `dragonCrest_new_01` and return to the **UV Editor**. Using the right-click marking menu, switch **to UV Shell** mode and manually select all the UV shells that correspond to the same UDIM regions used by `dragonCrest_part_01`.
5. Since both meshes share the same UV layout in these areas, this selection allows us to isolate exactly the vertices that received the updated sculpted information during the **Transfer Attributes** workflow.

   These UV shells will be used in the next steps to precisely define which areas should preserve the updated vertex positions and which areas should continue using the reconstructed blend shape deformation.

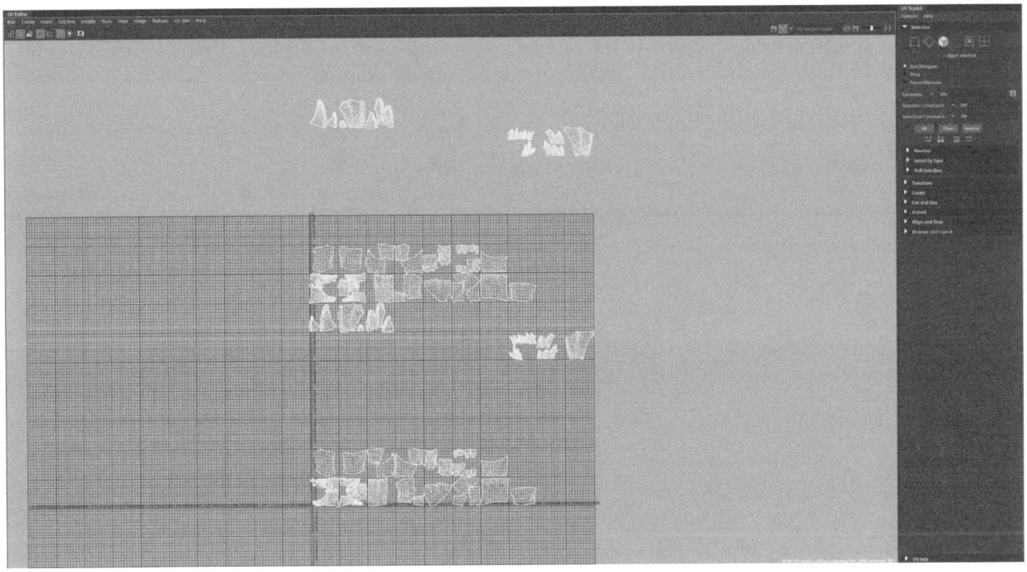

Figure 8.22 – UV layout of dragonCrest_part_01 showing the UDIM tiles and UV shells corresponding to the updated sculpted region

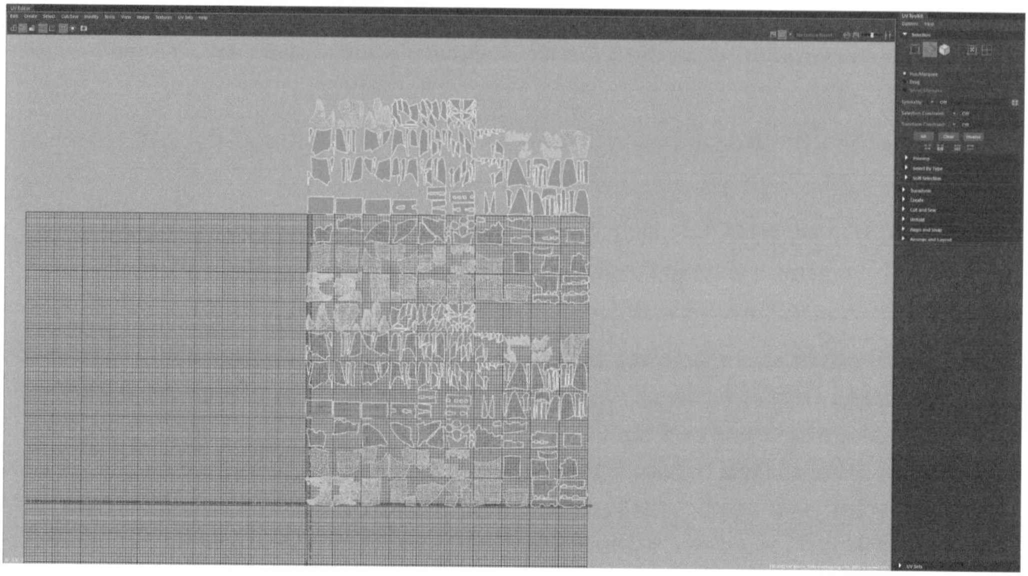

Figure 8.23 – Matching UV shells selected on dragonCrest_new_01 using the same UDIM regions identified in dragonCrest_part_01

6. Once all the required UV shells are selected, hold *Ctrl + Right Mouse Button* inside the **UV Editor** and choose **To Vertices** from the marking menu.

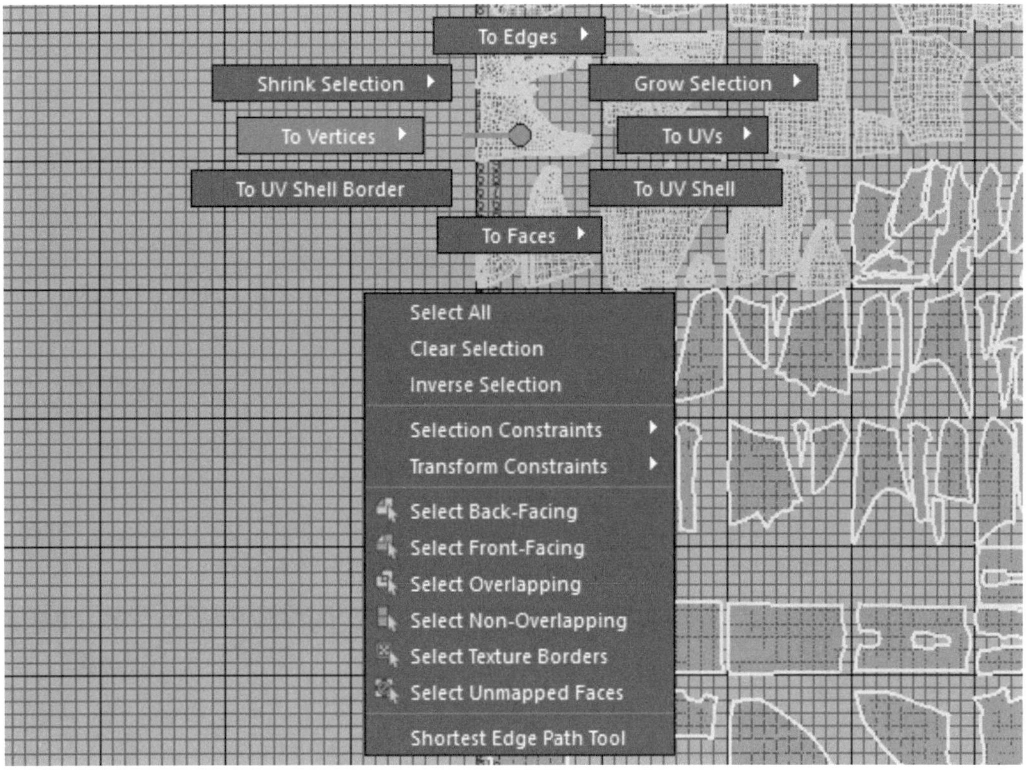

Figure 8.24 – Converting the selected UV shells into a vertex selection using the To Vertices command inside the UV Editor

7. After converting the UV shells to vertices, hold *Ctrl + Right Mouse Button* again inside the **UV Editor**, navigate to the **To Vertices** submenu, and choose **To Vertices**. Be careful not to select **To Vertex Perimeter**, as it creates a different selection than the one required for this workflow.

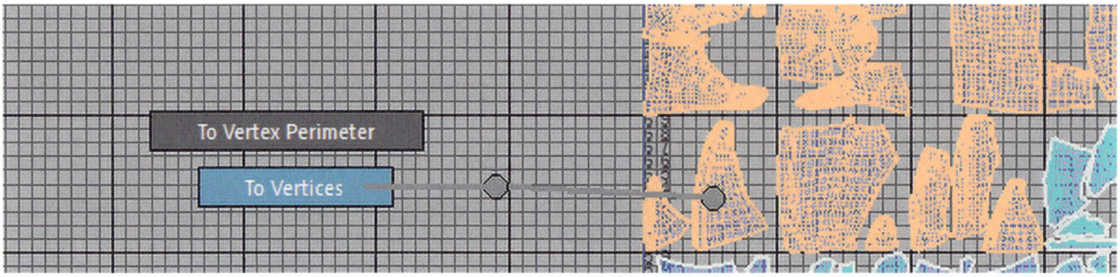

Figure 8.25 – Performing the final conversion to vertices to obtain the complete vertex selection corresponding to the chosen UV shells

Figure 8.26 shows the vertex selection generated from the previously selected UV shells. Verify that only the updated sculpted region is selected before continuing.

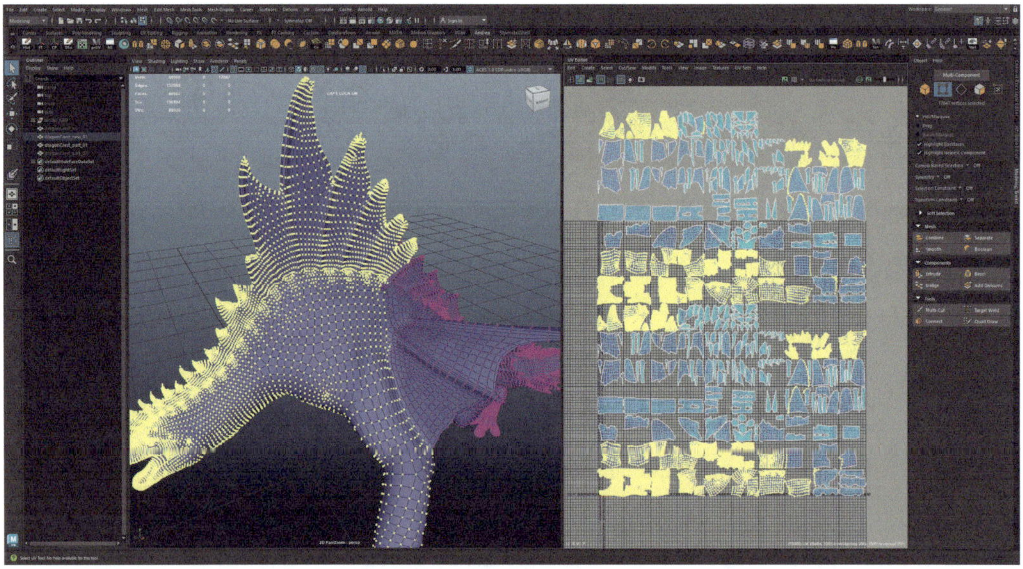

Figure 8.26 – Vertex selection generated from the previously selected UV shells

8. With the vertex selection still active, press < once to shrink the selection by one edge loop. This operation removes the outermost vertex ring from the current selection. We intentionally exclude these vertices because they belong to the transition area shared with the separate sculpted section.

   At this stage of the workflow, these border vertices still contain temporary positions inherited from the partial **Transfer Attributes** operation and do not yet represent the final reconstructed geometry. Excluding them ensures that only the fully validated sculpted region will preserve the updated vertex positions, while the transition area will be reconstructed correctly by the blend shape deformation.

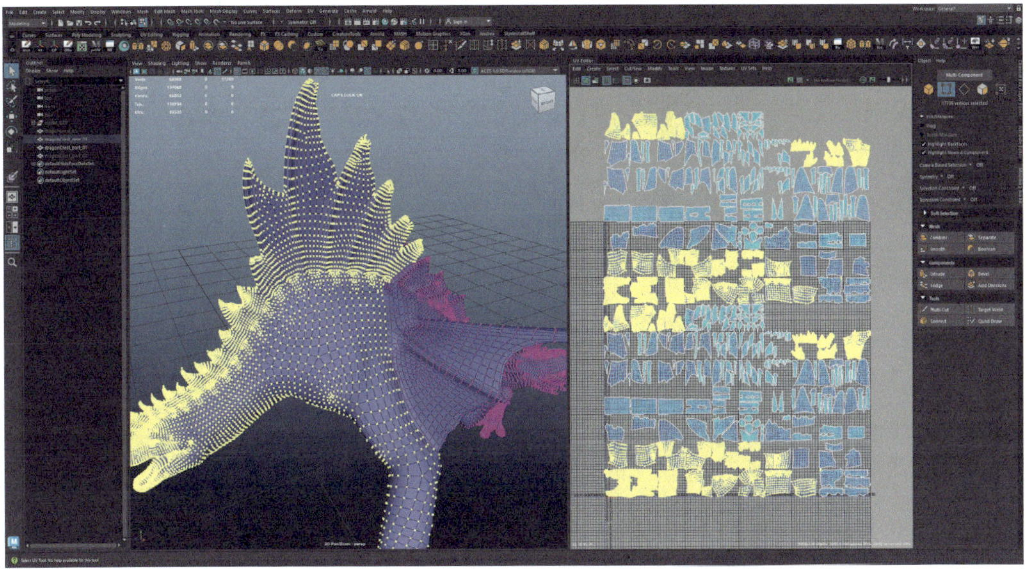

Figure 8.27 – Shrinking the vertex selection by one loop to exclude the transition border shared with the separated sculpted section

9. Return to the **Paint Blend Shape Weights Tool** settings and, under the **Paint Weights** section, set the **Value** parameter to `0`. Since a blend shape weight of `1` uses the reconstructed shape and a value of `0` removes its influence, we will use this setting to preserve the updated vertex positions transferred from the sculpted section.

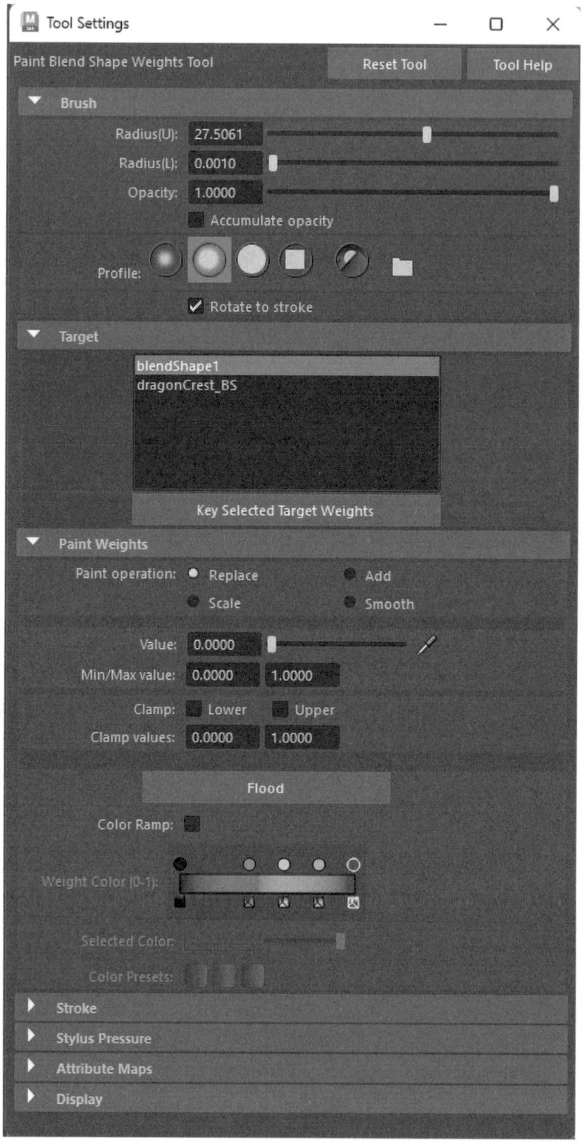

Figure 8.28 – Setting the blend shape paint value to 0 before applying it to the selected vertex region

Preserving and validating the updated sculpt

The final stage uses blend shape weight painting to preserve the transferred sculpted information, verify the result, and prepare the mesh for production use:

1. With the vertex selection still active, activate the **Paint Blend Shape Weights Tool**. You can adjust the brush size interactively by holding *B* and dragging with the *middle mouse button*. Dragging left decreases the brush radius, while dragging right increases it.
2. Choose a brush size large enough to comfortably cover the selected region while still allowing precise control near the transition borders, as shown in *Figure 8.29*:

Figure 8.29 – Adjusting the Paint Blend Shape Weights brush radius by holding B and dragging with the middle mouse button before painting the selected vertex region

3. With the **Value** set to `0`, start painting over the selected region using the *left mouse button*. The goal is to gradually turn the entire selected area black.
   In the **Paint Blend Shape Weights** workflow, black represents a value of `0`, meaning the blend shape influence is completely disabled on those vertices.

   By disabling the blend shape in this region, we preserve the updated vertex positions generated by the **Transfer Attributes** workflow while preventing the original `dragonCrest_BS` deformation from affecting the area.
4. Continue painting until the entire updated sculpted section becomes black.

Figure 8.30 – Beginning the blend shape weight painting process on the updated sculpted region

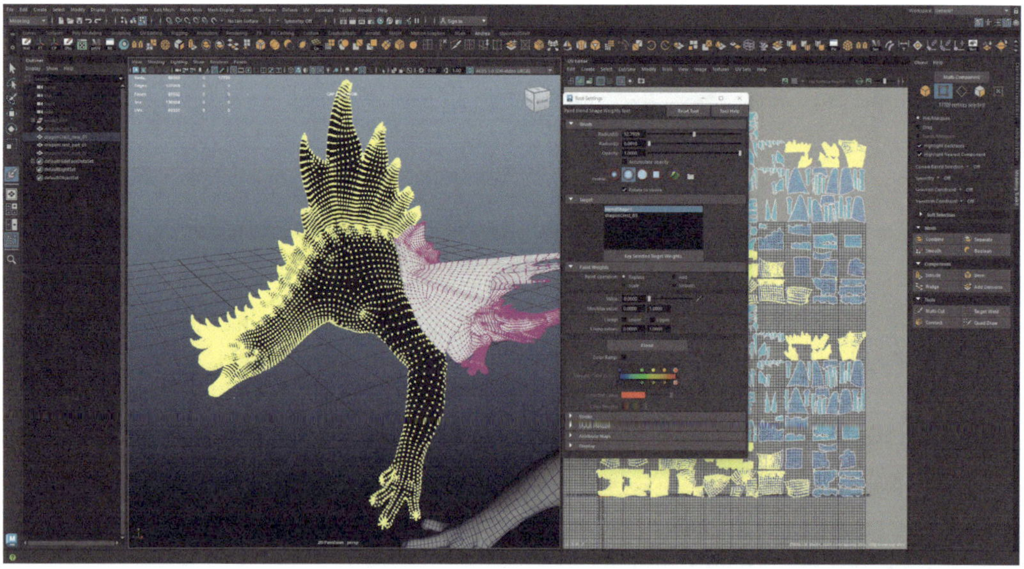

Figure 8.31 – Completed blend shape weight painting with the updated sculpted region fully isolated

5. Once the entire region has been painted and the blend shape weights have been updated, position `dragonCrest_part_01` directly on top of `dragonCrest_new_01` and compare the two meshes.

The updated sculpted region should now match perfectly. This confirms that the **Transfer Attributes** workflow, blend shape reconstruction, and weight painting process have successfully preserved the updated vertex positions while rebuilding the rest of the creature from the original production mesh.

The result is a unified mesh that contains the new sculpted information while still maintaining the original topology and vertex order required by the rigging pipeline.

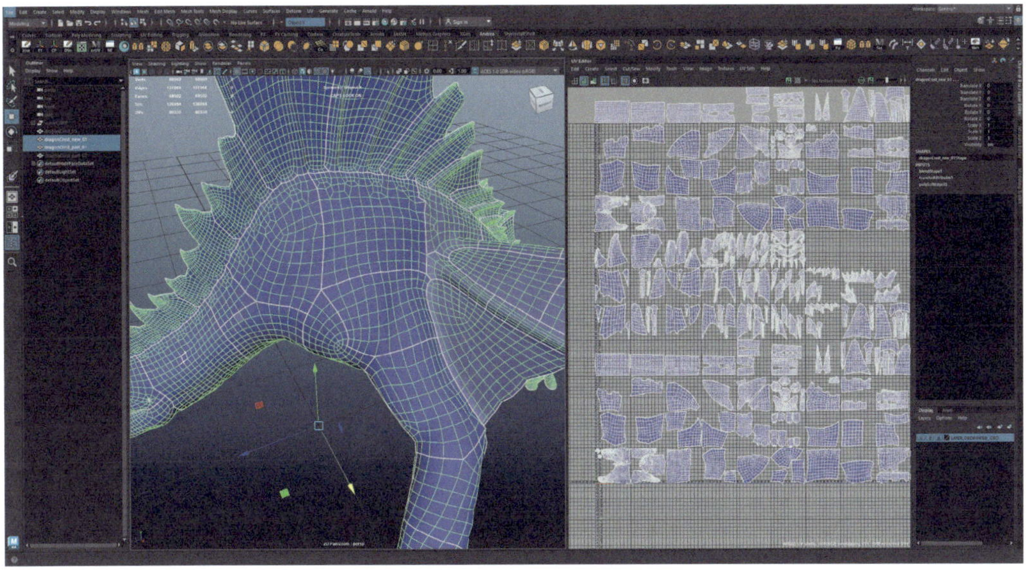

Figure 8.32 – dragonCrest_part_01 positioned directly on top of dragonCrest_new_01 to verify that the updated sculpted region matches perfectly

6. Once you have verified that the updated sculpted region matches correctly, you can safely delete the construction history on `dragonCrest_new_01`. At this point, `dragonCrest_new_01` becomes the new production base mesh and replaces the previous version of the creature.

From here, repeat the same workflow using `dragonCrest_part_02`. Transfer the updated vertex positions, reconstruct the remaining geometry through the blend shape workflow, isolate the corresponding UV shells, paint the blend shape weights, and validate the result.

In production, this process can be repeated as many times as necessary. Whether the creature is divided into two, three, four, or even more sections, the workflow remains identical until the entire model has been updated and reassembled into a single production mesh.

How it works...

One of the most challenging situations in production occurs when a large portion of a creature has been re-sculpted after the asset has already been integrated into the pipeline. At this stage, the model may already contain approved UVs, skinning data, rigging information, and other dependencies that rely on the original topology and vertex order.

Replacing the geometry directly is usually not an option because even small topology changes can break compatibility with the existing rigging and deformation setup. For this reason, the goal of this workflow is not to replace the production mesh, but to transfer the updated sculpted shapes while preserving the original topology, UV layout, and vertex order.

One of the main advantages of this workflow is that it allows large sculptural updates without forcing the production asset to restart downstream departments. Because the original topology, UV layout, and vertex order remain unchanged, rigging, skinning, look development, animation, and lighting can continue using the same production mesh while only the sculpted information is updated.

Another important production benefit is that only the modified regions need to be validated. Instead of rebuilding and rechecking the entire asset after every sculpting revision, artists can focus their quality control on the updated sections, significantly reducing iteration time on complex creatures.

The workflow also scales well to very large assets. Once one production section has been validated, the same process can be repeated on every additional sculpted region until the entire creature has been updated. This allows extremely high-resolution creatures to be developed in manageable sections without sacrificing production compatibility or sculptural continuity.

9

Exporting Meshes and Creating Maps for Texturing and Lookdev

Throughout this book, we have followed the complete creation of our dragon creature, starting from the initial blockout and continuing through retopology, UV layout, primary, secondary, and tertiary detailing, the creation of additional geometry, and the optimization techniques required to manage a high-resolution production asset. At this stage, the creature is fully completed in its neutral A-Pose and is ready to move beyond ZBrush into the next departments of a production pipeline.

However, creating a finished sculpt is only part of the process. Before the asset can be textured, shaded, and rendered, it must be exported correctly and accompanied by the maps required to reproduce all the sculpted information created during the previous chapters. A poorly prepared asset can cause unnecessary problems for downstream departments, while a clean, well-organized export package enables the rest of the pipeline to work efficiently.

In this chapter, you will learn how to prepare your creature for the final stages of production through the following recipes:

- Exporting a mesh from ZBrush for texturing and look development
- Creating normal and displacement maps with Multi Map Exporter
- Using Decimation Master to prepare high-resolution meshes for texturing
- Hand-painting a cavity map for more control

By the end of this chapter, you will have all the files needed to move your creature from ZBrush into a professional texturing and look development workflow.

Figure 9.1 shows the production assets generated from the completed dragon sculpt, including the decimated mesh and exported maps used for texturing and look development:

Figure 9.1 – Overview of the production assets generated from the final dragon sculpt

Technical requirements

To complete this chapter, you will primarily work inside **ZBrush**, using the creature project developed throughout the previous chapters. Although the workflows demonstrated here focus on preparing assets in ZBrush, the exported files are intended for use in texturing and look development applications, such as **Mari** and **Substance 3D Painter**, as well as in rendering packages used in production pipelines.

To complete the recipes in this chapter, you will need:

- **ZBrush 2024** or later.

- **Maya 2024** or later (as used throughout the previous chapters).
- **Mari** or **Substance 3D Painter** (not covered in this chapter but referenced as downstream applications).
- A completed creature project containing finalized geometry, UVs, and subdivision levels.
- At least 20 to 50 GB of free disk space is recommended for storing exported meshes, texture maps, and temporary files. The exact amount depends on the number of UDIMs, the texture resolution, and the file format used. As a general reference, a single 4K normal or displacement map typically occupies between 30 MB and 50 MB, so projects containing dozens of UDIMs can quickly consume several gigabytes of storage.

To follow the workflows in this chapter, use the decimated production meshes provided in the `Chapter06_07` folder of the book's GitHub repository.

The required files for this chapter are:

- `dragonCrest_body_tertiary_dec_v001.obj`
- `dragonCrest_accessories_dec_v001.fbx`

The following files are examples of the texture maps generated during this chapter for **UDIM 1001** and are available in the `Chapter09` folder in the GitHub repository:

- `body_CAV.1001.tif`: An example cavity map generated during the export workflow.
- `body_DSP.1001.exr`: An example displacement map generated during the export workflow.
- `body_NRM.1001.tif`: An example normal map generated during the export workflow.

You can download the example project files for this book by following the instructions in the *Download the example code/resource files* section in the *Preface* of this book.

This chapter's code/resource files are included in the downloadable code/resource bundle.

Exporting a mesh from ZBrush for texturing and look development

Before we can generate displacement, normal, or cavity maps, we need to prepare and export the correct versions of our creature. Although the high-resolution sculpt contains all the information required to reproduce every detail created throughout the sculpting process, it is not practical to use this version directly across all departments in a production pipeline.

Instead, production workflows rely on lighter meshes combined with maps that transfer information stored in the higher subdivision levels. This approach allows different departments to work more efficiently while preserving the visual quality of the original sculpt.

In this recipe, you will learn how to prepare and export the meshes required for downstream workflows, creating a solid foundation for rigging, texturing, look development, and map generation. By the end of this recipe, you will have two production-ready meshes: a low-resolution mesh for rigging and other downstream departments, and a mesh exported at Subdivision Level 2 (or another subdivision level that best fits your production pipeline) for texturing, look development, and map generation in the following recipes.

Figure 9.2 – Final dragon sculpt exported to downstream departments

Getting ready

For this recipe, we will work entirely inside ZBrush using the final version of the creature created throughout the previous chapters. I will use the `dragonCrest` asset developed during the book, but the same workflow can be applied to any creature or character project.

Open your project and make sure the model is loaded at its *highest subdivision level*. Before proceeding, save an incremental version of the file so you always have a backup of the original sculpt.

How to do it...

Before exporting any geometry, I like to spend a few minutes cleaning the project and removing anything that is no longer required. By this stage of the workflow, it is common to accumulate backup SubTools, temporary meshes, test geometry, old Insert Mesh assets, or duplicated elements created during the sculpting process. While these assets may have been useful during production, they only increase the file size and can complicate the export process. Let's begin:

1. Start by reviewing the SubTool list and identifying any geometry that is no longer needed. If you are confident that a SubTool will not be required in the future, select it and delete it using **Tool** | **SubTool** | **Delete**.
2. Continue this process until only the geometry intended for delivery remains in the project. The goal is to create a clean export file containing only the assets that will be used by the downstream departments.

Figure 9.3 – Reviewing the SubTool list and removing temporary geometry before export

3. Once the project has been cleaned, review the active layers on each SubTool and verify that their intensity values are set correctly. Create a dedicated export version of the project, then navigate to **Tool** | **Layers** | **Bake All** and bake the layers for each SubTool

that contains layer information. Continue until all sculpted details have been permanently stored in the geometry and the asset is ready for export.

4. After baking all the layers, switch every SubTool to its lowest subdivision level by navigating to **Tool** | **Geometry** | **All Low**. This allows you to quickly verify that all subdivision levels are intact and prepares the asset for the export operations that will follow in the next steps.

Figure 9.4 – The All Low button in the SubTool palette

5. Before proceeding with the export process, save a dedicated version of the project specifically for asset delivery. Navigate to **File** | **Save As** and create a new file using a clear naming convention such as `dragonCrest_EXPORT_v001.ztl`. This allows you to keep your original working file intact while preparing a clean version for downstream departments.

6. Open **ZPlugin** | **FBX ExportImport** and review the export settings before creating the FBX file. Set the export mode to **Visible** if you only want to export the SubTools currently visible in the scene. Alternatively, select **All** if you need to export every SubTool contained in the project regardless of its visibility state.

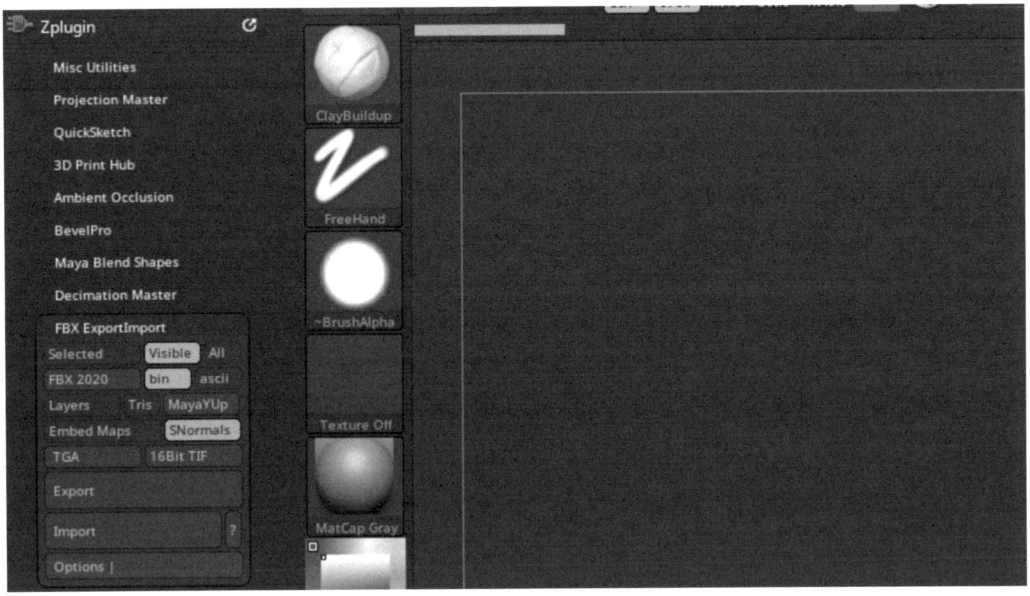

Figure 9.5 – Configuring the FBX ExportImport plugin before exporting the creature

Tip

Once the FBX has been exported, I recommend importing it into Maya and organizing the asset before delivering it to the rigging department. Create a dedicated group named `dragonCrest_lp_GRP` and place all the imported geometry inside it. Then, rename each mesh using a suffix such as `_lp_GEO`. For example, `body_lp_GEO`, `head_lp_GEO`, and `claws_lp_GEO` (`lp` means low-poly mesh).

This extra step only takes a few minutes but helps maintain a clean hierarchy, improves communication between departments, and makes it immediately clear which meshes are intended for rigging.

Although I could have introduced the **Multi Map Exporter** earlier in this book, I prefer introducing it at this stage because it marks the beginning of the map generation workflow and will be used extensively throughout the following recipes.

Unlike the FBX exported in the previous step, which is intended as the low-resolution production mesh for downstream departments such as rigging, the mesh exported with the **Multi Map Exporter** preserves the selected subdivision level and will be used to generate the normal, displacement, and cavity maps. Before continuing, make sure that all the SubTools you want to export are visible and that any geometry you do not want to include in the export is hidden.

7. Open **ZPlugin** | **Multi Map Exporter** and disable all the map generation options, leaving only **Export Mesh** enabled. Then, under the **Mesh Export** section, set **SubDiv level** to 2. This will generate the subdivision level that will be used for texturing, look development, and map generation in the next stages of the pipeline.

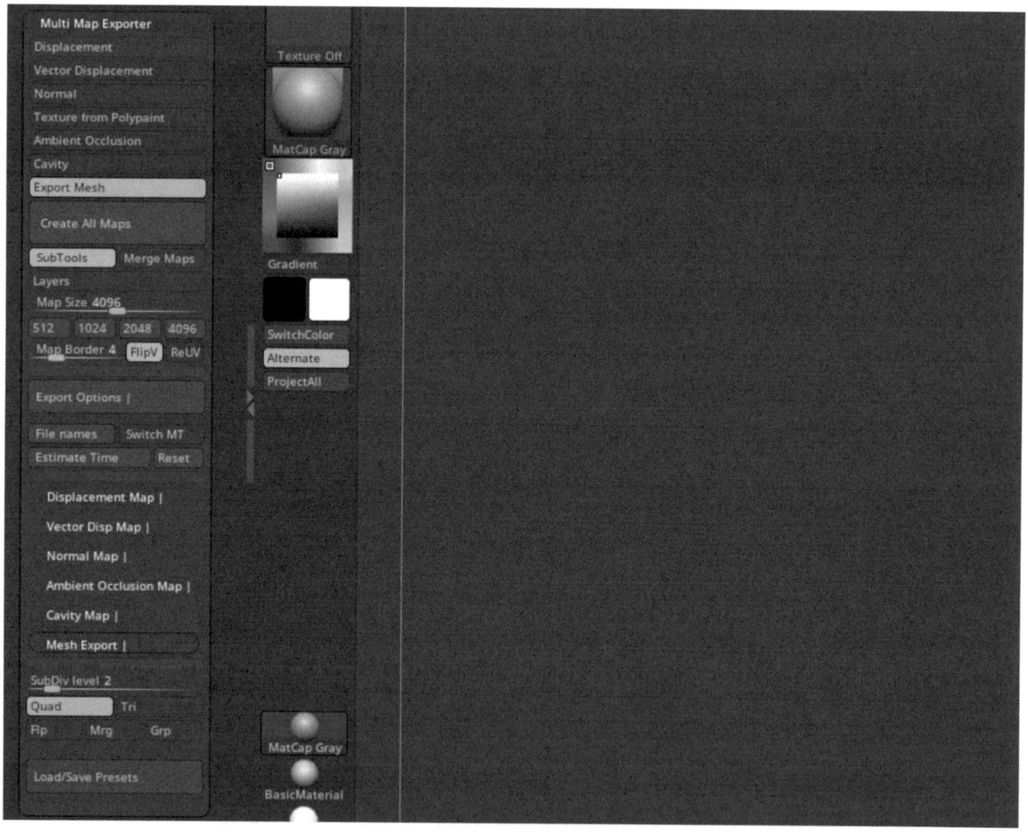

Figure 9.6 – Configuring the Multi Map Exporter to export only the mesh at Subdivision Level 2

Note

The subdivision level used for export is not a fixed rule and may vary depending on the studio pipeline, the complexity of the asset, and the final quality requirements. In this book, I use **Subdivision Level 2** because it provides an excellent balance between accuracy and performance for most creature workflows.

However, many studios choose to export **Subdivision Level 3** for hero assets or highly detailed creatures, especially when working with close-up shots, high-resolution textures, or look development workflows that require additional surface fidelity. Always adapt the exported subdivision level to the needs of production rather than following a rigid workflow.

8. Once the export settings have been configured, click on **Create All Maps**. Even though map generation is currently disabled, the **Multi Map Exporter** will still process the mesh export according to the settings defined in the previous steps.
9. When prompted, choose a destination folder for the exported files. I recommend creating a dedicated folder for this export directly from the **Save** dialog to keep all generated assets organized. After selecting the folder and defining the file name, click **Save** to begin the export process.

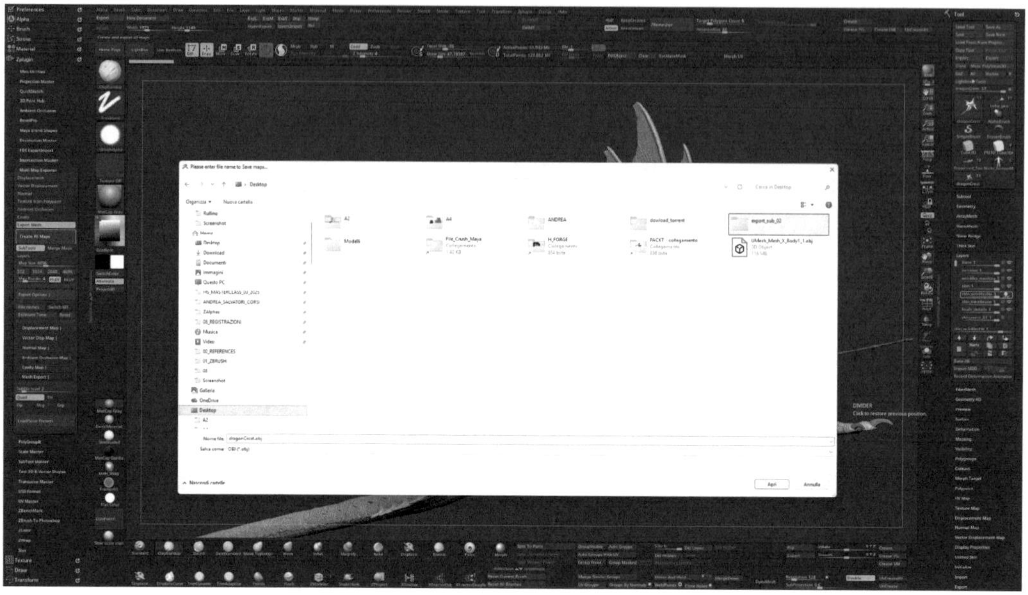

Figure 9.7 – Selecting the export directory and creating a dedicated folder for the generated assets

Once the exported mesh has been imported into Maya, I recommend organizing it using a dedicated naming convention that clearly identifies it as the high-resolution version. Create a group such as `dragonCrest_hp_GRP` and rename the individual meshes using the `_hp_GEO` suffix. For example, `body_hp_GEO`, `head_hp_GEO`, and `claws_hp_GEO`.

> **Tip**
>
> **Common causes of artifacts in exported maps**
>
> If your exported normal or displacement maps contain unexpected artifacts, seams, repeated details, or distorted areas, the problem is often related to the UV layout rather than the export settings.
>
> Before exporting your maps again, check the following:
>
> - No UV shells overlap unless intentionally mirrored
> - Every UV shell is completely contained within its assigned UDIM tile
> - No UV shell accidentally extends into a neighboring UDIM tile
> - The exported mesh uses the same UV layout and vertex order as the sculpted model

> Most of these issues become visible only after the maps are generated or later during texturing, especially when using generators, masks, or procedural effects. A quick inspection of your UV layout can often solve the problem before you spend hours exporting the maps again.

How it works...

The purpose of this workflow is not simply to export geometry from ZBrush, but to prepare an asset that can be efficiently used throughout the rest of the production pipeline. While the final sculpt contains all the information created during the modeling and detailing stages, this version is often too heavy to be shared directly with every department.

For this reason, production workflows typically rely on multiple versions of the same asset. A lighter mesh can be provided to rigging artists, while a higher subdivision level is used for texturing, look development, and map generation. This approach allows each department to work with the level of detail it actually needs while keeping file sizes manageable.

Before exporting, it is also important to clean the project and remove any temporary geometry, backup meshes, or experimental assets that are no longer required. Keeping the file organized reduces the risk of exporting incorrect geometry and helps maintain a cleaner pipeline. It also reduces the overall file size, making the export process more efficient.

Another important step is baking all active layers before starting the export process. At this stage, the sculpt has already been approved, and the layers are no longer required for further adjustments. Baking them directly into the geometry helps reduce the overall complexity of the file and creates a cleaner export version of the asset. When exporting multiple meshes and generating large numbers of maps, keeping the project as lightweight as possible can help improve stability and reduce the risk of crashes or unexpected issues during the export process.

The subdivision level chosen for export plays a critical role in balancing quality and performance. In this recipe, we export a subdivision level 2 mesh because it preserves the overall forms and proportions of the creature while remaining relatively lightweight. However, some productions may require higher subdivision levels depending on the complexity of the asset and the quality requirements of the project.

Finally, organizing exported assets using clear folder structures and naming conventions helps maintain consistency across departments. Creating dedicated export versions, organized folders, and clearly named meshes allows artists from rigging, texturing, and look development departments to immediately identify which files they should use. A well-organized export package is easier to track and update, and reduces the possibility of mistakes later in production.

Creating normal and displacement maps with Multi Map Exporter

Once the production meshes have been prepared, the next step is generating the maps that will be used throughout the texturing, look development, and rendering pipeline. Among the most important are *normal maps* and *displacement maps*, both designed to reproduce the details of the original sculpt, but in very different ways.

A **normal map** stores surface direction information and creates the visual illusion of small details such as wrinkles, pores, scales, and surface texture without modifying the actual geometry. Because it only affects shading, it is lightweight and fast to render.

A **displacement map**, on the other hand, stores height information that physically modifies the geometry at render time. This allows larger sculpted forms and high-frequency details to be recreated with much greater accuracy, making displacement maps an essential component of most creature and character workflows.

In production, these maps are rarely considered alternatives. Most creature and character assets use both together. The normal map captures fine surface details efficiently and improves rendering performance, while the displacement map recreates the larger sculpted forms and the finest surface variations at render time. Combining both maps provides the best balance between visual quality, rendering accuracy, and performance.

Using only a normal map is more common in real-time applications, such as video games, where maintaining high performance is often a priority. Although modern real-time engines increasingly support displacement techniques, they usually come with a higher performance cost. For high-end VFX and cinematic rendering, using both normal and displacement maps remains the preferred production workflow.

The **Multi Map Exporter** in ZBrush provides an efficient way to generate these maps across multiple UDIM tiles while maintaining consistent naming conventions and export settings. In this recipe, you will learn how to configure the exporter and generate production-ready normal and displacement maps for the `dragonCrest` creature.

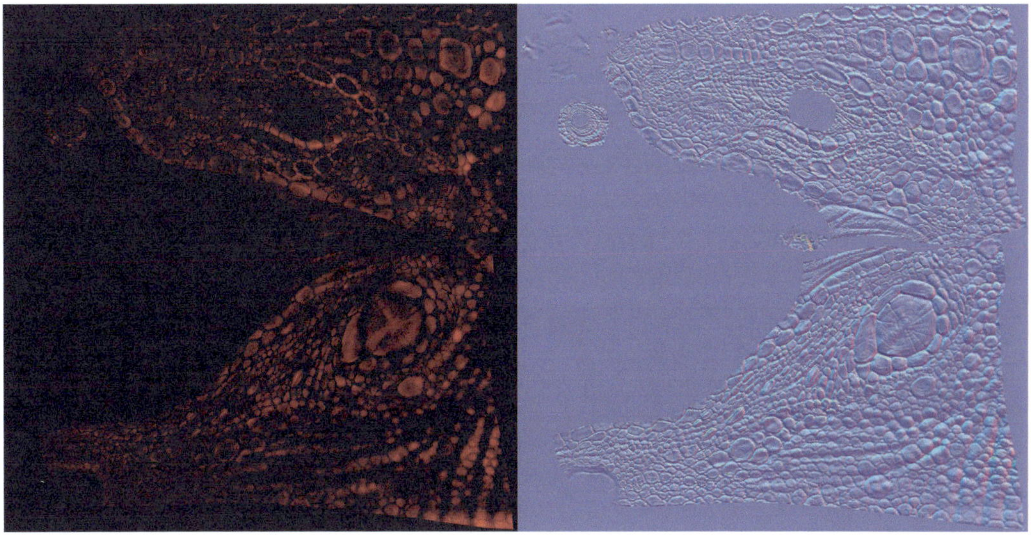

Figure 9.8 – Comparison between the displacement map (left) and the normal map (right) generated from the dragonCrest sculpt

Getting ready

For this recipe, we will continue working inside ZBrush using the final approved version of the `dragonCrest` creature. Before proceeding, follow these steps:

1. Make sure all sculpting work has been completed and that the project has been cleaned following the workflow described in the *Exporting a mesh from ZBrush for texturing and look development* recipe. Ideally, all unnecessary geometry should already have been removed and all sculpting layers baked into the mesh.
2. Before generating the maps, verify that all the required SubTools are visible and switch the model to its lowest subdivision level. This will be the base mesh used by ZBrush when calculating the normal maps and displacement maps from the higher subdivision levels.

How to do it...

Before generating any maps, we first need to configure the **Multi Map Exporter** and enable only the outputs required for this workflow. Let's get started:

1. Navigate to **ZPlugin** | **Multi Map Exporter** and enable **Displacement** Map and **Normal** Map. Disable all other map types to keep the export process focused on the assets required for texturing and look development. This also helps reduce export times and keeps the generated files organized.

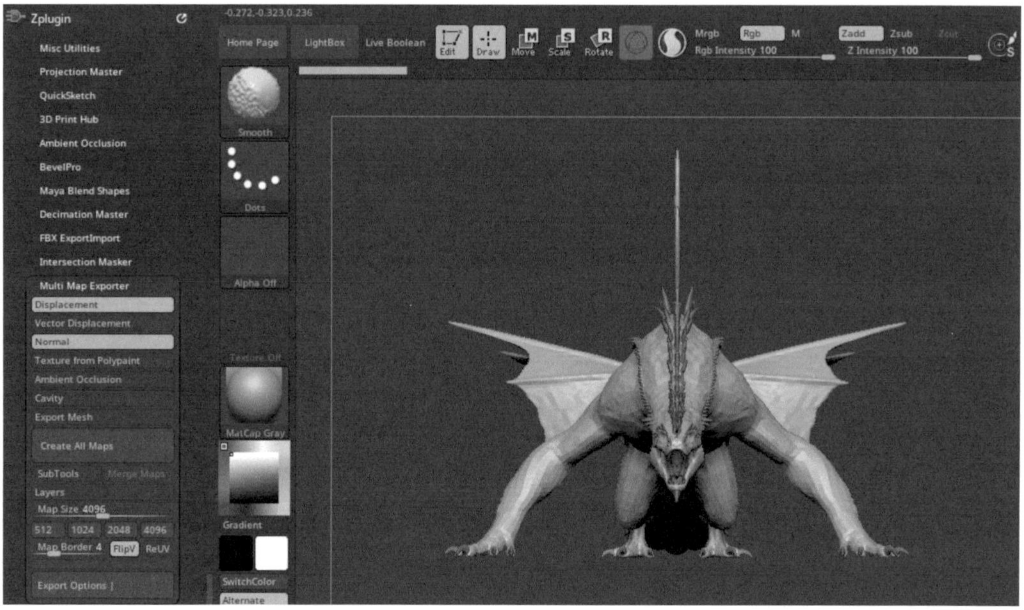

Figure 9.9 – Enabling Displacement and Normal maps in the Multi Map Exporter while disabling all other map types

2. In the **Multi Map Exporter** settings, enable **SubTools** to ensure that maps are generated for all visible SubTools in the project. Then set the **Map Size** to `4096`, which provides a good balance between detail quality and file size for most production assets. Leave the remaining settings at their default values for now, as we will adjust additional options later in the workflow.

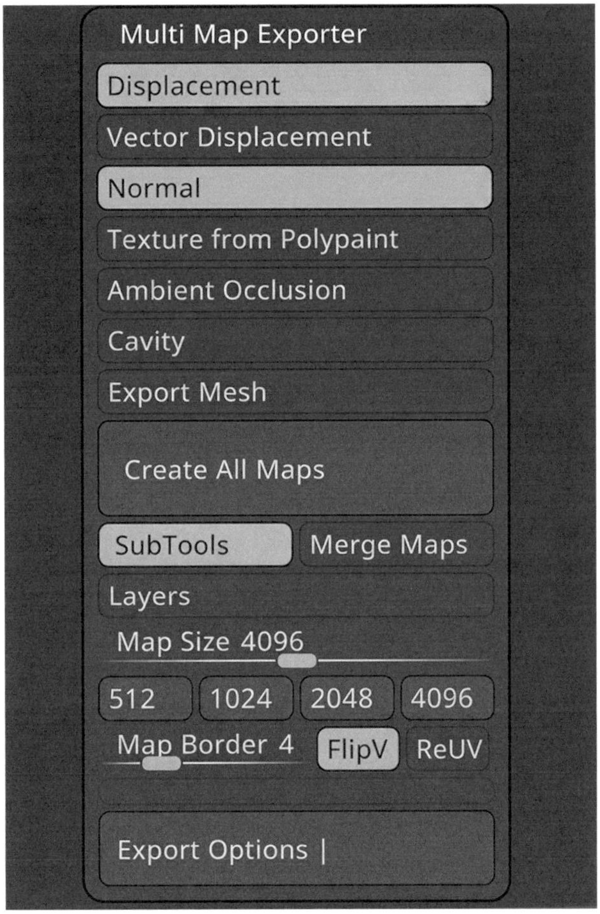

Figure 9.10 – Enabling SubTools and setting the map resolution

3. Expand the **Displacement** Map settings and configure the export options before generating the maps:
    - Enable **SmoothUV** to ensure that the displacement is calculated using the same smoothed UV borders that will be used during rendering.
    - Set **Mid** to `0` and increase **DPSubPix** to 2 to achieve greater accuracy when generating the displacement map.
    - Enable **32Bit** output and **exr** to export a 32-bit EXR displacement map.
    - Set **SubDiv level** to 2, as this will be the subdivision level used as the render mesh and will represent the base geometry on which the displacement will be calculated.

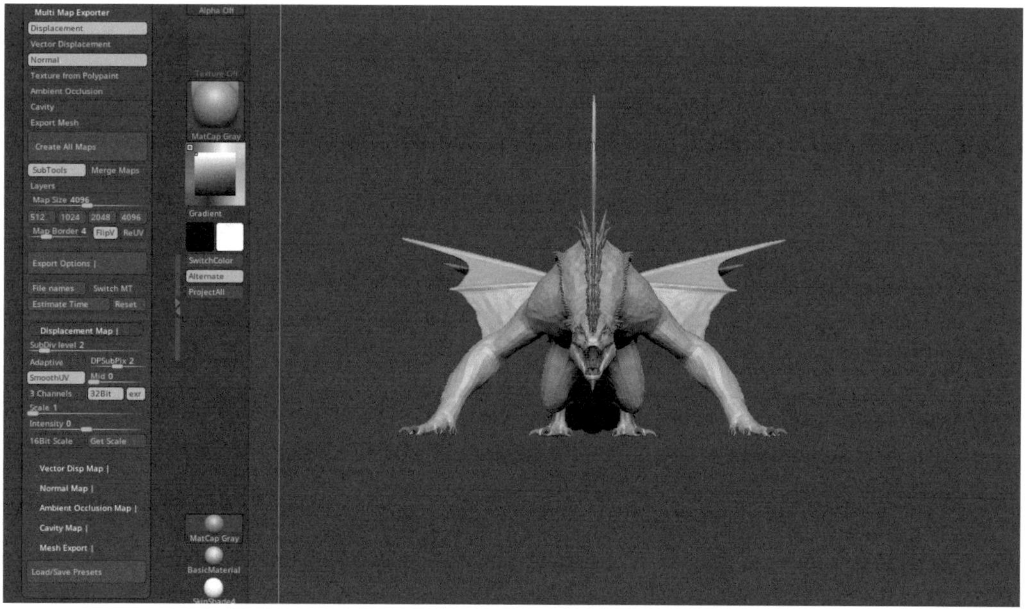

Figure 9.11 – Configuring the Displacement Map export settings

4. Expand the **Normal** Map settings and configure the export options:
   - Set **SubDiv level** to 2 so that the normal map is generated using the same base mesh employed in the displacement workflow.
   - Enable **Tangent** space, **SmoothUV**, and **SNormals** to ensure compatibility between the exported maps and most modern texturing and rendering pipelines.

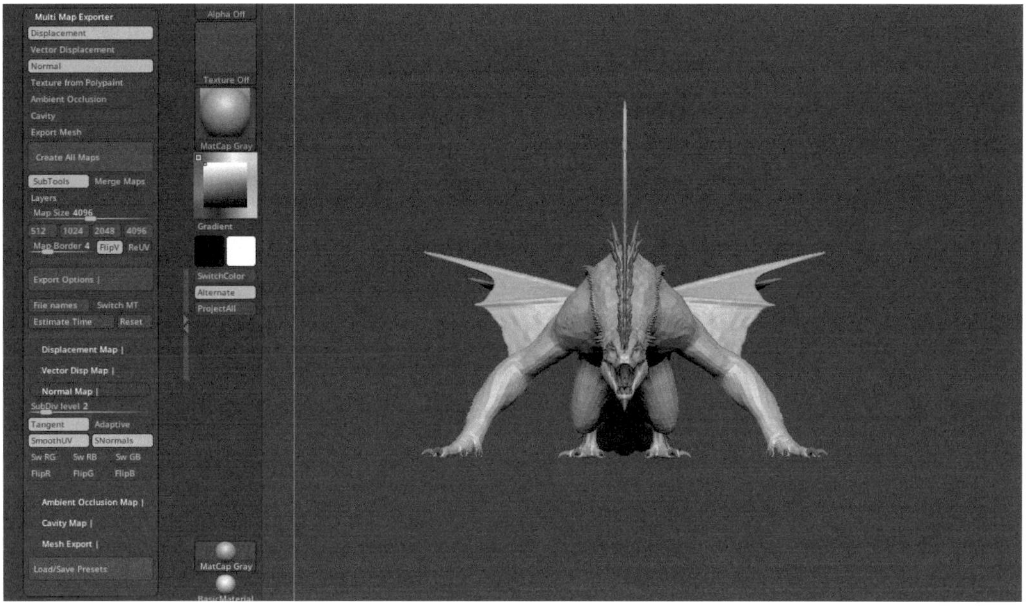

Figure 9.12 – Configuring the Normal Map export settings

5. Before exporting the maps, open **Export Options | File Names** and configure the naming convention. Rename the **Displacement map** suffix to `_DSP.` and the **Normal map** suffix to `_NRM.`, as shown in *Figure 9.13*.
6. Then, under **UV tile ID format**, select **<UDIM>**. This ensures that every exported map follows a production-friendly naming convention and includes the corresponding UDIM number in the file name, such as **1001**, **1002**, **1003**, and so on.
   Because the **SubTools** option is enabled, the exported maps will also inherit the name of the corresponding SubTool. For example, a displacement map generated from the body geometry may be exported as `body_DSP.1001.exr`, while the corresponding normal map would be named `body_NRM.1001.tif`. This naming convention makes it immediately clear which asset and UDIM tile each map belongs to, greatly simplifying texturing and look development workflows.

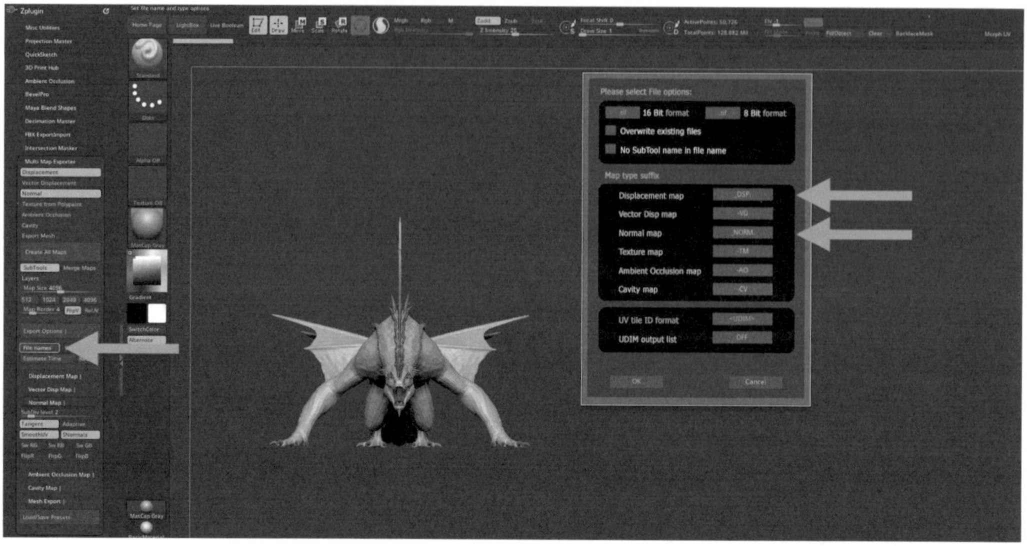

Figure 9.13 – Configuring map suffixes and enabling the UDIM naming convention inside the Multi Map Exporter

7. If you need to regenerate only specific UDIM tiles, open **Export Options | File Names** and enable **Use List** under **UDIM output list**.
8. Then click the **X** button (see *Figure 9.14*) to define exactly which UDIMs should be exported. This feature can save a significant amount of time when working with large texture sets. For example, if ZBrush crashes during the export process, if a map becomes corrupted, or if you later discover that a specific UV tile contains overlapping UVs that need to be fixed, you can simply regenerate the affected UDIMs instead of exporting the entire texture set again.

   You can specify a single UDIM by entering its number (for example, `1001`), export multiple individual UDIMs by separating them with commas (for example, `1001,1002,1005`), or define a range using a hyphen (for example, `1001-1005`), as shown in *Figure 9.15*. You can also combine both methods when necessary.

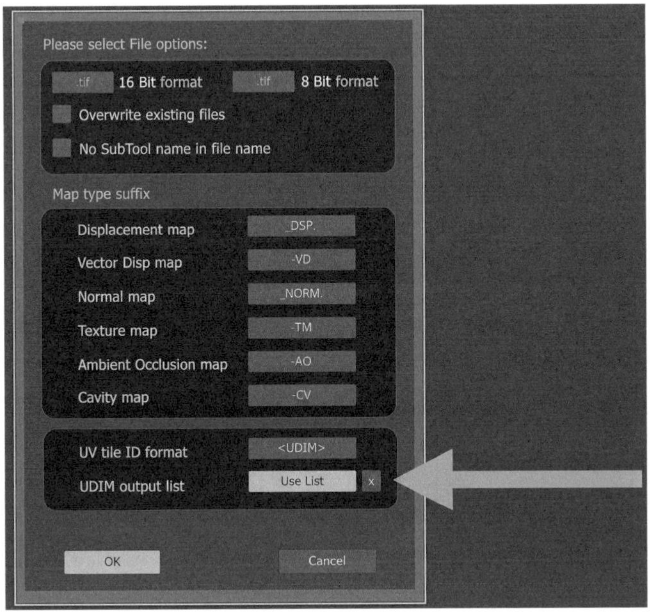

Figure 9.14 – Enabling Use List to export only selected UDIM tiles

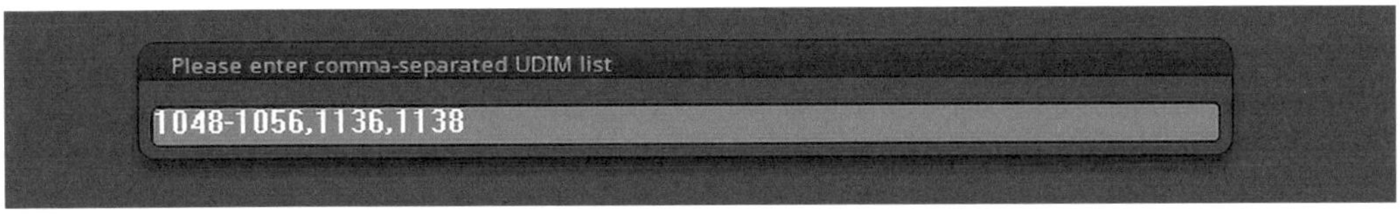

Figure 9.15 – Defining specific UDIM numbers and ranges for partial map exports

9. Once all the export settings have been configured, click **OK** to confirm the file naming options and return to the main **Multi Map Exporter** panel. Then click **Create All Maps** to begin the export process.
10. When prompted, choose a destination folder for the generated maps. I recommend creating a dedicated export directory, such as `v001`, to keep different versions organized and make future updates easier to manage.
11. After selecting the folder and confirming the file name, click **Save** and allow ZBrush to generate all normal maps and displacement maps for the project.

Figure 9.16 – Creating a dedicated export folder and starting the map generation process

Tip

When working with production assets that use a large number of UDIMs, be prepared for significantly longer export times. A creature containing 100 to 200 UDIM tiles can take anywhere from several hours to multiple days to generate all maps.

The total export time depends on several factors, including the number of UDIMs, the complexity of the sculpt, the map resolution, the types of maps being generated, and the performance of your workstation.

In some cases, exporting high-resolution displacement and normal maps for a large creature may require one to three days of continuous processing. For this reason, many artists prefer to launch large exports overnight or during weekends to avoid interrupting their daily production work.

How it works...

The purpose of this workflow is not simply to generate texture maps, but to create a reliable bridge between the high-resolution sculpt created in ZBrush and the assets that will be used throughout texturing, look development, and final rendering.

In a production pipeline, these maps are rarely used inside a single application. Instead, they travel through multiple Digital Content Creation (DCC) applications, such as Maya, Substance 3D Painter, Mari, Houdini, and the final rendering software. Each application must interpret the same sculpted information consistently, making it essential that the exported meshes and maps always remain synchronized throughout the pipeline.

It is important to understand that the subdivision level used during map generation must always match the subdivision level that will receive those maps during rendering. If your rendering workflow uses *Subdivision Level 1* as the base mesh, both the displacement and normal maps should be generated using **SubDiv level 1**. Likewise, if the rendering mesh is exported at *Subdivision Level 2*, the maps should be generated relative to **SubDiv level 2**. Maintaining this consistency ensures that the displacement values and surface details are reconstructed correctly at render time.

This consistency also helps avoid one of the most common causes of baking artifacts. Using a different mesh version, changing the subdivision level, or modifying the UV layout after the maps have been generated can lead to visible seams, incorrect displacement, or unexpected shading issues. By keeping the exported meshes, UVs, and generated maps synchronized throughout the workflow, assets can move reliably between departments with minimal troubleshooting and predictable results.

Saving the map as a 32-bit EXR preserves the full precision of the sculpted details and helps avoid stepping or precision loss when rendering highly detailed surfaces such as the scales, wrinkles, and skin folds of our `dragonCrest` creature.

Using Decimation Master to prepare high-resolution meshes for texturing

A successful texturing workflow typically relies on three essential components: a clean low-resolution mesh with proper topology, a well-organized UV layout, and a high-resolution version of the asset containing all the sculpted information. While the retopologized mesh and UVs provide the foundation for texturing, the high-resolution model is used to transfer surface detail and generate the data required by modern texturing workflows.

In the previous recipes, we prepared and exported the production meshes and generated the maps required to reproduce the sculpted detail during rendering. However, many texturing applications, such as **Mari** and **Substance 3D Painter**, also benefit from having access to a high-resolution reference mesh.

This geometry can be used to generate additional maps, such as **curvature maps**, which highlight convex and concave surface details, **ambient occlusion maps**, which simulate soft contact shadows, and **thickness maps**, which measure the volume of the mesh and are commonly used for subsurface scattering and material effects. These maps also drive masks, generators, and many procedural texturing tools, helping create more realistic and detailed textures.

Decimation Master provides an efficient solution by dramatically reducing the polygon count while preserving the visual appearance of the original sculpt. The resulting mesh retains most of the high-frequency surface information while becoming significantly lighter and easier to manage inside texturing applications.

In this recipe, you will learn how to create a production-friendly decimated version of the `dragonCrest` creature that can be used as a high-resolution reference mesh during texturing workflows, improving performance while maintaining the visual fidelity of the original sculpt.

Figure 9.17 shows the dragon model after all SubTools have been decimated:

Figure 9.17 – All SubTools decimated

Getting ready

For this recipe, we will continue working inside ZBrush using the final approved version of the `dragonCrest` creature. Before proceeding, make sure that:

1. All sculpting work has been completed, and the asset contains the final primary, secondary, and tertiary details approved for production.
2. Additionally, ensure that all SubTools are loaded at their highest subdivision level, as **Decimation Master** relies on the highest available resolution to preserve as much sculpted detail as possible during the decimation process.

How to do it...

Before starting the decimation process, make sure that all the SubTools you want to include in the decimated version are visible. If you completed the previous recipe, your project should already be clean and contain only the geometry intended for production and texturing workflows. Now, follow these steps:

1. Navigate to **ZPlugin** | **Decimation Master** and open the plugin settings. This tool allows you to dramatically reduce the polygon count of the creature while preserving as much visual detail as possible from the original sculpt.

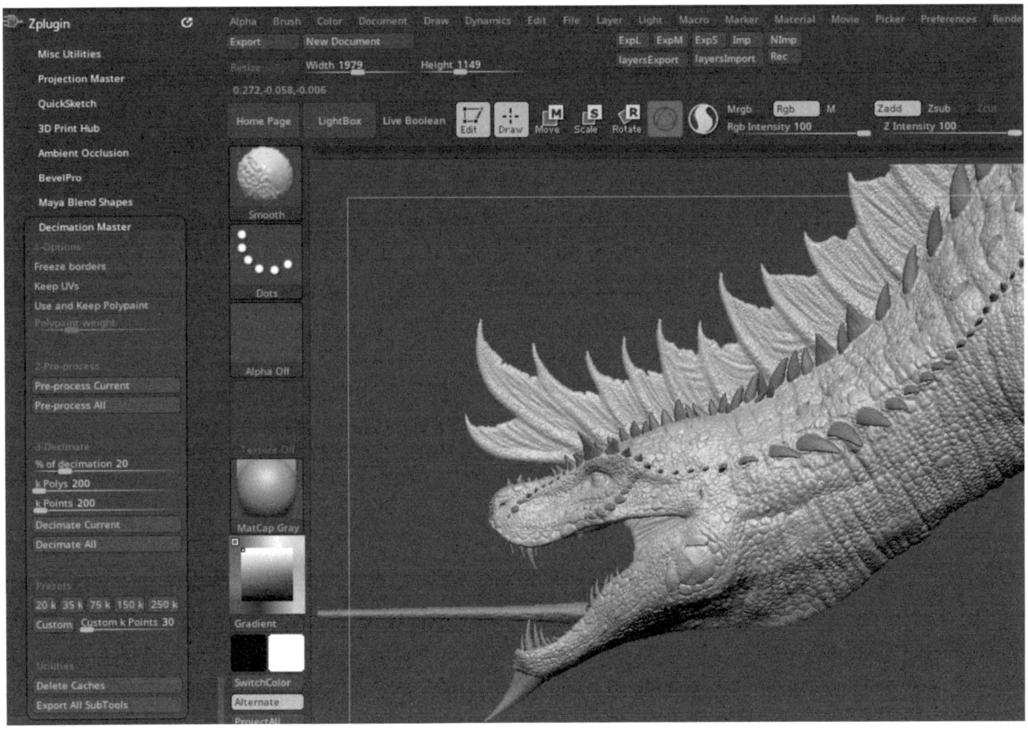

Figure 9.18 – Opening the Decimation Master plugin inside ZBrush

2. Click **Pre-process All** to calculate and analyze all visible SubTools before decimation. During this stage, **Decimation Master** evaluates the geometry and prepares the data required to preserve the sculpted details during the decimation process.

   In general, the more subdivision levels and polygons your creature contains, the longer the preprocessing stage will take. For complex production assets, this operation can range from a few seconds to several minutes.

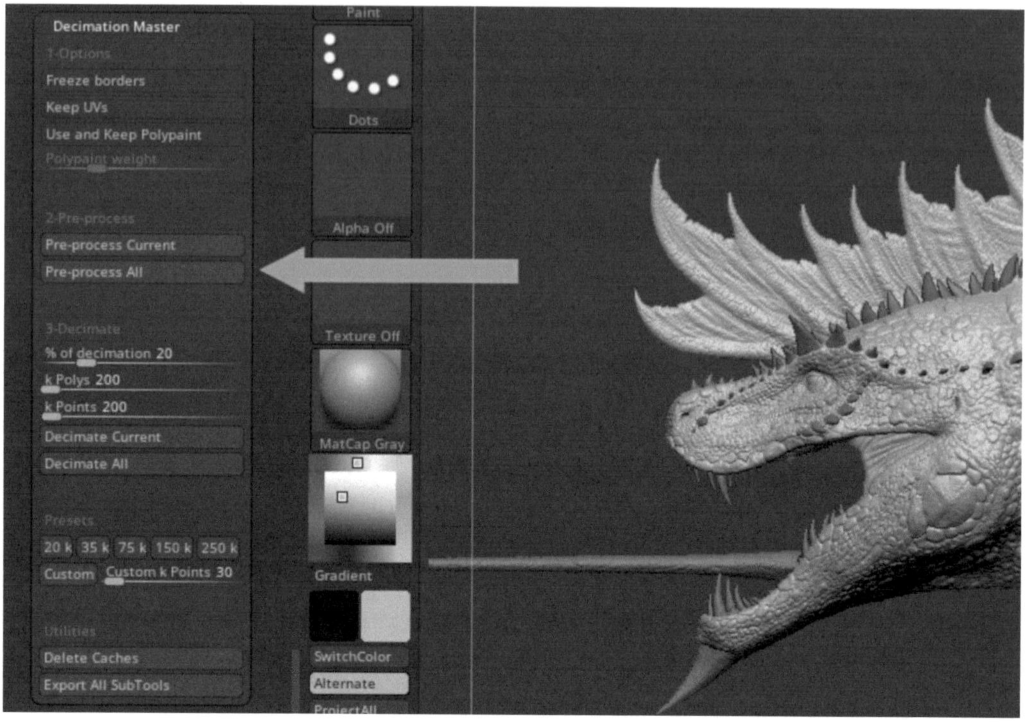

Figure 9.19 – Using Pre-process All to analyze all visible SubTools before decimation

> **Tip**
>
> If the **Pre-process All** operation takes an unusually long time, causes ZBrush to become unresponsive, or results in instability, consider using **Pre-process Current** instead. Processing one SubTool at a time often provides better stability when working with extremely dense assets, large creatures, or projects containing many SubTools. Although this approach requires a little more time, it can help prevent crashes and reduce the risk of losing progress during the decimation process.

3. In the **Decimation Master** settings, choose how you want to control the final density of each SubTool. You can either specify a percentage of the original polygon count using the **% of decimation** slider or define a target count using the **k Polys** or **k Points** control. Adjust these values to match each asset's requirements and preview the estimated polygon count before proceeding with decimation.

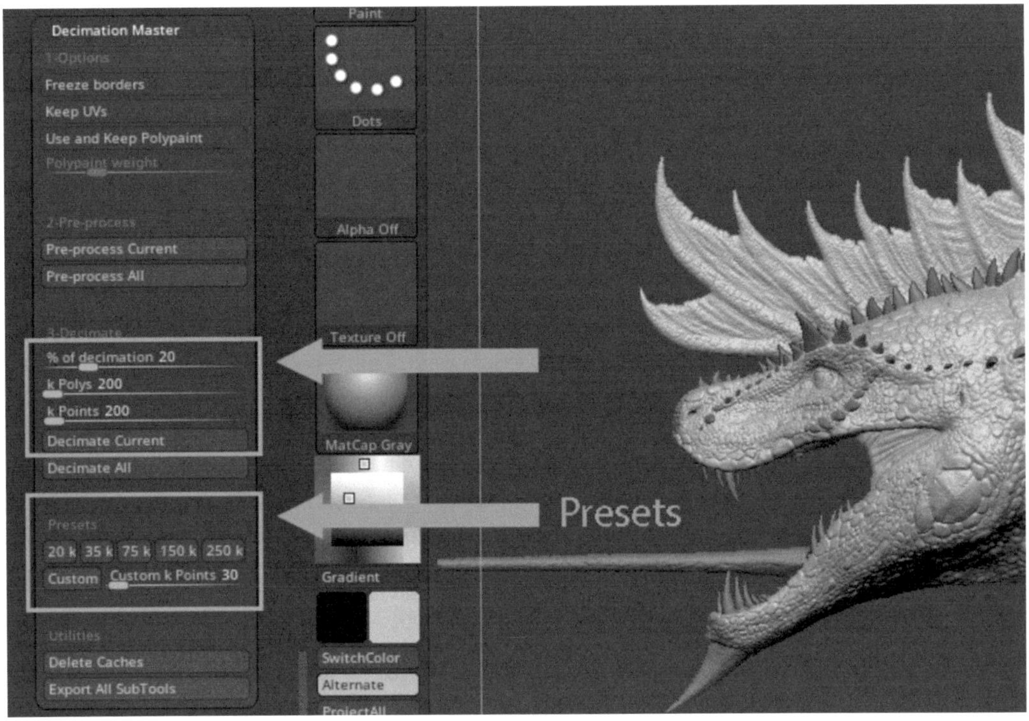

Figure 9.20 – Using either percentage-based decimation or a target polygon count to control the final density of the mesh

4. Once all the required SubTools have been pre-processed, start defining the decimation values for each asset. Rather than applying the same percentage to every SubTool, I recommend adjusting the polygon count according to the importance of each element in the texturing workflow.

   As a general production guideline, the main body of the creature can often be reduced to approximately *1 to 2 million polygons*, while secondary elements such as teeth, claws, and the tongue can usually be reduced to around *100,000 to 200,000 polygons* without any noticeable loss of detail.

   Smaller assets such as spikes, scales, or horns can often be reduced even further. In the case of the `dragonCrest` creature, I typically keep individual spikes between *200,000 and 400,000 polygons*, while the chin horn can be reduced to approximately *50,000 polygons*. Eyes generally contribute very little to the baking process, so they can often be heavily optimized. For this project, I kept the iris and cornea at approximately *10,000 polygons* each, while the pupil was reduced to roughly *1,000 polygons*.

5. Once you have decided the target polygon count for a specific SubTool, select it in the SubTool list and enter the desired value inside **Decimation Master**. You can work either with a percentage reduction or by adjusting the resulting polygon count according to your production needs.
6. After setting the value, click **Decimate Current** to generate the optimized version of the selected asset.
7. Repeat this process for all remaining SubTools until the entire creature has been prepared for export.

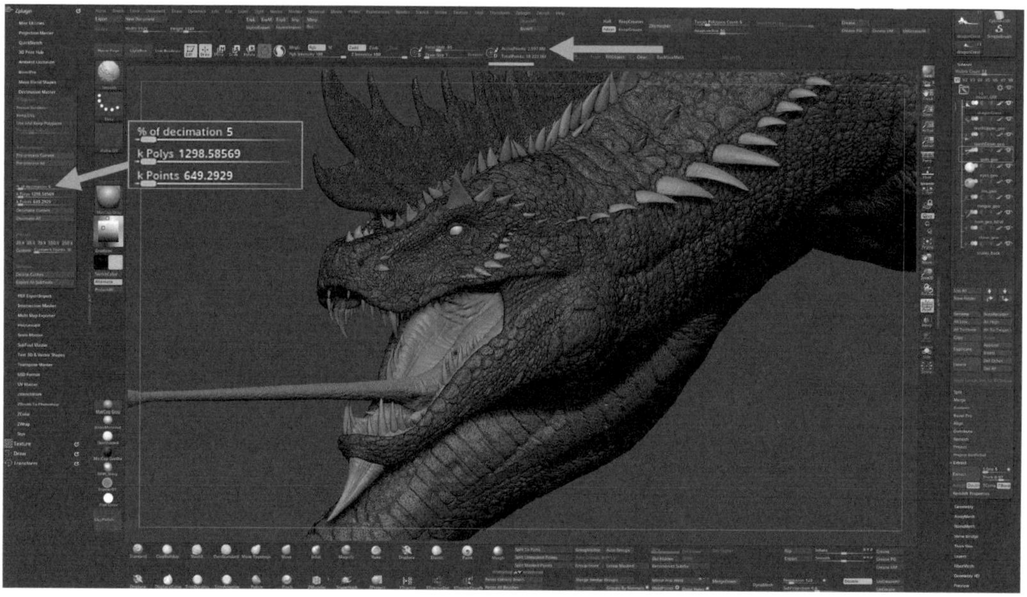

Figure 9.21 – Using Decimate Current to generate an optimized high-resolution mesh while preserving the essential sculpted detail

8. Once all the required SubTools have been decimated, export the optimized high-resolution version of the creature. Navigate to **ZPlugin | FBX ExportImport**, review the export settings, and create an FBX file containing the decimated meshes.

This file will serve as the high-resolution reference mesh used during texturing workflows in applications such as Mari and Substance 3D Painter.

How it works...

A common misconception among junior artists is that decimation is simply a way to reduce file size. While reducing polygon count is certainly one of its benefits, the primary purpose of a decimated mesh in production is to provide an optimized, high-resolution reference that can be used efficiently throughout the texturing pipeline.

Unlike the original sculpt, which can easily reach tens or hundreds of millions of polygons, a decimated mesh preserves most of the visible surface detail while dramatically reducing the computational cost required to load, display, and process the asset. This allows artists to work with complex production assets more efficiently while preserving the information required for accurate texture generation.

The preprocessing stage performed by **Decimation Master** is an important part of this workflow. During this process, ZBrush analyzes all visible SubTools and calculates how their geometry can be simplified while preserving the overall appearance of the sculpt. In the case of our `dragonCrest` creature, this includes everything from the large body surfaces to the individual teeth, claws, eyes, tongue, dorsal scales, and the distinctive horn located beneath the chin.

This preparation ensures that each component retains the level of detail required for texturing while remaining as lightweight as possible.

Another important aspect of production decimation is that not every asset requires the same polygon density. Large surfaces such as the body of `dragonCrest` contain most of the sculpted information that will later contribute to the texturing process, making them good candidates for higher polygon counts. Smaller elements such as teeth, claws, pupils, or individual horns can usually be reduced much more aggressively without affecting the final baking quality.

The same principle can be applied to any creature or character asset. Rather than using a single decimation value across the entire model, it is often more effective to evaluate each component individually and allocate polygons where they will provide the greatest benefit.

For example, the large dorsal scales of our creature contain far more visible information than the pupils inside the eyes. Similarly, the horn beneath the chin benefits from preserving its silhouette, while internal elements, such as the tongue, can often be optimized more aggressively. Understanding where the important visual information is located allows artists to create lighter assets without sacrificing the quality of the texturing workflow.

Once the decimation process has been completed, the resulting geometry can be exported as an FBX file and shared with texturing artists. The exported mesh remains visually very close to the original sculpt while being significantly lighter and easier to handle inside Mari, Substance 3D Painter, and other applications commonly used in production.

Hand-painting a cavity map for more control

Automatic **cavity generation** can produce excellent results in many situations, especially when working with clean sculpted details and well-defined surface information. However, no automated solution can fully understand the artistic intent behind a creature design.

In production, it is often necessary to enhance specific regions, reduce unwanted noise, or emphasize important details that would otherwise be lost using a purely procedural approach. Areas such as facial wrinkles, skin folds, scales, horns, claws, or membrane transitions may require additional control to achieve the desired texturing result.

One effective solution is to create a cavity map directly through ZBrush **Polypaint**. By combining masking tools, cavity extraction, and manual painting, artists can build customized black-and-white masks that provide far greater artistic control than an automatically generated cavity map. A **cavity map** identifies recessed areas and fine surface creases, allowing them to be isolated and used to drive masks, material variation, and additional texturing effects.

In this recipe, you will learn how to create a hand-adjusted cavity map using Polypaint and export it through the **Multi Map Exporter**. This workflow can be particularly useful when texturing hero creatures, such as our `dragonCrest` asset, but it can be applied to any production model that requires additional control over surface detail masks.

Figure 9.22 demonstrates the completed hand-painted cavity map generated from the dragon model, highlighting recessed details and surface transitions used to enhance texturing and material definition:

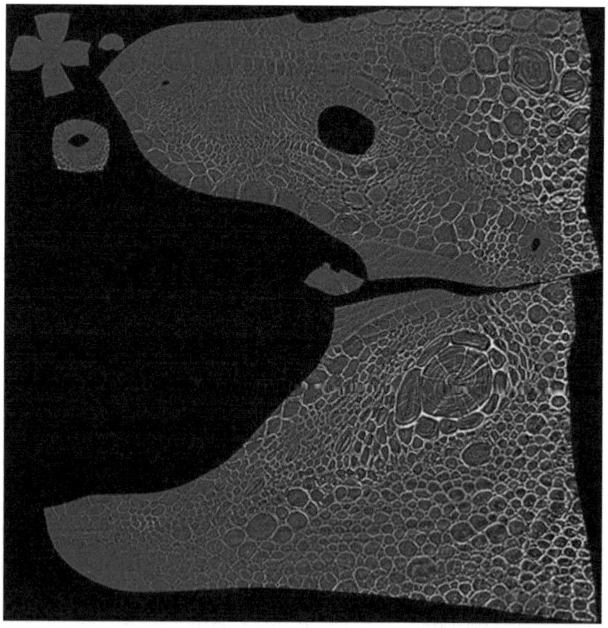

Figure 9.22 – A hand-painted cavity map generated from the dragonCrest model

Getting ready

For this recipe, we will continue working with the final approved version of the `dragonCrest` creature inside ZBrush. Before starting, ensure the following:

1. The project should be clean and organized, with all sculpting work completed.
2. Because the cavity extraction process relies on the smallest surface details present in the sculpt, the model should be loaded at its highest subdivision level. This ensures that wrinkles, scales, pores, skin folds, and other tertiary details are fully available when generating the cavity mask.

How to do it...

This workflow uses ZBrush's cavity masking tools together with Polypaint to create a customized cavity map that can later be exported as a texture and used throughout the texturing process. Now, follow these steps:

1. Before generating the cavity mask, switch the Viewport material to **Flat Color**. This removes all lighting and shading information from the model, allowing you to evaluate the cavity extraction more accurately throughout the workflow.

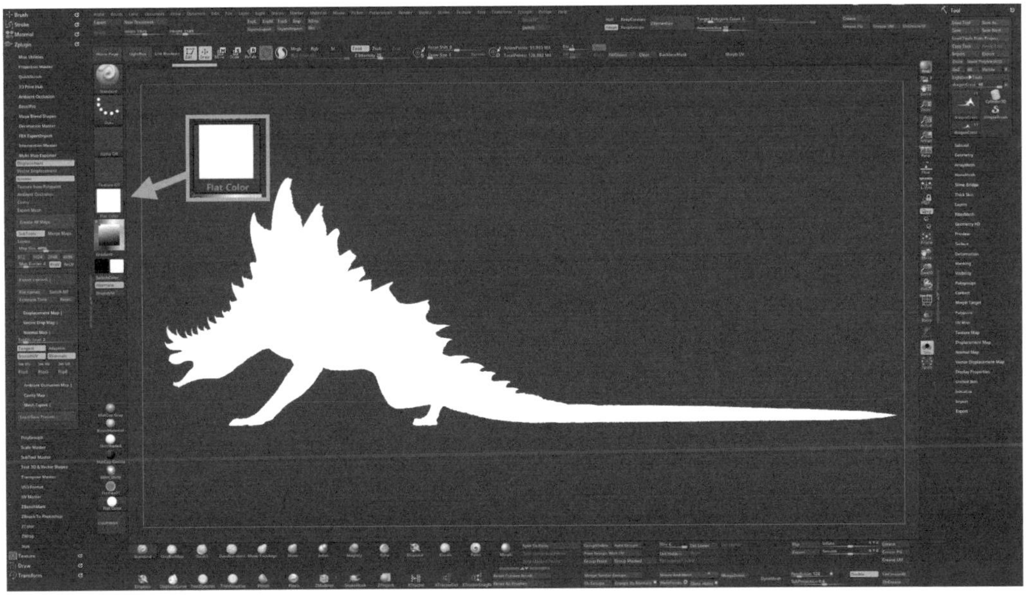

Figure 9.23 – Switching the material to Flat Color mode before generating the cavity map

2. Select the **Paint Brush**, make sure that only **RGB** is enabled, and disable **ZAdd**. Choose a pure white color and use **Color | FillObject** to fill the entire creature with white Polypaint. Starting from a completely *white* surface provides a clean foundation for the cavity extraction process and makes it easier to visualize the *black-and-white* information that will be generated in the following steps.

Figure 9.24 – Using Color | FillObject to apply a uniform white Polypaint color

3. Navigate to **Tool | Masking | Mask By Cavity** and click directly on the **Cavity Profile** graph to open the cavity settings.

Figure 9.25 – Locating the Cavity Profile graph used to control how the cavity mask is generated

4. In the **Mask By Cavity** settings, set **Focal Shift** to `0`. This provides a neutral starting point for the cavity extraction and helps produce a cleaner mask before making any additional adjustments.

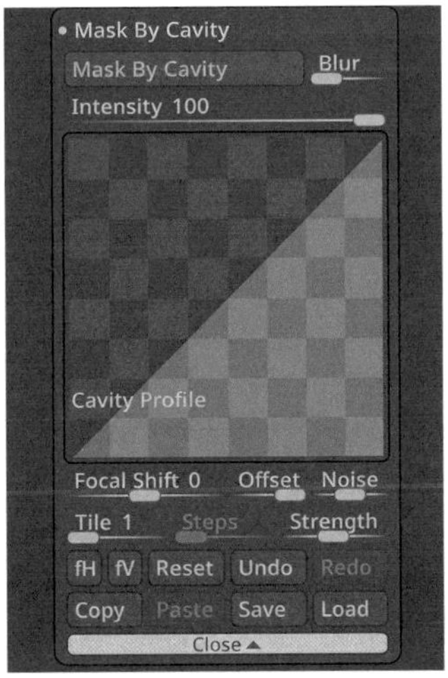

Figure 9.26 – Setting the Focal Shift value to 0 before generating the cavity mask

5. Once the **Cavity Profile** and **Focal Shift** settings have been configured, click **Mask By Cavity** to generate the cavity mask. ZBrush will analyze the high-frequency details

present on the model and create a mask based on the cavities and recessed areas of the sculpt.

Depending on the complexity of the creature and the amount of tertiary detail present, the resulting mask may already provide a strong foundation for the cavity map or may require additional refinement in the next steps.

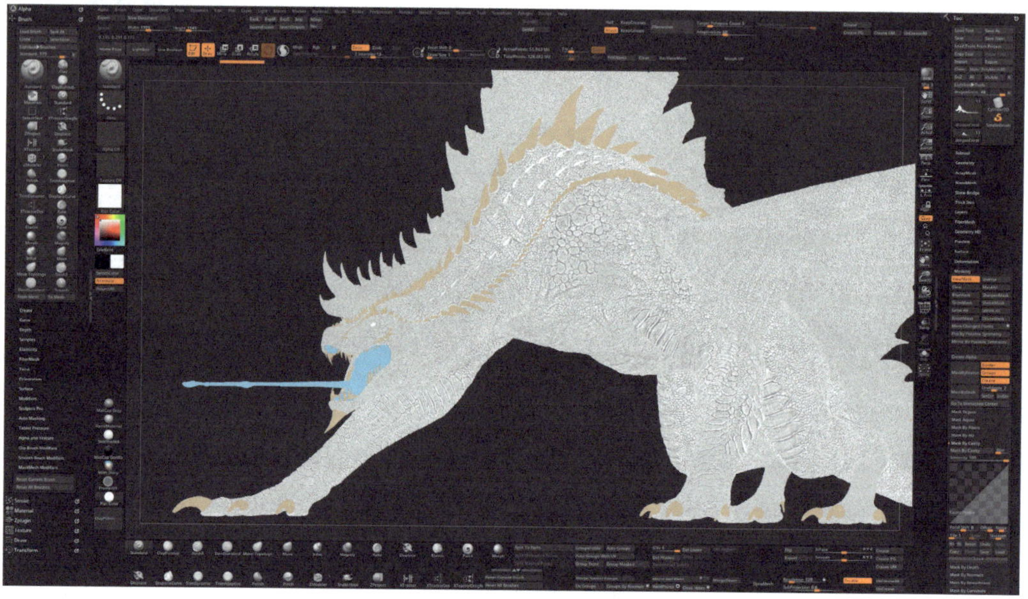

Figure 9.27 – Generating the cavity mask using the Mask By Cavity function

Tip

The settings shown in this recipe are simply the values that worked best for the `dragonCrest` creature. Depending on the type of asset you are working on, you may achieve better results by adjusting the **Cavity Profile** curve differently. Don't be afraid to experiment with the shape of the curve until the mask captures the specific details you want to emphasize.

ZBrush also provides several useful mask refinement tools that can help improve the result before converting it into Polypaint. For example, **BlurMask** can soften harsh transitions, **SharpenMask** can increase contrast, **GrowMask** can expand the masked areas, **ShrinkMask** can reduce them, and **Clear** can quickly remove the current mask and allow you to generate a new one using different settings. These tools can be combined freely to create cavity masks tailored to the needs of each asset.

6. After generating and refining the cavity mask, click **SwitchColor** to make *black* the active color. Then use **Color** | **FillObject** to apply the color to the visible, unmasked portions of the model.

   Since the mask protects the cavity information, only the exposed areas will receive the color, effectively converting the mask into black-and-white Polypaint information stored directly on the geometry. This Polypaint data will later be exported as a cavity texture map for use during texturing and look development.

Figure 9.28 – Using SwitchColor to set black as the active Polypaint color before baking the cavity mask into the model

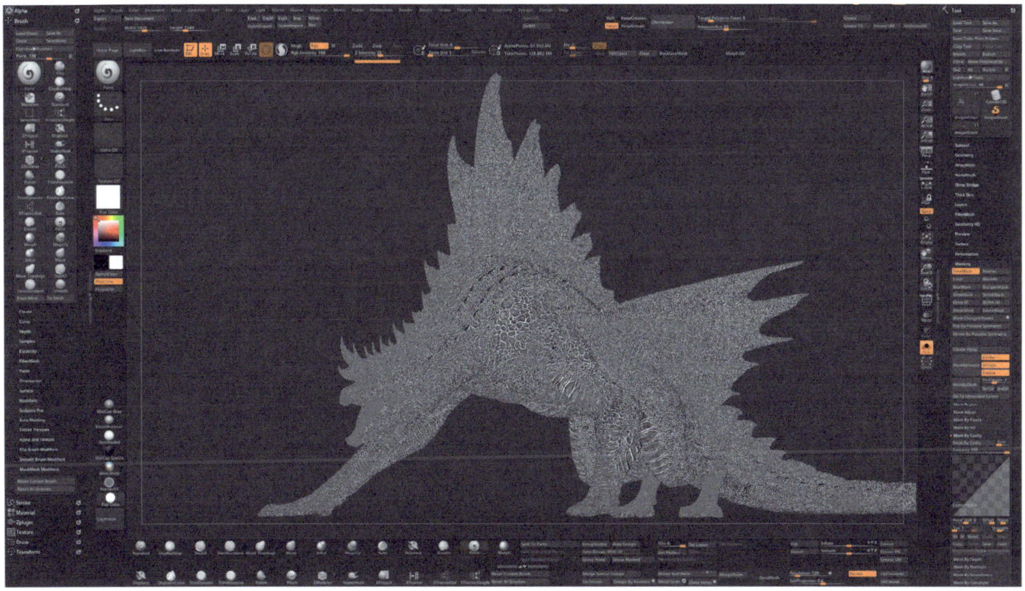

Figure 9.29 – Final cavity mask converted to Polypaint and ready to be exported as a texture map

7. Repeat the same process for all the remaining SubTools that require a cavity map.

8. Once all the required SubTools have been converted to Polypaint, open **ZPlugin | Multi Map Exporter** and enable **Texture from Polypaint**. Disable any map types that are not needed for this export to keep the process clean and organized. Since the cavity information is now stored directly as Polypaint data, ZBrush will generate texture maps from the *black-and-white* information painted onto each SubTool.

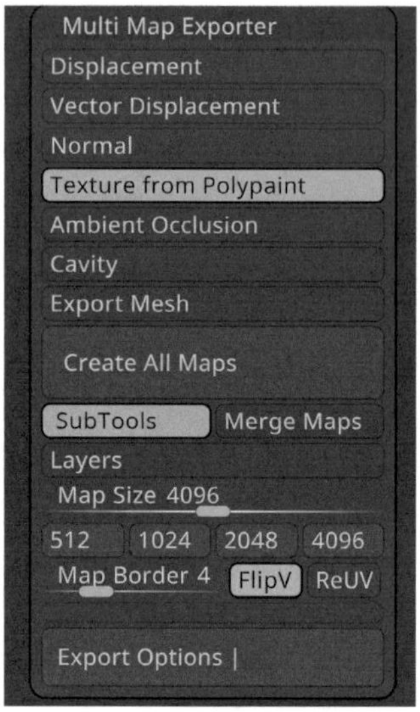

Figure 9.30 – Enabling Texture from Polypaint in the Multi Map Exporter before generating the cavity texture

9. Open **Export Options | File Names** and update the **Texture map** suffix to `_CAV`. This naming convention makes it immediately clear that the exported texture is a cavity map and helps distinguish it from the other maps generated during production. Combined with the SubTool name and UDIM number, the final file names will remain clean, readable, and easy to identify throughout the texturing pipeline. For example, a cavity map generated from the body geometry could be exported as `body_CAV.1001.tif`. Before proceeding, make sure the texture export format is set to `.tif`, as this format is widely supported across texturing, look development, and rendering applications while preserving the quality required for production workflows.

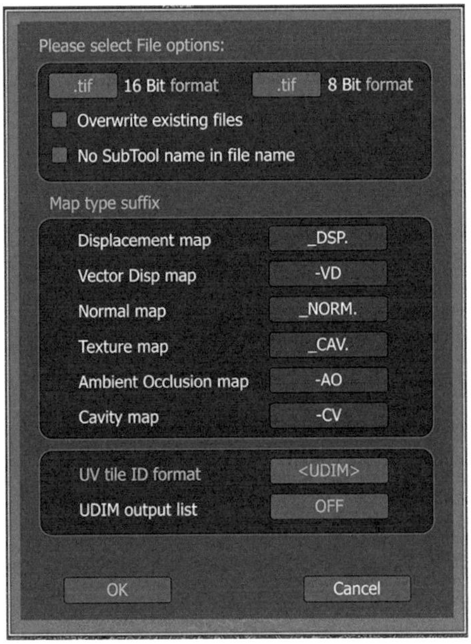

Figure 9.31 – Renaming the Texture Map suffix to _CAV. and verifying that the export format is set to .tif

10. Click **OK** to confirm the file naming options and return to the main **Multi Map Exporter** panel. Then click **Create All Maps** to begin the export process. When prompted, select the destination folder where the cavity maps will be saved. As with the previous recipes, I recommend creating a dedicated folder, such as `Cavity_v001`, to keep different versions organized and make future updates easier to manage.

How it works...

This workflow combines ZBrush's cavity masking tools with Polypaint to create a cavity texture that offers significantly more artistic control than an automatically generated cavity map. Instead of relying entirely on baked information extracted from geometry, this method allows you to decide exactly which details should appear in the final texture and how strongly they should be represented.

The reason we switched the Viewport to **Flat Color** at the beginning of the process is to remove all lighting and material influence from the evaluation. When creating masks and *black-and-white* texture information, shadows and highlights can easily make certain details appear stronger or weaker than they actually are. Working in **Flat Color** mode provides a much more reliable preview of the information that will eventually be exported.

The **Mask By Cavity** system analyzes the surface curvature of the sculpt and identifies recessed areas such as wrinkles, scale separation, skin folds, and other tertiary details. On the `dragonCrest` creature, this allows us to quickly isolate details such as the separation between the dorsal scales, the folds around the neck, and the finer skin information sculpted throughout the body. The **Cavity Profile** curve controls how aggressively this information is extracted, which is why different creatures often require different settings.

Converting the mask into Polypaint provides an important advantage. Once the information is stored directly on the geometry as color data, it becomes completely editable. You can blur it, sharpen it, repaint areas manually, regenerate sections, or combine it with other masking techniques before exporting the final texture. This flexibility is often difficult to achieve when relying solely on automatically baked maps.

Using **Texture from Polypaint** allows the exported texture to preserve exactly the information visible on the model. Since the cavity information is already stored as *black-and-white* Polypaint, the export process becomes extremely predictable and easy to art direct.

One of the biggest advantages of this approach is that the resulting cavity map is not limited to texturing alone. In production, cavity textures are frequently used to drive procedural masks, dirt accumulation, color variation, roughness breakup, edge wear, and many other effects. Because the information is artist-controlled, the final result is often cleaner and more useful than a purely automated cavity bake.

There's more...

Now that the cavity map created in this recipe is ready, together with the normal and displacement maps exported earlier in the *Creating normal and displacement maps with Multi Map Exporter* recipe, the asset has the main maps required to move into the texturing stage.

Modern texturing applications can paint seamlessly across UV shells, but tools such as generators, Smart Masks, blur filters, Fill Layers, and procedural effects may still produce small inconsistencies across UV boundaries or UDIM transitions. These are normal situations during texturing and can usually be corrected with minor manual adjustments.

The amount of cleanup required often depends on how the UV layout was organized. A clean and logical UDIM structure generally keeps these corrections to a minimum, while an unnecessarily fragmented layout may require more attention during painting. This does not make the layout unusable, but it is useful to understand that UV decisions continue to influence the asset even after the maps have been exported.

Reaching the final page of this book is both exciting and emotional for me.

I truly hope these pages have given you not only new techniques but also a deeper understanding of how professional workflows operate in production. Every step, from the first DynaMesh sketch to the final exported map, was designed to demonstrate that great results are rarely the product of talent alone. They come from structure, consistency, curiosity, and a willingness to keep learning.

Thank you for dedicating your time to this journey.

I encourage you to keep experimenting, keep asking questions, and keep creating. The best artists are not those who know all the answers, but those who never stop learning.

If you would like to share feedback, ask questions, or simply connect, feel free to reach out through **LinkedIn** (*Andrea Salvatori*) or **Instagram** (*@andreasalvatori3d*). You can also visit my website: `www.andreasalvatori.com`.

I would be delighted to hear about your work and your progress. All the best!

10

Unlock the Code/Resource Bundle and the PDF Version

Your copy of this book includes the following exclusive benefits:

Complete Code Bundle

Download the full source code for this book's examples and projects.

DRM-Free PDF Version

Download DRM-free PDF and ePub copies of this book.

7-Day Packt Library Access

Get 7-day unlimited access to 8,000+ books and videos. No credit card required.

Available for first-time Packt+ trial users only.

Next-Gen Reader Access

Read this book on Packt Reader with progress sync, dark mode and note-taking.

Follow this guide to unlock them. The process takes only a few minutes and only needs to be completed once.

Unlock this book's free benefits in three easy steps

Step 1

Have your purchase invoice ready for *step 3*. If you have a physical copy, scan it using your phone and save it as a PDF, JPG, or PNG.

For more help on finding your invoice, visit `https://www.packtpub.com/unlock-benefits/help`.

> Note
>
> **Note**: If you bought this book directly from the Packt website, no invoice is required. After *step 2*, you can access your exclusive content right away.

Step 2

Scan the QR code or go to `packtpub.com/unlock`.

On the page that opens (similar to *Figure 10.1* on desktop), search for this book by name and select the correct edition.

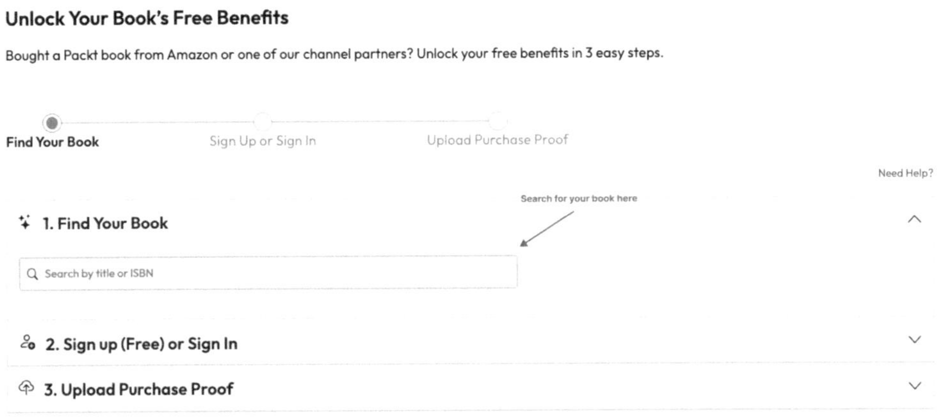

Figure 10.1: Packt unlock landing page on desktop

Step 3

After selecting the book, sign in to your Packt account or create one for free. Then, upload your invoice (PDF, PNG, or JPG, up to 10 MB). Follow the on-screen instructions to finish the process.

Need help?

If you get stuck and need help, visit `https://www.packtpub.com/unlock-benefits/help` for a detailed FAQ on how to find your invoice and more. This QR code will take you to the help page.

> **Note**
>
> **Note:** If you are still facing issues, reach out to `customercare@packt.com`.

Other Books You May Enjoy

If you enjoyed this book, you may be interested in these other books by Packt:

Sculpting in ZBrush Made Simple, First Edition

Lukas Kutschera

ISBN: 9781803235769

- Enhance your sculpting skills to craft a variety of organic and hard surface objects
- Create humanoid characters, focusing on basic anatomy and proportions
- Explore sculpting techniques for intricate details in human heads and hair
- Sculpt objects such as armor, clothing, and accessories
- Create custom brushes to enhance your sculpting workflow
- Develop skills in detailing and surfacing to add texture and depth to your sculpts
- Use Polypaint and Materials to add color and enhance your sculptures
- Render and export your sculpts to share them with others

Packt is searching for authors like you

If you're interested in becoming an author for Packt, please visit `authors.packt.com` and apply today. We have worked with thousands of developers and tech professionals, just like you, to help them share their insight with the global tech community. You can make a general application, apply for a specific hot topic that we are recruiting an author for, or submit your own idea.

Share your thoughts

Now that you've finished *ZBrush Cookbook*, we'd love to hear your thoughts! Scan the QR code below to go straight to the Amazon review page for this book and share your feedback or leave a review on the site that you purchased it from.

https://packt.link/r/1836207611

Your review is important to us and the tech community and will help us make sure we're delivering excellent quality content.

Index

Made in the USA
Las Vegas, NV
31 October 2026

57052326R00225